After Broadcast News
Media Regimes, Democracy, and Environment

MW00837541

The new media environment has challenged the role of professional journalists as the primary source of politically relevant information. *After Broadcast News* puts this challenge into historical context, arguing that it is the latest of several critical moments – driven by economic, political, cultural, and technological changes – in which the relationship among citizens, political elites, and the media has been contested. Out of these past moments, distinct media regimes eventually emerged, each with its own seemingly natural rules and norms, and each the result of political struggle with clear winners and losers. The media regime in place for the latter half of the twentieth century has been dismantled, but a new regime has yet to emerge. Ensuring that this regime is a democratic one requires serious consideration of what was most beneficial and most problematic about past regimes and what is potentially most beneficial and most problematic about today's new information environment.

Bruce A. Williams teaches in the Department of Media Studies at the University of Virginia. He received his Ph.D. in political science from the University of Minnesota and has taught at Pennsylvania State University, the University of Michigan, the University of Illinois, and the London School of Economics. He has published four books and more than forty scholarly journal articles and book chapters. His book *Democracy, Dialogue, and Environmental Disputes: The Contested Languages of Social Regulation* (with Albert Matheny) won the Caldwell Prize for best book in 1996 from the Science, Technology, and Environmental Politics section of the American Political Science Association. His textbook *The Play of Power: An Introduction to American Politics* (with James Eisenstein, Mark Kessler, and Jacqueline Switzer) was selected by the Women's Caucus of the American Political Science Association in 1997 as the political science text that best deals with women's issues and diversity. His most recent book is *The New Media Environment: An Introduction* (with Andrea L. Press). Also with Andrea Press, he is the editor of the *Communication Review*. Over the past five years, he has been active in a number of initiatives in the area of media policy and ethics.

Michael X. Delli Carpini, Dean of the Annenberg School for Communication, received his B.A. and M.A. from the University of Pennsylvania (1975) and his Ph.D. from the University of Minnesota (1980). Prior to joining the University of Pennsylvania faculty in July 2003, Delli Carpini was Director of the Public Policy program of the Pew Charitable Trusts (1999–2003) and a member of the Political Science Department at Barnard College and the graduate faculty of Columbia University (1987–2002), serving as chair of the Barnard department from 1995 to 1999. Delli Carpini began his academic career as Assistant Professor in the Political Science Department at Rutgers University (1980–1987). His research explores the role of the citizen in American politics, with particular emphasis on the impact of the mass media on public opinion, political knowledge, and political participation. He is author of *Stability and Change in American Politics: The Coming of Age of the Generation of the 1960s*; *What Americans Know about Politics and Why It Matters* (winner of the 2008 American Association of Public Opinion Researchers Book Award); *A New Engagement? Political Participation, Civic Life and the Changing American Citizen*; and *Talking Together: Public Deliberation and Political Participation in America*. He has also authored or edited numerous articles, essays, and edited volumes on political communications, public opinion, and political socialization. Delli Carpini was awarded the 2008 Murray Edelman Distinguished Career Award from the Political Communication Division of the American Political Science Association.

Communication, Society and Politics

Editors

W. Lance Bennett, *University of Washington*
Robert M. Entman, *The George Washington University*

Politics and relations among individuals in societies across the world are being transformed by new technologies for targeting individuals and sophisticated methods for shaping personalized messages. The new technologies challenge boundaries of many kinds – among news, information, entertainment, and advertising; between media, with the arrival of the World Wide Web; and even between nations. Communication, Society and Politics probes the political and social impacts of these new communication systems in national, comparative, and global perspective.

Other Books in the Series

(Continued after the index)

After Broadcast News

Media Regimes, Democracy, and the New Information Environment

BRUCE A. WILLIAMS
University of Virginia

MICHAEL X. DELLI CARPINI
University of Pennsylvania

CAMBRIDGE UNIVERSITY PRESS
Cambridge, New York, Melbourne, Madrid, Cape Town,
Singapore, São Paulo, Delhi, Tokyo, Mexico City

Cambridge University Press
32 Avenue of the Americas, New York, NY 10013-2473, USA

www.cambridge.org
Information on this title: www.cambridge.org/9780521279833

First published 2011

Printed in the United States of America

A catalog record for this publication is available from the British Library.

Library of Congress Cataloging in Publication data

Williams, Bruce Alan.
After broadcast news : media regimes, democracy, and the new information environment /
Bruce A. Williams, Michael X. Delli Carpini.
   p.   cm. – (Communication, society, and politics)
Includes bibliographical references and index.
ISBN 978-1-107-01031-4 (hardback) – ISBN 978-0-521-27983-3 (paperback)
1. Mass media – Political aspects – United States.   2. Broadcast journalism – Political
aspects – United States.   3. Press and politics – United States. 4. Popular culture – Political
aspects – United States.   5. Democracy – United States.   I. Delli Carpini, Michael X.,
1953–   II. Title.
P95.82.U6W54   2011
071′.3–dc22   2011009191

ISBN 978-1-107-01031-4 Hardback
ISBN 978-0-521-27983-3 Paperback

For our fathers,
Domenick Delli Carpini
and
Stanley Williams

Contents

Acknowledgments

The longer a book takes to write, the longer the list of people and institutions that deserve thanks for helping along the way – and this project has lasted a very long time indeed. The origins of our collaboration go back several decades and are lost in the mists of time, along with the beer-soaked napkin upon which some notes and diagrams were scribbled. However, Lance Bennett and Robert Entman, colleagues and friends, have been there since this book began to take shape, and without their support and encouragement you would not be reading it now. Over the years, at too many conferences to remember, they have both been valuable sounding boards. In 1998 they invited us to a series of small workshops they had organized on the future of political communication. Hosted by the University of Pennsylvania's Annenberg School for Communication, it was here that we first began to develop the ideas that have shaped our thinking about the democratic implications of a dramatically changing media environment. This opportunity to try out and hone our ideas in front of a talented and engaged group of political communication scholars was an invaluable experience. Since submitting our manuscript to their series with Cambridge University Press, we have added to our indebtedness as they proved to be incredibly generous and thorough editors. Their careful reading and responses to several versions of our manuscript have, needless to say, made this book much better than it would have been otherwise.

Many other colleagues and institutions have helped both of us along the way. Barnard College, Columbia University, the Annenberg School for Communication at the University of Pennsylvania, the Institute of Communications Research at the University of Illinois at Urbana-Champaign, and the University of Virginia have all provided the support, colleagues, and students that have nurtured us during our work on this book. We owe a special debt to our students who have read, reacted to, and dramatically improved this book. We have also benefited from the comments and criticisms of discussants and panel participants at the many conferences where we have presented parts of this book.

In the years we have worked on this project so many colleagues have contributed that we cannot even begin to reconstruct a complete list, but we thank them all. Several individuals deserve special mention for the help they gave us in developing and sharpening our arguments: Geoff Baym, Menachem Blondheim, Pablo Boczkowski, Clifford Christians, Nick Couldry, James Curran, Elihu Katz, Tamar Liebes, Sonia Livingstone, Peter Lunt, Richard Marks, Robert McChesney, John Nerone, Andrea Press, John Zaller, and Barbie Zelizer. Two graduate students, Keren Tenenboim at Annenberg and Michael Wayne at Virginia, deserve special thanks for their help. We also thank Lew Bateman, Anne Lovering Rounds, our anonymous reviewers, and all the other folks at Cambridge University Press who have contributed so much to this book.

In 2008, a two-week residency for co-author Bruce A. Williams at the Centre for Global Media and Democracy in the Department of Media and Communications, Goldsmiths University, offered an exceptional opportunity to revise our manuscript. In January 2009, a conference on media and public opinion in times of national crisis organized by Tamar Liebes at Mishkenot Sha'ananim, Jerusalem, provided a timely opportunity for us to present and discuss the core ideas in our manuscript to an interdisciplinary and multicultural set of scholars as well as to an interested lay audience in a complicated yet inspiring environment.

It is traditional for authors to thank their families for their support and for accepting the neglect and distractions that go with working on a book. Our debt is much greater, since we have worked on this book for so long that it was less a specific project than a way of life. Andrea Press, Jane Whitaker, Jessie Press-Williams, and Joshua Press-Williams all get our special thanks for living with this project for as long as we have.

Is There a Difference Between Tina Fey and Katie Couric? Policing the Boundaries Between News and Entertainment

The range of fiction extends all the way from complete hallucinations to the scientist's perfectly self-conscious use of a schematic model, or his decision that for his particular problem accuracy beyond a certain number of decimal places is not important. A work of fiction may have almost any degree of Fidelity, and so long as the degree of Fidelity can be taken into account, fiction is not misleading. In fact, human culture is very largely the selection, the rearrangement, the tracing of patterns upon, and the stylizing of, what William James called "the random irradiations and re-settlements of our ideas." The alternative to the use of fictions is direct exposure to the ebb and flow of sensation. That is not a real alternative...

– Walter Lippmann, *Public Opinion*, 1922

A federal judge yesterday sharply questioned an assertion by the Obama administration that former Vice President Richard B. Cheney's statements to a special prosecutor about the Valerie Plame case must be kept secret, partly so they do not become fodder for Cheney's political enemies or late-night commentary on "The Daily Show."

– R. Jeffrey Smith, *Washington Post*, June 19, 2009

The Strange Media Odyssey of Sarah Palin

On August 29, 2008, Republican presidential candidate John McCain announced that the little-known, first-term governor of Alaska, Sarah Palin, would be his running mate. The photogenic, former beauty queen's acceptance speech at the convention, her formal introduction to the nation, drew 37.2 million television viewers, only around 1 million less than for the acceptance speeches by Barack Obama and John McCain and far more than any other speech at either convention (Hechtkopf 2008). Given the degree to which Palin's selection was a surprise and her lack of a record in national politics, there was great uncertainty in the media over how to tell her story. Initially, the media narrative followed along the lines suggested by decades of political communication research. Following their profession's definition of nonpartisanship and balance, journalists relied on "reliable sources" – primarily spokespersons for both parties – to define the range of opinions about Palin.

At first, this meant a generally positive treatment of the Republican vice presidential nominee. Although the narrative of Palin's rise to national prominence was cast in gendered terms, it tended to work to her advantage (in contrast with the more negative impact of gendered frames on the candidacy of Hillary Clinton). One study of the first two weeks of press coverage of the nominee found that "[she was] viewed through gendered lenses, but in ways that actually benefit[ed] her – toughness, good looks, mother[hood]" (Harp, Loke, and Bachmann 2009, 9). This generally positive coverage resulted not from any measured judgment or independent investigation by journalists, but rather from their strategy of simply reporting the two sides of the story, defined by the political parties. Barack Obama's campaign was initially reluctant to criticize the Alaskan governor, fearing it would draw attention away from their focus on McCain, create sympathy for the political newcomer, and lead to accusations of sexism (Lott 2008). Democratic reticence led to Republican advantage in shaping the narrative. Creating a kind of feedback loop, Palin's positive coverage enhanced her poll standings, which has been demonstrated to influence the ways in which journalists write about candidates: popular candidates receive favorable coverage, and those whose poll numbers are low or falling receive more negative coverage, even when it is the same candidate who first benefited from the positive coverage that comes with rising poll numbers (Patterson 1994).

Typical of this early coverage of Palin was Joe Klein's adoring cover story in the September 10, 2008, issue of *Time*:

[Her] real message is: I'm just like you want to be, a brilliantly spectacular... average American. The Palins win elections and snowmobile races in a state that represents the last, lingering hint of that most basic Huckleberry Finn fantasy – lighting out for the territories. She quoted Westbrook Pegler, the F.D.R.-era conservative columnist, in her acceptance speech: "We grow good people in our small towns... " And then added, "I grew up with those people. They're the ones who do some of the hardest work in America, who grow our food and run our factories and fight our wars. They love their country in good times and bad, and they're always proud of America."[1] (http://www.time.com/time/politics/article/0,8599,1840388,00.html)

Klein went on to question whether it would be possible for the Obama campaign to find a similarly populist vision of America with which to challenge the "primal" appeal of Palin. By September 7, when polling revealed Palin with a 58 percent favorability rating, Democratic supporters began to question the Obama campaign for not attacking the political newcomer more forcefully (Madden 2008).

Even if professional journalists completely controlled the agenda, such favorable coverage of Palin would not have continued. Almost certainly, Democrats would have devised more aggressive strategies to attack her, and their attacks would have come to define one of the two sides presented by the press. Reversing the feedback loop between popularity and journalistic coverage, more negative coverage would tend to lower Palin's popularity with the public, thus freeing the press to be more negative. Yet given the sensitivity of journalists to accusations of bias or partisanship in their treatment, there would have been limits to this trend. For example, on September 2, Fox News ran a story arguing that Palin's coverage was already more negative than that of Democratic vice presidential candidate Joe Biden (Lott 2008). Coverage of Palin's first extended interview with a journalist, conducted by ABC's Charlie Gibson, followed the pattern: it was praised by supporters and criticized by opponents, leading to coverage concluding that she had hurdled the, perhaps, low bar: "Despite ... some ... hiccups the Alaska governor passed her first major media test in the ABC Charles Gibson interview with a six out of ten" (Spillius 2008). Based on past campaigns and the conventional wisdom of scholars, journalists, and pundits, the overall outcome would have been increasing criticism of Palin, given both her vulnerability and the development of more effective critical strategies, but this would have been balanced by the defense of Republicans and the rules of professional journalism, which demand that journalists present two sides to the story.

As we all know, the coverage of Sarah Palin did not follow the pattern of many past campaigns, and most significant, her story was not defined by professional journalists. Competing with the reports of journalists was the work of a variety of late-night television performers, especially

---

[1] Klein's article is particularly noteworthy in its casual mention of Palin's using a quote from Westbrook Pegler. In a few weeks, use of such an obscure (dare we say "even learned") quote would have drawn much comment, given the questions that were raised about the governor's reading habits and intellectual curiosity.

Tina Fey, which thoroughly disrupted the emerging journalistic narrative of Sarah Palin. The former *Saturday Night Live* (*SNL*) regular returned to the show on September 13 to lampoon Palin, using an uncanny physical resemblance and spot-on accent to parody Palin's intellectual shortcomings as a candidate for high national office ("I can see Russia from my house"). Ten days later, an extended interview of Palin by *CBS Evening News* anchor Katie Couric aired over two nights. With Tina Fey's satirical performance helping prime audiences (including journalists), the Couric interview was widely viewed as a disaster for the Alaskan. Following the CBS interview, Fey returned to *SNL* and skewered Palin by liberally sprinkling her parody with actual quotes from the Couric and Gibson interviews. The ratings of *SNL* hit levels they had not seen for years as the show became a significant voice in shaping media and public understanding of the 2008 election. Unlike the rules employed by journalists, which limited their ability to independently comment on the governor's obvious lack of experience, preparation, and perhaps intellectual ability and curiosity, satirists like Fey (along with Jon Stewart, Stephen Colbert, and late-night comedians like Jay Leno and David Letterman) faced no such rules. Satirical and comedic portrayals of Palin became a central component of the way journalists themselves portrayed the Alaskan governor, thus freeing them to be more independent and critical in their portrayals of the Republican nominee. It soon became almost impossible to find extended discussions of Palin that did not reference the Tina Fey lampooning. Even Palin herself seemed to recognize the significance of *SNL* and appeared on the show opposite Fey (attracting the show's largest audience – 17 million viewers – in more than fourteen years). Looking back on her campaign in January 2009 (and searching for ways to blame the media for her failures), Palin made no distinction between *SNL* and *CBS Evening News*, accusing both Fey and Couric of taking advantage of her to further their own careers. In July 2009, in the wake of Palin's surprising decision to resign as governor, it was hard to find coverage that did not mention the impact of Tina Fey on Palin's political fortunes. A story in *The New York Times* is typical:

If one of Ms. Palin's goals was to erase the perception of her as flighty – a perception encouraged by some McCain lieutenants in the rough aftermath of the failed campaign – it certainly could not have been helped to have staged an out-of-the-blue announcement that shocked even her closest aides and whose theatrics probably tempted Tina Fey and the "Saturday Night Live" production crew to abandon their vacations and head to the studio. (Nagourney 2009, A14)

Fey's influence was, of course, only a small example of dramatic changes in the way media now operate in American elections in particular and in American democracy more generally. By the 2008 campaign, it had become commonplace for candidates or potential candidates to make appearances and announcements on *The Daily Show* or *Late Night with David Letterman*. As well, the internet and social networking sites like Facebook and Twitter all became accepted components of the campaign. Hillary Clinton announced her candidacy on her webpage and appeared on both *Saturday Night Live* and *The Daily Show* in the week before the crucial Texas and Ohio primaries. Former U.S. Senator (and television and movie actor) Fred Thompson announced his run for the Republican nomination on *The Tonight Show with Jay Leno* while skipping a Republican candidate debate.[2] John McCain's last-minute cancellation of an appearance on David Letterman's show became a minor controversy, fueled by both journalists and comedians. Earlier, McCain tried to revive his then-flagging campaign for the GOP nomination with multiple appearances on *The Daily Show*, whereas Hillary Clinton used a sketch on *Saturday Night Live*, which poked fun at the press's infatuation with Barak Obama, as evidence for media coverage slanted to her opponent. A wide variety of videos – from "Obama Girl" to cell phone images from the campaign trail and clips of the latest *SNL* sketch or Jon Stewart quip – were viewed by millions of citizens on sites like YouTube and Facebook. On those sites, they might also encounter videos made by other citizens as well as by the campaigns themselves. It also seemed unsurprising that candidates from both parties were being interviewed on YouTube or that unregulated and controversial political advertising appearing on the internet would be routinely covered in the mainstream outlets. Bloggers altered the strategies employed by the two campaigns, as when, wishing to avoid direct attacks on Sarah Palin, the Democratic Party targeted negative messages to sympathetic bloggers, hoping the blogs would be picked up by mainstream journalists (as they often were) and enter public discourse without the direct fingerprints of the Obama campaign.[3]

---

[2] Thompson's campaign manager explained the choice by saying, "It makes a lot of sense" for Thompson to appear on Leno's show instead of at the GOP debate because the candidate would reach "everyday normal Americans who don't live in the 202 area code."

[3] One blogger, for example, reported, "On Tuesday [September 9, 2008] alone, more than two dozen e-mails about Palin from the [Democratic National Committee] or the Obama campaign landed in my in box, highlighting everything from her habit of taking a per

Changes in the relationship between media and politics are not, of course, limited to elections. Consider Sarah Palin's postelection activities. She regularly uses both her Facebook page (which has more than a million "supporters") and Twitter to opine on the issues of the day. These postings and tweets are then routinely circulated on blogs, cable-news talk shows, and occasionally newspapers and network news shows. She also engaged in a widely covered argument with David Letterman over his jokes about her daughter Bristol, and she battled with Levi Johnson (who fathered an out-of-wedlock child with Bristol and later appeared nude in *Playgirl*) over his involvement with his daughter and Palin's granddaughter.

Following the advice of Newt Gingrich for building a political career (write a book and then land a television show), in 2009, Palin published the best-selling *Going Rogue* and embarked on a heavily publicized book tour. Although there is nothing new about politicians writing books (or having them ghostwritten) and going on book tours, even these older forms of political communication have been transformed. In a perceptive article in the *New Yorker*, Sam Tanenhaus (2009, 84) compares the media environment leading to the circuslike atmosphere around Palin's book tour with that of Colin Powell's more serious-seeming book and tour in 1995:

In 1995, cable news remained the bland civic pasture of CNN and C-SPAN; Fox News and MSNBC were not founded until the following year. Rush Limbaugh was a bumptious presence – an honorary member of the Republican caucus that he had helped exhort to victory in the 1994 elections. But other noisemakers had yet to catch up. Bill O'Reilly was between jobs, having left the tabloid gossip program "Inside Edition." Lou Dobbs was still a business specialist, and not yet the ringmaster of anti-immigration furor and the "birther" controversy. And no one had ever viewed a YouTube clip.

Taking the rest of Gingrich's advice, it was announced in January 2010 that Palin would join the "noisemakers," becoming a political analyst and occasional host of her own show on Fox News.

The story of Sarah Palin illustrates the central issue we address in this book: the precipitous decline in the power of journalists to control, for better or worse, the media narrative and an increase, again for better or worse, in the importance of other forms of communication, some new and some old, to influence and/or dictate media coverage of politics.

diem for sleeping in her own home to the flood of stories poking holes in her claim she stopped the 'Bridge to Nowhere' in Alaska" (Madden 2008).

There is little disagreement that the media environment has dramatically changed over the past two decades and that these changes have had significant implications for American democracy. Yet the way these changes have been generally understood – by scholars, journalists, political elites, and citizens – has obscured our ability to grasp fully their extraordinary potential for improving and/or degrading the operations of media and politics in the twenty-first century.

Most scholars and journalists, as well as many citizens, view these changes with alarm and emphasize two lines of argument. First, there has been a precipitous decline in the attention paid to traditional and reliable sources of political information, especially to professional journalists. This contributes to an increasingly polarized and coarse public discourse, too often based on little more than rumor and innuendo. Second, and related, is that changes in media have accelerated a blurring of the distinction between news and entertainment, which results in less attention being paid (by both producers and consumers of media) to "serious" coverage of the political world. Although there is something to each of these perspectives, we argue that they provide an exceptionally poor starting point for any full appreciation (or criticism) of the changes currently under way in the media environment.

Changing Sources of Political Information

A major source of anxiety about the changes in the media environment is the public's, especially young people's, turning away from traditional sources of political information. By the 2004 elections, the Pew Research Center for the People and the Press reported that 21 percent of eighteen- to twenty-nine-year-olds named *The Daily Show* and *Saturday Night Live* as their regular source of campaign news (up from 9 percent in 2000). Twenty-three percent in this group named one of the three nightly network news broadcasts as their source of campaign news (down from 39 percent in 2000) (Pew Research Center for the People and the Press, 2004a). In the year between March 2007 and March 2008, the three network news broadcasts lost 21 percent (CBS), 13.5 percent (ABC), and 10.1 percent (NBC) of their eighteen- to thirty-four-year-old audience (Fitzgerald 2008). The figures for those who regularly seek out political information on the internet are similarly skewed by generation. So, for instance, in 2007, 26 percent of those between thirty and forty-nine years of age and 15 percent of those older than fifty years of age said that the internet is their main source of campaign news (Pew Research Center for

TABLE 1.1. *Internet's Broader Role in Campaign 2008*

Among the Young, TV Losing Ground to the Internet			
Get most election news from ...*	2004 %	2007 %	Change
Television	75	60	−15
Newspapers	30	24	−6
Internet	21	46	25
Radio	10	10	0
Magazines	1	4	3
Other	4	6	2

Based on 18–29 year-olds.
*First or second mentions.
Source: "Social Networking and Online Videos Take Off, January 18, 2008 Pew Research Center for the People and the Press http://people-press.org/reports/display.php3?ReportID=384.

the People and the Press 2008a). In contrast, Table 1.1 lists the main sources for those between the ages of eighteen and twenty-nine in 2004 and 2007.

Such results are usually viewed as evidence that the lines between "news" and "entertainment" are blurring. Typically, this blurring is viewed with alarm, seen as a sometimes economic and sometimes cultural challenge to journalism's preeminent status as the nation's gatekeeper of the public interest. According to this view, news professionals are the appropriate determiners of what is politically relevant for citizens to know. Thus, survey evidence that one-third of Americans younger than thirty years old say they get their news primarily from late-night comedians such as David Letterman, or that 79 percent of this age group (and half of the adult population more generally) say that they sometimes or regularly get political information from comedy programs such as *The Daily Show* or nontraditional outlets such as MTV is cause for alarm (Tucher 1997). It is a further cause for alarm, from this perspective, that in 2009, Jon Stewart was named in an online poll conducted by *Time* as "the most trusted newscaster" in America, swamping the anchors of the three nightly network news broadcasts (*Time* 2009).

Yet it is far from clear that any lack of knowledge by young people can be blamed on their use of nontraditional sources of political information. Privileging professional journalism is further undermined by surveys finding that those who say that they rely primarily on nontraditional sources of political information (e.g., *The Daily Show*, Fox's *The O'Reilly Factor*) may be better informed than those who rely primarily on traditional sources (e.g., newspapers or the nightly network news broadcasts). Consider the results of a 2004 Pew Research Center survey that asked four knowledge questions about current affairs (Pew Research Center for the People and the Press 2004b).[4] The survey then calculated the percentage of respondents who got all four questions correct according to their self-reported primary source of news and found the following ranking: *Daily Show*, 47 percent; *O'Reilly Factor*, 47 percent; talk radio, 45 percent; PBS's *NewsHour*, 46 percent; Sunday political talk shows, 44 percent; National Public Radio, 36 percent; daily newspaper, 34 percent; nightly network news, 33 percent.

If both journalists and late-night comedians are useful sources of political information, then why should we care whether comedians interject themselves into the political process or if people get their political news from late-night comedians rather than the evening news or the daily newspaper? We believe that we should care where and how citizens acquire political knowledge and that this is an important question with far-reaching implications for political communication. An adequate answer, however, is far from simple and must address explicitly the changing contours of the media environment rather than relying on unexamined, a priori distinctions between sources of political information. Too often, concerns over the changing sources of political information assume a clear distinction between news and entertainment, the former being the appropriate place for citizens to seek out factual political information. Moreover, this distinction also assumes that the news does a better job at informing citizens than entertainment outlets. Yet as we saw with the Sarah Palin story, professional journalists, because of the ways they approached their goal of being "fair and balanced," were much slower than (and in many ways dependent on) entertainment media (especially *SNL*, but also *The Daily Show* and *The Colbert Report*) to critically investigate the limitations of the Alaskan governor.

Certainly most journalists assume that the distinction between news and entertainment is clear and reasonable. Alex Jones (2009), a former journalist now at the Joan Shorenstein Center on the Press, Politics and Public Policy at Harvard University, assumes this distinction when he

---

4 The questions and the percentage of respondents answering correctly were as follows: 79 percent were able to recall that Martha Stewart had been found guilty in her recent trial; in an open-ended question, 71 percent volunteered that al-Qaeda and/or Osama bin Laden were behind the 9/11 attacks; 56 percent knew that the Republicans then maintained a majority in the House of Representatives; and 55 percent were able to correctly estimate the current number of U.S. military deaths in Iraq.

discusses the implications of the declining role of journalism in *Losing the News*. All newspapers, because they are the outlet for professional journalism, are considered desirable and worth saving, so he makes few distinctions between *USA Today* and the *New York Times* as useful sources of political information. Conversely, he considers all entertainment outlets as equally unsatisfactory, lumping together *The Daily Show*, *The O'Reilly Factor*, *The Tonight Show with Jay Leno*, and *Late Show with David Letterman*.

Political communications scholars have produced a large literature that either implicitly or explicitly assumes the validity of this information hierarchy, documenting the impact of the news and other clearly labeled political media (e.g., campaign advertising, political talk shows) on the political knowledge, beliefs, and behaviors of citizens. Much less systematic attention has been paid, however, to the political impact of other forms of media, a clear indication that these genres are not thought of as likely or appropriate carriers of politically relevant information. But what is the difference between news and entertainment, between Tina Fey on *Saturday Night Live* and Katie Couric on *CBS Evening News*?

The Inherent Arbitrariness of the News-versus-Entertainment Distinction

Despite the seeming naturalness of the distinction between news and entertainment media, it is remarkably difficult to identify the characteristics on which this distinction is based. In fact, it is difficult – we would argue impossible – to articulate a theoretically useful definition of this distinction. The opposite of "news" is not "entertainment," as the news is often diversionary or amusing (the definition of entertainment) and what is called "entertainment" is often neither of these things. One might instead use the terms *public affairs media* and *popular culture*, but these distinctions also collapse under the slightest scrutiny. Does the definition of public affairs media require that it be unpopular? Does the broadcasting of a presidential address shift from public affairs to popular culture because it is watched by too many people? And how does one classify the many magazine stories, novels, movies, websites, and television shows (in all their rapidly changing formats such as melodramas, docudramas, docusoaps, blogs, reality programs, and talk shows) that address issues of public concern? Clearly, the concept of popular culture does not provide a counterpoint to public affairs. To the contrary, the *public* in public affairs is meant to signal that the issues discussed are of importance to a substantial segment of the citizenry, and most of what is studied under this heading is popular by any reasonable definition of the term.[5] The invention of hybrid terms like *infotainment* do nothing to clarify these definitional problems, because they are almost always used as terms of derision, assuming the naturalness of the news-entertainment distinction and that the penetration of the latter into the former results in a polluted form of political information.[6]

The difficulty in even naming the categories on which we base so fundamental a distinction is more than semantics. It cuts to the heart of the complexity and artificiality of this distinction. A more useful approach might be to identify the key characteristics that are assumed to distinguish politically relevant from politically irrelevant media. But this does more to blur than to salvage the traditional "news" and "non-news" categories. Public affairs media address real-world issues of relevance or concern to a significant percentage of the citizenry, but so, too, does much of what traditionally would fall outside of this genre: one would be hard pressed to find any substantive topic found in the news that has not also been the subject of ostensibly non-news media. And public affairs media in general, and the news more specifically, regularly address issues of culture, celebrity, and personality. No less a student of journalism than Walter Lippmann in 1922 defined news as simply "the signalizing of an event." And yet so-called entertainment media often play this role, drawing the public's attention to issues and events of social and political import (Delli Carpini and Williams 2001; Fiske 1996). A final response, born largely of frustration with the definitional difficulties summarized here, is to simply argue that what is in the newspapers or on television news is the news and what appears outside them is not. This approach, which is implicitly adopted by most journalists and political communication scholars, does not prevent debates over the appropriateness of news content (e.g.,

---

[5] For example, the final episode of the first season of the television "reality" show *Survivor* received extensive press coverage for being watched by more than 50 million viewers. However, the first presidential debate in 2008 drew more than 52 million viewers; the second, more than 63 million; and the vice presidential debate between Sarah Palin and Joe Biden drew more than 70 million.

[6] We have not been immune to the use of such hybrid terms. Indeed, in 2001, we published a book chapter that used the term *infotain* in its title (Delli Carpini and Williams 2001). Such terms imply that between the categories of news and entertainment, there has emerged a third distinct genre: infotainment. Changes in the media environment that have continued unabated since 2001 make such terms unhelpful, depending as they do on distinctions that have long outlived whatever usefulness they might have once had.

concerns over the growth in "soft" news and infotainment or about the legitimacy of certain sources), but it limits those debates to explicitly public affairs media. It also ignores the degree to which the very definition of news is politically, economically, culturally, and technologically determined and so has changed, often quite dramatically, throughout American history. Distinctions such as news versus entertainment, public affairs versus popular culture, hard news versus features, and so forth – and the belief in their usefulness – emerged in the 1920s and certainly did not much exist before the Progressive Era (1880–1920). Understanding the historical specificity of these distinctions is crucial for understanding the political significance of the changes currently occurring in the media environment.

We are not arguing that there is no difference between fact and fiction, news and entertainment, politically relevant and irrelevant media. We are suggesting, however, that such distinctions are not self-evident. Rather, they are distinctions that should be made and defended in public discourse, not simply unreflectively assumed. The relationships among these categories of meaning must also be carefully articulated. For example, the distinction between fiction and nonfiction cannot be conflated with the difference, either in theory or in practice, between a news story and other stories – all narratives have elements of fiction and nonfiction (Paget 1998). Consider the "fiction" of Iraqi weapons of mass destruction that dominated news during the crucial period leading to U.S. military intervention. Late-night talk shows, comedians, and satirists, to say nothing of bloggers, may be much more able than professional journalists to challenge this sort of fiction.[7]

Attempts to assert these distinctions and hierarchies are specific examples of a broader reaction to the changes that have occurred in the media environment over the past two decades. The explosion in the sources of political information attended to by segments of the public, the confusion among formerly stable genres of political media, and the blurring of the distinction between the producers and consumers of political information all challenge established political and journalistic elites. These changes have been regularly noted by many scholars and journalists. However, they have usually been viewed from the perspective of the very media system being challenged. As a result, the breakdown of distinctions such

[7] On the failure of the press in the run-up to the 2003 invasion of Iraq as an example of the systematic problems with the American press, see Bennett, Givens, and Breunig 2007.

as that between news and entertainment, the emergence of a hybrid form labeled "infotainment," the declining influence of professional journalists, and so forth, are seen as a threat to democracy itself. Yet ironically, being firmly rooted in the assumptions of the media system under challenge severely limits the solutions to the "crisis."

In *Losing the News*, for example, after chronicling the enormous threat to democracy posed by the declining fortunes of newspapers and journalism, the solutions seem both limited and vague. Jones (2009, 199) concludes that "an enduring solution for preserving the iron core of news and traditional journalism standards has to be a commercial one." By limiting himself to the basic structures of the commercial model and failing to consider alternative models (e.g., public service models, actually considered in the United States in the 1930s and adopted in many other democratic societies) the solutions seem meager: "So how can the news be saved? Journalists must hold fast and persevere. Owners must do the right thing. And citizens and news consumers must notice and demand the news that they need" (Jones 2009, 222).

We are not arguing that these changes necessarily further democracy or that the passing media system did not have many advantages. When journalists actually lived up to their profession's best practices, they played a central role in American democracy by providing vital information to the public and holding elites accountable. Further, a great advantage of having professional journalists act as gatekeepers is that the rules and values they are supposed to use are explicit and so provide both standards for evaluating performance and a clear basis for critiquing the adequacy of the rules and values themselves. Unfortunately, when it comes to the evaluation of journalistic performance, much scholarship finds that professional standards are commonly honored only in the breach. Moreover, even at its best, this system ceded the public sphere to journalists and political elites. For these reasons, criticism rooted in that passing system, too often made from the perspective of the very elites – journalists and political leaders – who dominated that system is a poor place to start understanding the implications of a rapidly changing media environment. In the end, these arguments are more than mere definitional exercises, they are about political power in a democratic society; who will get to speak with authority; the form political information will take; what will be on the political agenda; the boundaries of political and commercial speech and responsibility; and perhaps most significant, what will constitute citizenship in America.

Going Forward

The rest of this book is our attempt to understand the changing media environment and its implications for American democracy. In the next chapter, we develop the concept of *media regimes* as a way of analyzing, from an historical perspective, periods of both change and stability in the relationship between media and politics. We then sketch the different media regimes that emerged in America from the eighteenth to the twentieth century to demonstrate the changing understandings of media, democracy, and the interconnections on which they were based. Highlighting these dramatically different media regimes and their underlying assumptions allows us to avoid uncritically limiting our analysis of the current changing media environment to the presuppositions of the media regime that they have so thoroughly undermined.

Chapter 3 provides a close analysis of the emergence, institutionalization, and collapse of the media regime we call the *Age of Broadcast News*. We highlight this regime's considerable advantages and limitations as a response to the changes in both media and politics of the second half of the twentieth century. We then turn to a consideration of how social and economic changes, as well as a changing media environment, systematically undermined the Age of Broadcast News over the past two and a half decades.

In Chapter 4, we develop our own approach to defining and analyzing political communication, one that is appropriate for the transitional period in which we live. This involves developing a new definition of politically relevant media that, by avoiding unexamined assumptions about where citizens should acquire political information, can capture the richness of the changing media environment. Rejecting the limits of definitions rooted in the Age of Broadcast News makes it possible to identify and preserve what is best about this passing regime while squarely facing up to its failures. Rooted in the broad sweep of American media history, our more expansive definition of politically relevant media also opens up consideration of the advantages and disadvantages of the full range of American media regimes, which is especially useful for coming to grips with the challenges of the changing media environment of the twenty-first century.

The following three chapters apply our theoretical and historical arguments through a series of case studies. Chapter 5 examines political scandals, especially the Clinton-Lewinsky scandal, which occurred at an especially dramatic time of media change. Chapter 6 explores media coverage of the environment, especially the climate-change debate. Here we evaluate the severe limitations of the coverage provided by professional journalism on this issue, especially when it comes to informing the public. We also examine how new sources of political information open up possibilities for improving (and worsening) coverage of global climate change. Chapter 7 analyzes how a broad range of politically relevant media addressed the terrorist attacks of 9/11 and the ensuing run-up to the invasion of Iraq. Drawing on the case studies, Chapter 8 concludes by sketching out normative criteria for evaluating the changing media environment and the issues being raised in debates over media policy that will likely shape a new media regime.

2

Media Regimes and American Democracy

The true poem is the daily paper.
— Walt Whitman, 1852

Rather than falling back on unexamined information hierarchies or indefensible definitions of *news* and *entertainment*, a more fruitful avenue of inquiry is to consider the larger context within which such definitions emerge and become reified. To help do so, we introduce the notion of media regimes. By a media regime, we mean a historically specific, relatively stable set of institutions, norms, processes, and actors that shape the expectations and practices of media producers and consumers. We choose the word *regime* to signal the degree to which any stable media system depends on actions by the state – whether in the form of public subsidies, the enforcement of laws regarding ownership, intellectual property rights, rules regarding public access, and so forth – and not simply on the nature of communications technologies and the preferences of individuals expressed through markets or social action. Media regimes, then, are held in place by the authoritative actions of government and so are always political and so always structure the nature of democratic politics. But they are also shaped by the institutionalized practices of private corporations, universities, professional associations, and so forth.

Media regimes are fundamentally affected, but never determined, by new developments in communications technology. In his seminal work, *Television: Technology and Cultural Form* (2003), Raymond Williams uses the concept of social formation to illustrate how the development of any new medium can never be explained simply by its technological characteristics but rather is always a function of the specific culture within which it is deployed. Drawing on this insight, we argue that the specific contours of any media regime develop in response to larger economic, cultural, and political trends. However, the relationship between particular media regimes and the economic, cultural, political, and technological contexts in which they operate is not purely a one-way interaction – once in place, a media regime determines the gates through which information about culture, politics, and economics passes, thus shaping the discursive environment in which such topics are discussed, understood, and acted on. At most points in time, the structure of this gatekeeping process is largely invisible, with elites and citizens alike at least tacitly accepting the rules by which information is disseminated as natural and unproblematic. Controversy, when it occurs, centers on perceived violations of the rules (e.g., when a journalist is seen as violating the norms of objectivity) rather than on the appropriateness of the rules themselves (e.g., should professional journalists be the primary source for political information?).[1] Periodically, however, economic, cultural, political, and/or technological changes lead to disjunctures between existing media regimes and actual practices (e.g., when new technologies, such as cable or the internet, challenge the dominant role of a particular set of media elites, such as the news divisions of the major broadcast television networks). When these disjunctures between existing rules and actual practice become too great to ignore, normally unexamined assumptions underlying particular media regimes become more visible and more likely to be challenged, thus opening up the possibility of "regime change." These periods of uncertainty, and reactions to them, have been described by Paul Starr as "constitutive moments." Such moments result in choices that "come in bursts set off by social and political crises, technological innovation, or other triggering events, and at these pivotal moments the choices may be encoded in law, etched into technologies, or otherwise embedded in the structure of institutions" (Starr 2005, 4). Robert McChesney (2007) defines such

---

[1] A good example of this tacit consensus is the shared use of "bias" as a critique of press coverage of politics. Political elites, journalists, and the public all agree that "bias" is a violation of the proper way for politics to be covered. So, despite all evidence to the contrary, Fox News identifies itself as "fair and balanced." A March 2007 Zogby poll found that 83 percent of those surveyed thought that bias was "alive and well" (*Washington Times* 2007). Predictably, however, there was sharp disagreement over whether the bias was toward the left or the right. What bias means, what it would mean to be unbiased, or whether that would be a possible or desirable goal are vital questions that rarely are addressed in a discursive environment that assumes that these issues are beyond debate.

moments as "critical junctures" and argues that we are at just such a critical juncture now.

Critical junctures are, of course, never unconstrained moments when past practices or media can be completely changed by either new social, economic, and political conditions or the development of new kinds of media. Keeping in mind the constraints of the past allows us to avoid inaccurate and ahistorical assumptions about the way new communications technologies operate or utopian and inaccurate predictions about their potential for social change.[2] Such faulty assumptions lie at the heart of the many claims made for how new communications technologies (e.g., the telegraph in the nineteenth century, the internet in the twenty-first century) would not just change but also transform society.[3] It is revealing to recall briefly past critical junctures and the resulting debates and policies over media and democracy that shaped previous American media regimes.

For example, as we discuss in more detail in Chapter 3, economic, political, and cultural changes occurring during the early part of the twentieth century, coupled with the emergence of radio and later television, challenged the existing media regime (dominated by newspapers and their owners) and its control of the discursive environment. This critical juncture was marked by a series of very public struggles over fundamental issues, such as the relative merits of newspapers versus radio or television as a source of public information, the appropriate balance between public and private ownership, the role of advertising, which elites should communicate with the polity and how should they do so, and even the appropriate role of citizens in a democracy. By the middle of the twentieth century, a more-or-less stable new media regime had emerged, consisting of the increasing dominance of electronic over print media, concentrated ownership of a shrinking number of media outlets, a limited public service obligation imposed on radio and television networks in exchange for the use of the public airwaves for private profit, professional journalists who would mediate between political leaders and the citizenry, and so forth. It was through the emergence of this new regime (labeled ironically by Jon Katz [1997] "The Golden Age of Broadcast News"), with its particular combination of media institutions, norms, processes, and actors, that familiar distinctions such as news versus entertainment

---

[2] For an excellent discussion of the staying power of older technologies, despite the invention of newer ones, see Edgerton 2007.

[3] For a trenchant critique of the utopian predictions of the internet made by George Gilder and Nicholas Negroponte, see Jenkins 2006.

came to take on their unquestioned, authoritative meaning. In turn, this regime determined the contours of the discursive environment in which public discussion occurred and public opinion formed. The "news media" became gatekeepers of the public agenda, the source of information about pressing issues of the day, and the public space in which (mainly elites) debated these issues.

Over the past two decades, economic, cultural, political, and technological changes have challenged the stability of the existing media regime, making visible once again (and thus opening for reconsideration) its historically determined roots, and thus raising questions such as the relative merits of *Saturday Night Live*, *CBS Evening News*, Fox News, Twitter, Facebook, the *Huffington Post*, and the *New York Times* as sources of political information.

We draw three conclusions about the debate over the eroding boundaries between news and entertainment. First, at best, what distinguishes news shows, comedies, dramas, and so forth, is not their content or democratic utility but their form, or *genre*, and how those genres are socially constructed and perceived. Second, how we define what is "politically relevant" or "newsworthy" cannot be determined a priori from its form, content, or source, but rather is itself a subject of political contestation and suppression, the outcome of which is often determined by the contours of the existing media regime. In turn, political debates over the "authoritative allocation of goods, services and values" (Easton 1965, 96) as well as over who participates in these debates, are shaped by these constructed and disputable definitions of relevance or newsworthiness. So, any particular media regime structures the ongoing (if only periodically visible) struggle for control of the discursive environment in which democratic deliberation about pressing issues of the day occurs, and so it shapes how deliberations are resolved and who resolves them. And third, this struggle over the appropriate contours of the discursive environment and who controls it has no permanent or objectively "right" resolution but is itself ultimately a matter of context and contestation.

This is not to say that there are no overarching continuities across these periods of regime change, however. Although the specific way in which the struggle over control of the discursive environment was resolved has varied in different historical periods, it has consistently revolved around enduring questions that cut to the heart of the relationship between media and democracy and that grapple with the most basic questions about citizenship. New media regimes emerge from debates over which citizens we believe should (or can) be part of democratic deliberation:

the entire polity, a smaller but activated and engaged portion of the citizenry, or an even more restricted group of political elites. A connected issue is how this "democratically relevant" portion of the citizenry is divided between consumers and producers of information. As well, struggles over the shape of new media regimes focus on the usefulness, sufficiency, and trustworthiness of the information provided by the media: Do the media provide us with the kinds of information that helps individual and collective decision making? Do media provide us with enough of this information? Do we trust the information provided by the media?

Although these questions have remained constant throughout American history, the answers to them have varied. In some periods, all or most citizens have been considered legitimate participants in democratic deliberation, whereas other periods have limited the relevant political community to a more select set of elites. At times, "average" citizens were seen as producers of politically relevant information, whereas in other times, this role has been reserved for political elites (e.g., political parties), economic elites (e.g., newspaper owners), or professional journalists. The content of what is considered newsworthy has also changed over time, varying from the lives and culture of ordinary citizens to the carefully orchestrated words and actions of political elites. Similarly, decisions regarding the appropriate line between public and private life – of everyday citizens and/or elites – have varied in different periods. The type of information presented has also varied, from the unedited transcripts of public statements to the quotes of authoritative sources and the interpretation and opinions of journalists and commentators. Even the dominant form or genre through which politically relevant information is provided – poems, narratives, novels, essays, letters, news articles – has varied in different periods.

Our point is more than that things change, however. For most of our history, the ways in which the questions discussed here were answered has resulted in well-defined media regimes that have reified those answers, making their contestable nature invisible and thus shaping the parameters of political discourse in ways that influence the outcome of this discourse. As Toby Miller (1998) argues, it is the implicit "collusion" between consumers and producers (i.e., the understanding that particular texts will be produced using particular rules and interpreted by particular audiences in particular ways) that guarantees that a genre and its role in society is recognized. It is only during critical junctures, when this collusion is disrupted by political, economic, cultural, and technological changes (as is the case today, with the audience for the nightly news and newspapers shrinking and aging, and with viewers seeking political information from a new and wide-ranging number of sources), that the naturalness of an existing media regime becomes contested, opening up a new struggle over how best to define the role of the media, and ultimately of citizens, in a democratic society. How these debates are resolved, how questions about mediated political information are answered, will determine the shape of democratic politics and political communications in the emerging media regime.

It is our argument that technological changes occurring over the past two decades (e.g., characterized by innovations like the internet, satellite and cable television, VCRs and DVD players, mobile technology, etc.) along with broader and quite profound political, cultural, and economic changes (e.g., the end of the Cold War, the rise of neoliberalism, increasing multiculturalism in the United States) have destabilized the media regime of the mid-twentieth century, challenging the premises on which the Age of Broadcast News were based and accounting for current debates over the eroding boundary between news and entertainment. Although these changes present new challenges for democratic politics, they also provide new opportunities. Understanding and addressing these challenges and opportunities requires first understanding their connections to the ongoing historical struggles discussed here, how they were resolved through the construction of prior media regimes, and the consequences of those prior resolutions for the practice of democracy in the United States.

Media Regimes in the Eighteenth and Nineteenth Century: The Decline of the Party Press and the Rise of Realism

It is not our intention to present anything like a comprehensive history of early American media or American journalism, several of which already exist (e.g., Emery and Emery 1997; Starr 2005). Rather, our first goal is to provide a little flavor of early media regimes that operated with very different values and assumptions than the ones that we now take for granted. Our second, more specific goal is to show how the enduring questions about the relationship between democratic politics and the media have been periodically revisited and temporarily resolved as a result of changes in the technological, social, political, and economic environments. These earlier debates help us better understand the current boundaries between news and non-news that are proving so problematic in our changing media environment.

Who Is the Father of Our Country? Lessons from the Dark Ages of American Journalism

A refreshing window on the partisan press of the early Republic (sometimes known as the dark ages of journalism) is provided in Richard N. Rosenfeld's (1997) *American Aurora: A Democratic-Republican Returns*. Rosenfeld recaptures the voice of the *Philadelphia Aurora* (later the *American Aurora*), a newspaper that opposed the dominant Federalist press and its views. The book recounts the day-to-day issues covered (between 1798 and 1801) in the *Aurora* and its Federalist antagonists, especially the *Gazette of the United States*, doing so almost entirely through reprinted actual newspaper articles.

The early American press, though beholden to their political masters, was also intensely personal, reflecting the views of the publisher, who usually served as editor, printer, business manager, and reporter (though reporting in anything like the current sense was rare, and papers usually waited for material to come in over the transom). A distinctive voice is quite clear in the *Aurora* – initially that of Benjamin Franklin Bache (Benjamin Franklin's grandson) and later (after Bache died awaiting trial on sedition charges) that of William Duane.

What is immediately evident to the modern reader is the near absence of any distinction between fact and opinion in the pages of the *Aurora* and its competitors. In its place were countervailing interpretations of current events, in which facts (or allegations) served as evidence to drive ideological and/or partisan arguments. These debates, argued with vigor, emotion, and drama, focused on fundamental issues of the day. For example, over its history, the *Aurora* claimed:

Washington and Adams opposed the French Revolution because they were enemies to democracy, and had been even during the American Revolution; that Washington was not the father of his country, but an inept general who would have lost the American Revolution had Benjamin Franklin not gotten France to intervene; that Washington, Adams, Hamilton, and other founding fathers had denied Franklin his credit (partly by under stating France's), had mythologized Washington's, and had adopted a British-style constitution to avoid Franklin's design (and many Americans hopes) for a democracy; and that Adams, Hamilton, and other Federalists really wanted an American king. (Rosenfeld 1997, x)

Whatever conclusions one might draw about the validity of these claims, the absence of a clear line between fact and opinion, the ideological and personal lenses through which contemporary events were viewed, and the presence of competing presses produced a much more active (and unfamiliar, for readers weaned on the Age of Broadcast News) role for the media. In this early regime, the press served unselfconsciously as a political actor, using its pages less to record events than to place them into different ideological narratives.

This perspective adds three twists to the maxim that "journalism is the first draft of history" (still a common assumption among today's journalists; see Konner 1996). First, journalism during this period was providing competing drafts of history, each with very different interpretations and implications – the perspective of the *Aurora* was quite at odds with the sense of the period one gets from the Federalist press. Second, this process was not simply a matter of preserving the past for future generations, but it was central to the way in which events themselves unfolded. And third, the press did not play this role as a neutral observer but was deeply involved in the very political struggles they reported on. Indeed, they were so involved (and the stakes of their involvement were so high) that John Adams used the Alien and Sedition Acts to jail Benjamin Franklin Bache and so silence the voice of the *Aurora*.

Another characteristic of this early media regime relevant to current debates over the place of the press in a democracy is the very different role played by reader-citizens. No one could read the *Aurora* or its antagonists and think he or she was getting a neutral, factual, or detached vision of the political world. Rather, the newspaper assumed that it was in a struggle with other papers to convince and persuade readers about issues over which there was great disagreement. Consider the following passage from the *Gazette of the United States* on December 2, 1799:

> The gin-drinking pauper who is said to conduct Bache's paper [the editor William Duane] boasts of having been highly complimented by a respectable English merchant of this city. The aspersion is undoubtedly a lie, as there is no such man...who would not be ashamed and afraid to perpetrate such an act of humiliation and disgrace. The exultation with which the vagabond mentions it shows, however, that the compliments of a gentleman are not "renewed upon him everyday." (Rosenfeld 1997, 722)

Press opinions were not limited to casting personal aspersions. Many of the most fundamental issues of the day (e.g., property qualifications for political participation, the definition of freedom of the press, the appropriate powers of the executive branch, relations with foreign nations) were addressed with a similar blend of emotion, fact, allegation, and opinion, with competing papers presenting often diametrically opposed "evidence" and drawing radically different conclusions (on the centrality of these struggles to the development of democracy in America in the late eighteenth and early nineteenth century, see Wilentz 2005, especially part 1).[4]

In this media regime, it was up to the reader to actively sort through these claims and counterclaims. Whether citizens were able to do so is, of course, an open question. The readership of newspapers was restricted by distribution practices (the price of the newspapers meant that they were often read only in clubs and other social settings, although this practice did encourage discussions about what was read). For example, the actual subscription base of the *Aurora* was only about 1,500 in 1798. Nonetheless, it has been estimated that, by the end of the eighteenth century, the United States had two-thirds the number of newspapers as England but only half the population. And although accurate figures are difficult to establish, literacy appeared to have been widespread, at least relative to other nations, including England.[5]

Regardless of the actual reach of newspapers in the eighteenth century, what is important for our purposes is that this model of journalism implicitly (and at times explicitly) assumed that readers were actively engaged in the process of creating political meaning. As the *New York Gazette* told its readers (tellingly, in lyric verse) in a 1770 edition:

> 'Tis truth (with deference to the college)
> Newspapers are the spring of Knowledge,
> The general source throughout the nation,
> Of every modern conversation.
> (Postman 1985, 37)

Especially significant in the model of the press articulated by the *Aurora* and captured in its ongoing exchanges with the *Gazette of the United States* is that questions of adequacy, trustworthiness, and usefulness were to be answered by the readers of an ideologically diverse and contentious press.

Of course, we are not suggesting that the early press was filled with weighty dissertations supported by complicated arguments and well-researched facts. Nor do we mean to imply that editors assumed a

---

[4] It is also worth pointing out that the same is true for the heated, vituperative exchanges between folks like Keith Olbermann and Bill O'Reilly, which hearken back to this period in terms of both their ad hominem nature and their connection to very basic issues of political ideology.

[5] Literacy in other parts of the country was lower. For example, male literacy in Virginia in the mid-eighteenth century is estimated to have been at slightly more than 60 percent, and limited education for women and slaves meant that three out of four adults were functionally illiterate. See also Postman (1985, 30–434) and Starr (2005, 52–53).

readership that would study their words in Talmudic fashion and then reach their own positions on the issues of the day. As Michael Schudson (1998) argues, citizenship in the early Republic was trust based and worked largely to endorse existing values and elites.

Finally, we are not arguing that similar examples of personal or political bias, of sensationalized reporting, or of assumptions of sophisticated readers cannot be found in the twentieth-century press.

We do believe, however, that within the political, social, and economic context of the time, the exchanges between the *Aurora* and its ideological competitors demonstrate a model of democracy that assumes very different relationships among the press, the public, and political elites than existed in the later half of the twentieth century. This relationship took as a given that many of the most important issues of the day were contestable and that both the press and citizens were critical actors in this ongoing debate. It also assumed that, in this debate, no one actor had full authority in determining "the truth." Exchanges between papers like the *Aurora* and the *Gazette* regarding property rights for voting and office holding remind us that, although citizenship of the era may have depended to some degree on deference to elites, which elites were worthy of trust was very much in question during the late eighteenth and early nineteenth centuries.[6]

A final conclusion we draw from this era is that, although the debates taking place in the press were intensely political in their substance – elections, events abroad, and so forth – the newspapers of the time adopt nothing like the distinctions between hard and soft news or, for that matter, between news and entertainment that we assume today. As a result, newspapers such as the *Aurora* provided a rollicking combination of serious debate, fantastic accusations, sexual innuendo, and vituperative attacks. The claims and counterclaims, turning on accusations about the sex lives of the founders (especially Jefferson and Hamilton), conflict of interest, secret plans, ad hominem attacks, and so forth, seem to the modern reader much closer to the *National Enquirer* than the *New York Times*. One cannot escape the conclusion that current figures like Bill O'Reilly, Rush Limbaugh, Michael Moore, Keith Olbermann, Jon Stewart, and Stephen Colbert would have felt right at home during the late eighteenth and early nineteenth centuries.

---

[6] For arguments that support the notion that Schudson and others have overemphasized the degree of trust and deference in this period, see Nash (1979) and Zuckerman (1998). Indeed, Wilentz (2005, 58) argues that controversies over deference to elites was at the center of the struggle between Federalists and the Democratic-Republicans, of which the *Aurora* was a primary voice, in the 1790s.

Clearly, the media environment of the late eighteenth and early nineteenth centuries was fundamentally different from that which characterized most of the latter half of the twentieth century. However, many modern-day retrospectives of this era, while often noting these differences, view them through the lens of today's embattled media regime. For example, Rosenfeld's recovery of the *Aurora* and its exchanges with other newspapers of the day is at odds with the interpretation of this period provided in the 2001 best-selling book *John Adams*, authored by the popular historian David McCullough and on which the 2008 big-budget HBO miniseries was based. The spectacular success of McCullough's biography of Adams and the high ratings for the television version are evidence of how this period still resonates in American public discourse. *John Adams* is much more than a simple biography of our nation's second president, however. Rather, it is a celebration of the "wisdom" of the Federalist founding fathers, implicitly legitimating their decidedly elitist answers to the enduring questions surrounding the role of the press and of citizens in a democratic society. McCullough writes from the perspective of John Adams and the Federalists – a perspective more akin to the views of political and media elites embedded in the norms and practices of the Age of Broadcast News – whereas Rosenfeld provides a glimpse of what the period looked like to those in conflict with them.

Consider, for example, the current debate over the newsworthiness of the private lives of political elites. Such debates can be understood only in the context of the particular media regime (and resulting discursive environment) in which they take place. As Schudson (1999, 3) suggests, during the late eighteenth and early nineteenth centuries, "[t]he whole of citizens' informational obligations was to recognize virtue well enough to be able to know and defeat its counterfeit." Although we believe citizens' obligations extended beyond this, if one task of citizens was to recognize the virtue or lack thereof in their leaders, then investigation of the private lives of public figures was germane to public debate. Indeed, one might further argue that viewing the early days of the U.S. Republic from the perspective of Federalist papers like the *Gazette* (as both McCullough and, to a lesser extent, Schudson do) while ignoring the competing perspective of outlets like the *Aurora* leads to overemphasizing the extent to which this era was dominated by a politics of trust.

Other insights into current controversies flow from such a historical perspective. The Yale law professor Jack M. Balkin (2009) notes the different definitions of journalism that have existed within what we are calling different media regimes. He argues that current controversies over

Fox News and attacks on it by the Obama administration must be understood within the context of a transition from twentieth-century ideas of nonpartisan journalism to an older model of the party press (which we have just described):

The irony of the Administration's response to Fox News is its declaration that Fox is not a "legitimate" news organization. It is not a legitimate mid-twentieth century news organization. But it is a legitimate nineteenth century news organization and it could well be what twenty-first century news organizations increasingly look like. The concept of "legitimacy" in news gathering and reporting is not timeless and forever fixed; the point is that it is now very much up for grabs. What the Obama Administration is trading on in its attacks is the notion that "legitimate" journalism is "objective" twentieth century journalism, and since Fox is not that, it is not legitimate journalism. Fox, for its part, actually plays into this framing because it insists that it is fair and balanced and objective, when it is anything but. Fox has been trying to have it both ways since it began; the Obama Administration is now calling its bluff, and attempting to redefine it as not legitimate according to a previous (but increasingly challenged) conception of legitimate journalism. (Balkin 2009)

We are not judging the appropriateness or accuracy of these competing points of view as they apply to either the past or the present. Rather, we are suggesting that it is such context-dependent definitions of citizenship and the relationship between media and politics that determine what is or is not appropriate media behavior. The role of ordinary citizens, the nature of the press, and the implications of these questions for the structure of the media and democratic politics animated debates between the *Aurora* and its critics. So, too, they animated debates during later periods, including our own. What distinguishes media regimes is not the existence of such debates but the specific way in which they are resolved.

The Emergence of the Penny Press: Media as Public Conversation

By the 1830s, political, economic, and technological changes were beginning to transform "news" into a product sold through the papers to a mass audience, although it remained quite distinct from twentieth-century notions of either news or newspaper content (Schudson 1978). And although the links between parties and the press had begun to break down during this period, the emergence of the penny press continued several tendencies of the media regime that preceded it. Somewhat paradoxically, newspapers became more personal as they became more concerned with news rather than editorial content. In addition, news of the time continued to be reported colorfully, although without the overt partisan ideology of the prior era.

As with earlier and subsequent transitions, changes in the media environment during the first half of the nineteenth century were crucial. One central change was the development of the post office system during the Jacksonian era and the reduced mailing rates it provided for newspapers. This development led to increases in the circulation of newspapers (in terms both of readership and of geographic reach). It also increased the prominence and visibility of newspapers as the source of news, first supplementing and then replacing private letters as the source of public information.[7] The development of the telegraph – labeled the "Victorian Internet" by Tom Standage (1998) – was also crucial, transforming the way information was transmitted; altering thinking about time, space, and community; changing the content of public information and the way reporters wrote their stories; and giving rise to a wave of utopian thinking about the possibilities for human emancipation immanent in new communications technologies (strikingly similar to the claims made for current transformations in communications technologies; see Standage 1998 and Carey 1989). Urbanization, immigration, and the expansion of suffrage (to white males at least) as a result of the elimination of property requirements provided a vast new political backdrop and audience for newspapers.

Emerging from these changes was the penny press. The "pennies" developed in the swirl of nineteenth-century urban America and chronicled the everyday life of the city and its inhabitants (especially of the deviant and the downtrodden) rather than the affairs of the national government or its leaders. It was during this period, for example, that the human-interest story emerged as a characteristic feature of daily journalism (Schudson 1978, 27). Although the partisan press of the early Republic reflected an ethic of the political being personal, the pennies were instrumental in making the personal political, or, in Hannah Arendt's disapproving words, creating "that curious hybrid realm where private interests assume public significance" (qtd. in Schudson 1978, 30). Despite this shift in emphasis, the focus of the pennies remained every bit as intensely political as the partisan press, addressing issues that cut to the heart of the role of the media in a democratic society. And in both style and substance, they continued to assume a readership that was actively engaged in the construction of political meaning. It was this growing readership (made possible in part by growing literacy rates, estimated as high as 91 percent among white Americans and 77 percent overall in the United States by the

---

7 On the significance this had for the development of a public sphere, see Habermas 1991.

mid-1800s; Starr 2005, 105), rather than a more select elite, that would answer questions of the trustworthiness, adequacy, and helpfulness of political information.

Another feature shared by both the partisan and the penny press (largely lost in the Progressive Era and its aftermath) was the notion that the media was part of a public conversation. The Age of Broadcast News would define the press as providers of information and citizens as consumers. The inverted-pyramid style of reporting, in which the information presumed to be most important (who, what, when, where) is provided first and the "least important" information (why and how) last, exemplifies this model. This style of reporting, still taught in journalism schools and used by most newspapers, assumes a very functional and hegemonic approach to the news. It also assumes that the flow of information moves in a single direction, from the newspaper or other source to the audience.

The roots of this model of reporting can be traced to the mid-nineteenth century and were originally designed to minimize the time taken to transmit a story over a telegraph, the space it took up in a newspaper, and the time spent reading it.[8] Nonetheless, during this period, one still finds, along with a growing one-way flow of information, a continuation of the more two-way, conversational approach to public communication. Characteristic of this model was a more interactive exchange involving a series of claims and counterclaims and the recognition by involved parties that others were part of the public discourse.[9] Although admittedly this conversation only occasionally directly included average citizens, and so remained largely the province of elites, it did assume an active citizenry that presumably continued the conversation in other public venues. Given the possibilities for reestablishing a more conversational approach to the communication of political information provided by the interactivity of much new communication technology of the early twenty-first century, it is worth recalling some of the features of this earlier model.

"Conversations" in nineteenth-century newspapers took a number of different forms. There were, of course, the ad hominem attacks characteristic of the notorious conflicts between James Gordon Bennett, editor of the upstart *New York Herald*, and James Watson Webb, editor of

---

[8] Mindich (1998) provides a fascinating discussion of the development of the inverted-pyramid form of newspaper writing, which he traces to the press releases of Edwin M. Stanton during the Civil War.

[9] Elsewhere, we have written about the importance of conversation as a metaphor for understanding public opinion, Delli Carpini and Williams (1994b).

the establishment *New York Enquirer* – conflicts so personal that they resulted in three separate physical assaults by the latter on the former. As with the battle between the *Aurora* and *Gazette*, these conflicts were driven in part by attempts to draw the boundaries between public and private life and in part by the desire to entertain readers. But aside from personal attacks between editors, there were other ways in which the newspapers of the nineteenth century were involved in a public conversation.

Stories appearing in one newspaper were quite commonly reprinted and commented on in other newspapers. Tellingly, this reprinting occurred because of the particular rules of the media regime in place, here the "subsidized postal swapping of issues across the country," called the exchange system, which subsidized the reprinting of content between newspapers and periodicals (Gitelman 2006, 27). The political significance of such exchanges is illustrated by the journalism historian David Mindich's (1998, 50) discussion of the influence of the abolitionist William Lloyd Garrison. The circulation of Garrison's own newspaper, the *Liberator*, was quite small, and it was banned in the South. However, he became an influential voice in the debate over slavery, because his articles were widely exchanged with and printed in other newspapers – even pro-slavery papers in the South, where they were criticized as illustrations of northernintolerance of slavery.[10] It is important to note that this conversation was facilitated by reduced postal rates for newspapers and magazines, government policies central to the mid-nineteenth-century media regime.[11] The nature of this conversation had profound political implications. As Mindich argues, Garrison illustrates a kind of nonpartisanship that is often overlooked by more recent models of journalism. Currently, *nonpartisanship* is defined as positioning oneself between the two political parties, allowing "both" sides of an issue to be considered and thus allowing the range of ideological disagreement to be defined

[10] This kind of direct exchange and/or criticism across media outlets would be largely unheard of during most of the twentieth century, which reflects the very different nature of the dominant media regimes in each period. However, they are more common today, as reflected in the exchanges between Fox News's Bill O'Reilly and MSNBC's Keith Olbermann. As with the *Liberator*, these cable shows have relatively small ratings, but their impact is multiplied to the extent that their contents are circulated in the wider media (including newer venues like YouTube). This is even more the case with the most widely read political bloggers, whose impact depends on their stories being circulated in the mainstream media.

[11] Similarly, the outcome of current debates over issues like public access cable, Net neutrality, and so forth, will shape the possibilities for political conversations in the media regime of the twenty-first century.

by existing political elites. However, Garrison adopted a nonpartisan stance that consciously rejected the position of both parties and insisted on the importance of slavery, despite the unwillingness of political elites to take the issue on. In this view, mediated political information was not trustworthy, adequate, or useful if it ignored voices outside the major political parties. The result was that, at a time when other political institutions, especially the political parties, did their best to avoid entering into a debate over slavery, newspapers played a vital role in engaging this central issue.

A second way in which newspapers in the mid-nineteenth century produced a public conversation was through the use of correspondents. In the nineteenth century correspondents were just that – acquaintances of a newspaper editor who wrote letters to (or corresponded with) the paper describing their travels. A reliance on letter writing as a source of information meant that there was nothing like the distinction between public life and private life or between news and entertainment that we take for granted today. Letter writers might comment on what we regard as political events, but they also described a cultural event they had attended or the details of a trip they had taken. Though odd to our modern sensibility, this seemed entirely natural in the world of the mid-nineteenth-century newspaper, which might publish poetry or a serialization of the latest novel by Charles Dickens on the front page alongside accounts of commercial transactions and transcripts of a politician's speech. Here again, more recent innovations such as blogs hearken back to this earlier era in ways that were foreign to the media regime dominating the latter half of the twentieth century. Indeed, the apparent oddness of these nineteenth-century newspapers helps us make explicit the degree to which our own understanding of what belongs in a newspaper is historically specific.[12]

Further, controversies over sources – the reliability and accuracy of correspondents themselves – were a major subject of debate between newspapers. Given the difficulties of actually verifying their accounts and their personal connections with a particular newspaper editor, letters published in one paper would often lead to accusations in other newspapers and questioning of their accuracy and motives. In interesting ways, the focus on the correspondents themselves created a kind of celebrity that anticipates modern concerns about the ways in which fame can affect the practice of journalism. As bylines became more common (as a way to provide a measure of the reliability of the writer), journalists

---

[12] On the evolution of newspapers, see Barnhurst and Nerone 2001.

themselves could become stars (Klein 1997, 3). Also, then as now, the role of correspondent, predating as it did the professionalization of journalism, could be filled by a variety of people, some of whom gained a voice in the newspaper simply because of their achievements in other cultural fields or because they were friends with the editor.

Constructing media as a conversation implies a very particular model of public opinion. The exchange of information characteristic of letter-writing correspondents, the reproduction and commentary on other newspapers' stories, and so forth, sees public opinion as social. It is constructed, rather than measured, through the public conversations that continuously create and re-create it. Indeed, we would go one step further and argue that the need to consider seriously the position of others, as in a conversation, is what distinguishes private life from public life and private opinion from public opinion. In contrast, close-ended, random-sample polling as a measure of public opinion, which emerged in the early twentieth century, is only poorly suited to an interactive exchange of ideas and information, as it consists of the gathering of discrete pieces of information (i.e., the individual poll results), which are then aggregated and authoritatively reported back to the public in the press. In addition, public-opinion polling treats citizens as isolated, individual decision makers rather than communal, social ones.[13] Here again, a changing media environment has opened up new possibilities for establishing a conversation around public opinion, as blogs like Pollster.com provide insights into how polls are constructed, the voter modeling behind their sampling strategies, expert analysis, and discussion boards for open discussions of the information they convey.

Whatever else one makes of the press through the mid-nineteenth century, it seems clear that the boundaries between different genres and their political relevance that came to dominate the media environment of the mid-twentieth century had not yet been drawn. In particular, the lines between news and entertainment, fact and fiction, objectivity and subjectivity, were much less clear, although the issues that underlie these distinctions (accuracy, fairness, who speaks and who listens) were very much under consideration and debate. The role of professional journalism as a gatekeeper and as the authoritative voice for the provision of political information had not yet emerged. As Schudson (1999) points out, newspapers during this period were still in competition with direct word of mouth and other forms of communication. As a result,

---

[13] For more on the implications of these competing models of public opinion, see Delli Carpini and Williams (1994b).

answers to questions such as the trustworthiness, adequacy, and usefulness of mediated political information remained a contested terrain that involved the larger reading audience and engaged polity. All of this would change beginning in the mid-nineteenth century and ending – until very recently – with the emergence of the media regime of the mid-twentieth century.

Newspapers, Novels, and Poetry: Realism and the News

Understanding the media regimes of the late eighteenth to mid-nineteenth centuries provides an appreciation of the diverse ways in which the connection between media and democracy have been constructed. It was, however, developments in the second half of the nineteenth century that constitute the specific origins of the media regime that emerged in the mid-twentieth century. Any full understanding of the late-nineteenth-century media regime must start with the rise of the Realist movement in American thought that raised many profound issues about how best to communicate the underlying truth of the dramatic changes taking place in society and the impact of those changes on ordinary people as well as the rich and powerful. Pioneering techniques that are still influential today, Realists used a wide variety of media and styles of expression to articulate the changing nature of American life. Using novels, newspapers, photography, poetry, and painting, they raised many profound questions about the connection between verifiable facts, artistic creativity, and media representation, on the one hand, and the underlying truth that they sought to portray, on the other hand.

However, although the Realist movement opened debate over questions that are still familiar to us in the twenty-first century, they inevitably and self-consciously stopped short of providing definitive answers to what are contestable issues. Later attempts to answer these questions by drawing distinct boundaries between fact and fiction, news and entertainment, and so forth, built on elements of Realist thought, but they were not a direct product of this movement. Indeed, the Realists would not have recognized such arbitrary distinctions. Rather, drawing such distinctions, based on a misreading of the Realists, was a strategy of the later Progressive movement. Yet most histories of media and democracy tend to emphasize the Progressive Era and slight the significance of the Realist Era that preceded it. Recovering a more nuanced understanding of the Realist impulse provides a view of the political role of the media that has much to add to the growing debates over the current media environment.

As we have seen, providing a definition that distinguishes between news and entertainment, or any of the other distinctions characterizing the modern press, is remarkably difficult. Such distinctions had still not become part of the worldview of nineteenth-century or early-twentieth-century journalists. Yet, paradoxically, it is in this period that we first hear what to the modern ear sounds like the creation of these boundaries. The riddle of this paradox is unraveled by understanding that the concerns of journalists in the late nineteenth century were part of a much broader cultural trend. Debates in this period over accuracy, informational models of newspaper writing, and the emergence of what we call today the doctrine of objectivity all occurred within a very different intellectual climate than would exist by the 1920s. Supporters of Realism, while searching for a way to get at "the truth" embodied in external reality, did not advocate facts as against values, objectivity as opposed to subjectivity, news as opposed to entertainment, or any of the other distinctions so familiar to us today. Realism was a broad intellectual movement that sought to bring greater truth to all areas of representation, whether in literature, newspapers, architecture, or elsewhere. Mindich (1998, 103) captures the broad-ranging influence of the Realist movement, arguing that by the mid-nineteenth century, "[t]he taste of Americans, from every level of society, was bending toward the real in areas as diverse as photography, art, literature, the social sciences, and philosophy." In the most general sense, Realism emphasized the power of observation over idealism's emphasis on invention. Realists identified reality with external phenomena, which they believed were subject to laws of science: "The world was disenchanted as never before, and the realists, embracing disenchantment to distinguish themselves from their literary fathers, were delighted" (Schudson 1978, 74).

Examining the origins of Realism helps explain its far-reaching consequences for the way Americans had come to understand the world by the end of the nineteenth century. David Shi (1995) traces its roots to the trauma of the Civil War and the role of Matthew Brady's photography, which in the words of the *New York Times* came close to bringing the horror of the war to the doorsteps and streets of ordinary Americans (Sontag 2003, 62–63). What Shi (1995) labels the "media of realism" – photography, advertising, and the movies – were all intimately connected with the rise of both modern journalism and modern popular culture. The public assumed that the new media captured reality in ways that other sorts of representation could not. This was the first in an ongoing series of claims that new media can pierce the veil between reality and its representation (Shi 1995, 104).[14]

The change in the look and feel of newspapers, especially those operated by Joseph Pulitzer and William Randolph Hearst, was dramatic:

> By the 1880s the perfection of the halftone print allowed photographs to be printed directly. Henceforth, cameras went everywhere, and the pages of the daily newspaper opened an infinite number of windows onto private and public, domestic and exotic experience. The newspaper journalist carried the possibility of seeing more than had ever been seen before into every nook and cranny of his city and his world. (Braudy 1997, 508)

Even more important, the distinction between the aim of journalism and fiction writing were not drawn as they are today. Indeed, the emergence of Realism was signaled by Walt Whitman's *Leaves of Grass* and his attempts to combine prose and poetry, all of which celebrated the everyday reality of American life (Shi 1995, 55). The literary style of the figures most closely associated with Realism – Whitman, Theodore Dreiser, Jack London, and Stephen Crane, for example – were heavily and self-consciously influenced by their experience as newspaper reporters.[15] At the same time, the purpose of news reporting (often by the very same figures who wrote novels and short stories) was not to simply describe the world in a value neutral fashion. Rather, the turn to observation was seen as part of both stated and unstated programs of social reform. Indeed, as Schudson (1978) points out, the debate over value neutrality and the sharp distinction between objectivity and subjectivity it assumes emerged only in the 1920s.

In his wonderful biography of William Randolph Hearst, David Nasaw (2000, 78–79) describes Hearst's *San Francisco Examiner* (which he began running in 1887):

---

[14] These claims always prove false. Civil War photographers, for example, routinely repositioned the dead, added props (like weapons, if absent on the battlefield), and retouched negatives to heighten dramatic impact. The well-known photographer Alexander Gardner carried around a stock of spare rifles to place with bodies to heighten the dramatic impact of his photographs, and in one of his most famous photos, he actually dragged a body forty yards to position it in a particularly photogenic trench (Evans 2001).

[15] Another well-known figure of the period, Karl Marx, was influenced both by his experience as a journalist and by the Realist acceptance of literature as a legitimate source of social arguments. Marx freely drew from both government statistics and literary works, especially Charles Dickens's *Oliver Twist* to make his case in *Capital*. See Wheen (1999 304).

While the prose was at times hackneyed, it was often first-rate. In the finest tradition of newspaper journalism (like the O. Henry stories that would appear in the *New York World* in the early 1900s), it was never easy to tell where reporting ended and fiction began.... The cult of objectivity which would define journalistic standards – if not always journalistic practices – later in the twentieth century was not yet in place. What readers expected of their newspapers was not literal, but figurative truth. They wanted a map of the city with the "feel" of events, the "sense" of being there, and this is what Hearst gave them every day.

Realism's social agenda, in many of its media manifestations, was defined by the struggle to focus on and understand the increasingly complex and often contentious social, political, and economic dynamics of a rapidly changing America. This led to an increasing concern with the experiences and problems of ordinary citizens and common life, which was reflected in newspapers' "discovery of the news" but also in the Realist turn in literature, painting, and philosophy (Shi 1995, 17; see also Schudson 1978). Leo Braudy (1997, 508) puts it well: "journalists immediately nominated themselves as intermediaries between their readers and those they wrote about, familiarizing the already famous and celebrating the previously anonymous, like so many Dantes deciding who should be allocated to hell, purgatory, or heaven." Illustrative of the broad reach of Realism, while the newspapers focused on the local events of the city, philosophers like William James and later John Dewey were insisting that philosophy be both scientific and concerned with the problems not of philosophers, but of ordinary people (Shi 1995, 77). Similarly, many women writers of the late nineteenth century focused on chronicling the details of actual domestic life (most famously Edith Wharton, but also Sarah Morgan, Mary Noailles Murfree, Sarah O. Jewett, and Mary E. Wilkins).

The difference between Realism and its tight connection to ordinary life and the Progressive Era's later adoption of an elite perspective is illustrated by the rise of statistics in the United States. A fascination with the potential of numbers and statistics for getting at the truth of society is an important part of Realism. However, the focus of measurement and statistics was considerably different in nineteenth-century America than it is today. From the Progressive Era on, the use of statistical techniques has been largely understood as a tool in the hands of trained professionals. This was not always the case, as the following description of mid-nineteenth-century Americans indicates:

Other industrializing nations like England, Prussia, and France demonstrated a greater sophistication in their collection and application of data and most of the major breakthroughs in mathematical theory occurred in Europe. But, as [historian Patricia Cline] Cohen notes, "What struck foreign travelers in America was the extent to which ordinary inhabitants had incorporated and internalized a tendency to measure, count, and calculate." Thus, a compiler of statistics, "assured of an audience that would understand his numerical messages and accord it a superior credibility, had only to choose the exact form his data would take." (Cohen 1982, qtd. in Tygiel 2000, 21)

We emphasize the broad range of both the influences on and impact of Realism to illustrate the degree to which its influence on newspapers was just a small part of a much broader change in the discursive environment shaping the way Americans thought about the world. Schudson (1978, 5) makes clear that journalists of this era did not make the distinctions between fact and fiction, objectivity and subjectivity, and so forth, that underlie later efforts to draw the line between news and entertainment: "at the turn of this century there was as much emphasis in leading papers on telling a good story as on getting the facts. Sensationalism in its various forms was the chief development in newspaper content. Reporters sought as often to write 'literature' as to gather news." He notes that the *New York Times* became the most prestigious newspaper by stressing an "information" model, rather than a "story" model, of reporting. "But into the first decades of the twentieth century, even at the *New York Times*, it was uncommon for journalists to see a sharp divide between facts and values" (Schudson 1978, 5).

Most significantly, Schudson argues that the struggle between the "prestige" and "sensationalist" press was not a battle between responsible, factual reporting, on the one hand, and irresponsible yellow journalism, on the other hand. Indeed, in his own study of political coverage in the *New York Times* and the *New York Herald*, he finds that both newspapers were equally influenced by their political biases. As in Jacksonian-era struggles between the mass-circulation pennies and the more-elite-readership party papers, so, too, in the 1890s, competition between styles of journalism were really about attempts to make newspaper ideals and practices consonant with the culture of dominant social classes – a tendency as true today as then.

The degree to which alternative models of journalism existed into the twentieth century is obscured by a focus on the emergence of journalism as a modern profession. Although journalism began to emerge as a profession in the 1890s (and paid reporting developed even earlier), this did not mean that it had achieved the dominance or adopted the values it would have three decades later. For example, "Edwin Shuman's

1894 *Steps into Journalism* (the first journalism textbook) noted that a reporter with 'sparkle' would be forgiven some inaccuracy, just as a reliable reporter would be forgiven some dullness, but the combination of accuracy and sparkle were the recipe for professional success" (Schudson 1978, 79).

The Realist movement searched for truth in all forms of media representations. This thirst for truth in what we today label "fiction writing" is illustrated by the common practice of period writers to subtitle their novels and short stories as "a true story" (Shi 1995, 95). This juxtaposition of true story to a novel seems odd to our sensibility today, but only because we map the quest for truth onto the Progressive Era's distinction between fact and fiction, which associates truth only with the former. Yet on reflection, it is obvious that there are many different kinds of truth that one might pursue – there is a kind of truth in a newspaper story but also an important kind of truth in a novel, poem, or movie.[16] Recognizing that truth is an unavoidable but essentially contestable concept is crucial to understanding current debates over the proper role of media in a democratic society.

The Complex and Contested Nature of Objectivity

Setting the "discovery" of the news in the context of the much broader development of Realism provides important insights into the development of the doctrine of objectivity in American journalism. It is, after all, the claim to being objective that allows journalists to argue that the news, as opposed to editorial analysis or other genres, provides the preferred factual account of political events.

In *Just the Facts* (1998), David Mindich makes clear just how complicated the development of the doctrine of objectivity was. He argues that, at a minimum, this doctrine consists of five separate stylistic commitments: detachment, nonpartisanship, the inverted pyramid, balance, and facticity. Each of these dimensions is more complex than it appears at first glance, and each developed somewhat independently. Indeed, what became in the 1920s the doctrine of objectivity was not recognized as such in the late nineteenth century. Further, each of these features was vigorously challenged by competing approaches to newspaper writing. The

---

[16] David Lodge (2002, 50), for example, argues that novels may be more effective at getting at the truth of consciousness than science: "For centuries, science and philosophy have grappled with the mystery of our inner life, but it is literature that has provided the most accurate record of human consciousness."

nature of this contestation is especially interesting and provides insight into today's criticisms of journalists for being biased and, more generally, arguments over the new media environment.

According to Mindich, one impetus for the increasing codification of objectivity in the emerging media regime was the struggle for circulation from 1883 through the 1890s between the Hearst and Pulitzer papers, both in competition with each other and the, by then, older and established penny presses (including the *New York Times*):

> The older papers recoiled with horror at the changes, for many journalistic and non-journalistic reasons, including that they quickly saw their readership dwarfed by that of Pulitzer and Hearst. Much the same way Dan Rather [now] assert[s] that he [is] "real" in the face of competition from below, the penny–elite-journalists asserted their "objectivity" and the immoderation of their rivals. The elite papers waged a "moral war" against the sensational and successful Pulitzer and Hearst, much like the one that the old elite conducted against the sensational and successful Bennett a half century before. (Mindich 1998, 129; for a discussion of the context within which Rather made this claim, see the opening of the next chapter)

This new journalism of the 1890s was characterized by the elite papers as "deviant, feminine, and uncivilized" (Mindich 1998, 130). Mindich, like Schudson (1978), draws the parallel between these struggles and those that occurred earlier and later in American media history: in the 1830s between the established newspapers and the pennies; in the 1890s between the former pennies and the Pulitzer and Hearst papers; in the 1920s to 1940s between newspapers and radios; and from the 1950s to 1980s between television and newspapers and radio. "Whenever the hegemony of elite news brokers is threatened, intense debates over the nature of news occur" (Mindich 1998, 138). In short, these are struggles over the question of who is to judge the trustworthiness, adequacy, and usefulness of mediated political information. Mindich sees current controversies over the new media environment as only the latest challenge to elite hegemony:

> We have so many storytellers (each of the thousands of home pages, for example, is a separate news source), and with so many departing from the information model of objective news, journalists are called on once again to define themselves. It is no surprise that the nature of news and objectivity should reemerge as an issue so important to the profession. (Mindich 1998, 139)[17]

---

[17] Of course, challenges to the notion of objectivity existed within the profession before the current period – consider, for example, the new journalism movement of the 1960s

Schudson (1978, 119) makes much the same point when he notes, "The moral war between information journalism and story journalism in New York in the 1890s was, like the moral wars of the 1830s, a cover for class conflict." However, he also adds a point we think essential for understanding current disputes over the nature of political media: the need for any media text to be entertaining, not as opposed to but as part of its role in providing political or any other kind of information.

In using his distinction between informational and storytelling models of journalism, Schudson (1978, 89) emphasizes the degree to which journalists at the time understood that both aspects were central to their trade: "While reporters subscribed concurrently to the ideals of factuality and of entertainment in writing the news, some of the papers they worked for chose identities that strongly emphasized one ideal or the other." However, both models serve important functions in democratic communication:

The moral division of labor between newspapers, then, may parallel the moral division of the human faculties between the more respectable faculties of abstraction and the less respectable feelings. People control themselves to read of politics in fine print; they let themselves go to read of murders or to look at drawings of celebrities. Information is a genre of self denial, the story one of self indulgence. (Schudson 1998, 119)

He goes on to argue that both models of newspaper writing contained implicit assumptions about the world of the reader:

The Times wrote for the rational person or the person whose life was orderly. It presented articles as useful knowledge, not as revelation. *The World* had a different feel to it; in tone and display it created the sense that everything was new, unusual, and unpredictable. There is every reason to believe that this accurately reflected the life experience of many people in the cities, the newly literate and the newly urban, members of the working-class and middle-class. Life was a spectacle as never before for many, and *The World* spoke faithfully to that experience of the many, as *The Times* did for the more ordered experience of a smaller group. (Schudson 1998, 119)

and 1970s or charges of liberal bias leveled at the press by conservatives during the Nixon administration. However, the latter charges assumed that objectivity could and should occur, and so they were not a direct challenge to the existing media regime. And new journalism, in many ways a precursor to contemporary challenges to objectivity, remained on the fringes of the journalistic profession, with its major advocates (e.g., Tom Wolfe, Hunter Thompson, Joan Didion) turning to novels, essays, opinion columns, and counterculture publications to express their views.

As changes in a media environment are triggered by political, economic, cultural, and technological changes, existing media regimes lose their authority, thus leading to a rethinking of who should be part of the production and consumption of politically relevant information and how best to ensure that this information is adequate, trustworthy, and useful. Understanding the insights drawn from such transitional periods and how they were resolved in the nineteenth century helps us understand the new media environment in which we currently find ourselves. Equally important is understanding the roots of our most recent media regime, found most clearly in the Progressive Era of the late nineteenth and early twentieth centuries. The inadequacies of the Progressive Era's answers to questions of who speaks for the public, what information and venues matters most, and so forth, still haunt our understanding of the role of media in a democratic society and limit our ability to effectively address the challenges and opportunities presented by the new media environment that emerged at the close of the twentieth century.

The Progressive Era and the Modern Common Sense about Political Communication: News, Journalism, Entertainment, and Citizenship

When we implicitly or explicitly create information hierarchies based on distinctions between news, compiled by professional journalists, and other forms of media (or between fact and fiction, or objectivity and subjectivity), we are drawing on a way of thinking that is largely a product of the Progressive Era. It was also, not coincidentally, during this period that the institutional structures and processes that would finally crystallize into the media regime we are calling the Age of Broadcast News emerged: the rise of electronic media (albeit radio and not television), the accelerating concentration of media ownership, the reduction in the number of information outlets, the founding of journalism schools, the emergence of journalism as a profession, and so forth. This transformation was part and parcel of a larger set of changes occurring in response to the emergence of modern capitalism.[18] The four decades straddling 1900 saw the rationalization and organization of American life as a national economy emerged, an economy characterized by large bureaucratically organized corporations competing in oligopolistic markets.[19] These developments

---

[18] Our discussion of the Progressive movement draws heavily on Williams and Matheny (1995, chapter 2).
[19] See, for example, Chandler (1977); Israel (1972); Lustig (1982); Wiebe, 1967.

posed a challenge to Progressive political thinkers: how to reconcile prosperity with the clear violations of American individualism modern capitalism seemed to represent? "[Progressives] were trying... to keep the benefits of the emerging organization of life and yet to retain the scheme of individualistic values that this organization was destroying" (Hofstadter 1955, 255). Further, Progressives represented the modern middle class, which stood between, and viewed with suspicion, the barons of big business and the poor and restless masses. They sought to use government to curb the excesses of corporate capitalism while avoiding the kind of mass democracy that might undermine the very economic order they sought to save.

Their solution was a reliance on trained professional experts, committed to the discovery of an objective public interest, who would work within bureaucratic organizations. Just as the engineering wonders of the age applied science to the physical world, and just as Frederick Taylor had developed a science of management, Progressives held that it was possible to develop a science of public administration to guide government actions. Progressive rhetoric held that scientific expertise could produce policies in the public interest and overcome the inadequacies of democratic decision making (Hanson 1985).

A characteristic of the Progressive movement was to draw sharp lines between fact and value, science and politics, objectivity and subjectivity. In turn, these categories became the justification for distinguishing neutral expert from political partisan. What is important to understand is that these distinctions, though often taken for granted and incorporated into common sense, are inherently contestable and deeply political. For example, the emerging "science" of public administration drew lines between policy and administration, the former the realm of elected politicians who are accountable to the public and the latter the realm of neutral experts trained to operate in the public interest. But held up to scrutiny, this distinction is untenable at the definitional level (i.e., there is no clear line between policy and administration) and inherently political (i.e., it gives power to bureaucratic administrators who are largely unaccountable to the public or its elected representatives; Lewis 1988; Williams and Matheny 1995).

The political nature of the Progressive movement's philosophy is best seen through the lens of the great German sociologist Max Weber's analysis of the connection among rational-legal bureaucracy, democracy, and the rise of the modern middle class. Weber argued that the increasing reliance on achieved characteristics for filling bureaucratic positions (e.g., advanced degree requirements, professional training, civil service testing) was justified on democratic grounds as replacing traditional methods of appointment, which favored corrupt and entrenched elites. However, the ultimate result of such a system is to institutionalize the advantages of the emerging middle classes, who could afford to send their children to prestigious universities, attain entry to elite professional schools, and otherwise obtain the credentials necessary to enter the newly emerging professions (Weber 1948).

The emergence of journalism as a modern profession and our current understanding of the role of the mass media in a democratic society are products of this transformation. Journalism followed the path of other new professions (e.g., engineering, public administration) that were struggling to define their roles within the large corporate structures emerging during this era. "In every profession, practitioners demanded the same thing . . . expertise should confer autonomy, social status, and economic security on those who possessed it, and they alone should regulate and restrict the members of their calling" (Diner 1998, 177). The development of specialized journalism schools and professional associations, as well as of formal codes of conduct, were designed to produce journalists capable of transcending the "distorting" influence of values and ideology.

Although it was part of larger changes occurring during this era, journalism (like other walks of American life) faced its own unique issues, driven by the shifting place of writing in general and the press in particular in democratic life. The emergence of modern capitalism (in this case, the mass literary marketplace) altered the position of the writer. Emphasis on market forces transformed literature into a product of labor rather than of romantic inspiration. Writers and editors stressed their responsibility to a definable public interest, as opposed to some inner calling: "All of these ideological alterations served to enlarge the scope of the author's social role and give that role a new agenda" (Wilson 1985, 3). The result of this process was the replacement of the "gentleman author and journalist" with the professional journalist (Wilson 1985, 8). The journalist in this new formulation was a full-time writer who made his (or less frequently in this era, her) living from their profession and who was increasingly distinct in public and self-conception from other citizens and other kinds of writers, as well. "The modern journalist and photojournalist became experts not authors" (Barnhurst and Nerone 2001 p. 19). In short, journalism had become a career, with all the significance that Weber attaches to that term: selection on the basis of achieved credentials, dominance of positions by the emerging middle class, employment in large bureaucratic organizations, dependence on the market, and so forth.

The emergence of modern capitalism in the publishing and broadcasting industry was especially challenging for Progressive Era thinkers. Reflecting the general trends toward oligopoly noted earlier, this period saw the centralization of newspaper ownership, the beginnings of radio, and the nationalization of advertising and marketing, thus reducing the number and diversity of media voices at the same time that the reach of the remaining voices was greatly extended. These conditions seemed to violate notions of a marketplace of ideas that were fundamental to liberal democratic thought and the existing media regime. They also raised the possibility – in combination with the developing science of market research – of a mass public manipulated into quiescence by economic elites or into rebellion by political demagogues. Neither outcome was particularly appetizing to the emerging middle class, which increasingly included professional journalists themselves. And yet these same changes were at the heart of the journalists' new status. The result was a set of tensions and contradictions in Progressive thought of the time: "beneath the confident rhetoric of the day, we see a series of modern problems in their embryonic stages: the imprisonment and anxiety of celebrity, the unreal theatrics of the pseudo-event, the distortion of potentially democratic causes in the media" (Wilson 1985, xv).

It is not surprising that journalists, while engaging in this debate, would ultimately defend themselves by deploying the same strategy as the other emerging professions – attempting to establish clear lines between what its practitioners did (i.e., objective news gathering and reporting) and what other nonprofessionals might write. The irony of this strategy is that it emerged at precisely the moment when objectivity was most challenged by developments in the political economy and thus, in retrospect, was rendered least tenable (Schudson 1978, 4). That is, the Realist movement had embraced a wide range of approaches (e.g., novels, newspapers, poetry, pictorial art) for getting at what Realists took to be the truth or reality (one and the same for them) of the world. The Progressive Era response to this increasingly inadequate and challenged notion of truth and reality was a series of specific procedures to guide the day-to-day practice of professionals. These practices depended on the institutionalized power of professional expertise, rather than open debate and individual reflection, to assert the existence of an objective public interest that constituted both political truth and political reality.

For example, as in the other emerging professions, journalists developed writing strategies that would maintain an appearance of objectivity. Central to the maintenance of objectivity in scientific writing (and adopted by the emerging social sciences) is what Evelyn Fox Keller (1994, 322) calls the "disappearance of the self": findings are presented in an impersonal way, especially through the use of quantitative data, but also through other writing strategies (e.g., the avoidance of personal pronouns) so that the research results seem independent of the specific persons producing them (Porter 1994; see also Keller 1994). The emerging profession of journalism adopted writing styles that also seemed to remove the writer from the story and thus created the illusion that the information was not so much produced by individuals but rather emerged from reality itself.

With respect to enduring questions about the role of the press in a democratic society, the Progressives assumed that it would be trained professional elites who would answer them. Further, although the Realist answer to the question of when do we have adequate, trustworthy, and useful political information is "when we have the truth," the Progressive answer was "when we have the facts." In short, the media regime advocated by Progressive thought replaced the Realist search for truth (which is always messy and unavoidably full of ethical considerations) with an emphasis on professional objectivity, a concept that elides many of the most important issues raised by the role of a modern mass media in a democratic society. Nowhere are the inherent tensions in such solutions clearer than in the influential writings of Walter Lippmann.

Walter Lippmann and the Model of the Modern Media Professional

No person better represents the Progressive Era line of reasoning about media and politics than Walter Lippmann, arguably the most influential print journalist of the twentieth century. His theoretical perspective on media and democracy continues to guide the thought and practice of both journalists and political communication scholars. Before World War I, Lippmann had been optimistic about the prospects for American democracy. However, his wartime propaganda work for the U.S. government convinced him of the ease with which the facts presented to the public could be distorted and suppressed (Rogers 1994). In his postwar writing (most notably, *Public Opinion* in 1922 and *The Phantom Public* in 1927), Lippmann articulated a much more pessimistic view of American democracy. In these writings, he challenged the notion that citizens, even if presented with objective facts by the press, could make intelligent judgments on public issues, and he found two problems with this model of democracy.

First, he understood the complexity of the concept of truth and, at the same time, the degree to which it is central to democratic governance. So, he argued that the press, though essential, cannot provide the truth because truth and news are not the same things. The function of news is to signalize events, whereas the function of truth is to bring to light the hidden facts. The news was like the beam of a flashlight that moves restlessly about, bringing one episode and then another out of the darkness into vision. This was an important problem because in a modern, complex society, knowledge about the world was almost never firsthand. People, in his now-famous phrase, responded not to the world, but to "the pictures in their heads." And for most citizens these pictures came from the press:

In all these instances we must note...the insertion between man and his environment of a pseudo-environment. To that pseudo-environment his behavior is a response. But because it is behavior, the consequences, if they are acts, operate not in the pseudo-environment where the behavior is stimulated, but in the real environment where action eventuates. (Lippmann 1922, 10)

Second, even if the press could provide an accurate picture of the world, the average person had neither the time nor the ability to digest this information and use it to get at the truth of the political world, on which good governance depended. Ordinary people were incapable of being the omnicompetent citizen presumed in much of democratic theory, especially in the complex world of modern politics.

For Lippmann, this argument led to a new version of democratic theory that sharply reduced the role of ordinary citizens. In this theory, most citizens' participation would be limited to voting for representatives, and their views on substantive issues would be expressed (if at all) through aggregate public opinion (as would come to be measured by scientific polls). In place of direct citizen input, elected officials would rely on neutral, scientific experts. Ronald Steel (1980, 82), Lippmann's perceptive biographer, summarizes how these two arguments led him to a quintessential Progressive solution:

This ruthless analysis left Lippmann with the conclusion that democracy could work only if man escaped from the "intolerable and unworkable fiction that each of us must acquire a competent opinion about public affairs." The task of acquiring such competent opinions had to be left to those specially trained, who had access to accurate information, whose minds were unclouded by prejudice and stereotypes. These people would examine information, not through murky press reporting, but as it came from specially organized intelligence bureaus untainted by prejudice or distortion. With their advice the legislature and the executive would be able to make intelligent judgments to submit to the citizens for approval or rejection.

In the media scholar James Carey's view, Lippmann's version of Progressivism shifted the public and ordinary citizens from being the subject of political life to being its object. It was professional elites who would answer the perennial questions about media and democracy, and the actual conversation that defines politics and culture would take place without the public's voice being heard (Carey 1989).

Lippmann's arguments were crucial for the development of modern understandings of journalism. He suggested that journalists would mediate between the complexity of politics and the limited interest and intelligence of the public. Journalists, in this gatekeeping role, would decide what was and was not politically significant and so ultimately what was important for the public to know. Elections, now more firmly the linchpin of democracy, would provide periods in which the public's fleeting attention was drawn to politics, thus holding political leaders accountable for their actions.

This model would seem to grant more political power to journalists than either Lippmann's views of the limits of journalism or his belief in democracy would warrant. However, Lippmann (and other Progressives) believed that if journalists were trained to report political information in an objective and fair manner, they would serve no purpose but the public interest. The media would simply provide a mirror (or in Lippmann's own metaphor, a flashlight in a dark attic) on the political world. This model of the press requires strict and self-evident distinctions between the journalist and the politician, expert and citizen, fact and fiction, objectivity and subjectivity – in short, all the couplets that have come to distinguish political news from other media genres. Professional journalists were positioned at the gates between political elites and the public, but their professionalism would ensure that they did not abuse this position. As Steel (1980, 183) notes, Lippmann's views reflected the ideological contradictions found more generally in Progressive thought:

The strength of Lippmann's analysis lies in a lucidly conceived and relentlessly argued thesis; the weakness, in a conclusion that looks to a specialized class for salvation. Even if the average self-centered man is a victim of his own stereotypes, one must ask, do not the experts, like all human beings, have their own stereotypes? Do they not have pictures in their heads?

Despite these now well-rehearsed problems with Lippmann's line of thought and the Progressive Era beliefs on which it was based, his ideas continued to dominate media theory and the media regime of much of the twentieth century. However, although many later ideas about media and democracy can be traced back to Lippmann and the Progressives, much of importance also dropped out. Lippmann's work clearly reflects the transitional period in which he was writing, a period in which the distinctions he was making seemed nowhere near as natural as they would for those who would later use them in often overly simplified ways, stripped of their underlying complexity. For instance, the quote from *Public Opinion* with which we opened Chapter 1 (a quote no doubt surprising to those who have read Lippmann from a more contemporary perspective) makes clear the extent to which he understood the inherent contestability of distinctions such as fact versus fiction. In addition, Lippmann's arguments constituted only one side of an ongoing debate with other public intellectuals, especially John Dewey, about the possibilities for more thoroughgoing reform of the democratic process and the empowerment of average citizens. In contrast, much later writing took Lippmann's side of the argument as self-evident. It is only very recently, as the media environment has changed, that the presumed naturalness of these inherently ideological distinctions has once again been brought starkly into question.

The study of political communication in the social sciences has been shaped by these Progressive Era developments no less than the practice of journalism has. During the 1930s, the Rockefeller Foundation sponsored a series of influential academic seminars attempting to set the agenda for communications research.[20] Attended by luminaries like Paul Lazarsfeld, Harold Lasswell, and Robert Lynd, the backdrop was the concern of many scholars about the apathy of the American public when it came to the rise of fascism in Europe. Some in the seminar self-consciously adopted the Lippmann approach, with its pessimistic assumptions about the possibilities for enlightened citizenship, and favored the management of public opinion by elites. In Lasswell's terms, the only way to combat propaganda in support of one position was by propaganda in support of

---

[20] For our discussion of the Rockefeller seminar, we rely on the wonderful article by Brett Gary (1996).

an opposing position. Yet at the seminar, others (e.g., Lynd) adopted an approach drawing on John Dewey, arguing that the apathy of the public required the creation of two-way communication models that would facilitate effective dialogue between elites and the public.

Participants struggled to reconcile the dismal lessons they took from the World War I experience of government propaganda and their belief in the need for U.S. involvement in the struggle against Hitler. These are truly complex issues, raising unresolvable questions about propaganda versus education, elite versus mass models of participation, and the ethical implications of scholarly cooperation with the state. Yet the lasting contribution of the seminar is remembered as Lasswell's reductionist model of communication ("who says what to whom in what channel and with what effect?"), which set the stage for quantitative mass communication research. Consistent with Progressive ideas, these questions would be answered by objective, professional social science researchers. As Brett Gary (1996) argues, this model focused research on a narrow set of questions that made the broader and more politically significant issues raised by the seminar recede into the background. And yet, although it claims to be disinterested and value free, Lasswell's model is undeniably a response to the value conflicts in the seminar and in the broader society.

Conclusion

The recent and growing instability of our current media regime has reintroduced questions about which citizens should be part of democratic deliberation; who should produce information and who should consume it; and how best to ensure that the information available to citizens is trustworthy, prevalent, and useful. However, as we argued in Chapter 1, to date, the resulting debate has been too narrowly circumscribed by the lingering influence of still underexamined assumptions, such as the distinction between producers and consumers, experts and laypersons, news and entertainment, facts and values, and objectivity and subjectivity. In this chapter, we used our concept of media regimes to demonstrate the different ways that the definitions of and relationships between media and democracy have been constituted throughout American history. Highlighting these various regimes provides us with a richer and more sophisticated understanding of media and democracy in the United States, as well as a wider range of possibilities for maximizing the current environment's democratic potential.

Past conceptualizations of political communications – as a partisan struggle requiring engaged citizens, a public conversation, storytelling, commentary on the lives of ordinary citizens, and a multigenre search for truth (in all its essentially contestable complexity) through Realism – provide useful perspectives on our more modern concerns. So, too, does realizing that accepted providers of political information have included not only journalists but also partisan and publicity-seeking editors, letter writers, poets, novelists, and even "average" citizens, and that these voices have all been found in the pages of the daily newspaper.

None of this is to suggest that many (not all) of the underlying motivations leading to modern notions of professional journalism, the importance of facts, the need for neutral or balanced observers, and so forth, are misguided. Nor is it to suggest that any or all forms of entertainment or opinion are automatically politically relevant. Clearly, any thoughtful vision of what a democratically useful media regime and the resulting discursive environment should look like would include space for media whose purpose were to provide accurate and useful information about pressing issues of the day in a timely fashion.

But to create such an environment, five often ignored points must remain foregrounded. First, what we currently term *news* falls far short – partly because of political, cultural, economic, and technological factors and partly because of the inherent difficulty of its avowed mission – of providing the factual, fair, relevant, and useful information it seeks to provide. Second, even if it could do so, providing objective information alone is not enough to sustain a democratically vibrant discursive environment. Third, other genres typically not thought of as playing a role in political discourse can and have done exactly that. Fourth, at their best, such genres can combine both fact and opinion in narrative structures that inform, educate, motivate, and capture the imagination of citizens. And fifth, if the real and potential political impact of non-news media is acknowledged, then the media regime defining the discursive environment we live in must include norms and rules that can apply across a range of media and genres, and that work to enhance their democratic utility. We return in depth to these issues in Chapter 4 and the concluding chapter. Before doing so, however, it is important to fully understand the political, economic, cultural, and technological forces that led to the media regime we call the Age of Broadcast News, as well as those that are responsible for its demise. This is the task of Chapter 3.

3

And That's the Way It (Was)

The Rise and Fall of the Age of Broadcast News

This medium [radio] – and until the rise of video and VCR its successor, television – though essentially centered on individual and family, created its own public sphere. For the first time in history people unknown to each other who met knew what each had in all probability heard (or, later, seen) the night before: the big game, the favorite comedy show, Winston Churchill's speech, the contents of the news bulletin.

Eric Hobsbawm, *Age of Extremes*, 1996

He's a working journalist. I'm impressed. Anyone who can reach into the data swarm and pick out what's newsworthy has my respect.

Ryan Bingham, in Walter Kirn's novel *Up in the Air*, 2001

Television is dead.

Elihu Katz, "And Deliver Us From Segmentation," 1996

On February 11, 1993, as the media regime in place for the latter half of the twentieth century was already showing signs of strain, *CBS Evening News* closed with a story on the increasing number of docudramas – made-for-television movies based on events and people in the news – being aired on prime-time television.[1] The segment focused on the plans of all three major networks to air docudramas about Amy Fisher, a young woman who was convicted for shooting the wife of her sleazy

---

[1] Our discussion of this broadcast is based on David Mindich, *Just the Facts: How Objectivity Came to Define American Journalism* (New York: New York University Press, 1998), 2–3, and the Vanderbilt Television News Archive (http://tvnews.vanderbilt.edu/) summary for that evening.

lover Joey Buttafuoco.[2] In response to the segment, Dan Rather ended his broadcast by facing the camera and, referring to the news broadcast he had anchored for more than a decade, saying, "*This* is real." Of course, the notion that what is real or true is contestable and socially constructed is as old as the idea of the modern fact itself (Poovey 1998). What is telling about Rather's impromptu comment is less its naïveté than that he felt the need to make it at all, a clear indication that the norms, practices, and institutions that for more than half a century had served to distinguish news from entertainment were collapsing. Were the comment made during the height of the Age of Broadcast News, it would have taken on a very different meaning, much like Walter Cronkite's signature closing of *CBS Evening News*: "And that's the way it is." During a period of regime stability, this nightly mantra, made by the most trusted man in America (according to polls of the time), signaled the acceptance by both viewers and journalists that the news media provided a useful and accurate picture of political reality. By 1993, however, Rather's unrehearsed comment, tinged with exasperation (and coupled with the fact that *CBS Evening News* chose to treat the docudrama battle as newsworthy at all, in the process providing free advertising for its own network's version of the Amy Fisher story), connoted little more than a desperate attempt to maintain the distinction between news and entertainment. And it is a comment that, were a news anchor to even consider making today, could be received only as ironic or satirical.

Seven years later, *CBS Evening News* provided another example of how changes in the media environment had destabilized the practices of journalism when it was revealed that, on New Year's Eve 2000, the network had used computer graphics to replace an NBC logo – visible on a building in the background of its "live" shot from Times Square – with a virtual advertisement for CBS's *The Early Show*.[3] In reporting on the controversy, the *New York Times* noted that the computerized insertion of advertising logos, though increasingly common in other live broadcasts, has "generally been considered out of line on news shows, a type of programming in which the assumption of reality is considered sacrosanct

---

[2] The appeal of the story of the "Long Island Lolita" was transatlantic. In 1995, all the British networks (even the BBC and BBC1) broadcast one or another of the American-made docudramas. See Derek Paget, *No Other Way to Tell It: Dramadoc/Docudrama on Television* (Manchester, U.K.: Manchester University Press, 1998), 9.

[3] Adding to the bizarre nature of this "journalistic" spat was the fact that NBC had purposefully put its logo in Times Square so that it would be visible in the CBS broadcasts (see, e.g., Kurtz 2007).

and not informing viewers is considered a breach of journalistic guidelines" (Kuczynski 2000, A1). The *Times*'s use of the word *assumption* to modify *reality* indicates how contestable the very notion of reality had become by the start of the twenty-first century, and with it the journalistic practices originating in the Progressive Era that were assumed to reveal it.

The doctoring of the New Year's Eve background visual stirred a by-then-familiar media debate decrying the decline of journalistic norms and standards. Attempts to honestly represent reality and frank evaluation of the rules used by any media outlet to do so are of vital importance, especially in the unsettled media environment we live in. This particular debate missed its mark, however, at best lamenting a loss that was no longer recoverable and at worst attempting to maintain distinctions that were always artificial and problematic. For example, missed was the by-then-common practice of using computer-generated sets in news broadcasts. When viewers watch television news, they are increasingly viewing sets and backgrounds that do not actually exist. Instead, journalists are performing in front of blue screens (as do movie actors in special effects scenes), with the accoutrements of a newsroom or, less frequently, a location shot added by computer (Taub 2002). Indeed, during part of his tenure as interim anchor of *CBS Evening News*, Bob Schieffer broadcast from cramped, temporary quarters, as the main studio was being refurbished in preparation for Katie Couric's debut as the new anchor. These dingy surroundings were masked from viewers through the use of a projected background image of a more professional-looking news studio. On his last night as anchor in September 2006, Schieffer wanted to let the viewers in on this secret by dropping the background image, but CBS News president Sean McManus ultimately decided against it, worried that it might leave the "impression that we go around phonying up stuff all the time" (Kurtz 2007, 266).

Although creating the illusion of a bustling news room or an on-site reporter may seem a trivial concern, it can have deeper consequences, as when "local" news broadcasters create the illusion of being imbedded within a community, when in fact they are broadcasting from other regions of the country, with little or no real connection to or knowledge of the town or city they purport to cover (see Klinenberg 2007). As well, given the strained budgets of many local news operations, the perceived need to use expensive computer equipment to appear professional (i.e., to have the same computer-generated look as the national news broadcasts) may lessen the resources devoted to actual reporting.

More generally, it provides a graphic (no pun intended) illustration of how difficult it is to maintain the distinction between what is real and what is not in today's media environment.[4] It also, upon only slight reflection, raises larger questions about the ways in which these distinctions were maintained in the past. Why, for example, does news become more trustworthy when accompanied by the familiar trappings (real or not) of a newsroom or when the reporter is physically located "on the scene"?

As final examples of how much has changed over the past twenty years, flash forward to two (out of the many that could be highlighted) 2009 segments of *The Daily Show*. On March 12, Jon Stewart interviewed Jim Cramer, host of CNBC's *Mad Money*, raking him over the coals for the news media's failure to adequately cover (and even for their collusion in) the problems leading to the financial industry's historic 2008 collapse, an exchange that 45 percent of the American public reported having heard about (Pew Research Center for the People and the Press 2009a). And on December 29, Stewart first skewered Fox News for its claims to being unbiased in the face of its clearly opinionated and supportive coverage of the conservative "Tea Party" march in Washington (coverage Stewart labeled "opiniotainment"), and then called CNN's Wolf Blitzer to task for "fact-checking" the accuracy of a *Saturday Night Live* news skit while ignoring CNN's own wildly inaccurate reporting on the estimated deficit reduction likely to result from the administration's budget proposal. Where does one begin to draw the lines between news and entertainment, fact and opinion, or journalist and celebrity? Is it truly as absurd as Stewart suggests for CNN to fact-check *Saturday Night Live* (or for that matter, *The Daily Show*) when, for example, 72 percent of Americans reported having heard about Tina Fey's caricatures of Sarah Palin during the 2008 presidential campaign (Pew Research Center for the People and the Press 2008b)?

In this chapter, we explore the rise and fall of the Age of Broadcast News, the media regime that dominated the latter half of the twentieth century. We begin by tracing the emergence of this regime from the Progressive Era model of the press with which we closed the previous chapter. We also examine the ways this regime became naturalized through a variety of government policies reinforced by journalistic (and scholarly) assumptions, norms, processes, and institutions. We then turn

---

4 Indeed, *The Daily Show* routinely lampoons this practice by having its "correspondents" seem to appear in exotic settings when they are clearly in the studio.

to an exploration of the radically changing political, economic, cultural, and technological environments of the past two decades, and how these changes challenged the tenets of the existing media regime, thus leading to its ultimate demise. We conclude by arguing for a reconceptualization of the media's role in a democratic society, one that questions the arbitrary and counterproductive distinctions between news and entertainment, fact and opinion, politics and culture, and producer and consumer that dominated the latter half of the twentieth century.

The Emergence and Institutionalization of the Age of Broadcast News

Recall that media regimes are characterized by a relatively stable set of state institutions, regulations, norms, processes, and actors that shape the expectations and practices of media producers and consumers. They develop in response to (but once formed, subsequently help to shape) technological, economic, cultural, and political trends, largely by controlling the environment in which such topics are discussed, understood, and acted on.

Although media regimes begin and end in response to larger societal trends, their specific characteristics are not preordained. Rather, they are the result of political struggles that play out over time, often invisibly, but at key moments in more public ways. The actors in these struggles can vary, as can their relative influence, but they usually include representatives of government (e.g., elected officials, relevant federal agencies), business interests (e.g., media owners, advertisers), practitioners (e.g., editors, producers, journalists), scholars (e.g., researchers, theorists), nonprofits (e.g., foundations), and the public (e.g., public advocacy groups; on occasion, citizens themselves). During these periods of struggle, enduring questions regarding the purpose of the media in a democratic society become more explicit in public debate than is usually the case. As a result, controversies that are often limited to the academy find their way into public (or at least elite) discourse. In short, ideas matter during these transitional periods. It is the interplay of theory and practice that determines and justifies the contours of the resulting media regime.

Although few contemporary reporters or journalists might be aware of it, Progressive Era ideas about the role of journalism in a democratic society became the bedrock on which mid- to late-twentieth-century understandings of journalism in a television-dominated media environment were built. Yet though rooted in the arguments of Progressives, the institutionalization of these beliefs in the mid-twentieth century attained

a commonsense status that eventually stripped them of the context, sub-
tleties, and uncertainties characteristic of the approaches of thoughtful
writers such as Walter Lippmann and his contemporary critics. Formal-
ized by the 1950s in the "social responsibility theory" of the press, these
ideas continue to shape (albeit often invisibly) our understanding of and
expectations about politically relevant media.

Although the tenets of the social responsibility theory can be traced
back to Lippmann and the Progressives, much had changed in the three
decades separating the two – most notably the rapid expansion of radio
and film and the emergence of television, the related acceleration of concentrated media ownership, and the ability to reach increasingly large
audiences with the same message.[5] As well, bitter political struggles
fought over the role of commercial interests (as opposed to educational
and democratic values) and how these struggles were resolved played a
major role in the emerging media regime. Especially important were battles over whether the broadcasting system would be publicly owned (on
the model of the British Broadcasting Corporation) and oriented toward
educational and cultural goals, or, as was the ultimate outcome, be a
privately owned system operated for profit and containing only limited
public interest obligations (see McChesney 1999). It was within this contested media environment that the social responsibility theory was worked
out, institutionalized, and ultimately naturalized.

One of the most important legacies to emerge from Progressive Era
thought was that, by the mid-twentieth century, "truth" as an inherently contested concept containing both ethical and descriptive elements
dropped out of journalistic theory and practice, to be replaced with gathering "just the facts." We saw in the previous chapter that the Realist
movement adopted a notion of truth that could be revealed through a
variety of media – novels, poetry, newspapers, and so on. Although the
Realists' underlying assumptions about the nature of truth may seem
naive by today's standards, the Progressive Era assumption of sharp and
clear distinctions between facts and values, as well as between objectivity
and subjectivity, was even less satisfactory. As Progressive ideas became

---

[5] Although many of the characteristics that define this media regime (e.g., the notion of
professional journalists) began to form and become institutionalized in the print media
as early as the 1920s, its full shape did not emerge until the 1950s, largely as a result of
the growing dominance of radio and then television. For this reason, we talk periodically
about newspapers in the Age of Broadcast News, but much of our discussion focuses on
television and television news.

institutionalized, it was implicitly assumed that well-developed professional practices could replace explicit ethical dialogue. For example, although textbooks focusing on the ethical responsibilities of journalism were commonplace in journalism schools throughout the Progressive Era, by the 1930s, "the term 'ethics' and its cognates disappeared from mass communications book titles for forty years in North America" (Christians 2000, 22).

The institutionalization of increasingly simplified versions of Progressive Era views within media theory and practice was aided by a variety of academic and professional sources in the immediate aftermath of World War II. Especially influential was the work of the Hutchins Commission, convened to address postwar anxiety over the possibilities of a free press in the face of totalitarianism abroad (in the shape of fascism and communism), increasing concentration of media ownership in America, and the growth of mass media such as film and radio. While many of the commission's members, like philosophers William Ernest Hocking and Reinhold Niebuhr, proposed a view of press freedom based on a nuanced ethical perspective, and much of the discussion entertained innovative, even radical solutions, as with the Rockefeller seminars discussed in the previous chapter, the actual recommendations of the commission did not reflect the complexities of the issue (Pickard 2010). Instead, the commission's conclusions focused on a set of specific policy issues and recommended professional practices rooted in scientific naturalism and the fact-value dichotomy (Christians 2000, 24–26).

The implications of these recommendations for a "socially responsible" press were most fully articulated in the work of Theodore Peterson (1956) and his colleagues at the University of Illinois in the mid-1950s. The social responsibility theory served as a post hoc way to reconcile the long-standing assumption that democracy required a marketplace of ideas produced by competing media outlets and a competent, active citizenry, with the reality of growing centralization of ownership, decreasing competition in the printed press, the rise of an inherently centralized and expensive-to-own electronic media, and social science research and real-world events that raised concerns regarding the stability of democratic systems and the civic capacity of their citizens. It did so by reinforcing (and eventually codifying) three conceptual distinctions.

News versus Entertainment

First, the news and entertainment "functions" of privately owned media outlets were separated conceptually, with the former viewed as fulfilling the media's public interest obligations. This formulation served to justify, post hoc, the outcome of political battles fought between 1927 and 1935 over commercialization of the broadcasting system, during which period "the basic institutions and regulatory and business practices were established not only for radio but also for television when it would be developed in the 1940s and 1950s" (McChesney 1999, 190). Organizations such as the National Committee on Education and Radio had argued that the emerging electronic media system, which relied on the public airwaves, had a significant and overriding role to play as a pillar of democratic culture in America. They and others unsuccessfully advocated for a publicly owned system modeled on the British or Canadian Broadcasting Corporations. Such a model, had it been adopted, would have meant a very different notion of public affairs programming, one in which social responsibility was the concern not only of news divisions but also of all those who control media content. However, as a result of heavy industry lobbying, and despite overwhelming public opposition to advertising on radio, congressional action set in motion the privately owned, advertiser-driven system that we take for granted today. As a result, explicitly labeled "news" and "public affairs" programming alone would fulfill the responsibility to serve the public interest assumed by the broadcast networks in return for being given control of the public airwaves.

It is important to note that such a system (i.e., one that limits the media's public interest obligations to an unspecified but small portion of their content and that allows the government, and indirectly the public, to monitor the meeting of this obligation through the licensing process) requires an institutional distinction between news and entertainment, whether or not such a distinction makes substantive, theoretical, or ethical sense. Only in this way were the broadcast media assured that the bulk of their schedule (i.e., entertainment)[6] would be governed strictly by profitability and market considerations (McChesney 1999). But as we have argued, such distinctions are problematic at best, no less during the Age of Broadcast News than in the media environments of the nineteenth or the early twenty-first centuries. As the *New York Times* columnist Frank Rich (2002) notes, "Even Edward R. Murrow, his

---

[6] In the words of the television executive Grant Tinker, referring to his entertainment division, "In the civic education of the American public, I am recess" (at the page "Tinker, Grant," *Encyclopedia of TV*, Museum of Broadcasting History, http://www.museum.tv/eotvsection.php?entrycode=tinkergrant).

network's patron saint of journalistic purity, dispensed both 'high Murrow' (his legendary investigative reports on 'See It Now') and 'low Murrow' (the prototype of today's prime-time celebrity-interview 'news' shows, 'Person to Person')." In short, the line between news and entertainment is inherently blurred and contestable and never fully maps the boundaries between politically relevant and politically irrelevant media forms. It was only the regulations, institutions, norms, and practices that came to define the broadcast news media regime that made such distinctions seem natural.

Fact versus Opinion

Second, within the news media, fact would be distinguished from opinion, and news reporting would strive to be accurate, objective, and balanced. Although newspapers had long had separate sections for sports, women's concerns, comics, and the editor's opinions, it was during the 1930s that they developed the distinction between news and opinion that we recognize today. Ironically – because he continued to insist that his reporters reflect his editorial perspective in their news writing – it was Hearst's *New York American* that originated (in 1931) what we now call the op-ed page: essays by outside contributors to run on the page opposite from the editor's opinion page (Nasaw 2000). The institutionalized distinction between fact and opinion reinforced the Progressive Era vision of journalists as trained professionals, though in ways that ignored the more subtle, ethical, and epistemological concerns associated with journalism. As the communication scholar Clifford Christians (2000, 23) concludes, "Stretched across the fact-value dichotomy of scientific naturalism, journalistic morality became equivalent to unbiased reporting of neutral data." Further, the ability of journalists to live up to this ideal was far more than a simple (if ultimately unrealistic and philosophically naive) professional aim but a vital ideological prop of an increasingly centralized media regime. As media scholars Ben Bagdikian (1997) and Robert McChesney (1999) convincingly argue, the concept of objectivity allowed the media to claim to continue to serve the public's interest despite the monopoly of the three networks and the dramatic increase in the number of one-newspaper towns.

Democratic Elitism

Third, the public was distinguished from media elites and policy experts, with citizens viewed largely as consumers of information and elites as information gatekeepers who represented the public's interest in the construction of political and social reality. Reflecting the triumph of the democratic elitism espoused by Lippmann in the debate with advocates of more participatory democracy such as John Dewey, social responsibility theory and its practical applications conceded the inevitability of both a centralized, privately owned media and a less-than-engaged public, and transferred much of the civic responsibility of the latter to a new class of information elites. The "truth" about the social and political world was no longer (if, indeed, it had ever been) constructed out of enlightened public discourse, as had been assumed by earlier American media regimes, but instead it emerged from a more managed and limited exchange among experts in the news media. Answers to questions about the trustworthiness, adequacy, and utility of mediated political information would be answered by trained professionals. Citizens were redefined as unsophisticated consumers of information, and the public was redefined as an audience of spectators rather than participants in politics. That the development of a commercialized, advertiser-driven media system itself played a crucial role in this redefinition from citizen to consumer was unremarked on. Instead, the range of possible alternatives considered by Cold War writers like Peterson and most journalists themselves extended only to the totalitarian systems of the Soviet bloc and did not include the noncommercial models adopted in other democratic countries and bypassed in the United States.

The Rise of Television News

Central to the media regime that emerged in the mid-twentieth century was the growing dominance of television in general and the three television networks in particular as a source of "news." Throughout the twentieth century, the number of newspapers declined – while the U.S. population doubled between 1900 and 1950, the number of newspapers declined from 2,226 to 1,900 (Bagdikian 1997, 176). Daily penetration of newspapers was cut nearly in half, from an average of more than 1.3 newspapers per household in 1920 to fewer than .7 by 1985 (Bogart 1989, 16). In contrast, by the end of the 1950s, nine out of ten U.S. households had a television. At that time (1959), 57 percent of Americans said they usually got most of their news "about what's going on in the world today" from newspapers, compared with 51 percent who named television and 34 percent who named radio (respondents were allowed to name more than one source). By 1963, however, television and newspapers were evenly ranked, and by 1967, television had become the single most popular choice for news.[7] And by 1986 – just as the Age of Broadcast News was about to be challenged – 66 percent of Americans said they usually got their news from television, compared with just 36 percent who said newspapers and 14 percent who said radio (Bogart 1989, 243).

Over this period, television news also gained in credibility. In 1959, 32 percent of Americans said that they were more inclined to believe newspapers than television if the two presented conflicting information, compared with 29 percent who were more inclined to believe television. By 1968, however, television was twice as likely to be believed as newspapers, and by 1986, 55 percent of Americans were more trusting of television, compared with 21 percent who were more likely to trust newspapers (Bogart 1989, 243).

The growing dominance of television, coupled with the declining penetration of independent newspapers, produced a much more centralized and nationalized discursive environment than had been true in earlier media regimes. At a time when we are used to receiving hundreds of television stations through cable or satellite systems, and having access to several twenty-four-hour news channels, to say nothing of the internet, it is worth remembering that the average household had access to slightly less than three stations in 1950, six stations in 1960, and seven stations in 1970. And although by 1980 the average American home received ten television signals, national and international news remained almost entirely the purview of the thirty-minute (including commercials) evening broadcasts of the three national networks.[8]

This political, economic, and technological structure of the media created a set of common images and patterns of attention that were consistent with the power of journalists and professional experts advocated by Lippmann and assumed by social responsibility theorists. The commonality of these images, the concentration of the media system that produced them, and the inability to imagine preferable alternative models (given the stark choice between social responsibility and totalitarian models) are what

---

[7] This transition from print to electronic media prompted the same sorts of fears about the decline of knowledge among the polity as has the move of young people from the network news broadcasts to late-night comedians and *The Daily Show* that we discussed in Chapter 1.

[8] In 1948, CBS launched network television news with the fifteen-minute *Douglas Edwards and the News*. The broadcasts of the three networks were expanded from fifteen to thirty minutes in 1963 (Webster and Phalen 1997, 103).

accounted for the stable, if unstated, "collusion" between producers and audience that led to the widespread acceptance of the boundaries of the news genre.

News producers' contribution to this collusion consisted of a set of institutional structures and processes that also reinforced the news-entertainment distinction: the design of media organizations into separate news and entertainment divisions; the assumption that public affairs programming would be free from (or less tied to) expectations of profitability; trade distinctions between news and entertainment media; the physical layout and labeling of segments of publications and programs so as to distinguish news from analysis or opinion, and hard news from soft news or features; the routinization of program schedules (local news in the early evening followed immediately by national news; local news again at 10 or 11 P.M.; political talk shows on Sunday mornings); the professionalization of journalists; the development of formal and informal standard operating procedures to assist in determining newsworthiness; and the limited number of television stations available to citizens, all of which broadcast news at the same time.[9]

The audience also played a key, if indirect, role in maintaining the distinctions between public affairs and popular culture on which the news as a genre depends. Average citizens were assumed to have met their public responsibility by watching the evening news (and were effectively blocked by the small number of stations, all carrying the nightly news, from watching anything else). Readers of prestige news magazines and newspapers, and viewers of Sunday morning political talk shows, constituted the "attentive public," a self-selected segment of the population representing a more elite social, economic, and political stratum of citizens. This elite audience signaled the serious nature of what was being read or watched, distinguishing it from "popular" media. This distinction was even drawn within specific media texts, as when William Randolph Hearst saw his new op-ed page as "aimed directly at more educated and affluent readers" (Nasaw 2000, 248). As with the more general distinction between "highbrow" and "lowbrow" culture, political significance and

---

[9] Many of these distinctions were formerly codified in the 1920s through the early 1950s by, among others, the Federal Radio (1927) and Federal Communications (1934) commissions; professional associations such as the American Society of Newspaper Editors (1922), the National Association of Broadcasters (1923), and the Newspapers Guild (1933); the privately funded Commission on Freedom of the Press (1947); and codes of conduct created by the movie (1930), radio (1937), and television (1952) industries (Emery and Emery 1988; Peterson 1956).

insignificance were defined more by the organization of producing institutions and the makeup of the audience than by actual content (Levine
1988).

Pointing out the degree to which the Age of Broadcast News was the
outcome of economic and technological changes, as well as of political
debate and struggle – rather than of more compelling and theoretically
sound distinctions – does not diminish the considerable advantages that
flowed from it. Among these are the creation of an influential professional
class of journalists committed to informing the public in an unbiased way
and to investigating and holding elites accountable, all while insulated (at
least in theory) from the pressures that might be brought to bear on them
by these elites, including the owners of the media corporations employing
them. At least as significant, for the first time the broadcast system of the
middle years of the twentieth century created a national public that daily
considered a common set of images and mediated experiences. Colin Leys
(2001, 150) captures the central political advantage of the Age of Broadcast News and what is lost with its passing: "In retrospect, the era of two
or three channels may be seen as constituting a unique historical moment
in which complex modern societies had for a couple of decades something
like a single forum for their most important 'formative conversations'; not
a forum that offered universal or even broadly representative access to
the podium, but one that was at least more or less universally attended."
Yet it is important to note that this achievement of the electronic media
did not depend on making a distinction between news and entertainment.
This point is clear in the quote from Eric Hobsbawm (1994, 196) with
which we opened this chapter, where in calling attention to the historical significance of the electronic media, he lists examples from across a
wide range of genres: "the big game, the favorite comedy show, Winston
Churchill's speech, the contents of the news bulletin."

Gatekeeping and Agenda Setting in the Age of Broadcast News

Most mid- to late-twentieth-century social science research about the
influence of the mass media on public opinion implicitly and explicitly
accepted the assumptions of the social responsibility theory of the press
and the particular media regime within which it was institutionalized.
When it came to examining the political influence of the media, scholars almost exclusively examined media explicitly labeled "political" by
producers: news broadcasts, news and editorial sections of print media,
political advertisements, and so forth. From the early days of empirical
research by Paul Lazarsfeld and his colleagues in the 1930s and 1940s

through the methodologically sophisticated work of scholars like Shanto Iyengar and Donald Kinder (1987), Diana Mutz (1998, 1996), and Robert Entman (1989, 2004), the centrality of the news media as the nation's information gatekeepers was assumed.

Researchers assumed (sometimes explicitly, more often implicitly) that between the booming, buzzing, blooming confusion of the political world and the limited time and capacity of ordinary citizens stood professional journalists who, in negotiation (sometimes hostile, sometimes more amicable and cooperative) with political elites, would determine what information passed through these media gates to the general public. Two basic findings emerged from this body of political communication research, with (at least until recently) both gaining widespread acceptance among scholars, media practitioners, and the educated public. First, in contrast to the fears of many, the mass media were found to have only limited effects on public opinion. The conclusion of a wealth of studies was that political attitudes and opinions were shaped by a number of forces – early socialization, interpersonal interactions, and so forth – outside the media. Further, those with little political information and interest, though most susceptible to media influence, were also those least likely to seek out mediated political information, relying instead on the opinions of more interested and informed opinion leaders (see Klapper 1960).

The agenda-setting power of the media, the second consensus conclusion of this research tradition, did not emerge until the 1970s and served to modify the so-called "minimal effects" conclusion. Agenda-setting research found that, although the media could not determine what people think (i.e., their political attitudes and opinions), they did shape what people thought about. So, although the ideological predispositions of citizens were relatively firm, the issues to which these predispositions were applied were heavily shaped by the media. That is, when the news media focus on an issue, it is considered important by the public. Conversely, issues that are ignored by the news media have a difficult time attracting public attention. Through a variety of ingenious research designs and methods, researchers were able to specify the dynamics of this agenda-setting process (Iyengar 2001; Iyengar and Kinder 1987).

Reflecting the degree to which political communication research is always connected to ideological debates over the role of media in a democratic society, the findings of researchers were comforting to defenders of the extant media regime. First, they undermined the critical arguments of those who feared the power of the media and their potential for manipulating public opinion rather than simply reporting on political issues. Limited media effects meant that structural reform of the media system on the grounds of democratic values was unwarranted. At the same time, the finding that the media set the agenda validated the role of journalists as specified under the social responsibility theory of the press. Professional journalists were successful at defining what was important without actually shaping the political opinions of their audience, a finding reassuring to those who believed in objectivity. James Carey (1997, 17) well summarizes this line of research:

The settled and established consensus and conclusion . . . was that the media might have special and limited effects on some topics and some groups, that they might direct attention to some problems and away from others and therefore set a social and political agenda of sorts, but the media did not constitute a social problem, did not debase the culture or promote extremism; the media were, in short, in concert with rather than opposed to the fundamentally democratic and egalitarian forces in the culture.

In short, mainstream political communication research was built on an implicit acceptance of the media regime in place at the time. In turn, the research produced by it, focused as it was on news rather than entertainment, served to further reinforce and naturalize this regime (for three representative studies, see White 1964; Bleske 1991; Berkowitz 1990).[10] Largely ignored were the political implications of non-news genres such as movies, television drama and comedies, music, and so forth. For example, in the 1960s and 1970s, Hollywood movies like *Dr. Strangelove*, *Apocalypse Now*, and *Easy Rider* arguably were important political texts for a large segment of the public. Similarly, novels like *Catch-22*, *Slaughterhouse-Five*, and *Gravity's Rainbow* became important conduits for communicating a variety of political values and perspectives given short shrift in the news (Kakutani 2001). However, a priori assumptions of media professionals and scholars prevented them from fully understanding this political significance.

Whatever the advantages and disadvantages of this approach for understanding the mass media (and a generation of critical scholars have identified its limits even within the media regime of this time period), it is in serious need of reexamination. We say this because the media system

---

[10] Reflecting the degree to which the genre of news is a collusion between producers and consumers and not based on explicit definitions, empirical studies of gatekeeping have consistently revealed that, rather than depending on categories learned through professional training, journalists rely on instinct, experience, or the decisions of other gatekeepers (e.g., news wires, competitors) to distinguish between types of news stories and between what is included and excluded from newspapers or television broadcasts.

scholars sought to understand has fundamentally changed precisely in ways that undermine the assumptions (both examined and unexamined) on which their research was based. This new media environment, to which we now turn, requires a thorough rethinking – by scholars, practitioners, and citizens – of the role of the media in a democratic society and the very concept of politically relevant information on which any such understanding depends.

The End of the Age of Broadcast News

Although the social responsibility theory of the press continues to undergird our commonsense understanding of the role of the media in a democratic society, the world within which this perspective developed has changed almost beyond recognition. These changes, emerging from a number of sources during the last two decades of the twentieth century and continuing today, undermine virtually all of the assumptions on which the current media regime is based. It is not our intention here to provide a detailed history of this period. Nor, at this point, do we wish to fully engage in the important and contentious debates over the normative implications of this period. Rather, our goal is to briefly recall three significant developments that have particular relevance for the current discursive environment and its relationship to the media regime in place since the mid-twentieth century: the end of the Cold War and the resulting alterations in real and perceived relationships between markets and the state; the increasing understanding of the United States as a multicultural society and the resulting collapse of a unified notion of political and social reality; and economic globalization and its impact on the public interest obligations of media corporations. We then turn in more detail to a fourth development, one that acted as a triggering device in ensuring the inevitable demise of the Age of Broadcast News: the growth in new telecommunications technologies and their impact on the production and consumption of information.

A New World Order: From the Cold War to Culture Wars

The End of the Cold War and the Triumph of Neoliberalism: From the summit conferences at Reykjavik and Washington in 1986 and 1987 through the ultimate collapse of the Soviet bloc by 1991, the end of four decades of conflict between the Soviet Union and the United States shattered the basic frames of reference used to understand the post–World War II world. As Hobsbawm (1995, 4) puts it, "there can be no serious doubt that in the late 1980s and early 1990s an era in world history came to an end." Coverage of the events that marked the end of the Cold War were staples of the evening news, as vivid images of joyful Germans hammering at the Berlin Wall or Russians toppling statues of Lenin were beamed into the nation's living rooms. Ironically, these images also marked the beginning of the end of the very media regime that provided them. Just as these events and how they were interpreted challenged our preexisting understandings of the twentieth century, they also fundamentally challenged the Cold War presuppositions on which the social responsibility theory of the press depended.

Basic to this theory was a stark contrast between free and totalitarian media regimes and the assumed superiority of the former over the latter. Implicit in this analysis is the existence of a bipolar world characterized by two types of political-economic systems: a communist bloc of state-controlled economies, totalitarian political systems, and tightly controlled, government-owned media on the one hand, and a capitalist bloc of market economies, democratic political systems, and privately owned media systems on the other hand. As the historian Mark Lilla (2003, 28) argues, it is precisely such assumptions that are challenged by events of the last two decades of the twentieth century:

The birth of the fascist axis, its defeat partly through democratic mobilization and resolve, the postwar spread of the Soviet empire, the gulags and concentration camps, the genocide, the espionage, the nuclear arms race – these are the political phenomena for which the century is today remembered. Already we are beginning to see that this was not the whole story, that other developments – such as decolonization, the integration of world markets, the technological shock of digitalization – were also revolutionary. Conceptually and rhetorically, however, the twentieth century confrontation with totalitarianism still sets our intellectual compass.... For as long as anyone living can remember, the fundamental political problem of our time has been captured, well or not by the slogan "totalitarianism or democracy," a distinction thought useful for the purposes of serious political analysis and public rhetoric alike. That age is definitely past.

Two consequences of the collapse of the Soviet bloc affected the discursive environment of the late twentieth century, thus challenging the underlying logic of the existing media regime: the increasingly hegemonic neoliberal faith in markets and the increasingly tenuous connection between the interests of specific nation states and of multinational media corporations.[11] Although these trends did not originate with the end of

---

[11] We use the term *neoliberalism* to describe the political-economic philosophy advocating for domestic and global free markets and free-trade policies, which emerged in reaction to both Keynesian economics and more socialist or communist approaches to economic regulation.

the Cold War (e.g., broadcast deregulation began as early as the Carter administration), the collapse of the Soviet bloc and how it was interpreted accelerated them.

In superficial but commonsense ways (most basically through the assumption that "we" won and "they" lost), the end of Cold War has been taken as proof positive of the desirability of markets as the prime distributors of goods and services, including mediated political information. Conservative analysts, in particular, interpreted the end of the Cold War as the end of history, ushering in the eternal triumph of neoliberalism (Fukuyama 1993). Even somewhat more sober writers like Daniel Yergin and Joseph Stanislaw (1998, 63) interpreted the collapse of the Soviet Union as evidence that any type of government interference in the econ omy, even in democratic societies, was simply the camel's nose of communism and thus was doomed to failure and popular rejection: "As communism was the most extreme form of state economic control, its demise signaled an enormous shift – from state control to market mechanisms." Network news divisions themselves contributed to this understanding as nightly broadcasts routinely interchanged the words *capitalism, markets,* and *democracy* as if they had a single meaning when contrasted with the equally interchangeable words *communism, socialism,* and *totalitarianism.* The result was the implicit assumption that "markets enjoy some mystic, organic connection to the people while governments were fundamentally illegitimate" (Frank 2000, xii).

One impact of this interpretation of the end of the Cold War was the increasing dominance of what Thomas Frank (2000) insightfully calls "market populism," which equates private markets with freedom and democracy. In this formulation, markets are not just mediums of exchange but also mediums of consent (Frank 2000). As Frank notes, however, market populism is best thought of as an ideological tool rather than a statement of fact, based as it is on a simplified and inaccurate interpretation of history. Markets are hardly populist mechanisms of equality. Indeed, left to their own devices, they inevitably lead to vast inequalities, as even Adam Smith recognized. Nor have they ever existed (in modern societies at least) without government support (consider the important role played by government in the cheap distribution of newspapers and magazines, and in the development of the post office, the telegraph, radio, and the internet). Finally, markets and their proper role are contested terrain constantly subject to political debate and struggle, whether by labor unions, environmentalists, or capitalists seeking to protect themselves from competition (Polanyi 1944). Indeed, one of the triumphs of neoliberalism as an ideological tool is that its supporters have managed to make the spread of markets –in terms of both the types of goods and services they are used to allocate and their increasingly global reach – as natural and, therefore, inevitable. The widespread acceptance of the market populist perspective has meant fewer calls from mainstream voices for policies that seek to further democratic values by limiting or regulating markets.

In the realm of the media in general and broadcast media in particular, the triumph of market populism undercut the notion that the provision of information should be guided by anything other than supply and demand, as the logic of markets reduces media outlets and texts to simple products, stripped of their broader public implications (Leys 2001). From this perspective, media corporations' "responsibility" is simply to produce the programming that audiences demand, and any criticism of such market-governed mass media was labeled as elitist, antidemocratic and ineffective. As cogently argued by Edwin Baker (2007), an unregulated profit-driven market approach is particularly devastating for journalism for several related reasons. First, even by their own logic markets offer no guarantee of producing optimal results, as owners often make decisions that fail to capture consumers' true interests, even interests the latter would be willing to pay for to have met. Second, media owners are not dictated to by consumer interests; rather, they have power in this relationship and so shape as much as react to consumer demand. Third, media owners seek to maximize profit, and so "quality" is never a good in and of itself, always being subjugated to more demanding notions of an acceptable bottom line. And fourth, an exaggerated dependence on the logic of markets leaves no room for appeals to noncommodified values such as a politically informed public or a democratically accountable political system. Lost in this market populism version of democracy is any sense of the collective good other than that emerging from individual and highly constrained consumer behavior. As the legal scholar Cass Sunstein (2001) argues, because they inevitably serve a collective purpose in democratic societies, it is never adequate to evaluate communications systems simply on the basis of whether they give individual consumers what they want.

The market populist consensus emerging from the collapse of communism signaled the death knell for the already thin and contested public interest obligations that had been imposed on the broadcasting industry and that underpinned the news-entertainment divide. Absent some notion of a public interest standing outside consumer behavior, the arguments of journalists, media critics and scholars aimed to resist the increasing imposition of profit considerations onto news divisions rang hollow and out of touch.

The end of the Cold War also undermined existing conceptions of the "proper" relationship between journalists (and scholars) on the one hand, and the nation-state, on the other hand. Although the social responsibility theory explicitly argued for a watchdog function of the press, this role was clearer in the coverage of domestic than international affairs. Complicating the latter was the implicit assumption that American journalists and scholars shared a set of interests with the nation-state within which they operated, as it is only within a liberal democratic state that a free press can exist and within which professional journalists and scholars can have independence. It was this largely unexamined equating of national and professional interests that led to the collaboration between the American security state and many scholars and journalists during the Cold War.[12] The end of the Cold War and the rise of an increasingly globalized media system (discussed in more detail herein) challenged the logic of this relationship, however.[13] Absent a Soviet threat, and increasingly beholden to corporations that crossed national boundaries, U.S. journalism (whose advantages were constructed in sharp contrast to the disadvantages of totalitarian media systems) could less easily be placed in the service of American democracy. Rather, news divisions, like any other division of the media corporations of which they were a part, have become increasingly viewed as just another market-driven profit center.

Of course the Age of Broadcast News's tendency to view national interests as paramount was not universal. The most notable example of this was coverage of the last half dozen years of the Vietnam War, when relationships between journalists and the state were most contentious and when coverage was most challenging to and skeptical of national policy (Hallin 1986). Viewed as a whole, however, this six-year period stands out as a dramatic exception to the more typical pattern of coverage of international affairs that characterized the years from the 1950s through the early 1990s.[14]

---

[12] For an excellent exploration of the ways in which this collaboration distorted the development of the American social sciences, in general, and communications research, in particular, see Simpson, 1994.

[13] For an attempt to deal with this shift in the nature of sovereignty, see Hardt and Negri (2000).

[14] And, as Hallin (1986) demonstrates, post-1968 coverage of Vietnam was driven by interelite conflicts and growing public disagreement over what actually constituted the national interest of the United States.

A final impact of the Cold War's end on the media was the disruption in journalistic notions of newsworthiness. In the hierarchy of news, international affairs in general and war coverage in particular traditionally stood at the pinnacle, serving as the very definition of *hard news*. The career paths of successful journalists were measured by their move from local assignments to national and international ones. The end of the Cold War, coupled with the growing importance of consumer demand as the determinant of news content, both challenged the centrality of international news and created space (literally and figuratively) to be filled. The result was a growth in what, from the perspective of the Age of Broadcast News, appeared to be soft or entertainment stories.

Multicultural Society and Contested Truth: Throughout the 1950s, during which the ideological underpinnings of the then-emerging media regime of broadcast news were becoming institutionalized, there was widespread acceptance of the uniqueness and virtue of an American political culture shared by all citizens. True, there was room within this ideology to acknowledge flaws in the American system, most significantly racism or poverty. However, faith in progress ensured that such problems would ultimately be overcome once identified. More to the point, these flaws would be remedied by bringing people of color or the economically disadvantaged into the American dream of white, middle-class culture. Virtually unchallenged was the notion that the United States constituted a single society, with a single cultural heritage and a single (or dominant) set of political values. In this context, it is easy to see why Progressive Era beliefs – which assumed that trained professionals, armed with the appropriate methods, could discover an objective truth to guide elite decision making – would be so persuasive and uncontested. Professional journalists played a central role in this ideology, serving as experts who were uniquely suited to objectively identify places where the realities of American society fell short of this common dream.

Confidence in the possibility and/or efficacy of neutral techniques, as well as in the very existence of a singular truth for them to discover, were all casualties of social and intellectual changes in the last decades of the twentieth century. Just as the end of the Cold War and the increasing globalization of capitalism (discussed in more detail herein) challenged prevailing understandings of the political role of the media, so, too, did sea changes in political culture challenge the models of truth on which much of professional journalism during the Age of Broadcast News was based. Among myriad other changes beginning to take place in America by the 1970s, increasing ethnic, gender, sexual, and racial self-awareness;

declining social trust; and rising cynicism helped to unravel the existing consensus. At its core, the emerging politics of recognition and identity challenged the idea that a single narrative could encompass American politics and society. This slowly emerging and still only partially accepted view concluded that the experience of America was fundamentally different for women than for men, for people of color than for white Americans, for gays than for heterosexuals, and so forth. In turn, these developments slowly undermined the most basic assumptions of professional journalism (not to mention academic social science), by challenging the notion that it (or any other set of experts) could or should provide a single, objective picture of social and political truth.

Although the roots of the multicultural challenge to preexisting notions of a unified and knowable American experience date back to at least the 1970s, the full significance of the challenge did not emerge until the late 1980s and early 1990s. This was in part because of the end of the Cold War. Absent a bipolar worldview, room was created for both more nuanced understandings of cultural diversity and history, and for greater media attention to domestic social issues. Whether attacked by detractors such as Alan Bloom (1988) and William Bennett (1997) or defended by supporters like Stanley Fish (1994) and Lawrence Levine (1997), the so-called culture wars in American intellectual life came to replace the Cold War as the symbol of struggle over American values. The culture wars directly involved the media in two crucial ways. First, the media in general, and entertainment media in particular, were increasingly seen by all sides as a central source of public values and behaviors. Conservatives attacked the media in its various forms (print, television, music, film, video games, and more recently the internet) for excessive violence, profanity, drug use, and sex, whereas liberals lamented the absence and/or stereotypical portrayals of minorities, gays, and women. At the heart of these specific concerns were broader issues of the nature of American culture and society.

Second, notions of cultural diversity and relativity directly challenged the underlying premise on which the social responsibility model of the news was based. Without a unified notion of truth, facts, objectivity, or point of view, the idea that a single class of professional elites (i.e., journalists), distinct from and superior to other producers of information (e.g., film directors, bloggers, musicians), and working within a system of limited and highly centralized news outlets, could fulfill the media's democratic public interest obligations became increasingly untenable.

Globalization and the Erosion of Media Public Interest Obligations: Although the growth in multinational corporations in the latter decades of the twentieth century generally changed the relationship between corporate and national interests, in perhaps no other industry has globalization been more significant than in the media. The growth of global media conglomerates undermined the assumption that corporate interests were largely coterminous with the interests of the nation – an assumption that underlay the social responsibility theory's imposition of formal, if limited, public interest obligations on media organizations in exchange for their commercial use of the public airwaves. Just as it had been argued in the 1950s by the president of General Motors that what was good for the automotive giant was good for the nation, and vice versa, so, too, was it implicitly assumed that what was good for NBC, ABC, or CBS was good for the nation, and vice versa. However, once networks become parts of global media conglomerates or partnerships, and/or seek out international audiences, corporate media interests are no longer tied to a specific nation and vaguely drawn public interest obligations within specific nations mean less and less. In what meaningful sense, for example, can one suggest that what is good for the Fox network, part of an international media empire owned by the Australian media mogul Rupert Murdoch, is good for the United States? Should journalism that is beamed into nondemocratic regimes by Murdoch's sky satellite reflect democratic values? On what basis and/or within what jurisdiction would one make such an argument?

This dilemma is especially at play with the globalization of new media like the internet. For example, in June 2001, the then AOL Time Warner media conglomerate entered into a $200 million joint venture with the largest Chinese maker of personal computers to expand internet access on the Chinese mainland. What values ought to guide the policy of a putatively American firm like AOL Time Warner when it comes to issues of political censorship, especially considering that Beijing has blocked politically sensitive internet content and, more to the point, has censored CNN and banned *Time* magazine (both owned by Time Warner)?

In 2007, a similar controversy erupted over Google's negotiations with Beijing to provide its internet search services to computer users in China. As with Time Warner, Google agreed to censor search results in accord with the wishes of the Chinese government. Calling attention to Google's corporate commitment to "do good," Chinese internet users objected to the firm's collaboration in creating the "Great Firewall" built on "a complex system of filters and an army of tens of thousands of human monitors to survey the country's 140 million internet users' surfing habits and surgically clip sensitive content from in front of their eyes" (Reuters 2007a). Undeterred, Google announced in June 2007 that it had won a license to provide "news" content in China (Reuters 2007b). Not surprisingly, there continues to be considerable debate about the differences among what Chinese authorities, Western journalists, and *Google executives* might mean by the term *news*. This debate erupted again in January 2010, when Google discovered that it had been subject to a sophisticated and targeted effort, orchestrated by the Chinese government, to gain access to the e-mail accounts of Chinese human rights activists. As a result, Google decided it was no longer going to accept censorship of its China site and contemplated the possibility of shutting down the site, as well as its offices in China (Meserve and Ahlers 2010). A compromise of sorts was reached when the company split its services. The mainland Chinese webpage offers only searches that are not censored (e.g., music, products, translation). A separate webpage, located in Hong Kong, was created that offers an uncensored version of Google's search engine, videos, maps, and so forth. However, users must click a link that takes them from the mainland site to the Hong Kong page which, critics argue, allows tracking by Chinese authorities (Morrison 2010). The stakes in these debates are illustrated by the case of the Chinese journalist Shi Tau, who was sentenced to ten years in prison for subversive pro-democracy activities after records of his online activities were turned over to the Chinese government by Yahoo!, another American firm doing business in China (Associated Press 2007).

Additional controversies have surrounded international access to the online video site YouTube, purchased by Google in late 2006. For example, in 2007, the Thai government announced it was dropping its four-month "digital blockade" of the popular site, but only because YouTube executives agreed to take their own steps to ensure that Thai citizens could not view material that violated Thai law – specifically material that was deemed "insulting" to the country or the king. Taking a different tack, YouTube reached a 2007 agreement allowing access in Great Britain in exchange for monitoring its site for the posting of illegally copyrighted videos and either removing the videos or paying royalties for them. And in the same year, YouTube responded to complaints from the German government regarding videos containing Nazi-related images by blocking access to them, not only in Germany but also for all users around the world (Lyons 2007)

Conflicts such as these, increasing in number and involving countries around the globe, highlight how problematic is the very notion of the public interest assumed by Progressives and the degree to which that notion depended on a convergence of the interests of media corporations with the political values of a specific polity. Given the difficulties we have chronicled in defining *news*, debate that assumes the naturalness of this term will inevitably prove difficult and likely avoid the central question that underlies it: what is the appropriate relationship between media and politics in the new media environment? Predictably, global corporate and nation-specific interests routinely trump broader "democratic" values, such as freedom of the press. For example, the former president of AOL International, Michael Lynton, said the joint venture described here would try to find the most "appropriate form of internet service in China while respecting Beijing's rules on content" (Savadove and Munrow 2001).

Summary – The Beginning of the End of "The Public"?: The political, cultural, and economic disruptions discussed here not only exploded prior assumptions about the relationship between the media and the public interest but also challenged the very notion that there is a public. During the Age of Broadcast News, an audience of virtually all who were watching television viewed the news and, as a consequence, shared the same stock of political images and information. This set of circumstances meshed well with the belief that the United States constituted a single society with a single cultural heritage and a single set of political values. As a result, it was relatively easy to equate this audience with "the public," coming together each night for a glimpse of politically relevant truth revealed by professional journalists. In turn, the common experiences created by broadcast news acted to reinforce, even reify, this sense of a single, unified public. This equating of the audience for the nightly news with the public was crucial to naturalizing the norms and practices underlying the Age of Broadcast News.

As some media scholars have come to argue, the very idea of the audience is not now and never was a naturally occurring phenomenon but rather an administrative category constructed by media producers and advertisers (Ang 1991). Just as the artificial distinction between news and entertainment depends on an implicit collusion between producers and viewers, so, too, the contingent and constructed nature of the mass audience – and thus of a singular public – is obscured when there is an unexamined and widely shared set of common media experiences and a notion of a common culture. We have discussed the ways in which the emergence of multiculturalism contributed to making more visible the artificiality of these constructions, making clear that the United States consists of many different cultures and political identities and thus undermining the notion that there is a singular American identity or a singular idea of citizenship. For similar but even more compelling reasons, the globalization of media ownership and the related increase in the globalization of both the producers and the consumers of mediated information further erodes any meaningful notion of a singular audience or, more significantly, a singular public.

Similarly, the overriding notion of a global struggle between democracy and communism that defined the Cold War provided, at least in a negative sense, a shared sense of American common identity that seemed to outweigh ethnic, racial, class, or gender differences (Gitlin 1996). That this collective identification was artificial and constructed has been pointed out by a wide variety of social critics, from Karl Marx, who saw class as a more important point of identification than nation, to more recent scholars of race, ethnicity, and gender. Nevertheless, real or not, it served as a way of justifying the media environment that characterized the Age of Broadcast News, with all of its advantages and disadvantages. And just as the end of the Cold War challenged this, at best, oversimplified notion of a collective national interest by unleashing largely contained cultural differences within the United States, so, too, in conjunction with an increasingly global media, it added to this fragmentation both by unleashing long-muted international cultural conflicts (based on, for example, religion, ethnicity, and nationalism) and by making these differences visible to international audiences. Absent some organizing principle other than market populism, what remains to bind people together – nationally or internationally – is little more than their common identities as consumers.

In combination, the end of the Cold War, the resulting triumph of market populism, and the partially related rise in the politics of identity and globalization have challenged the hegemony of the existing media regime while also limiting the discursive resources available for identifying alternative mechanisms for reestablishing the public interest obligations of the media. As markets have become increasingly conflated with democracy in public discourse, appeals to public interest obligations as collective values in conflict with individualistic market forces, and thus in need of government protection, become less and less persuasive. But in and of themselves, these trends could not ensure the complete collapse of the existing media regime. For this to happen, one more crucial ingredient was necessary: the introduction of a host of new information and communication technologies that fundamentally changed the nature of information consumption and production.

Technological Developments and the Changing Discursive Environment

To list the developments in communications that have occurred over the past twenty-five years is to be reminded of how radically different the media environment of the early twenty-first century is from what preceded it. For example, in 1982, as Shanto Iyengar and Donald Kinder (1987) were doing the research for their seminal work on the agenda-setting power of television news, *News That Matters*, fewer than 2 million personal computers were sold in the United States; the average home received approximately ten television channels; only 21 percent of American homes had a VCR; and the internet and mobile phones were, for all intents and purposes, nonexistent. By the late 2000s, annual U.S. computer sales had grown to 250 million, more than three-quarters of U.S. households had at least one personal computer, the average number of channels received had increased to more than 130, greater than 90 percent of homes had VCRs and/or DVD players, more than three-quarters of U.S. households had an internet connection (and more than 50 percent had high-speed connections), the number of websites increased from about 100 (in 1993) to more than 160 million, more than three-quarters of adult Americans had a cell phone or PDA (Personal Digital Assistant), and nearly one-third of households had a digital video recorder (DVR) such as TiVo (Statistical Abstract of the United States 2009; Media Dynamics 2010).

These and numerous other technological changes have profoundly affected the way information is produced, disseminated, and consumed. Individuals have unprecedented and almost instantaneous access to mediated information of a greater variety (in the form, content, and sources) than at any point in history. In turn, these changes, in combination with the political, cultural, and economic changes discussed here, have challenged the institutions, norms, and processes underpinning the television-news-dominated media regime of the mid- to late twentieth century. The new media environment, with its potential to influence the agenda of the mainstream news media, bypass these traditional gatekeepers entirely, and subvert the very distinction between information producer and consumer also represents a direct threat to the political, economic, and media elites who benefited most from this rapidly collapsing regime.

In the remainder of this section, we provide an overview of some of these changes, an overview that is intended to capture in its form and content a sense of the chaotic, unfettered, almost anarchistic nature of the current media environment. But in doing so we remain aware – as should the reader – that this Wild West version of contemporary information flows is unlikely to last. Almost certainly a new media regime, with new institutions and norms, as well as new "winners" and "losers," will take hold.

The Changing Terrain of Television: At the height of the Age of Broadcast News, each of the three dominant networks broadcast similar programming designed to attract the largest audience possible. During prime time, the usual fare was dramas and comedies, with the preceding hour almost universally devoted to local and national news. This also meant that, with few exceptions, the makeup of the audience for any program was quite similar to that for any other broadcast during the same time slot. In short, not only were audiences for any one broadcast likely to be large, but also audiences across these broadcasts were somewhat interchangeable, as was the content of what they were watching: the very definition of a mass audience.

The dramatic increase in the number of available media channels has shattered this hegemonic environment. In 1950, the average viewer watched slightly less than three channels a week, devoting 11.6 hours to each of these channels. As recently as 1980, the average number of stations viewed per week was under six, with more than eight hours devoted to each. By 2009, however, the average viewer watched more than sixteen channels a week, devoting only 2.2 hours to each (ACNielsen 2009). Thus, although Americans are watching more television than ever before, the range of what they are watching is greater, and the audience for any particular program is smaller. Needless to say, the three broadcast networks have been the big losers in this change in viewing habits. In 1982, over the course of an average day, the three major networks had a 72 percent audience share (the percentage of all television sets in use that are tuned to a particular station), compared with 21 percent for independent commercial broadcast stations and 7 percent divided among cable and public broadcasting (Goldfarb 2003). Twenty years later (in May 2002), a watershed occurred when the network audience share – including Fox, WB, and UPN – dropped to below 50 percent (Goldfarb 2003). Network television was once the only game in town, but by 2003, the average adult American devoted only about a third of his or her weekly television viewing time (4.9 hours) to the three major networks and their affiliates, with the rest devoted to independent broadcast channels (4.3 hours), pay cable (2.9 hours), basic cable (2.1 hours), and public television (2.1 hours). These trends are even more dramatic for young adults, for whom the traditional broadcast networks hold no special meaning and elicit no special loyalty (Media Dynamics 2004, 30–32; 323–388). The impact of this increased competition is illustrated by a single example:

When *Seinfeld* was the number one program in America in 1995, it had a big share of audience. But that share of audience 20 years earlier, in 1975, would not have placed it in the top 20 shows on TV. It would have been the 21st most popular show in the United States in 1975. And 1995 was the year *Seinfeld* had its largest audience share. (Pruitt 2000, 15)

The genre of network news specifically and public affairs broadcasting more broadly has been particularly hard hit by the fragmentation of television audiences. Once dominated by the three networks, by 2003, there were more self-professed "regular viewers" of cable national news (68 percent) than of the nightly national news on ABC, CBS, and NBC (49 percent combined).[15] Indeed, two cable news channels (Fox and CNN) had more regular viewers (25 percent and 22 percent, respectively) than any of the three major network news broadcasts (which averaged between 16 percent and 17 percent each; Pew Research Center for the People and the Press 2004a). And although Nielsen ratings continue to show network news drawing larger audiences than cable during particularly important political events, the trends here are equally telling. For example, on election night in 2008, the big-three broadcast networks attracted an average of 32.9 million viewers between 8 P.M. and 11 P.M., down 9 percent from 2004. The three major cable news channels, by contrast, attracted an average of 27.2 million viewers, up 58 percent from 2004 (Pew Research Center Project for Excellence in Journalism 2009).

Additional evidence of the breakdown of the Age of Broadcast News can be seen in Figure 3.1, which shows the average November ratings (each rating point equals 1 percent of households in the United States with a television set) for the three national evening news broadcasts from 1980 through 2008 (Pew Research Center Project for Excellence in Journalism 2009). The audience for local news has followed the same trend. By 2010, all three local news broadcasts – morning, early evening, and late evening – were losing their audience at an accelerating rate. Local advertising revenues had fallen by 22 percent between 2008 and 2009 (in contrast, in the previous two nonelection years, revenues had declined

---

[15] Percentages total more than 100 percent because survey respondents could be regular viewers of more than one news source.

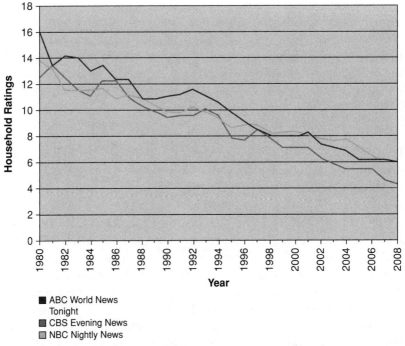

FIGURE 3.1. Evening News Ratings, November 1980 to November 2008
Source: Pew Research Center Project for Excellence in Journalism, "The State of the News Media," http://www.stateofthemedia.org/2009/narrative_networktv_audience.php?media=6&cat=2#NetAud1.

by 5 percent in 2005 and 6 percent in 2007), and there is some question about how much longer stations will be able to provide local news broadcasts (Pew Research Center Project for Excellence in Journalism 2010).

The shift away from network news has been most notable among young adults. The median age of network news viewers is older than sixty-one, and network news's share of the prized eighteen- to forty-nine-year-old segment of the audience has declined precipitously in the past two decades (Pew Research Center Project for Excellence in Journalism 2009). Although this decline in part reflects a shift to other news sources, it also reflects young people's more general abandonment of traditional news specifically and news as a genre more generally. For example, from 1998 to 2008 alone, the percentage of eighteen- to twenty-four-year-olds who reported "going newsless" the day before being surveyed increased from 25 percent to 34 percent (for the entire adult population, the percentage going "newsless" increased from 14 percent to 19 percent, with increases in every age category except fifty- to sixty-four-year-olds; Pew Research Center Project for Excellence in Journalism 2008).

Many in the media saw the increase in viewers (including young people) in the immediate aftermath of the terrorist attacks of September 11, 2001, as evidence that the news in general and network news in particular had begun to reestablish its relevance and importance. Quite predictably, however, this increase (like that in the early days of the war in Iraq or during moments of dramatic events such as Hurricane Katrina or the devastating 2004 tsunami) has proved a temporary spike in an otherwise larger pattern of steady decline. Indeed, the media critic Ken Auletta (2001) notes that even this temporary spike in ratings was a mixed blessing, as it resulted in dramatically increased costs and budgetary and ratings pressure on executives. Ironically, rather than a sign of the reemergence of "serious journalism," the aftermath of 9/11 may be remembered as the final deathblow to the broadcast news model of news:

The final proof, as if any was needed, came when the greatest natural disaster ever to strike the United States hit the coast of Louisiana and Mississippi in the summer of 2005. The networks did a fine job covering Hurricane Katrina, but their employers did not go wall-to-wall, did not blow out the schedule, did not forgo commercials as they had in the days after 9/11. If you wanted to know what was happening with the drowning of the city of New Orleans in mid-morning, or mid-afternoon, or mid-evening, you had to turn to CNN, or Fox News, or MSNBC, or the internet. (Kurtz 2007, xi)

Media scholars have noted that shifts in communication technology alter several fundamental expectations about media audiences and media content (Turow 1997, 2006; Webster and Phalen 1997). The increased competition within television in general and television news in particular brought about by new technologies such as cable, satellite, podcasts, and most recently online "television" has clearly had such an altering effect. The notion of a mass audience, at least as defined in the latter half of the twentieth century, is quickly being abandoned as networks and their competitors vie for audience share by marketing to different segments of the population. As a result, broadcast and cable networks (and their advertisers) seek to maximize differences in an effort to develop unique identities and brand loyalty. The combination of multiculturalism based on race, ethnicity, gender, age, sexual preference, religious beliefs and ideology, rapidly changing communication technology, deregulation, and the new media economics has led to more fragmented audiences and to greater diversity in genres and content.

An important impact of audience segmentation and genre diversity is a dramatic change in what constitutes news. As news executives struggle to maintain audiences, news programming (especially but not exclusively cable news) has increasingly focused on soft news and opinionated, often ideologically driven talk. For example, in March 2005, the prime-time lineup of Fox News drew an average audience of more than 2 million, compared to 775,000 for CNN. Jonathan Klein, the president of CNN, suggested that, to catch up with Fox, "the network's prime-time programs should spend less time reporting the news of the day and more time spinning out what he hopes are emotionally gripping, character-driven narratives pegged to recent events" (Steinberg 2005, E1). Following Klein's advice, in a story about an Atlanta courthouse killing by a defendant, CNN reporter Rick Sanchez demonstrated on himself the effect of a fifty-thousand-volt shock belt, which its manufacturers claimed might have prevented the rampage. When the device was activated, Sanchez groaned and collapsed to the floor. After being revived, he reported, "It hurts, but no one's dead." Klein was "euphoric" about the stunt, telling CNN editors and producers he "thought it was just great" (Steinberg 2005, E1).

More recently (and despite its name), CNN's HLN channel (formerly known as Headline News) has shifted from providing capsule accounts of the day's major stories to talk shows such as *Nancy Grace* and *The Joy Behar Show* – the February 16, 2010 (and typical) lineup of the latter consisted of a conversation with the comedian Kathy Griffin, plus "discussions" of the homophobic tirade by a cast member of the reality television show *Jersey Shore*, reality TV celebrity Heidi Montag's favorite body part, and "Octomom's" first date in four years. Other "news" programming exclusively focuses on specific topics (e.g., weather, sports, crime, entertainment) or specific demographic groups (e.g., African Americans, Hispanics, Christians, young people). At the same time, genres such as docudramas, satirical news, daytime and late-night talk shows, and even more traditional dramas and comedies blend public affairs and entertainment in ways that further blur any meaningful distinction between "news" and "non-news."[16]

Further complicating the new media environment is the growing ability of consumers to control much of the information they receive from television, although here as elsewhere the line between true control and

---

[16] So, for example, *The Daily Show* used the Rick Sanchez CNN piece mentioned earlier as a way to satirize and critique the degree to which cable networks had abandoned any pretense of seriously covering important events.

manipulation is a fine one. Television serves as a portal to other forms of media through increasingly common technology such as DVD players, Web TV, and video-game consoles. These and related technological developments have changed the way in which television is watched, thus altering the relationship between content producers and consumers. Consider the growth of a seemingly mundane technological device – the remote control. This simple innovation made it possible to shift easily between channels or between real-time programming, prerecorded programming on a VCR or DVD player, and even from television to the internet, all without ever getting up from the couch. As recently as 1985, only 29 percent of all households had a remote control, whereas by 1996 they were almost universal (94 percent; ACNielsen 2009).

Far more revolutionary are newer technologies such as digital video recording (DVR) systems like TiVo, estimated by Nielsen to be in more than 30 percent of households in 2009, up from just 12 percent two years earlier. These systems add to audience fragmentation by allowing viewers to easily record and play back television shows on the basis of personal preferences and schedules, and to skip through content that does not interest them (including, to the dismay of advertisers and media executives, commercials). Several versions can also "learn" from a viewer's past choices to suggest other related shows to watch or program. And they can gather information on specific viewer preferences that can then be sold to a variety of firms interested in aiming programming and advertising at precisely targeted segments of the audience. Web-based television ventures (e.g., Hulu.com) contribute further to the breakdown of the traditional relationship between television producers and consumers.

The fragmentation of television audiences, coupled with significant changes in content and the blurring of genres, has obvious though complicated and still-shifting implications for the nature of democratic discourse. As we discuss in subsequent chapters, the new media environment offers real opportunities for more varied, accessible, and citizen-driven communication than was possible during the Age of Broadcast News, as well as moments when unprecedented national and global audiences can attend to the same issue or event. At the same time, however, this media environment can result in trends that are anathema to such collective moments. For example, Robert Entman and Andrew Rojecki (2001) document the increasing divergence of television shows popular with black and white audiences, and the ways in which this audience fragmentation has led television producers away from airing integrated shows. According to Sandy Grushow, president of 20th Century Fox Television, "I don't think anybody's crying out for integrated shows. By pursuing advertisers and demographics rather than a mass audience, the networks have declared they don't need Blacks in the audience" (Entman and Rojecki 2001, 161). And several Pew Research Center polls have found significant ideological and partisan differences in viewers' choices of which television news broadcasts they regularly watch, as well as their ratings of the accuracy and fairness of different news networks (Pew Research Center for the People and the Press, 2004a, 2004b, 2009b).

In many ways, the new terrain of television hearkens back to earlier eras, a new marketplace of ideas that makes no clear-cut distinctions between fact and opinion or news and entertainment. But the new discursive environment is different in at least three important ways. First, the sheer volume and range of mediated information available on television dwarfs that of past media regimes. Second, the ubiquitous nature of television means that different segments of the population, though likely to gravitate to programming marketed specifically for them, have the ability to enter very different mediated worlds intended for very different segments of the domestic and even international population. And third, centralized ownership patterns mean that the appearance of unprecedented diversity and choice is bounded in sometimes invisible ways, providing at best "semi-autonomy" for citizens/consumers. In short, the new television environment combines elements of several earlier eras with new, unprecedented risks and opportunities.

The Rise of the Internet and Other Information and Communication Technologies: As dramatic as changes in television have been over the past two decades, they pale in comparison to the impact of the internet and related wired and wireless technology on the discursive environment of the early twenty-first century. On any given day in December 2009, more than seven of every ten adult Americans went online (Pew Research Center Internet and American Life Project 2010). And what do people do when they go online? Tracking polls conducted by the Pew Research Center Internet and American Life Project (2009) provide one answer to this question.[17] Three patterns emerge from this list of more than one hundred self-reported online activities. First is the dominance of search engines as the entry point into the web for most citizens (90 percent of those going online). Second is the extensive and diverse range of activities engaged in by sizable percentages of people who use the internet, ranging from sending or reading e-mail (90 percent), to seeking directions

---

[17] Statistics presented in text are the most recent available for that specific activity.

(86 percent), looking for medical information (80 percent), buying a product (75 percent), seeking news (72 percent), visiting a government website (66 percent), watching a video (62 percent), seeking out political information (60 percent), social networking (47 percent), reading a blog (39 percent), playing online games (35 percent), and donating to a charitable cause (19 percent). Third is the generally still small but collectively revealing percentages of "wired" adults who act as information producers by sending e-mails (90 percent), sending instant messages (39 percent), uploading photos (37 percent), sending text messages (35 percent), rating a product (31 percent), tagging online content (28 percent), sharing files (27 percent), posting comments to a newsgroup or blog (22 percent), participating in a chat-room discussion (22 percent), sharing something online that they created (21 percent), creating content specifically for the internet (19 percent), creating their own web pages (14 percent), working on someone else's webpage (13 percent), creating their own blogs (12 percent), remixing existing online material (11 percent), and/or creating an online avatar (6 percent).

The diverse, extensive, and fluid nature of use is matched by the content and form of the information created and provided. Indeed, more than any other medium, the internet and related new communication technologies dramatically highlight the inadequacy of late-twentieth-century distinctions between types of media and genres, producers and consumers, mass and interpersonal communication, and public affairs and popular culture. For example, Figure 3.2 reproduces the home page of Yahoo!, the most popular of the internet portals (Yahoo! gets more than 500 million hits a month and 3.8 billion page views a day, with one of every two internet users visiting a Yahoo!-branded site at least once a month (Yahoo! 2006). In ways evoking newspapers of the late eighteenth and early nineteenth centuries, the page contains (by the standards of the Age of Broadcast News) an unstructured combination of political, economic, social, and cultural information, with links to news, business, sports, weather, e-mail, advertisements, celebrity and popular culture stories, and recipes, although significantly absent in this mix is information about local public affairs. In ways evoking the Age of Broadcast News, however, the Yahoo! home page and other portals such as Google serve as centralized gateways (and thus potential agenda setters) for millions of people. And different from any prior media regime, these portals have the potential to connect vast numbers of people regardless of local, regional, or national boundaries to any of the billions of web pages in existence, websites that vary in unprecedented ways in their topics, sources, genres, and points of view.

FIGURE 3.2. Example of a Typical Web Portal Home Page: The New Gatekeepers?

The disruption of conventional ways of thinking about political media
posed by the internet, and the uncertain future it portends, extends
beyond the way information is organized on websites or portals. It also
includes the technologies used for gathering and sorting the information that passes through these gates. The search engine Google, for
instance, includes a feature called Google News, which uses so-called
"intelligent bots" to automatically search the internet for news stories,
which are then assembled in a list without any human being directly
taking part. Refining such automatic searches allows individual users

to specifically tailor the types of news they receive from this and other sites with similar technology. Taking this trend one step further was Newsblaster, a software program that scanned multiple news articles and then summarized and wrote its own story, again without direct human intervention: "Newsblaster's [writing] isn't jazzy ... but its ability to synthesize a dozen articles and summarize them is enough to give journalists pause – and to offer readers a new way to follow the news" (Campbell 2002).[18]

Such developments are often touted (or lamented) as providing citizens with the ability to gather information in ways that bypass traditional gatekeepers such as journalists. But this does not mean the end of gatekeeping, as the ways in which search algorithms are written has profound implications for the types of information that will be provided. Recall that Kurt Lewin (1947) in his formulation of the concept reserved the term *gatekeeping* for situations where the passing on of information was not simply automatic but required decisions to be made. Although the search techniques we describe here do not rely on the decisions of journalists, they are in many ways a more ominous form of gatekeeping, as those who write the search programs and algorithms make crucial decisions about what information will or will not be passed on, but they do so absent the training, norms, visibility, or accountability that, in theory at least, guide and tether the decisions of professional journalists (Vaidhyanathan 2011). In short, the writers of such programs become new and significant, but often overlooked, gatekeepers.

Numerous other examples highlight the ways in which the internet and related new technology are changing the discursive environment and thus challenging the underlying tenets of the existing media regime. The growing phenomenon of blogs (the blog aggregator and portal Technocrati has indexed more than 130 million blogs since 2002; Future Buzz 2009) is eroding the news-entertainment distinction, as well as the presumed lines between fact and opinion, and between journalist and producer and citizen and consumer. In several high-profile cases, bloggers have managed to maintain public attention on issues that had been dropped

---

[18] In something of an irony (to say the least), the now defunct Newsblaster was briefly hosted and run by the Columbia School of Journalism (CSJ). Although CSJ's home page insisted that Newsblaster would "absolutely not!" replace reporters, we have our doubts, at least when it comes to the larger array of new information and communication technologies that are increasingly filling the roles once exclusively played by professional journalists and their news organizations.

by professional journalists, eventually forcing mainstream news sources to revive them and thereby encroaching on one of the most significant roles of professional journalists, the ability to set the agenda. For example, Joshua Marshall's blog, Talking Points Memo, played a significant role in keeping Trent Lott from becoming the Senate Majority Leader in 2003.[19] At Strom Thurmond's hundredth-birthday party, Lott had expressed (jokingly, he asserted) his support for the aged South Carolinian's 1948 segregationist third-party run for the presidency. Though covered briefly by mainstream journalists, the story had begun to disappear from the news. As Marshall himself noted, "This was a story that the [established] press in DC was very well suited to miss. . . . [T]he way daily journalism works, a story has a 24-hour audition to see if it has legs, and if it doesn't get picked up, that's it" (qtd. in Burkeman 2002, 13). However, reflecting the weakening of professional journalists' and political elites' ability to set the agenda, Marshall and his audience of political activists were able to keep the Lott affair alive, forcing it back into the news and onto the political agenda. Similarly, in the 2004 election, rightwing bloggers played an important role in revealing the questionable practices of CBS News in checking whether documents used to show that President Bush failed to meet his Air Force Reserve obligations during the Vietnam War were genuine. Here, blogs managed to intrude on the priming role formally thought to be played by professional journalists: they successfully shifted the criteria used to judge the issue from the validity of the claims themselves to the narrower question of whether specific documents were real or forged (Pein 2005). Other aspects of the internet further complicate the information environment and the struggle for control of it. Chat groups and online discussions provide new venues for citizens to directly discuss public issues. Nonmainstream and/or international websites serve as alternative sources of information and opinion, challenging the agenda-setting and gatekeeping functions of the traditional news media. Networks of political and social activists use the web and various forms of mobile technology to mount virtual and real-world opposition to traditional political elites or to create alternative spaces for discussing issues ignored by mainstream media and elites.[20] Fringe candidates (consider, for example, the 2008 Republican presidential candidate Ron Paul's ability to use the web to generate followers, media

---

[19] Marshall himself was a little-known freelance journalist.

[20] These networks span the political spectrum from MoveOn.org on the left to the conservative FreeRepublic.com on the right.

attention, and substantial financial contributions) and other nonmainstream political actors are able to enter and even help shape public debate to an extent that would have been impossible in an earlier era.

Perhaps the greatest challenge to the existing media regime is the increasing ability of citizens to directly produce and access information about political, social, and economic life, bypassing both traditional and new media gatekeepers entirely. For example, the ubiquity of cell phones and other small, handheld video devices, coupled with the ease of uploading information, has led to numerous websites devoted to "citizen journalists" who can post their own "news" stories (Agence France-Press 2005). Social networking (e.g., Facebook), user-generated sites (e.g., YouTube), and microblogging services (e.g., Twitter) regularly demonstrate both the political utility of new media and the futility of distinguishing the news from other categories or providers of information. Even when not directly producing content, the internet empowers citizens through sites such as Newsknife and Digg, which allow them to rate the importance and quality of specific news stories and news providers. Indeed, the very notion of information producer and consumer has given way to the more encompassing and accurate role of "user."

Of course, traditional political, economic, and media elites are also "using" – and in many ways dominating – the internet and other new information and communication technologies. Candidates have made increasingly effective use of new media for everything from fund-raising to getting out the vote. Government officials use similar technologies to build and mobilize support for policy initiatives. For all its civic and political promise, the internet is better analogized to a shopping mall than a town hall. Traditional news media have incorporated at least the trappings of new media into their daily news-gathering and dissemination routines, and they increasingly invite readers, listeners, and viewers to provide them with video or other forms of content. The websites of the major news outlets are the most common destinations of citizens seeking information about public affairs (Hindman 2008). In addition, new corporate media players such as Google, Yahoo!, and Microsoft are vying for control of the discursive environment with one another; with more traditional political, economic, and media elites; and with less well-heeled competitors, such as independent journalists, alternative news organizations, representatives of nonmainstream ideological perspectives, and even citizens themselves. Consider, for instance, Google's purchase of YouTube for $1.65 billion, which resulted in a crackdown on the posting of copyrighted and/or libelous videos, or Rupert Murdoch's purchase of the social networking site MySpace for $580 million and the site's subsequent decline in popularity. And even when alternative media do play a role in shaping public discourse, to date, at least, this seldom occurs without the involvement of more mainstream media and political actors. For example, Joshua Marshall was trained as a journalist, his efforts were supported at least implicitly by Democratic Party strategists, and the full effect of his reporting did not set in until the Trent Lott story reemerged in the mainstream media. Similarly, right-wing bloggers would have been unable to put CBS News on the defensive without the involvement of mainstream Republicans and the megaphone provided by mainstream media.

For these and other reasons, it is important not to overstate the extent to which the internet – in control, content, or use – is unaffected by the principles and principals governing the Age of Broadcast News. Rather, we need to understand how these governing norms and actors are being explicitly and implicitly challenged even as they struggle to preserve their authority. Consider, as a last example, the inclusion of the section "In the News" on the Yahoo! home page reproduced in Figure 3.2, a label mirroring the "news" and "non-news" distinction that is a hallmark of the Age of Broadcast News. On the one hand, close examination reveals that what constitutes news as defined by the new gatekeepers at Yahoo! includes a much more diverse range of cultural, entertainment, and public affairs information than envisaged by professional journalism. In addition, the technology of the site gives users the revolutionary opportunity to individualize their own Yahoo! home page, thus turning individual citizens into gatekeepers–news editors of a sort. On the other hand, however, such users are still dependent on the initial choices already made for them by Yahoo! and other portals. As a result, even when individuals customize their Yahoo home page to reflect "their own" interests, most still include the "In the News" feature (Tewksbury 2003). In short, the new mix of form, content, scale, and access provided by the internet and other new technology has led to a fundamental but complex and contested shifting of who serves as the gatekeepers of information in this system (Vaidhyanathan 2011; Hindman 2008; Turow 2006).

In the end, what is clear is that the internet and other new information technologies have and will continue to change the way in which information is disseminated and used. And even as mainstream elites attempt to adapt to this new information environment, they are changing the ways they interact with the public, and so ironically they are helping to erode the tenets of the very media regime they are trying to preserve. That this regime is no longer tenable is, to us at least, also clear. What remains unclear, however, is the ultimate shape of the new media regime that will almost assuredly come to control this new discursive environment and the extent to which it will enhance or constrain democratic discourse.

The Shifting Relationship among Media, Politics, and Everyday Life

Americans spend an astonishing amount of time with media in the new information environment: an estimated average of nine hours and forty minutes a day by 2006, twelve minutes more than 2000, thirty-four minutes more than 1992, and more time than any other activity including work or sleep (Ohlemacher 2006)! In many ways, however, the increase in overall use is less dramatic than the change in the kind of media that people spend time with. For example, by 2006, more people played such popular online games as Warhammer or participated in virtual communities such as Second Life than watched the cable news networks (Teachout and Wu 2006). As the amount and type of interactions with media have increased, a number of assumed distinctions have lost their conceptual purchase. Most profoundly, the presumed line between the media and life outside the media is a casualty of our growing immersion into this ubiquitous, multidimensional, interactive, and often virtual new world. When we spend so much of our day attending to the media – be it watching television, DVDs, or movies; surfing the internet; playing video games; or interacting with others via instant messages, tweets, and social networking sites – life on and with the screen becomes inseparable from life in the "real world." To paraphrase Marshall McLuhan (1995), the new media are no longer bridges between people and life, not ways of relating us to "real" life; rather, they are real life and they reshape real life at will.[21] Or in Todd Gitlin's (2001, 17) words:

When one considers the overlapping and additional [to television] hours of exposure to radio, magazines, newspapers, compact discs, movies (available via a range of technologies as well as in theaters), and comic books, as well as the accompanying articles, books, chats about what's on or was coming up via all these means, it is clear that the media flow into the home – not to mention outside – has swelled into a torrent of immense force and constancy, an accompaniment *to* life that has become a central experience *of* life.

---

[21] The actual quote from McLuhan (1995, 272) is, "The new media are not bridges between man and nature; they are nature.... The new media are not ways of relating us to the old world; they are the real world and they reshape what remains of the old world at will."

Examples of this blurring that would have seemed remarkable two decades ago have become commonplace: the former governor of Virginia and potential Democratic presidential candidate Mark Warner creating his own avatar and holding a 2006 virtual town hall meeting on Second Life; governments exploring the possibility of taxing the millions of real dollars used in virtual online economies (Pasick 2006); Rod Blagojevich, the former governor of Illinois, starring, a year after being impeached and indicted for federal corruption, on the 2010 season of the reality television show *Celebrity Apprentice*; a 2010 public debate over the depiction of people with disabilities (covered on the front pages of the *New York Times* and a topic of discussion and debate on radio and cable television talk shows, and online blogs and websites) triggered by an episode of Fox's animated series *Family Guy* and drawing in both former vice presidential candidate Sarah Palin, whose son has Down syndrome, and Andrea Fay Friedman, the voice actress whose *Family Guy* character had Down syndrome and who herself suffers from this disability (Itzkoff 2010, A1).

What can we say about the relationship among media, politics, and everyday life in this new world in which we all increasingly live? Certainly, it is no longer a place where the always-porous borderlines that formed the basis of the Age of Broadcast News make any conceptual sense. Gone is any useful distinction between news and entertainment. Even within more traditional entertainment media, one can find much that constitutes the stuff of politics. Popular movies and television shows regularly deal either directly or indirectly with political personalities, institutions, and issues. Reality-based programs have serious political implications for how we think about the relationship between economic opportunity and the responsibility of the individual versus the government in providing it. Many popular daytime television and radio talk shows, magazines, music CDs, and music videos "cover" public policy issues or political issues of relevance to their readers and/or watchers.[22] Late-night shows like *The Tonight Show with Jay Leno* and *Late Show with David Letterman* feature a constant stream of political jokes and commentary on the events of the day. In short, even without watching the news as traditionally defined, many Americans are absorbing a media diet rich with political information.

Gone also is any meaningful ability to distinguish among various genres and media. Shows like *The Colbert Report*, *The Daily Show*, and

---

[22] In the most careful analysis of this type of show, which they call the audience participation show, the media scholars Sonia Livingstone and Peter Lunt (1994) highlight their intergenre nature, arguing that they are not classifiable as entertainment or public affairs.

Real Time with Bill Maher feature a wide variety of celebrities from the entertainment, academic, and political worlds discussing in humorous but often insightful ways major events of the day. Much of what passes as news on political talk shows bears little resemblance to what this term meant as recently as the late 1980s, as it focuses almost entirely on uncivil and aggressive confrontation to the virtual exclusion of either straightforward reporting or more thoughtful, informative deliberation about political issues. As old-media elites attempt to adapt to the new environment, news personalities, shows, and even entire organizations seek brand recognition that cuts across different media platforms. For example, the conservative talk show host Bill O'Reilly is a major presence on radio, television, and the web (including subscription services). Radio talk show host Rush Limbaugh maintains a popular internet site and has made several (to date unsuccessful) forays into the television talk show market. The radio advice-giver Dr. Laura has attempted similar moves across media. And, of course every major media organization – from the *New York Times* to CNN to ESPN to Disney – has a presence on the web. This multiplatform approach can go in the reverse direction as well: for example, after achieving celebrity recognition through his internet site, Matt Drudge has hosted both radio and television talk shows.

Also under assault in the new media environment is the prior regime's distinction between information producers and consumers. Because the internet is a more inherently interactive medium than print, television, or radio, at a minimum, it opens up new possibilities for talking back. More revolutionary, the almost incalculable number of interactive websites, blogs, online games, social networking sites, and so forth – created and maintained by traditional media elites and large media conglomerates, on the one hand, but also by upstart organizations and "average" citizens, on the other hand – have radically altered the media landscape, thus allowing citizens to graze across a wide range of sources and genres, share this information through a variety of media, remix and/or appropriate it in creative ways, and even produce and disseminate original content of public relevance.[23] For example, a survey by the Pew Research

---

[23] The media industry is well aware of this dilemma, which has direct implications for, among other things, its ability to set advertising rates. For example, in an effort to address viewers' increased tendency to rapidly switch between channels, Nielsen has the ability to provide television stations and networks viewer statistics broken down into ten-second segments, and some internet use statistics include more detailed information such as number of pages visited or length of time spent at a particular site (a measure called stickiness).

Center Internet and American Life Project (2010) found that 92 percent of Americans use multiple platforms to get their daily news.

The collapse of distinctions on which the Age of Broadcast News was based has made more visible the artificiality of these distinctions and thus the relevance of mediated information outside the realm of news, even during past regimes. The changes we have documented are more than perceptual, however. The proliferation of media outlets, the mixing of genres, the blurring of producers and consumers, the fragmenting of audiences and so forth, combined with the cultural, economic, political, and technological changes discussed earlier in this chapter, have materially altered the information environment, increasing the amount and the political relevance of ostensibly non-news media. These changes are only the most recent example of periodic shifts in how the relationship between media and politics is imagined and ultimately reified in the United States.

Will this new media environment promote vibrant and healthy forms of community, or will it result in the creation of a more fragmented, self-interest-based politics of competing groups and/or isolated individuals? Will it provide new opportunities for citizens to play more active roles in the production of social and political meaning, to engage more fully in politics of the day, or will it rather lead to their further reduction into consumers of information designed to entertain rather than inform? Will it create an open exchange of information and opinion in which the essential contestability of social meaning is accepted as fundamental to politics, or will it serve as a mechanism for greater and more corporate and government control? Will it preserve and even improve on the best features of prior regimes, including the Age of Broadcast News, or will it reproduce their worst aspects?

Answers to these questions are very much in doubt in the transitional period in which we live. For example, one result that could emerge from this new media environment is that the gatekeeping process that is controlled largely by professional journalists, network executives, advertisers, and a handful of political elites will pass, to varying degrees, to citizens themselves. Already citizens and/or audiences are more able than ever to "reach into the data swarm and pick out what is newsworthy" (Kirn 2001, 157), the traditional purview of professional journalists, through a variety of ways: zapping through commercials; flipping back and forth among the large number of programs, tapes, DVDs, and internet sites available to them; programming their own television schedules through the use of TiVo or replay systems; creating customized websites and e-mail alerts; creating their own content for others to consume; and so forth.

These new options arguably place much more power in the hands of view-ers to shape their (and others) individual media experiences, essentially creating their own texts and genres – a trend that will further accelerate with the increasing availability of broadband services and the concomi-tant convergence of television, the internet and telephones.

At the same time, however, new technologies from TiVo to the internet and mobile communication devices also increase the ability of marketers (of values and ideas, as well as of products) to target the individual preferences of consumers. Such use of these technologies seems likely to dramatically accelerate the fragmentation and manipulation of media audiences, with potential negative consequences for maintaining collec-tive national experiences, as well as for the ways in which individuals think about their connection to wider communities. As the *New York Times* reporter Michael Lewis (2000, 36) puts it, these technologies and others like them threaten to "spy on you, destroy prime time, and shatter the power of the mass market."

The evidence to date suggests that both scenarios are in play. Con-sider, for example, how citizens' news consumption habits are changing. According to a 2008 report of the Pew Research Center Project for Excel-lence in Journalism, contemporary news audiences can be divided into four news-consuming groups: *Traditionalists* (46% percent of the adult population) who still use traditional news media (television, newspapers, and radio) almost exclusively; *Integrators* (23 percent), for whom a tradi-tional news medium is their main news source but who also go online for news at least several days a week; *Net-Newsers* (13 percent), for whom online news is their main source for public affairs information; and *The Disengaged* (14 percent), who rarely seek out news of any kind. Tradi-tionalists are significantly older, more economically downscale and less educated, whereas Net-Newsers and Integrators are younger, more afflu-ent, and more educated. Significantly, Integrators spend the most time each day with news (see Table 3.1) and express the greatest interest in political news of any of the groups. And even these numbers mask the extent of change in Americans' news consumption, as "traditional news" such as television includes a wide range of cable programming, and many adults in general and younger adults in particular report getting at least some news from late-night talk shows, satirical news programming such as *The Daily Show* and *The Colbert Report*, and other forms of enter-tainment programming.

And what of the content provided by these different sources of infor-mation? A partial answer is provided by the Pew Research Center Project

TABLE 3.1. *Daily News Consumption (Minutes)*

Integrators Spend the Most Time with the News				
Average number of minutes spent...	Total	Traditionalists	Integrators	Net-Newsters	Disengaged
Watching TV news	31	35	37	23	13
Reading a newspaper	13	14	16	12	5
Listening to news on radio	14	14	21	15	7
Getting news online	8	1	14	28	4
Total	66	64	88	78	29

Source: Pew Research Center. August 17 2008. "Key News Audiences Now Blend Online and Traditional Sources: Audience Segments in a Changing News Environment." http://people-press.org/report/444/news-media.

for Excellence in Journalism's weekly tracking of stories found in traditional and new media. Figure 3.3 provides a comparison for the first week in February 2010.[24] As can be readily seen, the agendas of mainstream news media such as newspapers and national television news differed dramatically from that of blogs and other independent new media sources. Of particular note is that the blogosphere's agenda, though different and arguably more focused on hot-button issues, is every bit as newsworthy as that of the mainstream press.

Even within the world of professional journalism and political commentary, the expansion of sources and genres has, at times at least, unraveled the consensus found in the Age of Broadcast News. For example,

[24] The Pew Research Center Project for Excellence in Journalism's (2010c) weekly News Coverage Index examines the news agenda of fifty-two different outlets from five sectors of the media: print, online, network TV, cable, and radio. The weekly study is designed to provide news consumers, journalists, and researchers with hard data about what stories and topics the media are covering, the trajectories of that media narrative, and differences among news platforms. The percentages are based on the "news hole," or the space devoted to each subject in print and online and the time devoted to it on radio and TV. These reports also include a rundown of the week's leading newsmakers, a designation given to people or institutions who account for at least 50 percent of a given story. In addition, data are collected on leading blogs and other social media sites. See also Pew Research Center's Project for Excellence in Journalism, "List of Outlets," http://www.journalism.org/about_news_index/list_of_outlets. For a description of how blogs and other social media are selected, see Pew Research Center's Project for Excellence in Journalism, "Social Media Tackles Controversial Issues," http://www.journalism.org/index_report/social_media_tackles_controversial_issues. For a description of methodology, see Pew Research Center's Project for Excellence in Journalism, "Methodology," http://www.journalism.org/about_news_index/methodology.

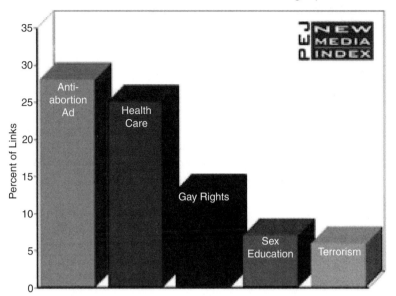

Hot-Button Political Issues Lead the Blogosphere...

Top Stories the Week of February 1–5, 2010

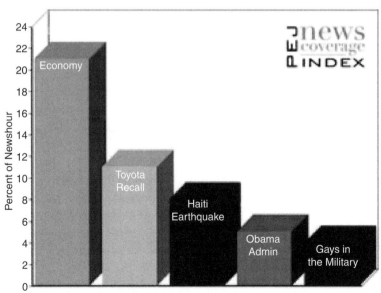

...While the Traditional Press Focus on the Economy

Top Stories the Week of February 1–7, 2010

FIGURE 3.3. A Comparison of Traditional and New Media Coverage
Source: Pew Research Center Project for Excellence in Journalism (2010c).

Figure 3.3 compares coverage of the health-care debate during the week of October 26–November 1, 2009 (the most covered story of the week overall and a time when legislation was being debated in Washington) for fifty-two different print, radio, television, and online professional news outlets. What is striking is, first, the great degree of variation overall in attention to this issue, and second, the relative lack of coverage in newspapers and network news compared with more opinionated media such as talk shows; radio; cable; and to a lesser degree, online news sites. A more comprehensive look at the Project for Excellence in Journalism's weekly comparisons suggests that such differences both across the various forms of professional journalism and between professional journalism and the larger blogosphere are common, though particularly dramatic events (e.g., the 2009 Iranian elections, the 2009 death of pop idol Michael Jackson, the devastating 2010 earthquake in Haiti) can lead to moments when these various information sources coalesce around a single topic.[25]

The picture becomes more complicated still when one considers another study conducted by the Project for Excellence in Journalism, this one a case study exploring the flow of local news in Baltimore. The study examined local news found in more than fifty different print, electronic, and online news outlets during the week of July 19–25, 2009. Among their findings were the following, taken verbatim from the Project for Excellence in Journalism report (2010b):

- The network of news media in Baltimore has already expanded remarkably. We identified 53 different news outlets that regularly produce some kind of local news content, a universe that ranges from blogs to talk radio to news sites created by former journalists. These are multi-platform operations that also make robust use of Twitter as a means of dissemination. Twelve of those outlets did not produce any local content during the days studied.
- Among the six major news threads studied in depth – which included stories about budgets, crime, a plan involving transit buses, and the sale of a local theater – fully 83 percent of stories were essentially repetitive, conveying no new information. Of the 17 percent that did contain new information, nearly all came from traditional media either in their legacy platforms or in new digital ones.

---

[25] In the subsequent chapter, we argue that these times when there is convergence on the same issue across both old and new media, what media scholars label "media events," have come to play an especially vital role in the new information environment.

- General interest newspapers like the Baltimore Sun produced half of these stories – 48 percent – and another print medium, specialty newspapers focused on business and law, produced another 13 percent.
- Local television stations and their websites accounted for about a third (28 percent) of the enterprise reporting on the major stories of the week; radio accounted for 7 percent, all from material posted on radio station websites. The remaining nine new media outlets accounted for just 4 percent of the enterprise reporting we encountered.
- Traditional media made wide use of new platforms. Newspapers, TV and radio produced nearly a third of their stories on new platforms (31 percent), though that number varied by sector. Almost half of the newspapers stories studied were online rather than in print.
- There were two cases of new media breaking information about stories. One came from the police Twitter feed in Baltimore, an example of a news maker breaking news directly to the public rather than through the press. Another was a story noticed by a local blog, that the mainstream press nearly missed entirely, involving a plan by the state to put listening devices on buses to deter crime. A newspaper reporter noticed the blog and then reported on the story, which led the state to rescind the plan.
- As the press scales back on original reporting and dissemination, reproducing other people's work becomes a bigger part of the news media system. Government, at least in this study, initiates most of the news. In the detailed examination of six major storylines, 63 percent of the stories were initiated by government officials, led first of all by the police. Another 14 percent came from the press. Interest group figures made up most of the rest.

These findings suggest that, although traditional news media continue to play a central role in originating local news (see Figure 3.4), they do so across a much wider range of platforms than was available in the past, and much of what they report originates from elite sources rather than from original, investigative reporting (Figure 3.5). Also telling is an additional finding that, although traditional news media still control the majority of local news that circulates, the amount of local news has declined precipitously: for example, the *Baltimore Sun* produced 23,668 stories on all topics in 2009, compared with 34,852 in 1999 and 86,667 stories in 1991, a decline of 73 percent in fewer than twenty years.

Clearly, extant data suggests that the new information environment and citizens' reactions to it is a complex mix of old and new habits and

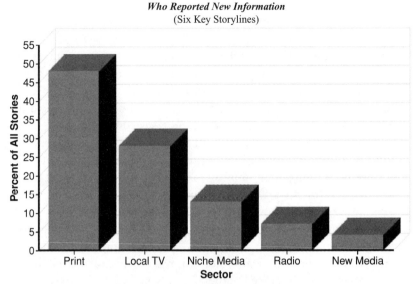

FIGURE 3.4. Reporting of New Local Information
Source: Pew Research Center Project for Excellence in Journalism, "Social Media Tackles Controversial Issues," http://www.journalism.org/index_report/ social_media_tackles_controversial_issues.

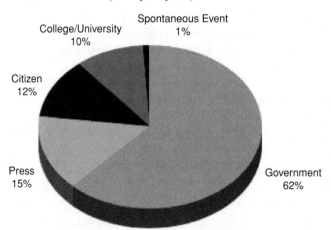

FIGURE 3.5. Originators of Local News Stories
Source: Pew Research Center Project for Excellence in Journalism, "How News Happens: A Study of the News Ecosystem of One American City," http://www. journalism.org/analysis_report/how_news_happens.

practices, which can combine in ways that auger both democratic promise and peril. Similar ambiguous and shifting patterns can be seen at a more macro level. On the one hand, the globalization of both the economy and communications offers new and exciting opportunities for expanding the sources, content, and form of politically relevant information, opening up the number and types of gatekeepers who control this information, and creating new ways of thinking about citizenship and community. On the other hand, these same developments challenge the authority of traditional state-based polities, risk exacerbating trends toward fragmentation and the dominance of market populism, and provide new and ominous threats to privacy. For example, Darin Barney (2000) argues that the creation of increasingly global computer networks produces new possibilities for monitoring and controlling workers worldwide. According to Barney, networks are not, as many technological utopians seem to believe, beyond control: they are mechanisms of control. It is possible, for instance, for a corporation with headquarters located in New York to monitor the keystrokes or help-line calls handled by workers in India (Barney 2000). This facilitates both the flow of jobs to the lowest-wage workers and a level of control over the activities of workers never before possible. Similarly, computer networks make it possible for governments to gather information about citizens on a scale never before possible.

These concerns are more than idle speculation. For example, part of the 2002 Homeland Security Act proposed by the Bush administration was the creation of a system of "Total Information Awareness" about every citizen. William Safire (2002) warned, "Every purchase you make with a credit card, every magazine subscription you buy and medical prescription you fill, every website you visit and e-mail you send or receive, every academic grade you receive, every bank deposit you make, every trip you book and every event you attend – all these transactions and communications will go into what the Defense Department describes as 'a virtual, centralized grand database.'" Although the proposal was not funded by Congress, at a minimum, it illustrates the possibilities for surveillance that are part and parcel of the information revolution, and by some accounts, the data gathering proposed in the Total Information Awareness system is continuing through other, less visible programs (Farrell 2009).

Such concerns about surveillance and the loss of privacy are not limited to government access and use of information. For example, in 2007, AOL purchased Tacoda, a private New York advertising firm specializing in helping websites keep track of information about their users to show users ads for products they might buy. This kind of behavioral targeting, based on inferring people's likely consumer interests from the web pages they visit, is increasingly used to establish the price of advertising on web pages (the *New York Times*, for example, uses Tacoda). But it also raises serious privacy concerns:

Tacoda says it doesn't look at information that can identify an individual – such as names and addresses. Rather it just tracks the surfing behavior of a computer. AOL, of course, has access to all sorts of information about the identity as well as the behavior of people who use its various services, so it will doubtless have a lot of privacy questions to answer. In one sign about the sensitivity of behavioral targeting, Microsoft announced Monday that it would give users the ability to opt out of its growing behavioral targeting system. (Hansell 2007)

Add the increasing willingness of private corporations to share their various databases with one another and with the government (as, for example, when several U.S. telephone companies shared information on their customers' phone calls with the federal government), and the Orwellian potential of the new information environment becomes of even greater concern. Making us aware of such threats requires a media that can fulfill the role to which professional journalism aspires but often fails to achieve. Crucial to the future of democracy is the ability of a new media regime to satisfy such tasks, whether by reinvigorating professional journalism or by creating opportunities for a wider range of actors to provide the public with the information needed to hold accountable public and private elites.

Conclusion

The changes of the past two decades of the twentieth century are clearly reshaping local, national, and international politics; economics and culture; and the role of the media in this new information world. Much of the controversies that now swirl around the media are driven by the rapidity of these changes and the inadequacy of extant answers to the perennial questions Americans have asked about the role of mediated political information in a democratic society, such as who decides the adequacy, trustworthiness, and usefulness of politically relevant information and who the major producers and consumers of this information are. To date, many journalists, scholars, and citizens continue to use intellectual frameworks rooted in the media regime of the mid-twentieth century, which are woefully inadequate for understanding the potentials and pitfalls of this new environment.

Equally clear is that answers to these questions will not emerge "naturally" from the changes we have discussed in this chapter. Rather, they will, in large part at least, result from the institutionalization and codification of elite and public expectations within the likely new media regime that will form in response to these changes. In this time of rapid change, as a new media regime is being constructed, it is particularly important to keep in mind the broad sweep of American media history and not be limited by the perspectives developed in the mid-twentieth century. It is somewhat ironic that a media regime of such short duration (the Age of Broadcast News lasted only forty years or so and was under challenge for much of that time) has been taken by so many as the "natural" state of affairs against which all other models are implicitly judged.[26]

We think it is particularly useful to reconsider the Realist assumption that the aim of media is to get us closer to the truth of politics, that "truth" is essentially contestable, and that this contestation serves the purposes of democratic practice when it is clearly situated within an open and wide-ranging public discourse. As James Carey (1997, 87) puts it,

Reality is, above all, a scarce resource. Like any scarce resource it is there to be struggled over, allocated to various purposes and projects, endowed with given meanings and potentials, spent and conserved, rationalized and distributed. The fundamental form of power is the power to define, allocate and display this resource.

To this end, in the next chapter, we explore the ways in which the new and complex discursive environment of the twenty-first century is changing the terms of this struggle to define, allocate, and display social and political reality and the stakes involved in how this struggle is resolved for democratic politics.

---

[26] We are indebted to John Zaller for making this point.

4

Political Reality, Political Power, and Political Relevance in the Changing Media Environment

> The important consideration is that opportunity be given ideas to speak and to become the possession of the multitude. The essential need is the improvement of the methods and constitution of debate, discussion, and persuasion. That is *the* problem of the public.
>
> – John Dewey, *The Public and Its Problems*, 1927

> I am a firm believer in the people. If given the truth, they can be depended upon to meet any national crisis. The great point is to bring them the real facts, and beer.
>
> – Abraham Lincoln, (attributed), 1864

> I've always gotten news through watching comedy shows. The coverage on CNN is something I honestly find boring.
>
> – Alexis, University of Illinois undergraduate

Throughout the spring of 2000, huge numbers of viewers across the country tuned into the final episode of *Survivor*, a new "reality-based" show airing on CBS. *Survivor* placed a group of sixteen "ordinary" people on a tropical island, staged a variety of obstacles for them to overcome (in addition to just surviving), and then had the participants vote one person off the island each week. The last show of the inaugural series, during which the final survivor Richard Hatch was chosen (and given a million dollars), was the second-most-watched show of the year, drawing 51 million viewers, behind only the 88 million of the Super Bowl, a much older form of reality programming.[1] The success of this show (and its

---

[1] We also should mention that the presidential debates of 2008 are another older form of reality programming, which can also attract large audiences. The three presidential

sequels) inspired networks to air any number of variations on the theme of ordinary people being placed in stressful situations for the chance to win fame and/or large amounts of money.[2]

The combination of potentially high ratings and routinely low production costs led to an explosion of this new genre of "reality" television.[3] *Big Brother*, currently in its eighth season on American television, originated in the Netherlands in 1999 and went on to become a hit in seventy countries.[4] The show placed a group of strangers in a small house in which their everyday lives could be minutely chronicled by television cameras strategically placed throughout the domicile. Each week, the roommates nominated two of their group for eviction, with the viewing audience ultimately deciding which of the two was actually eliminated from the show. *Who Wants to Marry a Multi-Millionaire?* placed fifty attractive women in a beauty-pageant competition (including the usual swimsuit segment) for the grand prize of an on-air marriage to a multimillionaire. In a particularly baroque variation, *Temptation Island* had couples in long-standing relationships test their commitments by being separated and placed on an island stocked with attractive singles. *Fear Factor* placed people in situations in which they had to carry out a terrifying task (e.g., eating a can of worms, entering a pool of spiders) selected because they played to specific fears or neuroses of the participants. Based on the hit British show *Pop Idol*, *American Idol* had contestants with a wide range (to put it kindly) of show-business talents perform on stage, with viewers voting one of the show's contestants as the most likely to become a celebrity, or American idol.

The producers of Fox's *Joe Millionaire* plucked a handsome young construction worker out of the crowd (not coincidentally, he was also a model and aspiring actor) and gave him the trappings of a millionaire. Throughout the series, he courted a group of women, all of whom believed

debates between John McCain and Barack Obama attracted 52.4 million, 63.2 million, and 56.5 million viewers. The vice presidential debate between Sarah Palin and Joe Biden drew even more: 69.9 million viewers. As a point of comparison, CBS's *Survivor: China*, the 2007 edition of the show, drew between 12 million and 15 million viewers per episode.

[2] We are heavily indebted to the advice of Rachel Dubrovsky for our discussion of reality programming.

[3] Without actors or scripts, reality shows can be produced for between $200,000 and $300,000 per episode, compared to about $1 million for the average television drama or comedy.

[4] The degree to which reality shows have been embraced internationally is an interesting phenomenon in its own right. See, for example, Kraidy (2009) on the popularity of the genre in the Middle East, and its political uses and significance.

he was a millionaire, only to find out later (on camera of course) that he was actually poor. The show's now defunct website promoted itself by asking, "Who is out for love? Who is in it for money? The answers will be revealed on *Joe Millionaire.*" In the final episode, "Joe" selects his mate and then tells her he is actually poor (and, by extension, a liar). In a "surprise" twist of relevance to the argument we develop later in this chapter, once the chosen woman decides to stay with Joe, both are told they would receive a million dollars, thus answering the, website's question with the answer, "You can have it all!"

Perhaps the variant most relevant to the topic of this book was Fox's *Anchorwoman*, which, according to its website, followed, "a gorgeous model and ex-WWE [World Wrestling Entertainment] diva with no previous news experience" who was brought in to anchor and bring up the ratings of a local news broadcast in Tyler, Texas.[5] The show's promotional material asked, "How will it turn out? Only the ratings will tell, so stay tuned." Ironically, we'll never know what happened to ratings in Tyler, as *Anchorwoman* was canceled after a single episode in 2007 (Variety 2007). One might also ask how different this show's premise is from what Frank Rich (2002 A15) calls "the Ken and Barbie dolls lately recruited as news 'personalities' to stem the hemorrhaging at CNN."

Reality programming and the various components that define it are, of course, neither new nor real. Since its earliest days, television has contained live broadcasts; contrived game, talk, and talent shows; hidden cameras exposing ordinary people in embarrassing situations; and the like. The roots of reality-based television go back as far as 1947 and 1948, when *Queen for a Day* and *Candid Camera* first aired. The current spate of romance-oriented reality shows has its roots in the 1965 Chuck Barris hit *The Dating Game.* Shows like *American Idol* hearken back to Barris's *Gong Show* and Ted Mack's *The Original Amateur Hour* (which aired on both radio and early television). Efforts to glimpse the lives of seemingly ordinary people can be traced to 1973, when PBS aired *An American Family,* a documentary series about an actual family (the Louds) who let cameras observe their day-to-day lives for seven months. Connecting the lineage between *An American Family* and its more recent offspring is MTV's long-running *Real World,* which follows a group of young people who have been brought together to live and work for a season as a made-for-television group of friends.[6]

---

[5] The site is available at http://www.fox.com/fallpreview/new/anchorwoman.htm.
[6] Applicants are picked partly because they film well, as evidenced by their demonstration tapes. Many, perhaps most, also aspire to a career in the entertainment field.

Even labeling these quite varied shows as a single genre is misleading, demonstrating that, as with the news, such categorizations are based less on clear distinctions in form and content than on the implicit collusion between producers and consumers.[7] There are, of course, certain commonalities. The current versions of reality television (which already has and will continue to change) plucks "real" people from the population and puts them in various situations that the audience will hopefully find entertaining and possibly informative enough to watch. The reward for the participants is usually monetary but often includes the chance for self-improvement (e.g., NBC's *The Biggest Loser* or A&E's *Intervention*) and/or fame. Even these definitional boundaries are vague, however. For example, the distinction between the "ordinary folks" of most reality programming and their struggle to become celebrities was challenged by MTV's *The Osbournes*, which turned this formula on its head by detailing the life of a celebrity (aging rocker Ozzy Osbourne) and his family struggling to be "ordinary." Shows about a wide range of D-list celebrities followed: from Victoria Gotti (daughter of mob boss John Gotti) to Victoria Beckham (former Spice Girl and wife of soccer start David Beckham) and the Kardashian family (ex-wife and children of O. J. Simpson's attorney Robert Kardashian).

The popularity of reality television, even the choice of this term for this genre, is yet another manifestation of the belief that new communication technologies can reveal the unmediated truth about the world. In this sense, it is not unlike the development of photography during the Civil War, of movies and radio during the 1890s to 1920s, or of the very early days of television in the 1950s. Just as Matthew Brady's Civil War photographs promised a look at the truth of a conflict that was, for those far from the battlefields, incomprehensible, so, too, the popularity of today's reality programming is arguably a response to the difficulty of coming to grips with the increasingly complex and fragmented world in which we live.[8] In short, reality programming represents another in a long line of mediated fixes that promise to get people closer to reality at a time when direct knowledge of that reality seems to be receding. Somewhat paradoxically, however, reality television, along with its equivalents from

---

[7] We faced the difficulties of classification when we debated whether to include *Who Wants to Be a Millionaire?* in our list of reality shows. In earlier versions of this chapter, we included it, as it met some of the criteria usually used to define the genre – ordinary people in tense situations competing for riches and record setting ratings – but we were then convinced by other readers that the "real" start of the reality phenomenon was *Survivor*.

[8] Although a comparison between *Survivor* and Matthew Brady's photography may seem strained, one must remember that Brady traveled with a collection of props, such as rifles, and carefully posed bodies before taking his pictures.

other media such as movies (e.g., *The Blair Witch Project, Paranormal*) and the internet (from chat groups to twenty-four-hour web cams) is also an attempt to escape from reality. What is "real" becomes increasingly problematic as shows blend together people drawn from everyday life, staged events, live broadcasts, subjects drawn from actual events, and so forth, all edited for production before airing.[9] Indeed, the degree to which reality television is real even within its own limited rules is debatable, as illustrated by complaints made to the Federal Communications Commission that much of what appears on these shows is staged and the outcomes rigged.[10] Television producers have responded to these accusations by arguing that editorial control and direction is necessary to improve a show's appearance and narrative flow. And as Jeff Gaspin, executive vice president of alternative series at NBC correctly noted, "Editing a show down from hundreds of hours of video is a form of manipulation anyhow" (Schlosser and McConnell 2001, 12).

The revelation that reality programs are not particularly real is hardly earthshaking, in large part because the implicit collusion between producers and consumers regarding this particular genre often includes, and is even based on, this understanding. Less appreciated – by both producers and consumers – is that all television genres, including television journalism, are inevitably edited, produced, and crafted for dramatic effect, and thus simultaneously help create and are a part of the partially real, partially fictional mediated environment in which we all live. The inevitability of this feature of mass media is obscured in television, however, by labels such as "reality television," "dramas," and "news," all of which serve to maintain socially and politically constructed, but ultimately artificial and increasingly challenged, boundaries of meaning. Objecting that reality shows are staged is akin to Dan Rather's plaintive claim that "*this* [meaning his news broadcast, as opposed to docudramas] is real," with which we opened Chapter 3. Both are attempts to define the relationships between various types of media representations and an objective reality. Yet it is precisely these distinctions – between types of genres and between media representations and the things they represent – that have fundamentally eroded over the past several decades.

---

[9] New media like the internet also grapple with this problem when, for example, the identity of the popular blogger Lonely Girl was revealed not to be a sixteen-year-old girl but a thirtysomething California scriptwriter looking for a movie deal (Foremski 2006).

[10] That the *Survivor* incident drew such little attention compared to the quiz-show scandals of the 1950s is also a telling example of how the norms of fact and truth have become implicitly accepted as essentially contestable.

Frank and Ernest

FIGURE 4.1. Political Conventions as Reality Television; Comic Strips as Political Commentary.

For example, one need look no further than presidential nominating conventions, or entire presidential campaigns for that matter, to see the degree to which political life, despite its appearance of being "live," is almost completely scripted and preplanned, with elaborately staged rituals designed (much like television commercials) to call forth particular responses from its audience. Further blurring the lines between entertainment and public affairs media, the similarities between political and reality programming were addressed in no less a source of social commentary than the comic strip *Frank and Ernest*. While watching television, one character announces, "I'm getting tired of all this reality programming. Let's try to find some political convention coverage (Thaves 2000)." How different is the public role being played by Frank and Ernest, or more accurately, Thaves, than that of the political journalist who, like a theater critic, evaluates candidates' performances in the live but heavily scripted dramatic series that campaigns have become? In the 2008 campaign, the role of critic was expanded beyond journalists as new media technologies allowed ordinary citizens to participate in this critical process of revealing the "real" campaign behind the managed facade through the creation of amateur video via cell phones and the like and then their widespread circulation through outlets like YouTube. Indeed, as we argue more fully here, a well-honed definition of politically relevant media would often conclude that, at times, comic strips, reality television, cell phone videos, YouTube, and other forms of purportedly entertainment media are more politically useful than much of the strategically oriented campaign coverage that is automatically assumed to be the venue in which democratic discourse takes place.

It is also instructive that people cast more votes by phone to help select a winner on *American Idol* than votes in the 2004 presidential election (Sweney 2006). The show's website encouraged this comparison with electoral politics by telling us that it is an example of "Democracy in Action" and "the beauty of this country is that we always protect our suffrage rights. Although let's hope this poll gets a little better turnout than an actual election. Vote now and tell us what you think of the Top 32!" In perhaps the most bizarre parallel with the 2000 presidential election, the final vote count in *American Idol* was so close and uncertain that it generated charges of voter fraud and demands for a recount! Some internet fan sites compared the problems with the *Idol* vote to the infamous butterfly ballot. It seems clear that any perspective on the current state of American democracy and the role of media in it must come to grips with the connections between participation in public rituals like the selection of pop idols and political leaders. What is needed is a public language that can capture these emerging and complicated forms of media representations, be they of survivors on a desert island voting on one another's right to stay or citizens in a nation voting for their next president.

The complex and intriguing political implications of reality television go beyond their borrowing of the rituals and language of democratic processes such as elections. For example, during the 2004 presidential election cycle, the Showtime cable network aired *American Candidate*, a reality show in which ten "average" Americans make the case that they should be the next president of the United States. As described on the program's website:

Week-by-week, candidates will face-off against each other in a series of challenges designed to identify one individual who has the qualities to be President of the United States. Episodes of AMERICAN CANDIDATE will feature well-known political experts who advise the candidates on the challenges they will face. These consultants help the candidates shape their messages and campaigns, as well as give advice on everything from political ad creation and media coaching to image consulting and polling.[11]

After ten episodes, the winning candidate, Park Gillespie, a thirty-eight-year-old teacher and small business owner with a strong free-market orientation, received $200,000 and a chance to discuss his platform. The show was less than a stunning hit, viewed by only 128,000 people. As the *Dallas Morning News* wryly observed: "Compared to that, the low-rated

[11] This quote is from the show's website: http://www.sho.com/site/americancandidate/home.do.

Democratic National Convention qualified as a veritable 'American Idol.' Its smallest audience, on either a broadcast or cable channel, was 1.07 million viewers for MSNBC's prime-time coverage of the convention's third night" (Bark 2004).

Though easily dismissed as exploitative, the show featured a number of intriguing elements, including opportunities for viewers to participate in online discussions about public issues such as same-sex marriage and medical marijuana use, to link to the sites of various political advocacy groups to find out more information or become engaged in the issue of interest to them, and to organize or participate in face-to-face political meetings to discuss public issues and show support for their favorite Showtime candidate. In short, the show is a blend of fiction and reality, the lines between which are difficult to ascertain. The show's creator is R. J. Cutler, director of *The War Room*, a documentary about the 1992 Clinton campaign, which itself has been accused of being carefully staged by James Carville and other campaign managers.[12] Further confusing the issue was the "fiction" of media pundits and campaign spokespersons touting candidates like George W. Bush and Sarah Palin as "ordinary" people and so especially qualified to represent the "average" American as president.

By the late 2000s, new questions emerged about the political implications of reality programming. Blogs and video from both American soldiers and Iraqi civilians, widely circulated on websites like Liveleak and YouTube, introduced a type of reality programming about the conflict in Iraq. In 2009, postelection street protests against the Iranian government were hailed as the "Twitter Revolution": the power of new media like social networking sites and cell phone cameras to organize and publicize resistance to repressive regimes. Critics, however, argued that new media were neither widely used or effective (as compared to traditional forms of organizing) and actually served as a new source of voyeuristic political entertainment for Westerners (Keller 2010). A similar debate regarding the role of new media in democratic revolutions emerged following the dramatic protests which spread throughout the Middle East in 2011. Closer to home, one might ask whether the fringe Republican candidacy

[12] It is also interesting that the laudable efforts of James Fishkin and colleagues (2009) to promote deliberative democracy during the 1996 elections through the device of airing shows on PBS were the subject of much debate and commentary among academic political scientists, despite that the shows drew small audiences (slightly more than 1.1 million viewers in the ratings). Why did *American Candidate* not receive comparable attention from academics? Was it because of a sophisticated analysis of the differences between the two shows or simply a dismissal of the latter as mere entertainment?

of Ron Paul was an actual candidacy or a new baroque variant of the reality genre. Paul garnered virtually no response from primary voters, but he did gain much publicity and money through his web-based campaign and colorful appearances on *The Daily Show* and *The Colbert Report*.

The political relevance of reality programming can be seen in only slightly less obvious ways in shows such as *Crime and Punishment*, which aired in 2002 and was produced by the entertainment division of NBC. Produced by Dick Wolf (creator of the highly successful "fictional" crime show *Law and Order*), *Crime and Punishment* followed actual trials from the point of view of the prosecutor's office of San Diego County. As is often the case in the worlds of both politics and Hollywood, the show's stars – two female district attorneys – were physically attractive (enhanced by obviously professionally arranged hairstyling, makeup, and clothing), a point that was widely touted by critics as one of the keys to the show's success. Unlike real-time coverage and commentary of trials such as those regularly aired by TruTv (formerly Court TV), the particular cases spotlighted on *Crime and Punishment* and *Crime V* had already been decided by the time they were aired.[13] This allowed a greater amount of editing and higher production values, thus creating a new kind of hybrid that draws on both fictional and nonfictional parentage. The resulting shows did much more than simply and objectively represent the criminal justice system. Rather, through the shows' heavily edited and inevitably ideological narratives, they both became part of and altered that system. They created celebrity prosecutors and defense attorneys who came to represent the criminal justice system in subsequent appearances as media talking heads. They also provided viewers with the illusion that they had witnessed the actual criminal justice system in action. In turn, this shapes what citizens expect when they sit on juries, assess the results of major court cases, or form opinions about the strengths and weaknesses of the criminal justice system more broadly. Of course, such influences are not limited to reality shows; episodes of the popular 1980s show *L.A. Law* shaped what clients expected their lawyers to look and behave like and have even been used in law schools to train future lawyers (Margolick 1990). Similarly, the popular series of shows in the CSI franchise, which focus on the wonders of new technologies to develop irrefutable forensic evidence of criminal guilt, have created what is called "the *CSI* effect": the raising of crime victims' and jury members' real-world expectations

---

[13] In 2008, Court TV changed its name to truTV, with the new slogan, "Not reality, actuality."

of forensic science, especially crime scene investigation and DNA testing (CSI effect 2010). So, too, avowedly public affairs media, such as the local or national news, have similar effects. Our point is that no one genre is automatically more or less likely to be the source of public understanding about the political and social world, and no genre can represent these worlds without also shaping them.

The political relevance of genres such as reality television is also not limited to occasions in which they explicitly reference or comment on political events such as campaigns or the criminal justice system. Foundational issues such as freedom, equality, community, fairness, individualism, and identity, on which explicitly political issues and their interpretation are based, are at the heart of drama, comedy, and other forms of entertainment genres. Of course, this is not a new phenomenon. Indeed, scholars, especially feminist media scholars, have produced a large and significant literature exploring reality television at this foundational level.[14] But the political significance of reality television has been lost on most political communication scholars, practitioners, and consumers because of the narrow definition of politically relevant media, rooted in the distinction between news and entertainment that became naturalized in the mid- to late twentieth century.

A useful correction to this blinkered approach is found in the work of the Frankfurt school theorists Theodor Adorno and Max Horkheimer. Their seminal 1947 article, "The Culture Industry: Enlightenment as Mass Deception" argues that part of the appeal to working women – secretaries, nurses, factory workers, and so forth – of Hollywood cinema was the common plotline in which ordinary women such as themselves were transformed by the studio system into movie stars. This made it possible for them to imagine being "discovered" by that very same industry (Adorno and Horkheimer [1947]2002). The underlying message being disseminated by these movies was that, in an industrialized system of cultural production, it was chance that determined who was turned into a star, and by extension, all that distinguished female audience members from the starlets on the screen was luck. Horkheimer and Adorno went on to argue that women's critical faculties were redirected away from any arguments against industrial capitalism and channeled instead into fantasies designed to make their dreary workdays more tolerable, and even potentially glamorous.

---

[14] For some of the more insightful work, see especially Grindstaff 2002; Shattuc 1997; Murray and Ouellette 2008.

Adorno and Horkheimer's insights are rich with implications for the impact of reality television on democratic life today. Reality-based shows arguably serve to redirect public discourse away from critical analysis of the economy through their messages of "you too can strike it rich," "you too can escape the drudgery of your daily life," and "success depends on individual ability combined with luck." It is little wonder that such shows have proved so popular, and their popularity may help explain why more than half of all Americans younger than the age of thirty expect to get rich at some point in their lives, and a majority of Americans – including the less affluent – support the elimination of estate taxes for the very wealthy (Moore 2003). It also helps explain why the details of traditional politics would seem so boring, irrelevant, and depressing in comparison.

We do not mean to suggest that the impact of "entertainment" media need always work to reinforce dominant political, economic, and social institutions and values. To the contrary, as we discuss throughout this book, often it is popular culture that provides the strongest critiques of these institutions and values.[15] Rather, we are saying that the political implications of the media can be understood only by expanding our notion of both media and politics. This is as true for our understanding of nominally public affairs broadcasting as it is for so-called entertainment programming. We have already noted the fictional aspects of campaigns and campaign coverage. Consider, as well, the dramatic images of joyous Iraqi citizens pulling down a larger-than-life statue of Saddam Hussein in the aftermath of U.S. troops entering Baghdad in the spring of 2003. The event, broadcast live and repeated hundreds of times on news broadcasts, came to symbolize both the success and the wisdom of the U.S. invasion of Iraq. But more than a year later, representatives of the U.S. government admitted that the event had, in fact, been staged by the psychological operations unit of the military in an effort to convince Iraqis that Hussein was no longer in control (and presumably, to convince the American public that the war effort was a success). In short, the event, much like President Bush's subsequent televised statement aboard a U.S. aircraft carrier that major fighting in Iraq was over, was as much or more fiction than fact, little more than the U.S. government's version of reality

---

[15] For example, anyone who is a fan of *The Simpsons*, as we both are, knows that the show often provides sharp satirical criticism of both specific events in and more general features of the American political economy. This criticism even extends to biting the hand that feeds it, in its frequent pokes at the Fox network and its owner Rupert Murdoch.

television. Further reflecting the porous line between fact and fiction these images continued to be circulated in a wide range of media even after it was revealed as a staged event.

Or consider the case of Private Jessica Lynch, who was wounded and captured by the Iraqi military. The American high command, aided by the Bush White House, claimed that Lynch was rescued from an Iraqi hospital in a dramatic mission by U.S. Special Forces. The "rescue," which was filmed by the U.S. military, was extensively used by the U.S. government (with the unwitting support of the various news outlets that extensively covered the story) to build support for the war and fuel a sense of patriotism at home. Yet it turns out that there was no rescue at all, the Iraqi doctors eagerly handed Jessica over to the troops, and there were no Iraqi military at the hospital.[16] Thus, the "news" footage provided by the U.S. Army was itself a docudrama of the worst kind: false propaganda masquerading as news. The concocted story made a celebrity of Private Lynch, much to her dismay. Central to the appeal of the story's narrative was the (mistaken) belief that Private Lynch had fought valiantly against her attackers, had been shot or stabbed during her capture, had been tortured and/or mistreated while in prison, and had been rescued by a stealth operation that took place under the noses of her inept Iraqi captors. The three major networks all competed for access to Lynch and her story, with CBS offering a deal (made possible by the breakdown of the lines between news and entertainment divisions and the increasing centralization of ownership) that included extensive news coverage; interviews on the network's morning, daytime, and evening talk shows; a book contract; and a made-for-television docudrama.

There is a final issue that a more useful definition of politically relevant communication can help to address: the impact of political media, broadly defined, on elites. In the rare instances when attention turns to non-news sources of political information, the emphasis is almost exclusively on the impact of such texts on "ordinary" viewers and/or the ability of elites to manipulate media for their own ends. Scholarly and popular authors use the Jessica Lynch story as an example of the ways in which the Bush administration manipulated a wide variety of media to distract the public

---

[16] We are grateful to Lance Bennett and Robert Entman for reminding us that there never was a military rescue of Private Lynch. Many sources have revealed the manipulation by government officials of the Lynch story. For an especially poignant retelling, see Krakauer (2009).

from its failures in the aftermath of the invasion of Iraq. Journalists criticize shows like *Law and Order* and *L.A. Law* for misleading gullible viewers into a naive view of the criminal justice system. And critical scholars accuse entertainment media of distracting the masses from more important and significant issues.

Yet political elites live in and are influenced by the same popular culture as ordinary citizens. For example, entertainment media can reinforce the policy preferences of political leaders, as when Richard Nixon repeatedly viewed the movie *Patton* before ordering the American military incursion into Cambodia (Perlstein 2008). Alternately, such media can help bring about shifts in the policy preferences of leaders, as when, according to the respected historian Richard Rhodes (2008), Ronald Reagan was deeply shaken by the made-for-television docudrama *The Day After*, which portrayed the impact of a nuclear war on Lawrence, Kansas. In *Arsenals of Folly*, Rhodes reveals that the television show challenged Reagan's belief in the possibility of a winnable nuclear war and helped convince him, against the advice of many of his advisers, to pursue nuclear disarmament with the Soviet Union. Popular culture also can structure in very specific ways the discourse of political elites when they debate policy alternatives among themselves. For example, as Jane Mayer (2008) reports, the exploits and practices of the fictional government agent Jack Bauer on the Fox show *24* was regularly referenced in support of enhanced interrogation techniques in the highest councils of the Bush administration.

Making Sense of the New Media Environment: Hyperreality and Multiaxiality

What are the boundaries of politically relevant communication? What are the politically relevant differences between *American Candidate* and actual campaign coverage? Where does reality end and fiction begin in the campaign process, in coverage of wartime events such as the toppling of Saddam Hussein's statue or the saga of Private Lynch, or in the airing of reality shows such as *Crime and Punishment*? How does one begin to make sense of the political implications of this interplay of fact and fiction within and across genres? How much influence do dramatic treatments of a wide range of politically significant issues have on both ordinary citizens and elites? Although the answers to these questions are not obvious, and ultimately depend on the contours of whatever new media regime emerges, we believe a starting point can be found in the concepts of hyperreality and multiaxiality.

As we saw in Chapter 2, central to the Realist movement was the development of media – photography and movies – which held the promise of
providing a more direct picture of reality. Underlying this belief in media
was an assumption that reality was objective and singular, waiting to be
discovered, independent of the method used to portray it. Although we
find much that is useful in the openness of the Realist movement to alternative media and genres, the movement's more basic assumption about
the nature of reality needs rethinking. The notion of a clear distinction
between objectivity and subjectivity has been thoroughly critiqued on an
intellectual level, but it also is brought under attack by the new media
environment; the sheer number and types of media easily available on
virtually any subject coupled with the large proportion of time people
spend with various media make reality itself an essentially contestable
concept.

The contestable nature of reality in the new discursive environment is
captured by the work of John Fiske.[17] Fiske argues that the central unit
of analysis in studying the media (and the driving force in public discourse) is not objective reality but "media events."[18] According to Fiske
(1996, 2):

> The term *media event* is an indication that in a postmodern world we can no longer
> rely on a stable relationship or clear distinction between a "real" event and its
> mediated representation. Consequently, we can no longer work with the idea that

[17] Although his reputation has suffered as his work attracted many vituperative attacks,
we believe that Fiske deserves a more balanced assessment. For us, as two quantitatively
trained political scientists, he introduced us to a range of "postmodern" theory with
which we were unfamiliar. One reason Fiske has been such a lightning rod is that,
unlike the theorists from which he draws, Fiske writes clearly and well. Although we
have criticisms of some of his arguments, in the end, Fiske helped us see the real value
of thinkers like Lyotard, Derrida, Baudrillard, and DeCerteau. We might have skipped
over citing Fiske and referred to the originals, with whom we are now more familiar, but
this would have been intellectually dishonest and most definitely ungenerous. Instead, in
the following discussion of multiaxiality and hyperreality, we acknowledge the influence
that John Fiske has had on our thinking.

[18] The concept of a media event has also been used by Daniel Dayan and Elihu Katz in
Media Events (Cambridge, MA: Harvard University Press, 1992). Although the two
uses are similar in some ways, there are several important differences. For Fiske, media
events provide opportunities for marginalized "publics" to enter mainstream discourse
by using such events to draw attention to their concerns (much as the O. J. Simpson
trial or Clarence Thomas–Anita Hill hearings raised broader issues of race and gender).
For Dayan and Katz, however, media events have the potential to tap into shared
foundational beliefs that can unify seemingly disparate segments of society: although
various media may cover the event in different ways, underlying assumptions about the
public agenda are shared across both outlets and audiences (as with the death of Princess
Diana or the explosion of the Columbia space shuttle).

the "real" is more important, significant, or even "true" than the representation. A media event, then, is not a mere representation of what happened, but it has its own reality, which gathers up into itself the reality of the event that may or may not have preceded it.

The complex intertwining of an event and its mediated representation produces what Jean Baudrillard has described as hyperreality, which Fiske (1996, 62) defines as "a postmodern sense of the real that accounts for our loss of certainty in being able to distinguish clearly and hierarchically between reality and its representation, and being able to distinguish clearly and hierarchically between the modes of its representation." In the new discursive environment, there is no clear distinction between a particular media text and the reality that text purports to describe. Instead, the media itself operates to construct alternative and competing versions of reality that cannot (except in the most mundane or limited ways) be objectively distinguished as more or less real.

The intertwining of media representations and our understanding of the events they purport to represent is captured by Susan Sontag (2003) when she notes that something becomes real to those not physically present through its media representation. At the same time, she goes on to argue, media representations more generally influence the way in which even those physically present understand particular events like the terrorist attacks of 9/11: "After four decades of big-budget Hollywood disaster films, 'It felt like a movie' seems to have displaced the way survivors of a catastrophe used to express the short-term unassimilability of what they had gone through: 'It felt like a dream'" (Sontag 2003, 22).

The point is not the rather absurd claim that reality does not exist. As Sontag (2003, 110) notes: "Reports of the death of reality – like the death of reason, the death of the intellectual, the death of serious literature – seem to have been accepted without much reflection by many who are attempting to understand what feels wrong, or empty, or idiotically triumphant in contemporary politics and culture." Claims that reality itself has been reduced to a mediated spectacle ignore most of the world, where media penetration and influence are nothing like they are in the wealthy nations, and they can be interpreted as implying ("perversely" and "unseriously" as Sontag notes) that real suffering does not occur.

The significant point is that, for contemporary American democracy, the hyperreality constructed in a mediated world is, itself, a kind of social fact (albeit contested), which shapes the understanding of us all, even when we experience events firsthand. There simply is no independent, objective, and unmediated position from which we can determine what is and is not political reality. As our examples of the influence of popular culture on presidents and their advisers indicate, this is often no less true for elites than it is for the rest of the polity. Rather, claims about the reality on which political arguments are based are essentially contestable and, in a democracy, open to contestation.

Although this sort of theorizing is dismissed by journalists and scholars who are rooted, consciously or unconsciously, in the assumptions of Progressive Era thinkers, we believe that it has much to recommend for understanding the new discursive environment and the portrayal of specific political events. For example, consider the 2000 presidential election. Beliefs in an objective reality independent of the techniques used for portraying it led naturally to the assumption that there was a "true" winner and loser determined by the vote count. Unsurprisingly, this was the underlying discourse used by most journalists, citizens, and scholars in struggling with the controversial results. Yet viewed through the lens of hyperreality, one is led to a very different interpretation of the election and coverage of it. In this interpretation, the vote count (more clearly in the 2000 election but true more generally) is not an objective fact but a constructed social fact, dependent on the definition and method one uses to count it. Count the hanging chads one way and Gore wins; count them another way and Bush wins. Further, the election and coverage of it highlighted the contestability and hyperreality of what we mean by a vote in the first place. Is it the intention of the voter, the computer-counted marked ballot, the dimpled ballot observable by humans, the views of the Supreme Court? Again, use one definition and Gore wins; use another and Bush wins.

One result of this postmodern interpretation of voting is that it foregrounds the role of media coverage in the determination of the outcome and what it means. At what point, for example, do the networks, cable stations, and so forth decide to stop covering the story and simply accept a winner (a decision made all the more hyperreal by the use – and misuse – of exit polls for announcing winners and losers before all votes are cast and counted)? Further, reflecting the futility of trying to distinguish news from entertainment, although news divisions chose to accept the election as over, the struggle over interpreting the outcome of the election continued in a wide variety of media outlets. Michael Moore's documentary *Fahrenheit 9/11*, for example, opens with the struggle by black Democratic House members to reject certification of the results of the election, an effort that was almost entirely ignored by journalists. And in May 2008 HBO aired the docudrama, *Recount*, a dramatized reenactment of the political machinations that followed the disputed vote count in Florida.

A second implication of hyperreality is that social reality is constructed through a struggle among competing actors. To continue with our example, the conclusion that George W. Bush had been elected president was not reached by a single set of actors, and it was certainly not the result of some objective set of facts. Rather, it emerged from a complex interaction that included journalists of different stripes; media corporations; political elites, including the candidates themselves; and citizen-viewers. Although the notion that political outcomes are the result of a struggle among competing interests is not new, the increasing complexity of the mediated environment changes the dynamics of this process. At a minimum, the related concepts of gatekeeping and agenda setting need to be rethought. The traditional gatekeeping model assumes a single vector for the flow of political information, determined by the interaction between political elites and journalists. This point of interaction constitutes the gate through which information passes to the public. However, the new discursive environment disrupts the single-axis system in three ways. First, the expansion of politically relevant media and the blurring of genres lead to a struggle within the media itself for the role of authoritative gatekeeper. Second, the expansion of media outlets and the obliterating of the normal news cycle have created new opportunities for nonmainstream political actors to influence the setting and framing of the political agenda (Kurtz 1998). And third, this changed environment has created new opportunities (and pitfalls) for the public to enter and interpret the political world.

Understanding this new environment must include recognizing the multiplicity of gates through which information now passes to the public. We need to come to grips with the sheer number of sources of information (e.g., the internet, cable television, radio), the speed with which information is transmitted, and the range of genres that the public uses for political information. These conditions create what Fiske (1996, 65) calls multiaxiality (the second critical concept we adopt from his work), which "transforms any stability of categories into the fluidities of power." Although Fiske focuses on three axes of class, race, and gender in his analysis, the concept of multiaxiality is useful for understanding the changing nature of mediated political discourse more generally. Its central value is reminding us that, even though the conduits through which information flows have expanded, this does not mean that they are no longer structured by specific (albeit changing) relationships of economic, political, or cultural power and influence. As we argue in the next chapter, although political scandals are driven by a new and greatly expanded array of media – from blogs to late-night satire, cable networks, cell phone cameras, and social networking sites – this seemingly anarchic (and to some, democratic) fragmentation reflects real struggles for power that still include structured and organized political forces. More specifically, multiaxiality suggests three things. First, the increase in the number and types of mediated gates through which information is disseminated means that traditional journalists are losing control of the agenda-setting process. Second, it means that a wider range of actors have the potential to influence the discursive environment. And third, it means that the ability of any set of actors to control the discursive environment is tenuous and unstable, with greater possibility of sudden shifts in either the agenda or how it is represented.

In summary, the concepts of hyperreality and multiaxiality help us understand how something as seemingly straightforward as, for example, the outcome of an election is ultimately the result of a complex social, political, economic, and media dynamic and not simply an objective reality determined by an indisputable vote, neutrally reported on by professional interpreters of that reality. To be sure, this was a close and contested election, but the same could be said of earlier elections (e.g., 1960, 1968), which were "decided" with much less angst and drama – in part, we would suggest, because of the very different discursive environment shaped by a well-established media regime within which those earlier elections were conducted (one that included a consensus over the existence of an objective social and political reality, and a limited number of professional elites who served as the gatekeepers of how that reality was understood).

Redefining Politically Relevant Media

If, as we suggest, hyperreality and multiaxiality are the defining characteristics of the new information environment, how does one avoid falling too deeply into a postmodern sensibility that anything goes? We believe that it is essential to begin with a definition of political relevance appropriate to this new environment.

Because we are concerned with the political implications of the new media environment and the steps that might be taken to maximize its potential for enriching democratic life, it is vital to avoid two limitations of most approaches to political communication. First, as we have argued in the previous chapters, we must discard definitions of political media that emerged from the media regime of the mid-twentieth century. Such definitions restrict us to a small slice of the media environment (i.e., media explicitly labeled political by producers, audiences, and analysts) while ignoring broad swaths of media that have always had political implications. Second, to avoid the equally unsatisfying conclusion that all media are political, it is necessary to develop a definition that provides guidance in identifying media likely to have significant impacts on political life.

In our view, a useful definition of politically relevant media requires a shift from categorizing by genre (e.g., news versus drama), content (e.g., a report on an upcoming election versus a story about the latest fashion fad), or source (e.g., professional journalist versus actor versus blogger) to categorizing by utility. That is, the extent to which any communication is politically relevant is dependent on what it does – its potential use – rather than what it says, who says it, and how it is said (Burke 1966).

So, our definition is as follows:

Politically relevant media shape opportunities for understanding, deliberating, and acting on (1) the conditions of one's everyday life, (2) the life of fellow community members, and (3) the norms and structures of power that shape these relationships.

We offer this definition not because it is the only one possible, but as a way to break the habit of relying on reified definitions of political relevance rooted in past media regimes. Our definition is meant to start a conversation about what constitutes political media in the new media environment.

There are several aspects of this definition that need elaboration. The emphasis on "the conditions of one's own and one's fellow community members' life" captures the ultimate purpose of politics in a way that is not overly constraining. At the same time, connecting these more intimate concerns to "the norms and structures of power that shape these relationships" helps ensure that our definition is tied to the collective institutions and processes that have authority to affect these day-to-day conditions. In addition, emphasizing communications' impact on "understanding, deliberation, and action" further delimits politically relevant media in a way that makes visible their presumed core functions in a democratic society – to facilitate citizen engagement in the determination and implementation of the public will. Finally, the phrase "shaping opportunities" places emphasis on utility without making a priori determinations about the normative implications of that use – communications can be politically relevant because they limit opportunities to understand, deliberate, and act, and because they enhance them.

Building on the approach taken by David Easton (1965), we define politics as the authoritative allocation of goods, services, and values. This definition emphasizes that the political system is far more than the daily activities of elected politicians, which tends to dominate media coverage labeled "political" by professional journalists. Consequently, it is important to understand that politically relevant information and discourse (and thus politically relevant media) operate on at least three interconnected levels. First is the level of *institutions and processes*: the formal channels of politics and government (e.g., elections, the presidency, the courts, local government, the press itself). Second is the level of *issues*: the debates and proposals for specific policies that are on the political agenda, that are becoming part of that agenda (e.g., social security, immigration, drug testing, criminal rights, international affairs) or that could become part of the agenda. When most journalists and social scientists discuss politics and political media, they are usually concerned with only these two levels. Yet politics also operates at a third *foundational* level: the processes and concepts on which the very idea of government and society is based (e.g., authority, power, equality, freedom, justice, community). Understanding and assessing the political relevance of the media requires consideration of its impact at all three levels. It also makes clearer the need to include non-news media in this consideration. For example, references to the connection between voting for politicians and for budding pop stars on *American Idol* or interpretations of the way the criminal justice system operates on *CSI* or *L.A. Law* have direct implications for how politics is understood and acted on at both the institutional and the issues levels. At the same time, echoing Adorno and Horkheimer ([1947]2002), reality shows (or news programs) that implicitly reinforce the notion that anyone can get rich have political implications that operate at the foundational level.

What purchase do these definitions of politics and politically relevant media bring us? First, they move us away from narrow and increasingly outdated categorizations that are based solely on genre and focus instead on the full range of mediated messages with which citizens interact. A Jay Leno monologue satirically pointing out the political ignorance of the general public, an episode of *The Simpsons* spoofing the consequences of different levels of voter turnout between younger and older voters, or an internet joke about the sex scandal surrounding former New York Governor Eliot Spitzer that generates discussion about the line between public and private behavior could all be considered as politically relevant as (or more relevant than) media such as the nightly news, a newspaper (either its print or web version), or political talk shows. Further, their relevance can be understood as operating at several different, though interconnected, levels of politics.

Second, our definitions change how we answer the question not only if a particular mediated message is politically relevant but also of how it is relevant. For example, the insider coverage of campaign strategy that makes up much of how professional journalists cover elections or the usual fare of sensationalistic crime and disaster coverage that dominates local news programs may be politically relevant, but their relevance comes from their tendency to limit rather than enhance opportunities for understanding, deliberating about, and acting on the relationship among the conditions of day-to-day life and the norms and structures of power that shape these relationships. Viewed in this light, it becomes clearer that cable talk shows like *The Sean Hannity Show* or *Hardball with Chris Matthews*, for example, often position their audiences as sports fans rather than citizens: "[t]he point is to disagree and develop good punch lines that score points for your side, rather than treat the issues seriously.... [T]he hosts of these shows focus on strategy to the virtual exclusion of issues" (Liebes and Williams 2000, 20). Suggesting that much of the content of news broadcasts and political talk shows is politically debilitating makes it more problematic to castigate the public for not paying attention to them. It helps explain why many of these shows appeal to no more than a small fraction of the population, many of whom are "political junkies" who see politics as a source of entertainment the way other people like sports, professional wrestling, or *Desperate Housewives* (Liebes and Williams 2000, 5). More important, it casts doubt on the value of treating such coverage (and the use of it by the public) as hallmarks of good citizenship and civic engagement.

Of course, this is not to say that everything found in traditional news media is debilitating or that the content of popular culture is always useful to democratic citizenship. Much of the former is both politically relevant and useful, whereas much of the latter is neither. The political relevance and utility of any mediated communications is not automatically self-evident and can always be legitimately debated. Such determinations regarding a particular mediated message ultimately depend on the political, social, and economic environments in which they occur. In short, any particular mediated political communication can be evaluated only with reference to the broader discursive environment.

Defining Who "We" Are in the New Discursive Environment

As we argued in Chapter 2, much of the debate and changing consensus over the appropriate role of the media in American democracy has been based on sometimes implicit and sometimes explicit answers to one of the enduring questions about the role of political media: who should (or is able to) participate in the authoritative allocation of goods, services, and values, and so who is in need of enough useful, trustworthy information to do so effectively? The concept of community in our definition of political relevance is meant to signal the importance of this question. Always contestable, in the new discursive environment, this concept is open to multiple, changing meanings, thus creating new and more fluid possibilities for how we define ourselves and the communities to which we belong. Indeed, we chose the phrase "fellow community members" carefully, because we think that one of the greatest powers of the mass media is to help define the nature of the community to which individuals think of themselves as members, a central act in democratic politics.

Community is one of those deceptively simple terms that, on careful analysis, actually prove quite complex. In his seminal work *Imagined Communities*, Benedict Anderson (1983) argues that there is nothing natural or inevitable about how we define the boundaries of any community. Even when it comes to the neighborhoods where we live, one of the most common definitions of community, identifying a common interest with others simply on the basis of geographical proximity and establishing the boundaries of this physical area (e.g., a number of city blocks, an apartment building, a homeowner's association, a town) is dependent on quite complex social interactions and the broader political economy (e.g., private ownership of homes versus renters, long-term residents versus more transient patterns of living). The definition of community is even more complex when we are referring to functionally defined communities of political interest – the gay and lesbian community, the farming community, the American pro-Israel community, and so on. It is a mistake to arbitrarily view any type of community as more real than another type of community – all are socially constructed, or imagined. As Anderson argues, once we move past face-to-face interactions, media play a central role in forging definitions of community.

The current environment provides opportunities for many heretofore-unimaginable communities. Consider, for example, the case of online role-playing games such as Ultima Online (UO), Second Life, or World of Warcraft, which as we noted in Chapter 3 are played by more people than watch the cable news channels. The UO game began in 1997 and is generally credited with popularizing the massively multiplayer online game (MMOG). It is an exceptionally open game with no beginning, end, or specific object. Players create avatars, which they negotiate through a computer world of spells; dragons; assorted creatures; and most important, other players' avatars. At its peak of popularity in 2003, UO claimed more than 250,000 subscribers who paid $9.95 per month and averaged thirteen hours a week of game play (Kolbert 2001).[19] Since its inception, UO has experienced a growing number of unanticipated "problems":

Ultima's appeal is clearly that of an escapist fantasy, yet the most striking feature of the games brief history is its perversely recurrent social realism. In its original design, the game gave players a choice of professions: they could train their avatars in any of some three dozen fields, ranging from archery and alchemy to animal taming. No sooner was U.O. up and running than a player introduced a new line of work by operating two characters, one named Jenny and the other Pimp Daddy. On top of hyperinflation, Britannia has suffered a wave of extinctions, paralyzing hoarding, and a crime problem so intractable that at one point the game was forced to, in effect, split itself in half. Considered as an inadvertent and largely unsupervised experiment, U.O. raises questions about whether people can manage to coexist peacefully even when they don't really exist. (Kolbert 2001, 90)

The players and operators of UO and other MMOGs constitute distinctive "communities" struggling to understand, deliberate over, and act on the relationships among their individual and collective (if virtual) lives and the norms and structures of power that affect those relationships. As such, it arguably constitutes a politically relevant form of media. The *Washington Post* columnist Michael Gerson (2007, A15) captures the foundational issues raised by Second Life:

It is, in fact, a large-scale experiment in libertarianism. Its residents can do and be anything they wish. There are no binding forms of community, no responsibilities that aren't freely chosen and no lasting consequences of human actions. In Second Life, there is no human nature at all, just human choices.

And what do people choose? Well, there is some good live music, philanthropic fundraising, even a few virtual churches and synagogues. But the main result is

---

[19] It is worth noting that this is a tiny figure by current standards of success for MMOGs. By 2009, the most successful game, World of Warcraft, claimed 11.5 million active subscribers.

the breakdown of inhibition. Second Life, as you'd expect, is highly sexualized in ways that have little to do with respect or romance. There are frequent outbreaks of terrorism, committed by online anarchists who interrupt events, assassinate speakers (who quickly reboot from the dead) and vandalize buildings. There are strip malls everywhere, pushing a relentless consumerism. And there seems to be an inordinate number of vampires, generally not a sign of community health.

To be sure, the impact of participation in such online communities on more traditional political values and behaviors is an empirical question (e.g., Are UO or Second Life players more or less likely to participate in "real" civic and political life, to keep up with current affairs, to be more trusting of fellow citizens, and so forth? Are there differences along these dimensions between participants in different kinds of MMOGs?). There is no doubt, however, that explicit political behavior occurs within these online worlds. During the 2008 presidential campaign, players of World of Warcraft regularly asked each other's avatars who they supported. Ron Paul supporters organized a march of avatars in support of their candidate, and one intrepid journalist created an avatar and interviewed others about their views on the election (GamePolitics.com 2008). There is also evidence that online activity affects certain behaviors offline. For instance, researchers have found that just as self-perception in the "real" world can affect behavior, so, too, can self-perception online (as measured by the attractiveness of one's avatar) affect behavior both online and offline (Dell 2008). But formulating propositions about possible political effects of online activities can emerge only once we have expanded our definitions of both politics and politically relevant media. Indeed, we think it is at least as useful to investigate the political implications of such popular gaming communities, as some are beginning to do, as it is to adopt the more dismissive language of disease and brand such activities as unhealthy addictions (for an example of treating video games as a health problem, see Tanner 2007; for examples of more open-minded and scholarly treatment, see Bogost 2007).[20]

Defining the communities in which we see ourselves belonging is central to the normative implications of politically relevant media. As John Dewey (1927, 154) observed, "To learn to be human is to develop through the give and take of communication an effective sense of being an individually distinctive member of a community; one who understands and appreciates its beliefs, desires and methods, and who contributes to a

---

[20] In fact, if one ignores the political and social context, it is just as easy to label as "addiction" the obsessive attention to the daily news that grips many older Americans.

further conversion of organic powers into human resources and values."
The philosopher Onora O'Neill (1996) argues that, in defining moral
responsibilities, we need to carefully and consistently define the individuals who are members of our own moral community. So, for example, if
we consume inexpensive food and clothing whose price is dependent on
low-paid foreign labor, it is morally inconsistent to then say that we have
no responsibility to such laborers simply because they live in faraway
lands about which we know little and care less. Whether we like it or
not, they have become members of our moral community because our
own day-to-day life is dependent on the conditions of their day-to-day
life (and vice versa).

The media are central to constructing, revealing, and at times disguising the communities to which we belong. Consider, for example,
the impact of the increasing globalization of media. The availability of
international news, entertainment, and one-to-one and one-to-many communications brought about by new technologies and their use allow previously impossible connections between individuals and groups widely
separated by space, class, and culture. Explaining the huge protests
against military action against Iraq in 2003, Madeline Bunting (2003,
21), writing in the British newspaper the *Guardian*, captures the power
of such moral communities and the political relevance of media often
overlooked by more traditional approaches to political communication:

The demonstration [the million-plus antiwar march in London] was driven by
one very powerful and very accessible emotion: a deeply felt revulsion against
modern warfare.... All this knowledge is underpinned by something much more
visceral. It is a sensibility formed by scores of war films such as *Platoon, Saving
Private Ryan*, and thousands of TV images of the suffering of war's victims. How
can we endure the suffering of Iraqi civilians on our television screens in two
months' time? The tears which have embarrassed us in our cinema seats and in
our armchairs may have been manipulated by Hollywood or newsmen, but they
have enlarged our emotional imagination. We can now imagine, in a way that
no previous generation has done, the families – just like our own – in a Baghdad
suburb whose lives are now hanging in the balance. And we can imagine the
suffering of those who prosecute the war, the sons and lovers – just like our own –
bracing themselves to kill, and to die.

Once the invasion took place, new media moved us past having to simply imagine the suffering mentioned by Bunting, as videos from soldiers
and Iraqi civilians circulating on sites like YouTube brought images that
opened up the possibility for forging communities with those actually on
the ground in Iraq.

Or consider how, in the 2008 election, the tech-savvy Obama campaign was able to mobilize supporters into an online community willing to contribute millions of dollars. To the extent that the resulting financial advantage over John McCain was significant in Obama's election, this is a case in which the skillful use of new media had implications for the distribution of political power.[21] After the election, the Tea Party movement used an equally skillful blend of old media (right-wing television and radio, to say nothing of phone trees and word of mouth) and new media (carefully moderated online discussion groups that ban liberal interlopers, YouTube videos, and the like) to create a community with an as yet unpredictable impact on American politics. In this vein, the political communication scholars Bruce Bimber and Lance Bennett have both begun to investigate the impact of new media on the creation of political interest groups (Bimber 2003; Bennett, Givens, and Breunig 2008; Bennett 2008).

In addition to providing opportunities to forge new and more varied interconnections across previously disconnected cultures, the media, in its role as a powerful tool for selling goods and services, forges economic connections that further bind us into increasingly global networks of moral responsibility.[22] The complexity of the new discursive environment and its impact on definitions of community can be seen in the political movements to ban the use of land mines, to stop the use of sweatshops and child labor in the production of shoes and clothing sold in the United States, to protest the negative impacts of the emerging global economy, and to provide greater political autonomy for Tibet. Cell phone video of the death of an Iranian woman at the hands of government authorized militia bands helped galvanize worldwide attention to the protests following the 2009 elections. In the aftermath of the Haitian earthquake of 2010, tweets from the stricken island and the ease with which money could be donated through texting helped forge bonds of community between individuals in the developed world and the victims in Haiti. In each of these cases, the media has been crucial in shaping opportunities for understanding, deliberating on, and acting on the relationships among the conditions of one's day-to-day-life, the day-to-day-life of fellow members of the community, and the norms and structures of power that shape those relationships.

[21] We are grateful to Lance Bennett and Robert Entman for making this point to us.

[22] One specific implication of this argument is that network news divisions have a growing moral obligation to cover global issues and the day-to-day conditions of the lives of individuals in nations with which we trade, particularly if the networks that own these divisions profit from airing advertisements for goods and services from such countries.

But the role played by the media has been much more complex than traditional categorizations based on content, genre, or speaker would anticipate. Actors such as Richard Gere, movie directors such as Martin Scorsese, and rock stars such as the members of Aerosmith have been central to the Free Tibet movement, to say nothing of the emergence of the Dalai Lama as a media celebrity. It seems to us that, absent the attention brought by such highly visible media figures, the protests against the Beijing Olympics would have been far less widespread and visible.[23] The anti-sweatshop movement grew in visibility (including in traditional news outlets) when television personality Kathie Lee Gifford and basketball star Michael Jordan were implicated through their relationships with companies such as Nike. The band U2's Bono has traveled to Africa to publicize both the continent's problems and potential solutions open to the international community.[24] The internet has been a central tool in identifying, informing, and mobilizing supporters of each of these movements and has done so in part by bypassing more traditional media channels and in part by influencing them. At the same time, in each of these cases, the media have played a crucial role in creating new definitions of community and, in so doing, in creating a new sense of responsibility that comes with community. Americans were suddenly bound to the plight of Buddhist refugees, child workers in Indonesia, immigrants from Mexico, and impoverished families in Africa or South America. In short, in the new discursive environment, it becomes easier to develop fresh definitions of community that are less bound by the traditional limits of space. It is less possible to escape the very real interconnections between people – interconnections based on economic, political, and cultural ties that transcend local and even national boundaries. This is especially true when these interactions are not limited to occasional exposure to a thirty-second news story but include exchanges through a host of media and genres.

It is easy to dismiss these emerging virtual communities, moral communities, and/or communities of interest as less real or meaningful than more traditional, place-based ones. It is also easy to argue that such connections can and had been made before the emergence of new media. Certainly,

[23] Similarly, the attention drawn to the issue by celebrities helped frame media coverage of these protests, as it largely ignored the perspective of the pro-Chinese demonstrators, who actually outnumbered the Free Tibet protesters in most locations.

[24] Indeed, his deep knowledge of the issues impressed and altered the position on aid to Africa of one of his traveling companions, then U.S. Secretary of the Treasury Paul O'Neill (Suskind 2004).

both these points have merit, but it is important not to overstate them. Consider, for example, the sense of moral outrage and collective self-reflection that accompanied the failure of local residents to come to Kitty Genovese's aid as she was attacked on a Queens, New York, street in 1964. Genovese's neighbors were castigated because they saw (or heard) her plight and failed to act in a situation where action was possible (at least by calling the police). In addition, national broadcast news and newspaper coverage of the incident sparked citizens around the country to reflect on the loss of community (in New York City, in urban areas more generally, and in the nation as a whole). This broader reflection did not, however, carry with it any deep-seated sense of obligation for viewers or readers to act – Genovese was not *their* neighbor. In the current environment, it is increasingly the case that media audiences are more like Genovese's neighbors than like the viewers and readers of her story. That is, we are increasingly in mediated situations in which we come to know other people (at least as well as Genovese's neighbors knew her); in which we see these people in need of help; in which we have a real economic, cultural, or political connection to them; and in which it is possible for us to do something. As Susan Sontag (2003) argues, viewing mediated events is a collective act that creates a kind of community, but at the same time, there is nothing predetermined about the nature of that community. The new discursive environment creates new and heretofore unimaginable communities of moral obligation – obligations that cannot be defined mechanistically but rather are essentially contestable and in need of constant public discussion and clarification.

This is not to say that the new discursive environment's impact on community is always a positive one. One can argue, for example, that participation in a virtual community such as that provided through World of Warcraft has the effect of drawing participants' attention away from other, more relevant communities to which they have a moral obligation. Similarly, the nationalization and globalization of media may be contributing to the deterioration of local community and the loss of local social capital (Putnam 2000). Even more alarming is the way in which the possibilities for online organizing have given new life to racist groups in the United States and across the globe. Of concern, as well, is the fragmentation of the audience, discussed in Chapter 3, which undermines the possibility of broader democratic dialogue and political engagement. As Colin Leys (2001, 164) asks, if "the idea of television as a medium of the public sphere, a forum for the 'main formative conversation of society,' come[s] to seem as quaint and outdated as the stagecoach ... then where, if anywhere, would such a conversation occur?" The answer to this question – and to the question of who participates in formulating it – is one of the crucial challenges facing the formation of a new media regime.

Equally troubling for notions of community is the dominance of market populism in setting the current discursive environment, which we discussed in Chapter 3. The danger is, as Cass Sunstein (2001) argues, that we will lose contact with a broader public, hearing instead, simply "the echoes of our own voices," as when mediated messages of all forms are tailored for and targeted at specific individuals on the basis of information gathered from their past selections. Politically, we are in danger of coming to believe that our preferences and values are more widely shared than they actually are, as more and more of the information we receive is specifically chosen to be consistent with those values and preferences.

In short, there is nothing inevitable about the impact of the new media environment on notions of community or democratic politics. As Sontag (2003, 116) has argued, the pervasiveness of images of suffering can only provide "an invitation" to pay attention. Constant exposure to the pain of others may actually encourage looking away through what Susan Moeller (1999) calls compassion fatigue. At its best, new media can provide unique and exceptionally appealing invitations not just to pay attention but also to actually participate. Yet the new discursive environment will not inevitably lead to either improved or degraded notions of community – this will ultimately depend on the rules and norms governing the media regime that will emerge over the coming several decades.

Given this, it is crucial that we remain aware of the political relevance of a much more varied set of communications genres and technologies than was the case in the past regime. What is clear already, however, is that the new environment has changed and will continue to change – for better or worse – current notions of community and the moral and political obligations associated with them. In doing so, it also changes the way in which we must assess the democratic potential of the new media environment.

Conclusion

In the first half of this book we have argued that significant changes in the role of media in a democracy result both **from** changing economic, political, cultural and technological conditions (including telecommunications technologies) and from the norms, processes, and institutions (what we call the media regime) that develop from political struggles over these changes. The emerging media regime shapes the resulting discursive environment and so, in turn, shapes future economic, political, cultural, and technological conditions. In the United States, this interplay has led to several very different media regimes, most recently, the Age of Broadcast News, which defined the latter half of the twentieth century. Recent changes have radically altered the media environment in which we live, overwhelming the ability of this existing regime to control the flow of information, to shape the discursive environment, and even to distinguish between politically relevant and politically irrelevant media.

The transitional period we are in will almost certainly lead to a new media regime. There is nothing inevitable, however, about the contours of this new regime and the discursive environment it shapes. As in the past, these outcomes will depend on political struggle and the specific policy decisions that result. The challenge in shaping this new regime is not to determine how to re-create the authoritative political-information hierarchy of the past – for better or worse, that battle has already been lost. Instead, the challenge is to create a media regime that can preserve the best features of past regimes, including the Age of Broadcast News, while fully realizing the potential of the new media environment to provide the opportunities for a wide variety of voices, interests, and perspectives to vie for the public's attention and actions. We believe that such a regime is preferable – more democratic – to assuming a priori that any particular group or interest should have the power to set the agenda. But whether or not one agrees with this assessment, there is no returning to the past regime, in which a limited set of elites served as sole gatekeepers and agenda setters.

Moreover, it is vital to not unreflectively accept the standards and values of the passing media regime as necessary or even desirable. If, for example, we judge a media regime by how well it fosters a more informed citizenry, the Age of Broadcast News did a remarkably poor job. As many scholars have noted, despite dramatic increases in the average level of education and an increase in access to sources of information, Americans in the 1980s showed no improvement in levels of political knowledge over the earliest days of survey research in the 1940s (Entman 1989; Delli Carpini and Keeter 1996). As well, this media regime witnessed precipitous declines in virtually all forms of political participation. We are not arguing that the Age of Broadcast News and the rise of television as its dominant medium caused these trends, only that this media regime clearly did nothing to improve matters.

We use the concepts of hyperreality and multiaxiality to highlight the degree to which the assumptions of the Age of Broadcast News are no longer applicable. Though often decried by scholars and journalists for suggesting a vertiginous relativity, these concepts do not challenge the existence of reality but make clear that defining politically relevant truth has always been essentially contested, even when stable media regimes obscure this contestation. Media in the United States have always played a central role in shaping contestation over how to define political reality and assertions about politically relevant truth that inevitably flow from such definitions.

Hyperreality and multiaxiality suggest the need for a definition of politically relevant media broad enough to capture the potential impact of the new environment on democratic politics. Making such definitions explicit is especially vital now, as political decisions are made that will institutionalize a new media regime with its own answers to enduring questions of media and democracy, such as which citizens should be part of democratic deliberation, who serves as producers, who serves as consumers of politically relevant information, how trustworthy the information available to citizens is, and whether the information received is adequate (in amount, form, and content) to increase the likelihood of informed and ethical political decisions.

As a starting point for debate, we outlined a definition of politically relevant media emphasizing their influence on the way citizens understand, deliberate over, and act on the conditions of everyday life of individuals and communities, as well as the broader structures of power that shape these conditions. We now use this definition, along with the concepts of hyperreality and multiaxiality, as guides for exploring the pitfalls and promises of the new media through three very different case studies of media and politics: the Clinton-Lewinsky scandal, public discourse regarding environmental policy, and the terrorist attacks of September 11, 2001.

5

Politics in the Emerging New Media Age

Hyperreality, Multiaxiality, and the Clinton Scandals

> President Clinton landed at lunchtime at Greater Cincinnati Airport.... Democratic politicians in the region who might have found a way to be there, had the President not been in such deep political trouble, stayed away.
> – R. W. Apple, *New York Times*, September 18, 1998

> After the game, I'm watching the news, and I see a commercial for that "Titanic" video where they show the hundreds of people jumping overboard and abandoning ship. Then I realize it's not the "Titanic" – this is the news. It's Democrats leaving the White House.
> – Jay Leno, *The Tonight Show with Jay Leno*, October 28, 1998

> We are living in an era where the wall between news and entertainment has been eaten away like the cartilage of David Crosby's septum.
> – Al Franken, *Rush Limbaugh Is a Big Fat Idiot and Other Observations*, 1999.

In mid-January of 1992, the *Star*, a national tabloid specializing in stories about the personal lives of celebrities, published an article in which Gennifer Flowers claimed to have had a twelve-year affair with Bill Clinton, then the front-runner for the Democratic nomination for president of the United States. The story was initially downplayed in the mainstream press, in part because the allegations were two years old. It was also initially ignored because the *Star*, described in one mainstream newspaper article as better than most of the national tabloids but still a step below the *National Enquirer*, was deemed an unreliable news source.[1]

---

[1] The blurring between news and entertainment is exemplified by the fact that the *National Enquirer*'s own reputation had been enhanced and begrudgingly acknowledged by members of the mainstream press as a result of its reporting during the O. J. Simpson trial.

The decision by Bill and Hillary Clinton to directly address the issue by appearing on *60 Minutes* (a choice made in part because the show would air immediately following the Super Bowl and thus give them access to a very large audience) brought it more centrally into the mainstream press.[2] The Clintons, who helped perfect the art of using the nontraditional media for political ends, also appeared on shows like *Primetime Live*, *Donahue*, *The Arsenio Hall Show*, and MTV either to directly refute or to deflect the allegation. Although the Clintons' efforts were successful in rallying public support and partially diffusing the controversy, the alleged affair had gained some legitimacy within the mainstream press as a campaign issue – members of the press could point to the existence of legitimate sources (e.g., the Clintons themselves) and to the fact that other traditional news outlets were covering the story to justify their expanded coverage. The press could also justify covering what was initially defined as a private matter by focusing on the issue of whether the president was "lying" to the public.

Nearly seven years later, the Clinton presidency stood at the brink of dissolution, rocked by another sex scandal and another controversial Star(r) report – this time that of Independent Counsel Kenneth Starr – focusing on, among other things, an alleged affair between President Clinton and a White House intern named Monica Lewinsky. By the fall of 1998, all notions that one could make clear-cut distinctions between serious and less serious news outlets, between news and non-news genres, even among sources, producers, and consumers of news, had been effectively destroyed. Whether one started the day by listening to National Public Radio or Howard Stern, by watching *Good Morning America* or CNN, by reading the *New York Times* or the *National Enquirer*, by seeking out information through traditional venues or emerging online sources, or by e-mailing a friend or- talking to a coworker, the topic was the same. Viewers of daytime talk shows such as NBC's *Leeza* could watch a panel – consisting of a Washington newspaper correspondent, a public relations expert who worked with celebrities, a gossip columnist, and a television star who had gone through a very public divorce – discuss the way Hillary Clinton was handling the media spotlight. An internet search for "Monica Lewinsky" would produce more than twelve

---

Indeed, the *Enquirer* has been nominated for a Pulitzer Prize for its reporting on the John Edwards sex scandal.

[2] Tellingly, the advent of *60 Minutes* is viewed by many as the point at which the networks began to view their news divisions as potential revenue sources.

thousand options, ranging from breaking news reports to "the Monica Lewinsky Fan Club."[3] E-mails sharing the latest Clinton-Lewinsky jokes were commonplace in offices around the country.

The early evening local and national news competed not only with one another but also with the online Drudge Report (fifty thousand hits per day at the height of the scandal, a large proportion of which were mainstream journalists themselves) and television tabloid shows like *Entertainment Tonight*, *Hard Copy*, and *A Current Affair* (the latter two whose names had taken on interesting double meanings) for the latest details and interpretations of the scandal. Prime-time dramas and comedies either made direct references to the scandal or their usual fare of sex, infidelity, power, and conspiracy took on new meanings. All-news cable networks like MSNBC, CNN, and Fox News, and their political talk shows such as *Hardball with Chris Matthews*, *Rivera Live*, *The O'Reilly Factor*, and *Hannity & Colmes*, became virtually all Monica, all the time. Late-evening news was no different, to be followed into the wee hours by more "discussion" of the scandal by news anchor Ted Koppel; comedians Jay Leno, David Letterman, Bill Maher, and Conan O'Brien; and crossover personalities like sportscaster-turned-newscaster Keith Olbermann. One could literally spend twenty-four hours a day watching, listening to, or reading about the latest chapter of the Clinton-Lewinsky affair and, should one choose, do so without picking up a daily newspaper or tuning into a network news show.

Reflecting the ability of the new media to obliterate time and space, the story flowed instantaneously across national borders, where it also crossed genres and audiences. For example, while "serious" commentary in Israeli newspapers focused on the impact of the scandal on prospects for a Middle East peace settlement, commercials for a spot remover on Israeli television spoofed the scandal (private detectives searching Lewinsky's closet are distressed to find a can of the advertiser's spot remover lying next to "the dress"). Similarly, the scandal dominated the mainstream British press and was also used in commercials to sell a newspaper's weekly job listings (a Clinton impersonator asks his aide why he should be interested in the new job listings, as he already has a job. After a pause, he says, "Oh, yeah, maybe I should take a look").

---

[3] These numbers, as well as those reported later herein, seem small by today's standards, but at the time, they were quite dramatic. Indeed, the fact that they appear so small to us today is further indication of the scope and rapidity of change in the new media environment.

The personal lives of public officials have been part and parcel of U.S. politics since the nation's founding. However, the gatekeepers who set and frame the process and establish the norms for covering such issues have changed over time. Central to this gatekeeping process is the media. For example, the degree to which sexual indiscretions have been considered newsworthy, the extent of coverage, and the political and social meaning attached to this coverage have varied over time in ways that can be illustrative of the shifting media regimes discussed in the first four chapters of this book.[4] During the Age of Broadcast News, media gatekeepers were in a powerful position to determine when and if sexual indiscretions became sex scandals. From the 1930s through the 1960s, extramarital affairs by major public figures such as Franklin Roosevelt, Dwight Eisenhower, and John F. Kennedy, though well-known to journalists, were considered private matters that fell outside the existing definition of news. This standard began to shift in the mid-1970s, with the disclosure of House Ways and Means Chair Wilbur Mill's relationship with the "Argentine Firecracker," stripper Fannie Fox. Between 1974 and 1994, the alleged sexual impropriety of no fewer than twenty-two congressmen and senators became news stories, including, in 1984, the emerging front-runner for the Democratic presidential nomination, Gary Hart.[5]

However, although standards for the newsworthiness of the sex lives of elected officials had begun to shift, during this period the primary justification for coverage remained tied to a particular definition of public relevance. As the journalist Ken Ringle, reflecting on changes that had occurred within the news profession, wrote in a 1998 *Washington Post* column:

Most veteran political reporters have sleuthed at some point after illicit relationships involving governors and attorneys general and legislators and congressmen, whether or not such escapades could be confirmed and written about. And most of us have walked away from more of those stories than we've written, sometimes because we couldn't document them sufficiently and sometimes because, however titillating or sordid we found the Democrat or Republican involved, we decided it was none of our business. Not every sex act of a politician involves the public's

---

[4] The accusations leveled at Bill Clinton were primarily about sexual indiscretion. However, as we discuss later in this chapter, they included allegations of other personal failings and political abuses that combined into a single narrative.

[5] Even in this period, journalists continued to successfully opt for not making reasonably well-established rumors of sexual indiscretion public, as with those surrounding President George H. W. Bush in the 1980s.

need to know.... [The difficulty] is deciding how much to investigate rumors of an officeholder's discreet but chronic sexual adventuring. Does it involve questions of character that reflect on performance in public office? Does it involve criminal conduct? If it's clearly predatory or the exploitation of a professional underling or becomes very public through legal proceedings... that's obviously a story. (Ringle 1998, B1)

Crucially, during this bygone period, it was professional journalists who decided what constituted newsworthiness and whether a particular allegation met that definition. And once such a decision was made, the news media's authoritative position usually meant that their interpretation was accepted – of the twenty-two cases of congressional sexual indiscretion reported between 1974 and 1994, seventeen congressmen either resigned or were defeated for reelection.

According to the journalists and media critics Bill Kovach and Tom Rosenstiel (1999, 2), "No event signals the changing norms [of journalism] as much as the Clinton-Lewinsky scandal." Indeed, the Lewinsky affair, coupled with a litany of other allegations of impropriety leveled at the Clintons (e.g., other affairs, sexual harassment, misuse of power, even murder) represented a sea change in media coverage far more dramatic and significant than that of Congressman Mill's affair, with more in common with the media regime of the late eighteenth and early nineteenth centuries than the mid-twentieth century. However, despite these similarities – the more overtly political use of innuendo and rumor, the parallels between media figures such as James Callender and Matt Drudge, the blurred lines between entertainment and public affairs – it would be a mistake to see media coverage of the Clinton scandals as they developed between 1992 and 2000 as simply a return to the dark ages of the press.[6] Nor, as many thoughtful journalists and media critics believed, should it be seen as simply a momentary failing that could be remedied by reestablishing the norms and practices of "traditional" (i.e., twentieth-century) journalism. That model of news and political communication – one based on clear-cut distinctions between fact and opinion, public affairs and entertainment, mainstream and fringe political actors, or producers and consumers – is of little help in understanding the dynamics of the information flows related to the Clinton scandals.

---

[6] The writer James Callender, while working at the behest of the anti-Federalists led by Thomas Jefferson, leveled accusations about the sexual and financial misdeeds of Alexander Hamilton. Later, disillusioned at being abandoned by the patrician Jefferson, he unearthed accusations about the patriarch of Monticello's illegitimate children with the slave Sally Hemings.

Rather, these scandals, the way they were consciously constructed and used by conservative opponents of the Clintons, and the way they came to dominate political discourse, need to be understood in the context of the profound economic, political, cultural, and technological changes discussed in Chapter 3 of this book. Occurring as it did at the very moment when the media regime that had dominated the second half of the twentieth century was breaking down, this nine-year media spectacle offers a unique window into the implications of the changing information environment for mediated politics in the United States, implications that, though perhaps less visible, are as relevant to the coverage of day-to-day politics as to moments of political turbulence.

In this chapter, we provide an interpretative recounting of this crucial period in American politics, a period that while consisting of a number of disparate subplots arguably constituted a single, nearly decade-long media event. This media event did not happen spontaneously but was the result of what Hillary Clinton described as "a vast right-wing conspiracy" and that the right-wing pundit Ann Coulter, in a flip response to Clinton's remark, described instead as "a small, intricately knit right-wing conspiracy" (Brock 2003, 196). Its construction, maintenance, and impact depended on many of "the usual suspects," including established leaders of both the Republican and the Democratic parties and journalists from the mainstream print and electronic news media, as well as many of the traditional levers of political power such as the electoral, legislative, and legal systems. And it required a president whose personal behavior before and once in office was morally questionable and politically risky. But, we argue, it also depended heavily on the breakdown of the media regime that dominated the latter half of the twentieth century and on the new information environment's emergent qualities of hyperreality and multiaxiality.

Hyperreality: The Clinton Scandals as a Media Event

As we noted in Chapter 4, Fiske (1996, 2) argues that the driving force in contemporary public discourse is not objective reality but "media events," defined as "an indication that in a postmodern world we can no longer rely on a stable relationship or clear distinction between a 'real' event and its mediated representation."[7] Also recall that this blurring is not a simple

---

[7] As we noted in Chapter 4, concept of a media event has also been used by Dayan and Katz (1992). Although the two uses are similar in some ways, there are several important

matter (as it might be seen through the lens of traditional journalism or social science) of a failure to distinguish truth from falsehood. Put another way, media events themselves become significant "social facts," regardless of their accuracy as representations of the real. Finally, recall that within the hyperreal, one can no longer "distinguish clearly and hierarchically between the modes of its representation" (Fiske 1996, 62).

The Clinton scandals were nothing if not hyperreal. As established by a careful reading of the independent counsel's own report (Starr 1998), as well as by a spate of post hoc investigative reports and tell-all confessionals by several of the principals (see, e.g., Conason and Lyons 2000; Brock 2003; Kovach and Rosenstiel 1999), with few exceptions, the various "events" that collectively constituted the Clinton scandals were a mix of past accusations that had already been publically vetted (e.g., the Clinton's Whitewater financial dealings, the Gennifer Flowers affair, the alleged use of Arkansas state troopers to facilitate and cover up other sexual encounters), unsubstantiated accusations (e.g., Kathleen Willey's claims of sexual harassment, Gary Aldrich's "sensationalized, fantastically exaggerated" account in 1996 of goings on in the Clinton White House), telling though relatively trivial excesses of power (e.g., the firing of the White House travel office staff), and outright absurdities (e.g., the "murder" of deputy White House counsel Vince Foster). The facts specifically surrounding the Monica Lewinsky affair – Did Clinton engage in inappropriate sexual behavior? Did he lie about this behavior? Did he commit perjury? – were both new and, for a period at least, in doubt, although whether uncovering these facts deserved the amount of attention it received was and remains questionable, especially among the very journalists who covered it. Indeed, members of the mainstream news media regularly and publically questioned and critiqued their own coverage as they engaged in it.

Ultimately, what mattered most in the ongoing media discourse of the Clinton scandals was the discourse itself. The "truth" surrounding the various events was inextricably tied to and ultimately overshadowed by their media representations – Bill Clinton's televised denials of inappropriate sexual relations to the American public; Hillary Clinton's claims of a vast right-wing conspiracy; the barrage of interpretations by partisan pundits, lawyers, and comedians; the nonstop release of rumors, leaks,

---

differences. For obvious reasons we believe the Clinton scandals come closer to Fiske's than to Dayan and Katz's type of media event. We return to the significance of these different definitions of media events in Chapter 7.

and reports; the sounds and images of private phone conversations and grand jury testimony. The sometimes serious, sometimes satirical or skeptical, representation of these and other moments through the news, talk shows, entertainment programs, websites, and e-mail exchanges often built on the same set of mediated "facts" but deployed them in distinct ways. On other occasions, these competing epistemologies met head-on, as on shows like *Politically Incorrect*, where guests drawn from entertainment, academia, politics, and the news media periodically discussed the latest revelations or rumors connected to the scandals.

These sometimes distinct, sometimes intersecting discourses blurred any notion of a hierarchy between fact and fiction, or between news and non-news.[8] For all the information available, and the speed with which it was available (President Clinton received Starr's report to Congress only an hour before the rest of the American public did), there was and still is no consensus on all but the most rudimentary facts, because there was no longer a meaningful distinction between facts and their representation. In a world in which we have the ability to use the science of DNA testing to "prove" the occurrence of an event, but in which such evidence has no guarantee of carrying any more authority than a comedian's satirical comment or a lawyer's definition of sex, what does it mean to talk about the objective facts?[9] In short, in the new information environment mediated representations become "social facts" on which elites and citizens alike base their understanding of and participation in political life – the very definition of *hyperreality*.

Our point is that the dynamics of the Clinton scandals are better understood in the way one might deconstruct a novel, film, or – perhaps most usefully – a long-running television drama, soap opera, or reality television show than through the more clinical, rational standards of professional journalism. At stake was not (or not only) the accuracy of the facts but the way their collective representation produced a narrative

---

[8] For an insightful "insider" account of the interplay among mainstream and new media, see Isikoff 1997.

[9] Of course, the DNA evidence did lead Clinton to finally acknowledge his sexual relationship with Lewinsky but had little discernable or lasting effect on public opinion. In contrast, in the O. J. Simpson case, the science of DNA testing itself could be challenged by further appeals to science, to beliefs in the corruption and/or ineptness of the police, and to inherent assumptions of racism, thus reducing this evidence to the status of opinion at best and even to "proof" that Simpson was being set up and thus was not guilty. More recently, as a result of the CSI effect, which we discussed in Chapter 4, DNA evidence has been seen by juries as so conclusive that its absence may make convictions in certain cases difficult.

structure, character development, moral and political lessons, and so forth. This nine-year saga had numerous plot twists constructed out of disparate (and often questionable or unsubstantiated) events, such as the Whitewater land deal; the alleged misuse of FBI files; the firings at the White House travel office; the suicide of Vince Foster; and the accusations of sexual misconduct leveled by Gennifer Flowers, Paula Jones, Kathleen Willey, Monica Lewinsky, and (on behalf of others) Linda Tripp. Absent the authoritative gatekeeping role of professional journalists, these separate "news stories" were transformed into a media event with its own complex, shifting, and competing meanings. In this hyperreal world, the specific "facts" – important as they were – became mere vehicles for political discussion, deliberation, and debate, operating simultaneously at various levels: from issues at the institutional level, such as the future of the Clinton presidency, to more deep-seated, foundational issues, such as political corruption, public and private trust, sexual mores, and workplace harassment.

From this perspective, the Clinton scandals were as much rooted in events as diverse as Watergate; the political and cultural movements of the 1960s; and the O. J. Simpson, Louise Woodward, and JonBenét Ramsey trials – as in the Whitewater, Paula Jones or Monica Lewinsky cases. It was also rooted in popular culture genres (films, television dramas and comedies, novels, and music) that addressed many of the same foundational issues. Sometimes these connections were obvious – terms like *Whitewatergate*, *Filegate*, *Travelgate*, and *Fornigate* tied the Clinton scandals to those of the Nixon administration and, in doing so, tied the former to the long-standing public cynicism about government that the latter engenders.[10] Films like *Wag the Dog*, *Primary Colors*, and *An American President*, and television shows like *Spin City* – direct commentaries on the contemporary state of politics – occasionally became part of the discourse about the Clinton scandals. For example, when the U.S. bombed a Sudanese pharmaceutical plant that was allegedly manufacturing chemical weapons, Kenneth Starr was asked by a reporter whether he had seen *Wag the Dog* (in which a fictional president creates a fake war as a diversion from a sex scandal) and whether he saw any parallels. If he didn't, Saddam Hussein did: earlier in the year, Iraqi television broadcast

---

[10] Indeed, the Clinton financial and sex scandals themselves have become part of this larger hyperreal narrative, as demonstrated by their resurrection (through the publication of several books on the topic, regular commentary by pundits such as Dick Morris, website and blog exchanges, and political humor) during Hillary Clinton's 2008 presidential bid.

a pirated copy of the movie at the height of tensions over U.N. weapons inspections and U.S. threats to launch air strikes. And an MSNBC story noted that a statement by President Clinton explaining his initial concerns over ordering the strike sounded remarkably like one made by the fictional president in *An American President* under similar circumstances.

Consider, as well, the best-selling novel *Primary Colors*, published anonymously (by reporter Joe Klein) in 1996 and released (during the height of the Monica Lewinsky scandal in 1998) as a major Hollywood movie starring John Travolta. This fictionalized but thinly veiled insider's account of the 1992 Clinton presidential bid provided a subtle, engaging, and insightful analysis of the motivations – both political and personal – of Bill Clinton that simultaneously challenged and reinforced those found in the other mediated representations, including the traditional news media.[11] In turn, this image of Clinton the man and the politician became part of the larger conversation surrounding the Lewinsky scandal, exemplified by Desson Howe's (1998) movie review in the *Washington Post*. The review moves seamlessly between plot summary and commentary on the film as a work of fiction (i.e., a traditional movie review), on the one hand, and explicit social and political commentary, on the other hand. For example, in the second paragraph of the review, Howe (1998, N47) writes:

But if you're living in Lewinsky-Tripp Hell – i.e. late 20th-century America – you could do worse than sit back and watch John Travolta and Emma Thompson playing the aspiring First Couple. "Primary Colors" is ... a thinly veiled excuse to relive the country's number one obsession: the transparent, yet enigmatic soul of William Jefferson Clinton.

The review is peppered with real-world parallels. He notes that the lead character (former Governor Jack Stanton) "is a guy who actually seems to give a damn about people – even if he does pull out false Reaganesque anecdotes to amplify his sensitivity"; that the idealistic aide "joins the campaign and starts the bumpy ride familiar to any of us with a living room, a TV and CNN"; that viewers will "relish the interface between reality (at least, the reality as learned from the accursed media) and fiction." Even his criticisms of the movie focus on the public interest aspects of the film: "First, the bad news: The final third of the picture

---

[11] In many ways, both the novel and the film version of *Primary Colors*, written by a journalist and based on real-world, contemporary events, hearkens back to the novelized "true" stories of the Realist Era discussed in Chapter 2.

becomes more fictionalized – and therefore useless to most of us looking for Stanton/Clinton parallels"(N47).

Or consider two television broadcasts – a 1999 ABC special and a 2002 HBO special – both of which featured Monica Lewinsky giving a personal account of her affair with Clinton and her reactions to its aftermath. The ABC special, which was watched by nearly 49 million viewers (twice the number of any other prime-time show broadcast that week) featured an in-depth interview of Lewinsky by Barbara Walters, whereas in the HBO special, Lewinsky fielded questions from a live audience of young adults. Though easy to dismiss as either mere entertainment or even exploitation, both broadcasts served, in ways that paralleled *Primary Colors*, to place a human face on "that" woman, Lewinsky, while also raising foundational issues ranging from gender relationships in situations of unequal power to generational politics to the role of the media in modern life.

Is *Primary Colors* "fact" or "fiction"? Is Howe's piece a movie review or a political commentary? Were the HBO or ABC specials public affairs broadcasts or a variant of reality entertainment programming? These are questions that are increasingly meaningless in the hyperreality of today's media environment. Often, the connection between popular culture and the Clinton scandals was more subtle, based on the similarity of the underlying issues, values, or beliefs that were tapped rather than on direct references to contemporary events or politics (e.g., the corrupt and promiscuous character of Mayor Quimby regularly featured on *The Simpsons*). But this larger media environment, even when it never made specific reference to the Clinton scandals, was critically important in setting the context in which the scandals were constructed and interpreted.

Viewed in this light, the journalistic touchstone of objectivity becomes nearly meaningless, and the somewhat deeper notions of truthfulness or truth seeking take on a very different, more complex meaning. The focus of traditional journalists and news reporters is on uncovering the truth as defined by standards of factual accuracy – who did what, when, where, and how. In a hyperreal world, however, the truth becomes a much broader concept (similar in many ways to that found during the Realist Era of the nineteenth century) intended to capture the extent to which the claims made explicitly or implicitly by and through the media help citizens understand, think about, and ultimately deliberate and act on the issues under discussion.

Even using the traditional journalistic notion of truth (defined by objectivity, balance, and factual accuracy), the news media often fell short in its coverage of the Clinton scandals, hence the ongoing lament within the profession regarding its poor use of sources, the publishing of unsubstantiated rumors, and so forth. And given the relatively limited set of knowable "facts" involved in this issue, using alternative media sources such as cable television, radio talk shows, tabloid newspapers and magazines, internet sites, late-night entertainment television (e.g., *The Tonight Show with Jay Leno, Late Show with David Letterman, The Daily Show*), and hybrid genres such as *Politically Incorrect* would have provided about as much basic factual information as the more traditional news outlets.

Focusing (as journalists themselves did) on whether the traditional news media got their facts right or on the relative accuracy of news coverage as compared to alternative media sources, though important, misses two larger and more important points. First, absent in such a discussion is the crucial question, "The truth about *what*?" Neither the question of whether President Clinton had sex with Monica Lewinsky (or whether any of the other allegations of sexual, financial, or political impropriety) were accurate, nor the question of would he be impeached and convicted, were, ultimately, the central issues. Rather, these were symptoms of more foundational political and social issues, such as the inter- and intraparty power struggle over control of the national agenda, public trust in government, ethics and morality, and gender politics. There is little reason to think that a regular viewer, listener, or reader of the national news would have come away with the information necessary to grapple with these issues in a meaningful way, in part because the structure and norms of journalism were not designed to allow or encourage such discourse.

Second, had the mainstream news media downplayed the scandals or covered them in a way that was more in line with their journalistic norms and ideals, would it have mattered? Such behavior may have led to a very different discursive environment with potentially different effects on the Clinton administration's ability to govern. But given that by the late 1990s alternative genres and mediums were already usurping journalists' gatekeeping role (though to a lesser degree than is the case today), it is equally possible that the Clinton scandals would have still dominated much of public discourse and thus the administration's behavior, with the only result of journalists' constraint being a greater and more rapid awareness of their declining authority. Indeed, it was just such a Hobson's choice that drove much of the mainstream news media's behavior during this period.

Politics in a Multiaxial Media Environment

Were hyperreality the only consequence of the changing media environment, one might conclude (as many postmodernists have) that political communication, at least in the traditional sense of information about the struggle over control of government, is no longer meaningful. To the contrary, however, the blurring of reality and its mediated representation increases the importance of political communication, as its role shifts from simply presenting the facts on which the traditional struggles over the authoritative allocation of goods, services, and values (Easton 1965) take place, to constructing and using those "facts." At one level, this is not new – from Walter Lippmann's (1922) "pictures in our heads" to the agenda-setting theory of McCombs and Shaw (1972) and Iyengar and Kinder (1987), George Gerbner and colleagues (1986) cultivation analyses, and Robert Entman's (1989, 2004) studies of media framing, researchers have understood the power that mediated politics holds in shaping public understandings of the world.

What is new, however, is that the hyperreality of media events, coupled with the breakdown of the traditional news media's gatekeeping function, has created what Fiske calls multiaxiality, or a more fluid and unstable notion of political power in which access to and even control of the media environment is no longer automatically ceded to a handful of political and media elites. Traditionally, the political agenda has been shaped by a symbiotic relationship between mainstream political actors and major news outlets (Bennett 1998; Hallin 1986). In this relationship, the media act as a monolithic gatekeeper while a limited set of political elites vie with one another (and the media) to shape the agenda and how it is framed. The public is reduced to a passive consumer, whose own attention to and interpretation of events is constrained by this limited information environment.

By the 1990s, this single-axis system was being transformed in four ways. First, the expansion of politically relevant media and the blurring of genres led to a struggle within the media itself for the role of authoritative gatekeeper – elite papers such as the *New York Times* competed with the *National Enquirer*, network news competed with twenty-four-hour cable stations and internet sites, journalists competed with comedians, and so forth. Second, the expansion of media outlets and the obliterating of the normal news cycle created new opportunities for a greater number and range of nonmainstream actors to influence (often in concert with more mainstream actors) the setting and framing of the political agenda.

Third, elements of the new media environment (e.g., e-mail, chat rooms, and, for more recent media events, instant messaging, text messaging, Twitter, social networking, and blogging) allowed citizens (as individuals and collectivities) to influence the public agenda, either indirectly through vertical communication with the plethora of old and new media outlets or directly through horizontal communication that completely bypassed more established venues of any kind. And fourth, this new system was quite fluid and unstable, allowing different media and different actors to ebb and flow in their influence, depending on the circumstances and their ability to effectively manipulate the circumstances. As a result of these changes, the gatekeeping role that had allowed the mainstream news media, in concert with a handful of established elites, to create and frame the political agenda was eroding. The traditional news media and traditional elites were in the unfamiliar position of vying or cooperating with numerous other actors for these gatekeeping and agenda-setting roles.[12]

Consider Salon.com's (1998) unusually candid explanation for publishing an online article revealing a twenty-five-year extramarital affair by Republican congressman and Clinton critic Henry Hyde. This unsigned editorial begins with a brief explanation of how the story was brought to Salon's attention:

Two weeks ago, Salon editor David Talbot received a phone call from a 72-year-old retiree in Aventura, Fla., named Norm Sommer. Sommer asserted that Henry Hyde, the chairman of the House Judiciary Committee, had between 1965 and 1969 carried on an extramarital affair with a married woman named Cherie Snodgrass. At the time of the affair Hyde was an Illinois state representative, married and the father of four sons. Sommer was told of the affair seven years ago by Cherie Snodgrass' ex-husband, Fred Snodgrass. During a tennis game, Snodgrass, a friend and tennis partner, had blurted out the story of the affair and how it had ruined his family.

It also acknowledges Sommer's political motives but also his political independence:

Norm Sommer, the man who did lead us to the story, categorically denied to us that he had any connection to the Clinton administration.... [However] Sommer's motivation, he readily admits, was political.... [H]e is a lifelong Democrat

---

[12] As we discussed in Chapter 2, such struggles between older established information sources and their newer challengers have been a staple of transitions in American media regimes. And as the media historians David Mindich (1998) and Michael Schudson (1978, 1998) demonstrate, theses battles are always about class, status, and political power.

who served as a Henry Wallace delegate at the 1948 presidential convention. Sommer says he was outraged by what he called the "bloodless coup" carried out by the Republicans over Whitewater and the Lewinsky scandal.

Later in the piece, they describe Sommer's circuitous route to Salon.com:

"Not only am I not connected to [the Clinton administration,] I couldn't get anyone there interested," he said, adding that he also called the Democratic National Committee but that he "never heard back from anyone." Sommer said he called the White House and the DNC to get advice on how to get his story out: "I tried to get the story out for seven and a half months. I've spent hundreds of hours and called dozens of people in the media, without success." Among the various publications he contacted in a futile effort to air the story were the Los Angeles Times, Boston Globe and Miami Herald. He finally turned to Salon, he said, when he heard the Web magazine mentioned on a TV talk show.

Finally, the editors attempt to justify their publication of the story:

Aren't we fighting fire with fire, descending to the gutter tactics of those we deplore? Frankly, yes. But ugly times call for ugly tactics. When a pack of sanctimonious thugs beats you and your country upside the head with a tire-iron, you can withdraw to the sideline and meditate, or you can grab it out of their hands and fight back.

The Salon.com piece captures many of the elements of the then still-emerging multiaxial media environment. The "source" was a seventy-two-year-old retiree with political motives but few political connections. The story was initially rebuffed by both mainstream political and news gatekeepers, who in an earlier era could have kept the story from ever seeing the light of day. However, Sommer had alternatives available to him – in this case, Salon.com – thanks to the proliferation of new entry points into the public sphere. The editors of Salon.com were hesitant to publish the story but did so because of the new politicized news environment that had muddied issue of newsworthiness, objectivity, propriety, and so forth. They were also unusually candid in explicitly discussing their rationale for publishing the story, an openness in stark contrast to the more traditional journalistic practice of making the news seem to come from nowhere. And once broken by Salon.com, the mainstream media were "forced" to cover (and mainstream political elites were "forced" to address) the very issue that they had rejected earlier.

Published postmortems of the Clinton scandals document numerous other examples of the mainstream media covering stories that they had initially deemed unreliable or not ready for airing or print because of the

fear or fact of being scooped by alternative media (Kovach and Rosenstiel 1999; Brock 2003; Conason and Lyons 2000; Isikoff 1997). Indeed,
throughout the Clinton scandals, the mainstream press frequently paused
to reflect negatively on its own practices in an effort to recapture its
preeminent position in the agenda-setting and issue-framing hierarchy.[13]
Ironically, this often meant acknowledging that the issue was garnering
more coverage than traditional definitions of newsworthiness would call
for. But the existence of multiple news outlets, seminews outlets, entertainment media, new hybrid genres, and the internet, all of which were
"covering" the scandals, made it impossible for either the mainstream
press or traditional political elites to ignore or downplay these scandals without further risking their own relevance to the agenda-setting
process. And of course, it did not hurt that covering the scandal was
at least perceived by media owners as good for the increasingly important bottom line. The result was far from mainstream journalism's finest
hour:

[Coverage of the Clinton scandals is] also the story of important journalists and
news organizations succumbing to scandal fever, credulously and sometimes dis-
honestly promoting charges against the Clintons in heavily biased, error-filled
dispatches, columns, bestselling books, and TV news specials, and thus bestow-
ing "mainstream" prestige upon what was often little more than a poisonous
mixture of half-truth and partisan malice. Some conducted themselves as if their
mission were less to inform the public than to guard their institutional prestige by
protecting their own erroneous reporting from correction. (Conason and Lyons
2000, xv)

The dynamics of this emerging multiaxial media environment can be seen
more broadly in the pattern of coverage that characterized the Paula Jones
allegations of sexual impropriety by Clinton.[14] While mainstream coverage ebbed and flowed throughout most of 1994 (driven largely by events
in the civil suit), and all but disappeared throughout 1995 (as a result of
legal appeals that put much of the case on hold), a number of alternative
media outlets stuck consistently to the story, keeping the issue firmly on

---

[13] Recent attempts by the news media to police itself also point to this crisis in defining
journalism; for example, the firing of several reporters and columnists at the *Boston
Globe* and *Washington Post* for inaccurate reporting, the resignation of Carol Marin, a
local newscaster, in protest over the hiring of talk-show host Jerry Springer, the decision
by ABC to not air a docudrama by Oliver Stone about the downing of TWA Flight 800
out of fear that it would confuse viewers, the ongoing criticism of public journalism by
mainstream members of the press, and so forth.

[14] A similar pattern existed for coverage of the Gennifer Flowers scandal, although it was
shorter in duration.

a subterranean agenda. It was not until 1997 that the Paula Jones issue became an ongoing news story in the mainstream press, driven largely by events surrounding the civil suit and the increasingly inflammatory rhetoric coming from both the Clinton and the Jones camps. Although in some ways this increased attention suggests that the mainstream news media had recaptured control of the political agenda, most of the stories written or aired during this period were initially generated through leaks, reports, and rumors that first emerged over the internet, from conservative publications, and/or from the cable talk shows. Thus, the mainstream press had more firmly embraced the issue as newsworthy, but it was still reacting to an agenda that was being framed largely by others. Mainstream news sources like the evening news and the prestige newspapers were also disadvantaged by the collapse of the normal twice-a-day news cycle and its rapid replacement with twenty-four-hours-a-day breaking news (Kurtz 1998).

For all the attention generated by the Paula Jones case, it paled in comparison to the explosion of coverage that began with the allegation in January of 1998 of President Clinton's affair with a White House intern. The last ten days of that month generated more newspaper stories on the new allegations than all the articles and commentaries written on Gennifer Flowers and Paula Jones combined. Although journalists continued to periodically stop and reflect on whether this was a topic worthy of so much attention, or to lament the decline in journalistic standards in reporting, by 1998, the mainstream news media had in practice essentially succumbed to the new system. Alternative media figures (most notably Matt Drudge) continued to indirectly shape mainstream media coverage but also emerged as commentators or guests on "serious" news shows like *Meet the Press*. At the same time, mainstream print journalists and news reporters appeared with greater frequency on network and cable talk shows, both a reflection of their increased celebrity and a concession to the shifting balance of power in the media. Major publications like *Newsweek*, the *New York Times*, and the *Washington Post* "prepublished" and updated their stories on the internet, allowing the public to see the normally hidden process of constructing the news. Competing news outlets began to use one another – and in at least one case indirectly used itself – as sources for their stories.[15] The commentary of comedians like Jay Leno, David Letterman, Bill Maher, and Al Franken occasionally

---

[15] One major news organization published what later turned out to be an erroneous story on its website. The story was then picked up from the website by a competitor, leading

became the topic of the next day's news stories, whereas the day's news was increasingly the subject of that evening's late-night monologue.

In short, in the six-year period from the publication of the *Star* expose to the publication of the Starr report, traditional journalism lost its position as the central gatekeeper of the nation's political agenda. For most of that period, the news media attempted to play its traditional role and found that the political agenda was being set without them. As a result, it adapted to the new, if still amorphous, "rules" by increasingly mimicking the form and substance of its new media competitors.

Just as the new information environment created multiple axes of power within the media, it also created new axes among the political actors who shape the media's agenda. Authoritative sources have been traditionally limited to largely mainstream political, economic, and social elites: elected officials, spokespersons for major interest groups, and so forth. These sources, while attempting to shape the media environment in ways that would benefit their particular political agenda, understood and largely operated within the rules of traditional journalism. But the new media environment, with its multiple points of access and more continuous news cycle, has increased the opportunities for less mainstream individuals and groups to influence public discourse, often in concert with more mainstream actors. This was certainly the case in the Clinton scandals (Kurtz 1998; Kovach and Rosenstiel 1999; Brock 2003; Conason and Lyons 2000; Isikoff 1997).

Though perhaps falling short of Hillary Clinton's claim of "a vast right-wing conspiracy," the attacks on Bill Clinton's financial and sexual behavior were orchestrated in large part by the religious and partisan far right. Of particular interest to us is the way this traditionally marginalized group effectively exploited the new media environment to create new axes of power.[16] For example, when Gennifer Flowers first went public with her affair, her contract with the *Star* was negotiated by John Hudgens, an Arkansas businessman who had been press secretary to two of Clinton's Republican challengers for governor. And it was Floyd Brown (head of the independent Presidential Victory Committee that produced the infamous Willie Horton political spot in 1988) who set up the 900 number on which

the first news organization to reaffirm the story using the second organization's story as confirmation!

[16] In the case of the Clinton sex scandals, it was conservative groups outside the mainstream that were best able to exploit the new media environment, but we make no claims that this was the only possibility: in other circumstance and certainly for other issues, very different groups could be equally successful.

callers could listen to excerpts from the taped conversations between Clinton and Flowers. The Flowers affair was also kept in the news when the ultraconservative congressman Robert Dornan read the entire *Star* expose into the *Congressional Record* while being broadcast on C-SPAN.

In December 1993, the *American Spectator*, a conservative monthly magazine, published the first reports that then governor Clinton had used state troopers to facilitate his rendezvous with Flowers and other women. The troopers' lawyer was Cliff Jackson, a former Oxford classmate of Bill Clinton and later critic who had been the source of the story about Clinton's draft dodging during the Vietnam War. It was Jackson who approached the American *Spectator* about doing the Troopergate story, which was then picked up first by CNN and subsequently by other major news outlets. Jackson also organized the 1994 news conference (sponsored by the Conservative Political Action Conference) in which Paula Jones announced her intent to file a sexual harassment suit against Clinton.

The Jones story was also initially kept in the news through conservative publications like the *Washington Times* and the *National Review*. When the mainstream press failed to cover the story with enough vigor, the conservative media-watchdog group Accuracy in Media ran ads in the *Washington Post* and the *New York Times* criticizing them for ignoring the issue. By that time, Floyd Brown, then heading an organization called Citizens United, was acting as a clearinghouse for incriminating information about Clinton and providing leads to conservative GOP congressional aides and reporters from both mainstream and nonmainstream media. The religious right also played an important role in maintaining the anti-Clinton media campaign. Jerry Falwell produced and distributed a video titled *Circles of Power*, which "documented" a host of alleged ethical and moral violations of the president. And the television evangelist and one-time Republican presidential candidate Pat Robertson interviewed Paula Jones on his nationally televised program.

Conservative groups found other creative ways to draw media attention to the Clinton scandals. In 1996, the former FBI agent Gary Aldrich published *Unlimited Access*, which alleged numerous (largely unsubstantiated) improprieties within the Clinton White House. In addition to becoming a best seller that was released in paperback as the Lewinsky scandal was at its peak, it was also given away free as an incentive to join the Conservative Book Club. In 1997, the Free Congress Foundation ran radio spots in Washington, D.C., offering to pay any "victims of Bill Clinton" who would step forward and tell their story. And in that same year, Judicial Watch, headed by Larry Klayman, initiated a suit on behalf of State Farm Insurance policyholders, alleging that the company wrongly paid for some of President Clinton's legal bills as a result of a personal liability policy he held. The suit allowed Klayman to depose a number of Clinton administration people and ask about a wide range of topics. Klayman then became a regular guest on a number of talk shows, such as *Rivera Live*, where he aired selected portions of the videotaped depositions.

To be sure, many mainstream conservatives and Republicans were often willing accomplices and even key players in this effort to discredit Clinton and recapture the reins of power. As Conason and Lyons (2000, xiv–xv) note:

[T]he effort to destroy Clinton began early on in the highest councils of the Republican National Committee, and included aides to former president George [H. W.] Bush. Arguably even the chief justice of the United States himself was not entirely aloof from the great crusade.

But as they and others also note, "[s]wept up in their movement's anti-Clinton fervor, these respectable figures sometimes eagerly joined forces with persons of considerably lesser repute" (Conason and Lyons 2000, xiv). These included

longtime Clinton adversaries from Arkansas and elsewhere; an angry gallery of defeated politicians, disappointed office seekers, right-wing pamphleteers, wealthy eccentrics, zany private detectives, religious fanatics, and die-hard segregationists who went beyond mere sexual gossip to promote rumors of financial chicanery, narcotics trafficking, and even politically motivated murder. Some were mobilized by spite, other by ideological zeal, and more than a few by the prospect of personal profit. Some shared all three motives. (Conason and Lyons 2000, xiv)

This multiaxial alliance between mainstream and fringe actors was strengthened with the Republican congressional victories of 1994, in which many representatives of the latter became part of the former, thus blurring the distinction between mainstream and fringe elements of this conservative insurgency movement. And crucial to our argument, this alliance and its successes were made possible by the changes in the information environment discussed in Chapter 3:

No president of the United States and no first lady have ever been subject to the corrosive combination of personal scrutiny, published and broadcast vilification, and official investigation and prosecution endured by William Jefferson Clinton and Hillary Rodham Clinton. In historical terms, certain of the mechanisms

necessary to inflict this kind of punishment – from the Office of the Independent Counsel to the twenty-four hour news "cycle" and the Internet – are quite
recent innovations. All have been brought to bear against the Clintons and their
associates with stunning effect. (Conason and Lyons 2000, xiii)

In summary, a network of conservative foundations, public officials, private citizens, and alternative media organizations was able to significantly
influence the course of politics at a crucial point in American history. They
did so by sometimes operating outside of mainstream politics, sometimes
in coordination with the mainstream, and ultimately taking control of
it. Though largely failing in more traditional institutional settings (e.g.,
the courts, the independent counsel's office, the impeachment process),
they succeeded in dominating the public agenda and public discourse for
much of Clinton's eight years in office. And, we argue, none of this would
have been possible were it not for the collapse of the media regime in
place during the latter half of the twentieth century, the resulting hyperreality of politics, and the newly emerging axes of mediated political
power.

Lessons from the Clinton Scandals

The media regime that dominated the second half of the twentieth century
was supported by a set of institutional structures and practices designed
to distinguish fact from opinion, public affairs from popular culture,
news from non-news, and expert producers from citizen-consumers. In
this system, politically relevant information, narrowly defined as recent
events involving the people, processes, and institutions of government was
the exclusive purview of professional journalists, the news organizations
for which they worked, and the political elites they covered; and it was to
this part of the media that the public was assumed to turn when engaging
the political world.

For better or worse, by the late 1990s, this hierarchical, Lippman-
nesque notion of citizens', elites', and journalists' involvement in public
discourse about politics was becoming dismantled by the technological,
cultural, political, and economic changes discussed in Chapter 3. New
technologies such as cable and satellite television, personal computers,
and the internet provided a plethora of competing new outlets for the
mass dissemination of information. Traditional news cycles were disrupted, as were the economics of news and public affairs genres. Relationships between journalists, citizens, and elites; between mainstream

and nonmainstream elites; and between consumers and producers of public information were altered. The socially constructed and institutionally maintained lines (in terms of both content and genres) between hard news and soft news and more generally between entertainment and news became simultaneously more visible and more porous. In this changed environment, the existing rules of the game regarding the definition, production, consumption, and use of politically relevant information became increasingly ineffective, irrelevant, and counterproductive.

Although the ramifications of these changes could be seen in coverage of several media events during this transitional period – most notably the video-game-style cable news coverage of the 1991 Persian Gulf War, coverage of Clarence Thomas's nomination to the Supreme Court and the subsequent allegations of sexual harassment brought by Anita Hill in 1991, and the media frenzy surrounding the O. J. Simpson murder allegations in 1994 and 1995 – the Clinton scandals constituted the first major media event that brought together the numerous elements of the new media environment. Playing out as they did over the last decade of the twentieth century, the scandals and how they were represented particularly illuminate what we have argued are the periodic and relatively discrete moments in time when external forces conspire to challenge the authority of existing media regimes. They are also instructive for understanding the emerging characteristics of the information environment in which we currently live.

As discussed in both Chapter 4 and this chapter, one defining characteristic of this new information environment is hyperreality. This concept is meant to capture the dominance (in shaping public discourse) of media representations over the underlying reality being represented. It is also intended to capture the diverse range of media and genres that play a role in the construction of these representations. The choices of what issue or event to emphasize (Clinton may have had extramarital sex with Monica Lewinsky, but there was no sex scandal absent its mediated representations), how to represent it (Was it a personal failing? A high crime or misdemeanor? A vast right-wing conspiracy? A trivial matter to be made light of?), and through what media or genre (Mainstream news? Documentaries? Late-night talk shows? Stand-up comedy? Fictional films or docudramas? Internet chat rooms and websites?) were as important as – or more important than – the protracted public debate over this issue than was any set of "objective facts" or any journalistic notion of "inherent" political relevance. In short, the Clinton scandals demonstrated how mediated representations can create "social facts" that are only loosely based on "objective facts," and how these social facts can drive subsequent deliberation and action.[17]

Reinstating the institutional and political controls that underpinned the Age of Broadcast News, even if it were possible, is no solution to these dilemmas, as it would neither curtail the more ominous tendencies of the new media environment nor take the greatest advantage of its democratic potential. We say this because the changes occurring in the late twentieth century did more than challenge journalistic norms regarding the determination of what was politically relevant (as illustrated by journalists' numerous laments and self-reflections during the Clinton era) and provide news organizations with greater pressures, incentives, and opportunities to decouple mediated representations from any meaningful underlying reality (as illustrated by the fact that journalists continued to cover the scandals even as they questioned the newsworthiness of what they were covering). They also challenged the mainstream news media's control of this process, thus eroding professional journalists' gatekeeping role (a hallmark of the Age of Broadcast News) and allowing a host of alternative "political" actors (including fringe political groups, comedians, and citizens themselves) to influence the social construction of the scandals.

The issue of who controls the flow of information is an important one, one that is often missed in much of the theorizing regarding the impact of the new media environment. This oversight is caused, we believe, because of its hyperreal, decentralized, even anarchistic tendencies. But as illustrated by the Clinton scandals (and discussed more broadly in the first part of this book), although the new environment has greatly complicated issues of who controls and shapes the mediated political agenda, it has not eliminated them. Specifically, this new environment, with its wide range of politically relevant media and genres, has altered power relationships from a single axis largely controlled by the mainstream news media and the mainstream elites with which they interact to one with multiple axes and a much larger, fluid set of potential political actors and coalitions. This multiaxiality – the second core characteristic of the new

---

[17] Although in its most extreme, Baudrillardian sense, *hyperreality* sometimes is interpreted to mean the literal inability to distinguish reality from its mediated representation, one need not go to this extreme to find utility in the term. Viewers and readers can "understand" that they are watching a docudrama or listening to a comedian, and even "know" that what they are watching does not comport with the "objective" facts, but still be affected by or make use of the information in the social construction of their opinions.

media environment – manifests itself in two ways. First, it allows previously marginalized publics (e.g., the right-wing groups that, albeit with the collaboration of key mainstream actors, were instrumental in fueling much of the Clinton scandals) to influence the substance and tenor of mainstream-mediated discourse by taking advantage of the numerous alternative media outlets available to them. Second, these same new pathways can be used, separately or in conjunction with each other, to bypass the mainstream media entirely, thus creating multiple discourses around the same topic.

Combined with hyperreality, multiaxiality creates a much more fluid, unpredictable, and polysemic discursive environment, one that Fiske (1996, 7) describes metaphorically as "a river of discourses":

At times the flow is comparatively calm; at others, the undercurrents, which always disturb the depths under even the calmest surface, erupt into turbulence. Rocks and promontories can turn its currents into eddies and counter-currents, can change its direction or even reverse its flow. Currents that had been flowing together can be separated, and one turned on the other, producing conflict out of calmness. These are deep, powerful currents...and these discursive "topics" swirl into each other – each is muddied with the silt of the others, none can flow in unsullied purity or isolation. Media events are sites of maximum visibility and maximum turbulence.

This new environment offers reasons for both concern and hope regarding its democratic potential. On the one hand, the loss of journalistic control of the media agenda, the absence (or inapplicability) of norms regarding the public interest responsibilities of various types of media, the devaluing of facts as a central component of reasoned public discourse, the ability of unrepresentative fringe actors with self-interested goals to capture or shape (either on their own or in partnership with mainstream elites) the media agenda, the potential loss of any sense of a larger national community or national conversation, and so forth, are worrisome. On the other hand, the new media environment has the potential to give the public new ways, as a collectivity and as separate social, economic, political, and cultural communities, to become one (or more) of the axes of power through which political discourse occurs, thus expanding the concepts of democratically relevant citizens and politically relevant media, blurring the lines between producers and consumers of news, and providing a more useful public sphere for deliberating about and acting on complex political issues.

These complicated dynamics and conflicting tendencies can be seen in media representations of the Clinton scandals, a media "event" that was, as Fiske describes, a site "of maximum visibility and maximum turbulence." As will become clearer in subsequent chapters, we believe that absent governing norms and practices (i.e., absent an established media regime), the new media environment is inherently unstable, and thus which issues become part of public discourse, through which media and genres, at what level of politics, and with what consequences is highly context dependent. In addition, the information environment has become even more complex since 2000, which makes conclusions drawn from this period tentative at best. Nonetheless, several tendencies that emerged from the Clinton scandals are worth noting.

This period suggests that even with the complex and decentered nature of the emerging new information environment, large-scale events that simultaneously capture the attention of the media (in its various forms), political elites, and the public are still possible. The Clinton scandals were a constant theme of mediated discourse throughout his administration and dominated this discourse during its last two and a half years. Although the public and political agenda was focused on these issues, however, the interpretation of events varied dramatically, producing the "rivers of discourse" described by Fiske (1996). These discourses occurred across a wide range of media and genres and involved a wide range of political and social actors. They resulted in a host of sometimes parallel, sometimes competing, and sometimes intersecting narratives, all of which were only loosely tied to or dependent on "the facts" as understood during the Age of Broadcast News. They moved in fluid ways across the three levels of politics (institutions and processes, substantive policy issues, and foundational issues) discussed in Chapter 4. And they varied in their usefulness for "understanding, deliberating, and acting on the conditions of one's everyday life, the life of fellow community members, and the norms and structures of power that shape these relationships," our definition of politically relevant media.

Underlying the seemingly anarchistic nature of these discourses, however, was a political struggle, a struggle for control of the media agenda and, through it, the authoritative allocation of goods, services, and values. Mainstream news media and political actors were no longer the sole arbiters of what does or does not become a media event and how it plays out. As often as not, professional journalists were reacting to rather than driving this process throughout the 1990s. And although established political elites – especially social conservatives – were able to use the multiaxial and hyperreal media environment to their advantage, they could do so only by "joining forces with persons of considerably lesser repute."

In addition, the very definition of mainstream elites shifted as moderate officeholders were replaced by more doctrinaire conservatives. Nonetheless, it would be a mistake to conclude from this that traditional elites no longer mattered. Rather, politics remains in large part a struggle over control of the reins of government, but in the new information environment, this struggle is more complicated, more fluid, and less predictable than in the past. Multiaxiality can, depending on circumstances and skill, advantage political insiders and outsiders, those in power and those in opposition; but it is a double-edged sword that is not easily wielded or controlled.

Finally, despite the hyperreal nature of the new media environment, the ways in which media events play out have real political consequences. Most obvious was the impeachment of a sitting president, the resignation or damaged reputations of several sitting members of Congress, the Republicans' winning control of Congress in the 1994 elections, and their subsequent losses in the 1998 congressional elections. The lost opportunities for the Clinton administration to address other important national and international issues and the narrow defeat of Al Gore in the 2000 presidential election could also be at least partially traced to the Clinton scandals and how they were mediated. And foundational public attitudes about everything from sex and marriage to trust in government were undoubtedly influenced by this extended and multifaceted media event.

Taken as a whole, the social construction of the Clinton scandals suggests to us that the new media environment contains important, often contradictory, and competing elements of all the past media regimes discussed in the first half of this book: the explicitly partisan discourses of the late eighteenth century; the sensationalism and populism of the penny press; the expansive notions of truth, truth seeking, and politically relevant media characterizing the Realist period; and the professionalization and elitism of politics and journalism that emerged during the Progressive Era and evolved into the centralized and hierarchical system that dominated the Age of Broadcast News.

What are the democratic perils and promises of this hyperreal, multiaxial, and as of yet ungoverned media environment? Although it is difficult to say with any confidence, again we believe the mediated construction of the Clinton scandal is instructive. We have argued that the new media environment allowed nonmainstream conservative groups to help set the news media's agenda, but its impact on the larger media agenda and, most important, on the public's agenda is much less obvious. Public-opinion polls throughout this period showed remarkably little movement, and much of the movement that did occur was in the direction of increased support for the president – exactly the opposite of what traditional agenda setting, framing, and priming theory would predict (Zaller 1998).[18]

This stability could be interpreted as evidence that in the new media environment the "public" (collectively and as separate economic, political, and cultural communities) is free to construct its own interpretation of political reality. Opinion surveys and media-market analyses suggest that the public followed the ongoing story (through a variety of media) and knew the central issues and "facts." Yet despite the efforts of the president's supporters and detractors to frame the issue, a large majority of the public created their own narrative that was consistent with neither group's interpretation: The president had an affair and lied about it to the public and in his deposition and testimony (despite his denials). This affair (and other allegations of sexual misconduct) lowered their estimation of Clinton's already-questionable moral character (despite his attempts to salvage his image). At the same time, and in the face of concerted efforts by Clinton's detractors, the public consistently separated this issue from his ability to govern; said that it was ultimately a private matter; and opposed resignation or impeachment, instead favoring either dropping the issue or imposing some form of mild censure. Arguably, the ultimate resolution of the scandal (with the significant exception of the president's impeachment) was closer to the public's preferred outcome than that of either the president or his opponents.

But there is another, less optimistic interpretation of these events and public reaction to them. Although Clinton ultimately remained in office, his sexual infidelity (and his opponents' exploitation of this personal failing) shaped a substantial part of the media's agenda for seven years and dominated it for another year; led to the impeachment of a popularly elected president for the first time in U.S. history; and turned both the public's and the government's attention away from other, more substantive issues. And all this was done with maximum media attention and minimal public response. From this perspective, the public's attention to this unfolding drama was no different from how it might have been to a particularly engrossing episode of *Survivor*, *American Idol*, or *The Osbournes*. In short, national politics had been reduced to a sometimes amusing, sometimes melodramatic, but seldom relevant spectator sport.[19]

---

[18] But see Keeter (1999) for an argument suggesting that political science theories of presidential approval may account for this pattern of stability and change.

[19] The fact that the public's reaction to charges of sexual harassment in the Paula Jones or Kathleen Willey cases (or to alleged campaign finance violations by the Clinton-Gore

Both of these interpretations of public reaction to the Clinton sex scandals suggest that media events may play a greater role in setting the public agenda than in framing it.[20] But determining whether reaction to such mediated events reflects an autonomous, reasoning public or massive public indifference is crucial to understanding the current and future state of democracy in the United States. At the heart of this issue is the new media environment's ability to help citizens move from observing the political world to acting in it. Our conclusion is that, at least at the level of the institutions and processes of politics, little in the media environment as it addressed the Clinton sex scandals effectively encouraged or facilitated such engagement. To the contrary, coverage by traditional news outlets, political talk shows, late night entertainment talk shows, political comedies, even the internet seemed much more likely to instill a sense of passiveness, frustration, alienation, and apathy. This is perhaps unsurprising given the news media's elitist frame and the entertainment media's largely cynical one.[21] Using our definition of politically relevant media, all of these genres were quintessentially political but not democratically useful.

Conclusion: Media and Politics since the Clinton Scandals

Viewed as curiosities in the early 1990s (to the extent they existed at all) and as unexpected and unpredictable political forces by the late 1990s, cable and satellite news and commentary, talk radio, documentaries and docudramas, fictional and fictionalized movies and dramas, daytime and late-night talk television, internet websites and blogs, and e-mail are now integral mediums and actors in all facets of politics. This hyperreal and multiaxial media landscape has changed the behavior of mainstream elites and brought new political actors – including the public – more centrally

---

campaign) were similar to those expressed in the Monica Lewinsky case supports this rather pessimistic view. Perhaps more tellingly, the involvement of U.S. military forces in Kosovo could not hold the public's attention at all.

[20] Unexplored in this chapter is the impact of the new media environment in the absence of an overriding media event. Under these quite common circumstances, the typical pattern is a fracturing of the ability of the media or political elites (mainstream or not) to even set an agenda that holds the attention of anything like a majority of the public; we turn to this type of issue in the next chapter.

[21] One of the few exceptions to this conclusion was Rush Limbaugh, who often connected his diatribes to specific actions people could take, or aspects of the internet that did encourage people to at least register their views through bulletin boards and chat groups of certain kinds.

into the mix. Although the implications of these changes are still in flux, four observations are worth highlighting.

The Transformation of Day-to-Day Politics

The new media environment has transformed the day-to-day operation of politics in important and increasingly institutionalized ways. National candidates, parties, and their affiliated political organizations regularly use the internet to raise campaign funds, a technique largely developed by John McCain's 2000 campaign for the Republican presidential nomination and refined in subsequent campaigns by Howard Dean (in 2004) and Barack Obama (in 2008). First exploited by Howard Dean and his national campaign adviser, Joe Trippi (2004), the internet now serves as an important medium for contacting, recruiting, organizing, and mobilizing supporters through a combination of candidate, party, and organizational websites; targeted and viral e-mails; social networking sites such as Facebook, MySpace, and MeetUp.org; and video-sharing sites such as YouTube. Alternative media also serve as increasingly common platforms for candidates to present themselves to the public in more relaxed, conversational settings, thus demonstrating their "authenticity." For example, the 1992 decisions by Ross Perot to announce his independent presidential run on *Larry King Live* and by Bill Clinton to appear on *The Arsenio Hall Show* and MTV created a firestorm in the journalistic community. Fifteen years later, Larry King seems more like a journalist than an entertainer, and national candidates routinely announce their political plans to the public (and the news media) through non-news television shows such as *The Daily Show*, *The Late Show with David Letterman*, and *The Tonight Show with Jay Leno*; more recently through their own websites and videos; and on occasion through an orchestrated combination of both (as with the announcement of former U.S. senator and actor Fred Thompson's 2008 presidential candidacy). Candidates also create serious, humorous, or eye-catching videos to be distributed on the web; for example, Senator Sam Brownback's introduction of his run for the presidency through a low-tech YouTube video of him casually dressed and speaking directly to the camera, Barack Obama's remix of a classic Apple ad originally aired during the 1984 Super Bowl, and Hillary Clinton's takeoff of the final episode of *The Sopranos*. Such videos then circulate throughout the new media environment, creating viral buzzes reinforced and fueled by cable and network news "coverage." Candidates also sometimes embrace videos created by independent sources; for example, the "I Love Obama" YouTube video that spawned "I Love Rudy" and "I Love Hillary" spinoffs. Even the virtual world has become part of candidates' political strategy, as when Democratic presidential hopeful Mark Warner (or more accurately, his avatar) held a town hall meeting on Second Life. And ideological talk radio (e.g., *The Rush Limbaugh Show*, Air America) and talk television (e.g., Fox News's *The Sean Hannity Show*, MSNBC's *Countdown with Keith Olbermann*) increasingly serve as outlets for candidates to make their case to a sympathetic host and audience.

The Double-Edged Sword of the New Media Environment

Although, as illustrated here, changes in the media environment provide significant opportunities for political elites, they also raise new challenges. On the one hand, they allow candidates to bypass and influence the mainstream news media, as well as to more effectively reach either sympathetic or new supporters. They also allow candidates to target and craft their substantive messages, requests for financial support, and voter mobilization efforts with much greater precision than ever before. On the other hand, they often require ceding greater autonomy to individual and group supporters who can use the social networking and user-produced content aspects of the new media to interpret "support" in their own ways, ways that can at times be at odds with the campaign's own message or strategy. They provide opportunities for opposing candidates and their supporters to use the new media to mount challenges in new, creative, and sometimes surreptitious ways. The result is a campaign and governing process that is sometimes more interactive and democratic, sometimes more manipulative and opaque, but always hyperreal, multiaxial and – as a result – more unpredictable.

Consider, for example, the struggle for control of the Republican Party in the aftermath of the 2008 Obama victory. Volumes of political theory and research would suggest that such a victory would move the opposition party (in a two-party system) to the center. And yet just the opposite has happened. Since Ronald Reagan's 1980 victory, Republicans had used a successful strategy of courting social conservatives during campaigns but governing from a more pragmatic perspective that allowed them to enact conservative policies (and dismantle more liberal ones) while maintaining control of government.[22] By the time of the Clinton presidency,

---

[22] In the twenty-eight years from 1981 to 2008 Republicans controlled the presidency for twenty years, the House for sixteen years (with two more years evenly split), and the majority of state governorships and legislatures. And where Democrats controlled the U.S. Senate for sixteen of those twenty-eight years, Republicans did so for twelve of the last fourteen.

however, this tiger-by-the-tail strategy, coupled with a changing media environment, had empowered the far right both within and outside the government, thus making moderate, pragmatic politics increasingly difficult. After eight years of an increasingly unpopular presidency of George W. Bush, the relatively moderate John McCain won the Republican nomination but, contrary to popular wisdom, was forced to move to the right during the campaign and selected the socially conservative Sarah Palin as his running mate. And since the Obama victory, members of the already quite conservative Republican Party have found themselves facing serious primary opposition from the far right.[23] More generally, the Tea Party movement, along with other fringe groups such as the Birthers (who claim that Barack Obama is not a U.S. citizen), 911Truth.org (whose members believe the U.S. government was responsible for the terrorist attacks), and the Oath Keepers (who want candidates for office to swear they will abide by their literalist interpretation of the U.S. Constitution) have continued to pressure Republicans to adhere to their ultraconservative views. These movements have energized the most conservative parts of the party's base; have forced candidates, officeholders, and the party as a whole to the right; have increased the power and/or visibility of fringe figures such as Sarah Palin, Ron Paul, and Michele Bachmann; and have contributed to gridlock in government.

The Democrats have not been immune from the complexities created by the new political and media environment. The 2008 Obama campaign clearly benefited from both its own innovative use of new media and from the support of a number of left-of-center organizations and individuals. At the same time, this loose and independent coalition (including the virtual interest group MoveOn.org, independent filmmakers such as Michael Moore, the recently defunct Air America Radio Network, left-leaning cable television talk show hosts such as Keith Olbermann and Rachel Maddow, and blogs such as The Huffington Post and The Daily Kos) has led to many of the same (though arguably less effective) pressures on Democratic candidates and officeholders that Republicans have faced from the far right. Caught on the horns of this dilemma, as the Obama administration engages in the compromises required to achieve legislative success, it is immediately confronted with threats from the newly mobilized and now quickly alienated left wing.

Although the difficulty of maintaining ideologically diverse coalitions is not a new phenomenon in U.S. party politics, the dynamics of this

---

[23] Debra Medina's challenge to Rick Perry in Texas, J. D. Hayworth's to John McCain in Arizona, and Mark Rubio's to Charlie Christ in Florida, to name but a few.

process have been altered significantly in the hyperreal and multiaxial new media environment. Insurgents on the right and left have effectively used e-mail, blogs, websites, social networking sites, user-generated content, ideologically sympathetic talk shows, and the like to spread their message, increase their visibility, organize and rally supporters, and raise money, thus creating unprecedented opportunities and challenges for established political elites. The new media environment also affects the speed, scope, and fluidity of these opportunities and challenges, all with uncertain implications not only for the Republican and Democratic parties but also more broadly for the state of democratic politics.

The Political Uses of Scandal (and Rumor and Conspiracy)

Our third observation about politics in the new media environment is the growing use of scandals, rumors, and even conspiracy theories as a political strategy in the new information environment. As we noted in the opening of this chapter, political scandal is not new in American politics. The same can be said about rumors and conspiracy theories. But the new media environment has made their strategic political use more possible and common. Hyperreality has blurred the distinction between a mediated event and its factual underpinnings, giving them greater credence and thus impact, regardless of their importance or even truth. Multiaxiality has increased the number and range of actors who can shape the discursive environment and the number of entry points into the mediated public sphere these actors have available to them. At the same time, the authority of professional journalists to act as authoritative gatekeepers, and so as arbiters of what is or is not accepted as true, has declined precipitously. The proliferation of mobile phones, cameras, video cameras, and databases increases the ability to uncover or allege personal or institutional impropriety. And the networked, multiplatform nature of the new information environment allows a mix of facts, rumors, and allegations to circulate, grow, and morph in unpredictable ways. For example, in just the past few years, racist statements by George Allen, Trent Lott, and Harry Reid; sex scandals involving John Edwards, Mark Foley, and Larry Craig; financial improprieties by Tom Delay, Charles Rangel and William Jefferson; and even far-fetched conspiracy theories such as U.S. government involvement in the destruction of the World Trade Center towers, the effort by Democrats to create "death panels" as part of health-care legislation, and the cover-up of President Obama's true citizenship have become part of the media and political discourse, sometimes distracting from and sometimes influencing struggles over the authoritative allocation of goods, services, and values.

Politics in the New Media Environment Is Unstable but Not Random

Our final observation is that, although the new media environment contributes to less stable and less predictable politics, its effects are not random. Rather, the contemporary relationship between media and politics reinforces a central argument of this book: the uses to which media are put, by whom, and to what end are and always will be a matter of political power and political struggle. Multiaxiality, hyperreality, and other characteristics of the new environment can shift power relationships and allow for a different and larger range of actors to enter this struggle, but they offer no guarantee as to whether this restructured playing field will enhance or detract from the substance and quality of democratic discourse. In the mediated world of politics, the politics of the media matters, a point that is true not only for the construction of dramatic and high-profile media events such as the Clinton scandal but also for representations of more ongoing but crucial public issues. It is to just such an issue – global warming – that we now turn.

6

When the Media *Really* Matter

Coverage of the Environment in a Changing Media Environment

> To me the question of the environment is more ominous than that of peace and war.... I'm more worried about global warming than I am of any major military conflict.
>
> – U.N. Weapons Inspector Hans Blix, March 14, 2003

> Through "balanced" coverage, the mass media have misrepresented the scientific consensus of humans' contribution to global warming as highly divisive.... Such coverage has served as a veritable oxygen supply for skeptics in both the scientific and political realms.
>
> – Boykoff and Boykoff (2004, 134)

> This is a movement about change, as individuals, as a country, and as a global community. Join the 935,104 supporters of the Stop Global Warming Virtual March, and become part of the movement to demand our leaders freeze and reduce carbon dioxide emissions now.
>
> – StopGlobalWarming.org, 2004

In May 2004, *The Day after Tomorrow*, a $125 million Hollywood blockbuster (with a $50 million advertising budget) opened in American theaters. Directed by Roland Emmerich (*The Patriot, Godzilla, Independence Day*), the movie told the story of a sudden ice age brought on by the collapse of ocean currents caused by global warming. The elaborate special effects depicted the destruction of New York City and Los Angeles by killer hurricanes and giant tidal waves. As is typical for many summer blockbusters, the film opened to decidedly mixed reviews but did well at the box office, grossing $187 million during its American theater run. Yet the movie was more than a mindless summer distraction, it was also a political text that initiated a fresh round of public dialogue, albeit brief, about global warming. Coming just a few months before the 2004

168

presidential election, the film's portrayal of a disengaged president, a venal and powerful vice president, and an administration in denial about global warming was seized on by both environmentalists and climate-change skeptics. The controversy over the movie and the actual threat of global warming became the subject of an intense flurry of newspaper coverage, which moved across the arts and entertainment, science, news, and op-ed sections. So, using the definition of politically relevant media that we suggested in Chapter 4, *The Day after Tomorrow* played a role in shaping opportunities for understanding, deliberating, and acting on (1) the conditions of one's everyday life, (2) the life of fellow community members, and (3) the norms and structures of power that shape those relationships. We also hasten to add that *The Day after Tomorrow* was by no means the first feature film to play such a role in coverage of the environment. *The China Syndrome* (1979, directed by James Bridges), a story about an accident at a nuclear reactor starring Jane Fonda and Jack Lemmon, was the subject of a similar debate, which was cut short, ironically, when the accident at Three Mile Island occurred twelve days after the movie's release.

Seeing *The Day after Tomorrow* as politically relevant, rather than ignoring it as mere entertainment, focuses our attention on how this particular text influenced debate over global warming. Most obviously, the movie set the agenda in ways both similar to and different from the role of more traditional sources of political information like the nightly news broadcasts. Just as the tabloid press set the agenda in the case of the Clinton-Lewinsky scandal, in this case, a movie set the agenda of the mainstream press, thus initiating a flurry of newspaper and magazine articles. According to a search of the Vanderbilt Television News Archive using the film's title, there were ten network news stories on the movie, five of which discussed the controversy over its accuracy, a remarkably high number given that, in 2004, there were only twenty stories about global warming or climate change, as we discuss here. At the same time, fears or hopes that the movie would have a lasting political effect were groundless, as the issue of global warming scarcely surfaced during the 2004 presidential election.[1] Further, as suggested by the notion of agenda setting, the film didn't seem to change many minds – it didn't tell the writers of these articles what to think, but it clearly worked to influence what people, at least newspaper writers and readers, thought about.

---

[1] We might also add that, absent a feature movie and given the focus on the economic crisis, the issue of climate change was even less in evidence during the 2008 election.

Those convinced that global warming was a pressing problem, that the U.S. government must take more aggressive action, and that it should be a central issue in the coming election recognized the limits of the scientific basis of the film but welcomed its impact on public discourse:

[I]f "Day" is a hit, it could conceivably fire the public imagination in a way that decades of scientific white papers and congressional testimony have been unable to do. So what if the speed of the climactic shift is absurdly rapid in the film – a matter of days, as opposed to the scores of years predicted by even the most pessimistic of experts? Dan Schrag, a real-life paleoclimatologist at Harvard, recently pooh-poohed the movie's science in *Variety* but admitted that "getting people excited about something that happens over decades is difficult, so I understand why they shortened it to a couple of days." (Burr 2004, N17)

Those who denied the seriousness of global warming were also prompted to join in the debate over the film. Joseph Perkins, a columnist for the *San Diego Union-Tribune*, focused on the problem of serious issues being debated through nonserious and one-sided media:

[T]he public dialogue, the political debate about global warming ought not be driven by Hollywood. Ought not be influenced by bad science in the form of cinematic entertainment. Indeed, filmgoers who attend "The Day After Tomorrow" will be none the wiser that there is continuing dispute about global warming within the scientific community.... The movie does not apprise them that many respected scientists believe that planetary warming is not nearly as pronounced as alarmists suggest. And that much of the warming that actually has been detected is natural, rather than anthropogenic (caused by human activity). (Perkins 2004, B7)

An article in the *Denver Post* starts by trying to reassure readers that, when it comes to the catastrophic impact of global warming portrayed in the film: "Most rational scientists think it will happen in 10 to 50 years, as opposed to overnight."[2] Assuming, as does Perkins, that there is scientific disagreement over the issue, the article then adopts the "he said, she said" approach so typical of American news organizations when it comes to global warming, by citing one scientist who says the science in the movie is flawed but the threat is real, and then citing another who says that science in the movie is flawed and the threat is not real (Booth 2004).

---

[2] How the statement that most rational scientists believe that we are facing the end of civilization as we know it in as little as ten years is supposed to reassure us is left unexplained.

The outrage by journalists over *The Day after Tomorrow* might have been more persuasive if they were doing a better job of covering global climate change. In early 2002, the Larsen B ice shelf (roughly the size of Rhode Island) in Antarctica fell into the ocean. Scientists estimated that this was the largest ice-shelf collapse in more than ten thousand years and was a result of warming temperatures in Antarctica. Somewhat ironically, this event occurred soon after the screenwriters of *The Day after Tomorrow* wrote a similar scene of a catastrophic ice-shelf collapse for their movie. According to one newspaper account: "After the Larsen B collapse, Emmerich and [Jeffrey] Nachmanoff reportedly joked that they should have been making a documentary, and the cream of the jest is that if they had, it would be playing to an audience in the thousands instead of the millions" (Burr 2004, N17). Although the *Day after Tomorrow* writers joked about the appropriate genre for their screenplay, the rest of the media largely ignored the Larsen B story. A LexisNexis search reveals that between 2002 and 2005 there were only forty total references to the ice collapse, of which only eight appeared in American newspapers. Television nightly news did even worse, with a total of three stories: a 20-second piece at the end of the February 14, 2002, *CBS Evening News*; a 2-minute, 10-second story on the March 19 *NBC News* that mentioned the ice-shelf collapse and connected it to unusual weather across the United States and the possibility of a connection to global warming; and a follow-up on *CBS Evening News* on March 22, 2002, which provided time for both climate scientists and global-warming deniers.

Hollywood blockbusters emphasizing the dangers of global warming aren't the only nontraditional source of information that have managed to place the issue on the public agenda. Reflecting the dynamic nature of the media environment, *An Inconvenient Truth*, the 2004 documentary by Al Gore, attracted large audiences, prompted another round of media and public discussion of global warming that repeated many of the same sorts of arguments as *The Day after Tomorrow*, won both an Oscar and a Nobel Peace Prize for Gore, and helped turn the former vice president and presidential candidate into a media celebrity. Interestingly enough, the movie caused a brief flurry of controversy in 2008, when it was revealed that some of the opening footage of the documentary depicting the collapse of Antarctic ice shelves was actually computer-generated footage taken from *The Day after Tomorrow* (Sheppard 2008).

But all popular nontraditional sources of information did not support the global-warming argument. In 2005, the best-selling author Michael

Crichton (*Jurassic Park, Airframe, Disclosure, Rising Sun*) published *State of Fear*, a novel that portrayed environmentalists as crazed terrorists who invented the idea of human-caused global warming to advance their radical goals. Their plans include carving off giant icebergs to raise ocean levels, inducing killer storms, and generally doing anything they can to "prove" that global warming is real. The heroes of Crichton's story, however, know it is a lot of hot air and junk science. Crichton signaled his intention that his book be taken seriously by using footnotes to actual scientific articles cited by characters in the novel and including a large appendix summarizing his conclusions after reading through the research on global warming in scientific journals. As with *The Day after Tomorrow*, the book was treated harshly by most critics, but it found a large audience, making it to the *New York Times* Best Seller List with an initial printing of 1.5 million copies. As with Emmerich's film, *State of Fear* sparked a brief flurry of mainstream media attention, with both those who accepted the reality of global warming and skeptics using the book as evidence for their positions.

Fiona Harvey (2005, 19), the *Financial Times*'s environment correspondent, took Crichton to task:

[I]n fact it is what scientists are saying in public that makes the views of Crichton, and other influential climate-change "deniers," increasingly difficult to understand.... [A] study led by the California-based Scripps Institution of Oceanography found the warming of the world's oceans could only be explained by anthropogenic (man-made) climate change. As one of its authors said when news of the report broke: "The debate over whether there is a global-warming is over now, at least for rational people."

In contrast, global-warming skeptics applauded Crichton's effort. A writer for the *Pittsburgh Post-Gazette* lauded *State of Fear* as a valuable education in the guise of entertainment, advising, "Do yourself a favor and buy it" (Kelly 2004, J7). Columnist George Will (2004, A23) endorsed the book and alluded to the enormous amount of scientific research supporting the author's conclusions:

"State of Fear," with a first printing of 1.5 million copies, resembles Ayn Rand's "Atlas Shrugged" – about 6 million copies sold since 1957 – as a political broadside woven into an entertaining story. But whereas Rand had only an idea – a good one (capitalism is splendid), but only one – Crichton has information. "State of Fear" is the world's first page turner that people will want to read in one gulp (a long gulp: 600 pages, counting appendices) even though it has lots of real scientific graphs, and footnotes citing journals such as Progress in Physical Geography and Transactions – American Geophysical Union.

Journalists React: A Profession's Own State of Fear

State of Fear and *The Day after Tomorrow* undermine traditional expectations that political issues are communicated to the public primarily through the gates guarded by professional journalists. Although these expectations have always been suspect, based as they are on the dubious distinction between news and entertainment, recent changes in the broader media environment both have made the limits of such assumptions clearer and have created new challenges for understanding the role of media in twenty-first-century American democracy. These changes have done far more than alter coverage of political scandals, as we discussed in the previous chapter. They have also altered the provision of information about more ongoing, persistent, and – dare we say – serious issues. In this chapter, we address the impact of a changing media environment on coverage of the earth's environment: arguably the most serious issue that faces humanity.

As the concept of hyperreality suggests, the mediated construction of global warming has become at least as significant, when it comes to public understanding and political action, as the actual scientific understanding of the issue. Further, as multiaxiality highlights, this mediated construction results from a much broader range of conduits of information than was the case in the Age of Broadcast News. The relative influence of these new conduits is not, however, random, but rather shaped by the structures of power – economic, political, and cultural – that produce them. As we will see, for example, climate-change "skeptics" used a wide range of new and old media to construct a hyperreality that global warming and its human causes either were not occurring or were in doubt. This mediated construction drove shifts in public opinion that bore scant relationship to either scientific consensus or actual changes in global temperatures. Though carried on in a wide range of new and old media, this hyperreality was the result of a very conscious strategy developed by the industries that stood to lose the most from policies addressing this environmental challenge.

Understanding mediated political communications, even dealing with this most serious of issues, requires abandoning a priori assumptions about the media conduits through which information flows and the relationship between mediated representations and the reality they claim to represent. We miss much of what is most important about media coverage of environmental issues if we restrict ourselves to outlets assumed to be serious (e.g., traditional news, documentaries, newspapers) while ignoring sources assumed to be less serious (e.g., movies, music, popular novels, prime-time dramas and comedies, mobile technologies, e-mail, blogs, and websites).

When dealing with environmental issues, or any other significant public debates in the new media environment, it is vital to see the debate as a field of discourse – what we call the discursive environment – crossing the boundaries of many types of media. The changes in the media environment we described in Chapter 3 have created both increased opportunities for fostering public debate and increased insecurity over the impact of these changes on the quality of that debate. So, in the examples we have just discussed, there was tremendous frustration expressed by journalists in traditional outlets over the quality of the information in *The Day after Tomorrow* and *State of Fear*. According to the science writer of the *San Francisco Chronicle*:

Indeed, if there's a moral to the cinematic debacle of *The Day After Tomorrow*, it's this: In a democracy, it's not enough to scare people into believing in global warming. You also have to trust their intelligence enough to show them the compelling evidence. There's strong scientific evidence for global warming, but you won't see any of it in the film because the filmmakers evidently think you're too stupid or easily bored to be bothered with the scientific details. (Davidson 2004, E1)

The frustration felt by journalists is, in our view, a result of at least three factors that we will examine throughout this chapter.

Unclear Truth Claims
Journalists have an understandable suspicion that, although movies and novels often make overt or covert claims about their basis in facts, the standards on which such claims rest are often, to put it charitably, unclear, which raises serious questions about how viewers should interpret them. The question of how to understand the truth claims made in a wide variety of conduits of political information is one of the most challenging facing citizens, experts, and political elites in the new media environment. Answering these questions must lie at the heart of media literacy, an essential for citizenship in the twenty-first century.

If we are to grasp both the potentials and pitfalls of this new media environment for fostering public debate, we must avoid blanket denunciations of the validity of information simply because it appears in a particular type of conduit – here, a Hollywood movie or best-selling novel. Just because something is presented in a dramatic fashion does not mean that the underlying truth claims are necessarily false or misleading. Rather, criticism must address the actual nature of the claims made, not simply the particular media conduit through which they flow. And indeed, there is reason to take the warnings of *The Day after Tomorrow* quite seriously. An article in *Scientific American*, which mentions *The Day after Tomorrow* in its lead paragraph, notes that there are researchers who believe that rapid and catastrophic cooling (though perhaps not quite as instantaneous as in the movie) might result from global warming: "the cooling would start right away and significant effects would be felt in Europe in the first winter after the currents failed. The full severity of the cooling would be established within a few years" (Reville 2005, 15). Equally interesting was the explicit comparison between the scale of the catastrophe in *The Day after Tomorrow* and the work of a British academic on the possibility of a killer tsunami hitting the East Coast of the United States:

The stage was set for the mega-disaster in 1971, when an eruption loosened a 12-mile-wide chunk of the Cumbre Vieja volcano on the Canary Islands.... If and when the 500 billion tons of barely hanging rock finally barrels into the Atlantic, it could make the disaster flick *The Day After Tomorrow*, look like a joke, experts say. Prof. Bill McGuire, of the Benfield Hazard Research Center at University College in London, said the largest tidal wave ever would race across the Atlantic at up to 600 mph and hit New York as well as shorelines from the Caribbean to Boston. (Standora and Shin 2004, 5)

At the same time, the truth claims of any outlet for politically relevant information must be subject to critical scrutiny. Michael Crichton is to be applauded for presenting footnotes and appendices citing the scientific sources on which his novel is based, thus making his truth claims easily verifiable. However, just because the means to verify sources is provided does not mean that verification has actually taken place, as sympathetic columnists like George Will assume. An article in the *Boston Globe* actually did the work of checking Crichton's sources and found them to be used out of context and in highly misleading ways, inaccurately casting mainstream scientists as global-warming critics (Mooney 2005).

Confidence in the Methods of Professional Journalists
A second factor underlying journalistic suspicion is an implicit argument that, in contrast to a moviemaker or a novelist, journalists themselves employ a set of procedures for making verifiable truth claims about the content of their own work. As we saw in the first portion of this book, these essentially contestable claims have their origins in the Progressive Era emergence of journalism as a profession and are

themselves being severely challenged by changes in the media environment. Moreover, there are serious criticisms made of the ways in which journalists themselves use and interpret scientific research (Mooney 2007; Gelbspan 2004).

It is important to note another failure of journalism that has its roots in the attempt to draw sharp lines between fact and opinion. In February 2009, George Will once again used his syndicated *Washington Post* column to claim that global warming was a hoax, perpetrated by liberal environmentalists and abetted by dishonest or confused scientists. After using predictions made in the 1970s that the climate would cool as evidence that climatologists basically have no idea what they are talking about, Will relied on two "factual" claims in making his case that current predictions of global warming were equally baseless. The first claim was that, contrary to the predictions of experts that sea ice was declining, "According to the University of Illinois' Arctic Climate Research Center, global sea ice levels now equal those of 1979" (Will 2009, A20). The second was that, over the previous decade, the climate was no longer warming. Both claims are incorrect. The Arctic Climate Research Center immediately disavowed Will, saying that he had misstated its research. The second claim depends on the statistical trick of ignoring trend lines and cherry-picking single observation points (which are affected by random variations): because four of the years between 1998 and 2009 were among the warmest ever recorded (and so fell on the high side of the long-run trend), when 2009 fell on the low side of the trend (but was still one of the warmest years ever recorded – warmer than any before 2000), it was possible for Will to claim that the globe was cooling. Both of these claims would have been revealed as false if there had been even the most modest attempt to fact-check Will's column. However, it turns out that the *Washington Post* does no fact-checking for its op-ed page (Breen 2009). Given the attention of journalism to getting the facts right, this practice can be understood only as being rooted in the Progressive Era's futile attempt to draw a sharp line between fact and opinion. Yet like so many other assumed dichotomies, this one also collapses on the slightest scrutiny. Here, for example, Will's opinions make sense only if they are backed up by false claims, or, as Daniel Patrick Moynihan once so eloquently stated, "You are entitled to your own opinions, but not your own facts."[3]

[3] It is also worth noting that the column became controversial when bloggers challenged Will's claims. The attention of these new media watchdogs resulted in a column by the *Post*'s ombudsmen, who criticized the paper's fact-checking policy.

As we have argued in previous chapters, rather than appealing to dubious information hierarchies, we believe that developing a full and sophisticated understanding of the truth claims made in various sorts of media texts dealing with serious public issues is essential to taking advantage of the new media environment's potential to enrich democratic politics. We argue in the conclusion of this book that all who hold the greatly enlarged public soapbox, be they movie producers, novelists, bloggers, or journalists, should be encouraged to take responsibility for the truth claims they make.

Boundary Maintenance

Finally, underlying much of the debate about *The Day after Tomorrow* and *State of Fear* is a concern with the subject of this book: anxiety about the erosion of the boundaries between news and entertainment. Debate about media coverage of environmental issues should be understood in the context of a broader turf battle about where citizens are turning, or should turn, to find out about serious public issues. As the number and variety of conduits through which political information passes increase, professional journalists have a strong incentive to argue that information about serious issues should be gleaned from trained professionals, like themselves. As we move from the single axis system of the Age of Broadcast News to the multiaxial system of the new media environment, battles inevitably erupt between new and old actors jockeying for influence (e.g., journalists, producers of feature and documentary films, bloggers) and the organized political forces with stakes in the outcome (e.g., energy industries, environmentalists, various political elites). If we are to fully realize the democratic potential of this new media environment, it is vital to assess the job journalists actually do when it comes to informing citizens about serious issues rather than simply accept their adequacy as privileged gatekeepers. It is equally important to analyze the potential advantages and disadvantages of new sources of mediated information opened up in the new media environment.

In the following section, we explore how, when it comes to environmental issues, journalists answer enduring questions about media in American democracy, such as, who needs to be informed, who produces and who consumes the information, whether the information is useful, whether the information is sufficient, and whether the information is trustworthy. We then examine the potentials and limitations of the new media environment for altering the answers to these questions in coverage of environmental issues. Finally, we glean several lessons from our analysis that are instructive regarding how one might shape a new media regime capable of addressing important issues such as global climate change.

Serious Media Addresses (or Not) a Serious Issue: How Well Does Mainstream Media Cover Environmental Issues?

There is no overstating the importance of environmental issues. The environment is not just one important public concern among many; it is, arguably, the most significant challenge facing human beings at this moment. A changing global climate threatens the continuation of life as we know it and raises the most profound questions about how we live and how human civilization affects the fate of the earth. Any adequate understanding of such connections depends on a solid grounding in cutting-edge scientific research (as well as in how science operates as an institution) and an analysis of the interconnections among economic, political, and social life on a global scale. Even seemingly unrelated issues are, in the end, connected to global environmental crises. For instance, in the most recent U.N. ranking of countries according to its index of human development, the lowest-ranked countries, many in sub-Saharan Africa, had the lightest carbon footprints but were also the countries most disastrously affected by climate change, a result of the heavy carbon emissions of the countries ranked higher on the list (Nizza 2007).[4] The journalist Robert Kaplan (2001, 19), who specializes in post–Cold War problems, makes this point eloquently:

It is time to understand the environment for what it is: the national-security issue of the early 21st century. The political and strategic impact of surging populations, spreading disease, deforestation and soil erosion, water depletion, air pollution, and, possibly, rising sea levels in critical, overcrowded regions like the Nile Delta and Bangladesh – will be the core foreign policy challenges from which most others will ultimately emanate, arousing the public and uniting assorted interests leftover from the Cold War.

Unlike many other issues, there is broad and enduring agreement between experts and the public about the severity of the environmental crisis. For example, Harris Interactive has asked the following question for many years: "Do you agree or disagree with this statement: Protecting the environment is so important that requirements and standards cannot be too high, and continuing environmental improvements must be made

---

4 The Human Development Index ranks nations mainly according to life expectancy, literacy, and income.

regardless of cost." Since 1983, the percentage of Americans agreeing strongly or somewhat strongly with the question has never been less than 58 percent; it reached 80 percent in 1989 and 1992, and it was 74 percent in 2005, the last year we found polling data (Teixeira 2007).

Reflecting their global character, environmental problems are of concern to people around the world. In a survey of forty-five thousand respondents in thirty-seven countries and the Palestinian territories, the Pew Research Center's Global Attitudes Project (2007) found that the environment was the top concern of a growing number of people in both rich and poor nations. As Table 6.1 reveals, these percentages were sharply up from Pew's 2002 survey. Especially in Europe, concern with global climate change and its human causes has grown rapidly (especially as compared to public opinion in the United States) among the general public (Crampton 2007). Moreover, the United States is blamed more than any other nation for global environmental problems in thirty-four of the thirty-seven countries surveyed (one-third of Americans agree with this assessment; Schaefer 2007).

Yet despite high levels of concern, levels of public knowledge about the specifics of environmental issues are quite low. Most studies reveal little understanding of relative risks posed by various environmental problems, the dynamics of global warming, how it connects to other issues like ozone depletion, and so forth (Suzuki 2006; Bord, Fisher, and O'Conner 1995). This lack of knowledge creates a disconnect between the views of experts and the general public, with alarming consequences for public debate and public policy. The Princeton engineering professor Robert Socolow comments:

I've been involved in a number of fields where there's a lay opinion and a scientific opinion. And, in most of the cases, it's the lay community that is more exercised and more anxious. If you take an extreme example, it would be nuclear power, where most of the people who work in nuclear science are relatively relaxed about very low levels of radiation. But, in the climate case, the experts – the people who work with climate models every day, the people who do ice cores – they are *more* concerned. They're going out of their way to say, "Wake up!" (qtd. in Kolbert 2006, 131–132)

Given the vital importance of the issue, long-term and widespread public concern (with even greater concern among climate experts), its impact on myriad other important public concerns (e.g., U.S. standing in the world, terrorism, national security, global justice), and its development from the 1970s on during the heyday of the Age of Broadcast News, environmental problems seem a natural test of the ability of the media regime and its

TABLE 6.1. *Worldwide Concern about Climate Change*

Percentage Naming Environmental Problems as Top Global Threat			
	2002	2007	Change
United States	23	37	14
Canada	43	54	11
Argentina	28	53	25
Bolivia	39	42	3
Brazil	20	49	29
Chile	–	44	–
Mexico	34	45	11
Peru	37	55	18
Venezuela	20	42	22
United Kingdom	30	46	16
France	29	52	23
Germany	27	45	18
Italy	39	51	12
Spain	–	46	–
Sweden	–	66	–
Bulgaria	28	45	17
Czech Republic	42	49	7
Poland	20	33	13
Russia	40	43	3
Slovenia	36	50	14
Ukraine	54	57	3
Turkey	22	27	5
Egypt	37	40	–
Jordan	–	30	−7
Kuwait	–	22	–
Lebanon	22	13	−9
Morocco	–	31	–
Palestinian territories	–	28	–
Israel	–	26	–
Pakistan	13	18	5
Bangladesh	28	30	2
Indonesia	76	37	6
Malaysia	–	37	–
China	69	70	1
India	32	40	17
Japan	55	70	15
South Korea	73	77	4
Ethiopia	–	7	–
Ghana	11	22	11
Ivory Coast	16	14	−2
Kenya	9	17	8
Mali	–	19	–
Nigeria	17	17	0
Senegal	–	13	–
South Africa	22	22	0
Tanzania	20	24	4
Uganda	8	22	14

Source: Pew Research Center Global Attitudes Project, 2007.

TABLE 6.2. *Number of Stories on Network News*

Year	Global Warming	Michael Jackson	Gasoline Prices
2007 (Jan. 1–Aug. 1)	79[a]	2	51
2006	67	27	112
2005	37	156	94
2004	20	112	52
2003	12	62	36
2002	22	7	23
2001	40	0	91
2000	34	1	85
Total stories	311	367	544

[a] Although this is a surprisingly large number, given past coverage, it should be noted that ten of these stories were focused on either Al Gore's documentary *An Inconvenient Truth* and/or the Live Earth concert to publicize global warming. We address this phenomenon of celebrity-driven agenda setting herein.
Source: Vanderbilt Television News Archive.

assigned gatekeepers, especially professional journalists, to inform and elevate public debate.

By almost any measure, the mainstream American media has done a poor job covering environmental issues, in general, and global warming in particular. Although it is impossible to define how much coverage would be adequate, it is clear that, by international standards, American print media does poorly. One study found that between September 1999 and March 2000, British newspapers had twice the coverage on environmental issues of American papers, and the disparity was even greater if one looked only at the prestige press. German newspapers provided dramatically more coverage as well (Gelbspan 2004, 70). Our own discussion here of media coverage of specific environmental issues reveals a similar disparity in the amount of coverage between American and foreign newspapers.

Broadcast news does no better than print media. We used the Vanderbilt Television News Archive to identify all the stories mentioning global warming on television news broadcasts between January 1, 2000, and August 1, 2007. The results are presented in the first column of Table 6.2. As a way to compare coverage of the issue of global warming with other topics, we also searched on Michael Jackson for a sense of how much coverage the news devotes to celebrity scandal. As Table 6.2 indicates, coverage of global warming has never come close to the level of intense coverage devoted to the accusations of child abuse leveled at the controversial singer during 2005 and 2006, when the networks devoted

156 and 112 stories, respectively, to the singer. As another point of comparison, the third column lists the number of stories devoted to gasoline prices, an ongoing issue with clear connections to environmental issues (although this relationship is never analyzed by television journalists). As the numbers indicate, with the exception of 2007 (when the numbers for global warming were artificially inflated by celebrity-driven stories covering the Oscar win for Al Gore's documentary *An Inconvenient Truth* and the Live Earth concert), global warming has never received the consistent coverage accorded to fluctuating gasoline prices.

Even if we cast our net wider than just the evening news to include the entire range of programs on cable television, the record is dismal. For July 2005, a month marked by a record-breaking heat wave during the second-warmest year on record and two months before Hurricane Katrina, we set up one of our TiVo DVR recorders to search all shows using the keywords *global warming* and/or *climate change*. The result yielded not a single documentary or special about these topics. Ironically, given the focus of this book, the only programs captured were showings of *The Day after Tomorrow* (in regular rotation on HBO) and episodes of the animated Fox program *Futureworld* (featuring the frozen head of Al Gore).[5]

Is Very Little Coverage Still Too Much? The Quality of Environmental Coverage during the Age of Broadcast News

When it comes to the American media, especially the prestige press – the *New York Times*, the *Washington Post*, and the *Wall Street Journal* – it turns out that the quality of coverage has actually had a deleterious influence on public debate, or the lack thereof, on global warming. Far from providing useful information to a public already concerned about environmental issues, American media coverage has worked to confuse the public, to limit timely consideration of policy alternatives, and to distort the results of the best scientific research bearing on climate change. These problems in the quality of media coverage are not aberrations or the results of departures from the best practices of professional journalists but rather follow directly from these practices. Consequently, even when dramatic events overcome the more normal practice of ignoring the issue by triggering flurries of increased coverage of environmental issues, this

---

[5] This does not mean that cable television ignores serious or actual events – a similar TiVo search for "World War II," for instance, turned up thirty-five shows, ranging from documentaries on the History Channel and Fox News to Hollywood movies and regularly scheduled series.

does little to improve the quality of public debate. Most troubling is the success of industries opposing policies aimed at climate change (e.g., cap-and-trade legislation) to shape media coverage by "gaming" journalistic practices through the hidden (at least to journalists who failed to investigate) funding of climate-change deniers and skeptics, which has created the illusion of scientific disagreement (Gelbspan 1997, 2004; Mooney 2007). In short, the practices and institutions that governed the provision of political information during the Age of Broadcast News are ill suited to providing useful political information on environmental issues in general and global warming in particular. Even before its collapse, the broadcast news media regime failed to adequately cover global climate change. We emphasize this point because it highlights both the limits of the past media regime and the need to creatively explore the possibilities of the new media environment for improving public discourse on this vital issue.

Before exploring the systematic problems underlying the quality of coverage of environmental problems, it is important to recognize that this is not an easy issue to cover well. In any specific area of environmental concern (e.g., global warming, ozone depletion, air pollution, water pollution), although there may be scientific consensus over broad outlines of the causes of the problem, there is often uncertainty and disagreement among scientific and technical experts over specifics, such as how rapidly conditions are changing, the actual magnitude of the threat, and the adequacy and cost of proposed solutions. Any sophisticated appreciation of environmental issues requires some familiarity with this sort of technical complexity and uncertainty (for a more detailed discussion of the issues raised in this paragraph and the next, see Williams and Matheny 1995). Media coverage that focuses on specific disagreements while ignoring broader scientific consensus can seriously distort public understanding. Likewise, assuming that broad consensus is equivalent to understanding all the specific details can lead to unrealistic expectations about the ease with which problems can be addressed.

The history of scientific debate over global climate change and its human causes well illustrates the relationship between broad consensus and specific disagreement and uncertainty. In 1988, although there was no final consensus among the scientific community, James Hansen, a NASA scientist, testified before Congress to warn that it was likely that human activity was leading to global warming and that it was vital to act immediately (Weart 2008, 155). This testimony, coupled with an unusually hot summer, moved global warming onto the public agenda. British Prime

Minister Margaret Thatcher, for example, said to the Royal Society in London, "[W]e may have unwittingly begun a massive experiment with the system of the planet itself" (Boykoff and Boykoff 2004). At this point in time, although there was a growing number of scientists who connected increasing average global temperatures to human activity, there was still much debate about the degree to which extant research supported such theories. Ten years later, a consensus among scientists had emerged. In 1997, D. James Baker, administrator of the U.S. National Oceanic and Atmospheric Administration, said that when it came to global warming, "There's a better scientific consensus on this than on any issue I know – except maybe Newton's second law of dynamics" (Boykoff and Boykoff 2004, 125). In 2001, the U.N.-sponsored Intergovernmental Panel on Climate Change (IPCC) recognized the international scientific consensus that global warming was occurring and that human activity was a significant cause. To be sure, there is still disagreement about the overall impact of human activity and about numerous specific details of the overall dynamic of global warming, but there is no longer any debate over the general question among scientists.[6]

The challenges of adequately covering environmental issues don't end with understanding scientific research, consensus, disagreement, and uncertainty: political and economic implications of environmental problems pose even more difficult issues. Because most causes of environmental stress in America are the by-products of private economic activity, dealing with them raises significant questions at all three levels of politics that we defined in Chapter 4. At the substance level, specific public policies designed to protect the environment must address questions about the appropriate trade-offs between economic growth and the health and safety of citizens and the environment. At the institutional level, environmental protection raises questions about the role (in terms of both what that role is and what it might be) of political institutions as regulators of the activities of private corporations. At the foundation level, environmental concerns address the overall meaning of and relationships among terms like *capitalism, democracy*, the *public good, fairness*, and so forth. All of these challenges are even more

---

[6] The consequences of a limited understanding of scientific agreement and disagreement was on display again during 2009, when revelations about some trivial mistakes in the U.N. Climate Report (e.g., exaggeration of ice loss in some glaciers, typos attributing research findings to environmental groups instead of the scientific researchers who actually produced the data) were taken by many climate skeptics and journalists as evidence that the case for global warming was coming apart.

severe when we add in the global dimension of the environmental crisis, which raises fundamental questions about the balance between national interests and global obligations, what rich nations owe poor nations, and so forth.

Why Isn't the Environment News?

Given these complexities, it is truly unfortunate that there is so little high-quality coverage of environmental problems. Yet given the rules of the mid-twentieth century media regime that we have been calling the Age of Broadcast News, this is hardly surprising. Further, the privileged role of professional journalists as gatekeepers makes these limitations especially significant given the lack of legitimate alternatives in the single axis of this passing regime. One advantage of the multiaxiality of the new media environment is that it allows a variety of approaches to gathering and communicating information. This holds the potential for finding an appropriate fit between the characteristics of any particular issue and the rules used by various information providers.

For a number of reasons, there is a poor fit between the rules used by the gatekeepers of the Age of Broadcast News and the characteristics of environmental issues. Central among them is that environmental issues seldom meet the definition of news adopted by professional journalists, the authoritative gatekeepers of this regime. News is defined as something different, something that has changed since the last broadcast or newspaper edition (after all, we call it the news, not the olds). Global warming in particular and environmental problems more generally are thus often ignored, as changes tend to be slow and incremental, and little happens on a day-to-day basis that would push environmental problems into the news. The result is a lack of timely and ongoing coverage of the impact of human activities on global climate change. Although scientists were beginning to be concerned as early as 1970, the issue was not mentioned in the prestige press until 1981, and then only in passing (Kolbert 2006). Because it is difficult for journalists to cover the issue on a sustained day-to-day basis, it is virtually impossible to provide citizens with the sort of in-depth information needed to appreciate the complex issues involved.[7]

---

[7] This lack of ongoing coverage of environmental issues has been particularly significant in the case of global warming, where, as we will see, the failure to provide such coverage has resulted in a systematic and serious distortion of the emerging scientific consensus over the anthropogenic influence on climate change.

By the time dramatic or catastrophic environmental events occur, thus making them newsworthy, it is often far too late to do anything about them. This is especially a problem for television, where compelling visuals are needed to push any ongoing story onto the news on any given day. Even when dramatic events do occur (e.g., Hurricane Katrina, the Exxon Valdez and BP oil Spills, or the tsunami in Japan), they are covered for brief periods of time and in ways that often overdramatize and simplify the issues involved. Further, as we saw with the absence of coverage of the collapse of the Larsen B ice shelf, when dramatic events occur, the American press often does a poor job of taking advantage of such opportunities to enrich the public dialogue.

Press treatment of the connections between global warming and hurricane severity provides a good example of how the lack of ongoing coverage of environmental issues can lead to flawed coverage when catastrophic events occur. Increasing routine coverage of the connection between weather changes and global warming ought to be possible, as Ross Gelbspan (2004) points out, given the dramatically increased news budgets for coverage of weather disasters, yet this connection is seldom made, despite the emerging scientific consensus that such connections are very real. In August 2005, the beginning of what would be one of the most severe hurricane seasons on record, a LexisNexis search of major newspapers revealed a total of five stories referring to global warming in American newspapers (as compared to twenty stories in foreign, English-language newspapers).

In the wake of Hurricane Katrina, which devastated New Orleans and the American Gulf Coast in September, concern was raised by scientists that global warming was intensifying the severity and frequency of hurricanes. At the time, many journalists and scientists were, quite correctly, reluctant to claim that Katrina, as a specific weather event, had been caused by global warming. But, as Chris Mooney (2007) points out in his book *Storm World: Hurricanes, Politics, and the Battle over Global Warming*, given the research on the connection between global warming and the increasing severity of hurricanes, this is no different from insisting that, although smoking increases one's risk of lung cancer, we cannot conclude that a specific case of lung cancer is caused by smoking. It would have been easier for journalists to make such connections had there been ongoing coverage of the research suggesting a connection between global warming, increasing ocean temperatures, and the severity of hurricanes.

One missed opportunity occurred before the hurricane in July 2005, when Kerry Emanuel, a leading climate researcher and professor of meteorology at the Massachusetts Institute of Technology's Department of Earth, Atmospheric, and Planetary Sciences, withdrew his name from an article to be published in a meteorology journal that found little evidence of a connection between climate change and hurricane severity. The withdrawal occurred after he reanalyzed the data and found that there was, indeed, a connection. He published his new conclusions online at the site of *Nature* magazine (Thomson 2005). However, this change in the views of an eminent meteorologist on a significant issue was not covered in any American newspaper.

The Limits of Balance as a News Value
The poor fit of the news values of novelty and immediacy with environmental problems are not the only reason for the poor quality of American press coverage. Even deeper problems result from the basic rules shaping professional journalists' approach to telling the stories they cover. Most significantly, defining *balance* as the requirement that there be two sides to every story has resulted in coverage that, over the long run, systematically understated the degree of scientific consensus about global warming and its human causes. Gelbspan (1997, 2004) has shown how interest groups representing industries opposed to government actions to reduce the production of greenhouse gases (especially the petroleum industry) have funded a group of global-warming skeptics who, though having little standing in the scientific community, were regularly cited by journalists in an attempt to provide two sides to their stories on climate change.

As we argued in Chapter 3, equating objectivity and fairness with the assumption that there are two sides to every story is problematic, even when covering political debates. It is simply extraordinary to apply such definitions of objectivity to scientific issues around which scientific consensus has emerged. Here it would seem to be journalists' responsibility to convey this consensus and, if there are skeptics, to explain what is motivating their rejection of that consensus. And as we noted earlier, around global warming and its anthropogenic origins there has been a strong scientific consensus since the end of the 1990s.[8] Although there is uncertainty about many of the specific dynamics of global warming, and

---

[8] For a careful treatment of the emergence of this scientific consensus, see Weart 2008.

these deserve adequate and thorough coverage, treating basic questions of global climate change as if they were still being disputed distorts the conclusions of virtually all respected researchers and has specific political consequences. Moreover, as *New York Times* columnist Nicholas Kristof (2007, A17) notes, in other areas of policy, uncertainty over specifics is not treated as an excuse for inaction:[9]

There is natural variability and lots of uncertainty, especially about the magnitude and timing of climate change. In the same way, terror experts aren't sure about the magnitude and timing of Al Qaeda's next strike. But it would be myopic to shrug that because there's uncertainty about the risks, we shouldn't act vigorously to confront them – yet that's our national policy toward climate change, and it's a disgrace.

The failure of journalists to independently check for themselves the truth claims made by their sources is a systematic problem, basic to the ways journalists go about their job, with implications far beyond coverage of the environment. As we discuss in the following chapter, this was certainly one of the reasons for the failure of the press to challenge Bush administration claims about the connection between Saddam Hussein's possession of weapons of mass destruction or his regime's connections to al-Qaeda. This problem is not limited to American journalism. Rodney Benson and Daniel Hallin (2007) find that the failure to evaluate truth claims is a problem for both the French and the American press (although they find that the former does slightly better on this score).[10]

Misguided adherence by journalists to definitions of *balance* were more than just an unfortunate mismatch between journalistic norms and the underlying truth of a story; it is clear that these rules were manipulated by interest groups to shape the coverage and its impact on public opinion for

---

[9] In Chapter 6, we discuss the American media's suspension of the notion that there are two sides to every story when it came to the aftermath of the 9/11 attacks.

[10] This systematic problem has implications for the current debate over the consequences of the "crisis" of journalism. Many defenders of the profession and its vital role in democracy base their argument on the ability of journalists and newspapers to provide the kind of neutral and factual information on which enlightened public discourse depends. Such arguments assume both that professional journalists are a good source of such information and that new media, for a number of reasons, is a poor source. Although there are good reasons to accept the latter, the former is often assumed mistakenly and without adequate reflection.

their own political ends. In 1998, a report compiled for industry opponents of action on climate change was leaked to the press and reported
on in the *New York Times*:

Among the ideas in the proposal was a campaign to recruit a cadre of scientists
who share the industry's views of climate science and to train them in public
relations so they can help convince journalists, politicians and the public that
the risk of global warming is too uncertain to justify.... Moreover, the plan
would measure success "by counting, among other things, the percentage of news
articles that raise questions about climate science and the number of radio talk
show appearances by scientists questioning the prevailing views." (Boykoff and
Boykoff 2004, 133)

It is ironic that the application of a notion of balance, developed as a way
to keep journalism nonpartisan, resulted here in partisan advantages for
those opposed to addressing climate change, as the false impression of
scientific dispute worked to block timely policy action. It is testimony to
how powerful and unexamined for journalists are ideas of balance and
nonpartisanship, such that, even when the strategies of industrial groups
to take advantage of those rules was revealed, coverage of climate change
continued to be shaped by those strategies.

Maxwell Boykoff and Jules Boykoff's (2004) careful analysis of the
prestige press's coverage of global warming between 1988 and 2002 provides a systematic and detailed picture of how, as Ross Gelbspan (2004,
67) notes "[t]he press's adherence to balance actually leads to biased
coverage of global warming." Using formal content analysis and more
qualitative readings, they examine a random sample of all articles mentioning global warming in the *New York Times*, the *Washington Post*,
the *Los Angeles Times*, and the *Wall Street Journal* to reveal how frequently discussions of climate change and its anthropogenic causes were
dealt with as matters of dispute, for which two sides needed to be presented, or matters of settled scientific consensus. They found that more
than half the coverage in the press provided "roughly equal treatment
to the view that humans were contributing to global warming, and the
other view that exclusively natural fluctuations could explain the earth's
temperature increase" (Boykoff and Boykoff (2004, 129). In contrast,
only slightly more than a third of the coverage (35.29 percent) reflected
the actual scientific consensus by "emphasiz[ing] the existence of anthropogenic contributions to global warming – as distinct from natural variation – but still present[ing] both sides of the debate." Finally, roughly
equal percentages treated the claim that humans were influencing climate

change as dubious (6.18 percent) or simply accepted the anthropogenic causes of climate change (5.88 percent).

Even more revealing is the Boykoffs' year-by-year comparison of press coverage of climate change and the published scientific research on the topic. They found that when newspapers first began covering global warming in 1988 and 1989, the vast majority of articles "emphasized anthropogenic contributions to global warming, thereby mirroring the scientific discourse of the time" (2004, 130). However, by 1990, coverage had shifted to a balanced frame, providing equal space to arguments for and against anthropogenic causes of global warming. Significantly, they attribute this change not to any shift in the scientific community (indeed, the scientific consensus was growing stronger, and in 1990, the IPCC released its first report identifying humans as a significant cause of global warming) but to the politicization of the issue and the growing reliance of reporters on political officials as sources (as opposed to scientists). The call by both government officials and efforts of industry-funded skeptics for more research created the impression in press coverage that there were many questions remaining to be settled at the same time that the scientific community was actually becoming more united than ever over the impact of humans on global climate change.

This analysis distinguishes between press coverage of the scientific research on climate change and press coverage of policy debates over how to respond to global warming. Initially, coverage of policy options tended to focus on mandatory government actions; later, as the issue became politicized, press coverage was more likely to balance discussions of voluntary and mandatory solutions. This is consistent with the underlying rationale for balance that developed as a strategy to provide nonpartisan coverage of politics. However, unless one believes that flat-earth supporters or gravity deniers are entitled to equal treatment, it is clear that norms of balance were never intended to apply to discussion of the state of scientific knowledge (Gelbspan 2004).

The combination of misapplication of norms of balance and the tendency to frame all issues as partisan political struggles influenced even the embrace, albeit belated, of anthropogenic influences on climate change by major media outlets in 2007. On August 13 of that year, *Newsweek* ran a cover story announcing that anthropogenic causes of climate change were a settled issue for scientists, and only the efforts of the industry-funded denial lobby had prevented such recognition in the press (Figure 6.1). Over a close-up of the sun, the headline "Global Warming Is a Hoax" carried a footnote: "Or so claim well-funded naysayers who still reject

FIGURE 6.1. *Newsweek*, August 13, 2007.

the overwhelming evidence of climate change. Inside the denial machine."
Both CNN and NBC News similarly declared that the debate over global
warming was over. Yet given the years-long divergence between balanced
press coverage of the issue and the scientific consensus that had clearly
emerged by 2001, such declarations by the press seemed both arbitrary
and themselves politically motivated. Indeed, even *Newsweek* ran a column by its own editor Robert J. Samuelson (2007) criticizing the story,
calling it "a vast oversimplification of a messy story" and "fundamentally
misleading." Conservative sources, from blogs to Fox News, and the outlets of the deniers themselves quickly branded the pronouncements by
Newsweek, NBC, and CNN as yet another example of liberal bias and an
attempt to cut off legitimate debate. In short, given the previous eighteen

years of press coverage, by 2007, there was little that could be done to treat scientific consensus as anything other than a partisan struggle for political advantage.

The legacy of press coverage of climate change as if it were a "he said, she said" partisan issue was visible again in 2009. Hackers made public a series of more than two thousand e-mails between climate researchers. Although the overwhelming majority discussed the details of data gathering and analysis or the preparation of scholarly articles, a small number discussed how to combat the arguments of climate-change skeptics (along with ad hominem attacks against them), how to present a united front to journalists so as to minimize publicity about data anomalies, how to limit the access of climate skeptics to data, and even a suggestion (never acted on) that certain data be destroyed. All careful reviews of the e-mails by scientists and mainstream journalists concluded that, although they reflected badly on the specific e-mailers (who never expected their messages to be made public) and demonstrated an unprofessional disdain for skeptics, in no way did they undermine the case for global warming. Yet the affair came to be labeled "Climategate" and was used by skeptics to bolster their claim that consensus on climate change was the result of a liberal political strategy based on dishonest research. In turn, this claim became one side of the stories told by journalists, even when their main point was to discredit the conspiratorial interpretation of the e-mails.

Finally, we need to mention the basic commercial nature of most mass media. As we argued in Chapters 2 and 3, although there was considerable debate at the time and ongoing public opposition, American media policy in the 1930s created a system of privately owned media corporations financed largely through advertising revenue. To the extent that environmental issues raise troubling questions implicating consumption-driven economic growth itself and the consumer lifestyle on which most advertising and media corporations depends, it is extraordinarily difficult for the existing media regime to cover such controversies well (Delli Carpini and Williams 1994a). Reinforcing this structural limitation is the rise of neoliberalism following the Cold War, which we discussed in Chapter 3. As Robert Kaplan suggested earlier, the global environmental crisis should have been a candidate for becoming the dominant template for framing American understanding of the world in the wake of the Cold War. However, the triumphalism about the supposed triumph of capitalism and neoliberal faith in the unfettered market made it quite difficult for journalists to adopt a new frame that fundamentally challenged these assumptions at a moment of intense celebration over their validity and worth.

Clearly, when it comes to informing public dialogue about environmental issues, there were severe problems with the rules used by professional journalists during the Age of Broadcast News. Consequently, as scientific consensus jelled around the existence of anthropogenic causes of climate change, American public opinion, following the arc of press coverage, actually became more skeptical about the human influence on global warming (Gelbspan 1997). As a new media regime develops, it is important to keep such failings in mind to avoid misguided and futile attempts to reinstate the flawed practices of the past. To the degree that the problems in coverage of environmental issues and the resulting disconnect between scientific consensus and press coverage of global warming stems from the very rules used by journalists to tell their stories, simply increasing the amount of coverage or reasserting their authority as gatekeepers will not address the problem.

Beyond the "News"

Although the limits of the passing media regime are many, it is also important to appreciate its achievements – but this is only possible if we focus on the full panoply of media, not just on what was produced by professional journalism. When it comes to environmental issues, one of the major achievements of the Age of Broadcast News was the ability, during media events, to fully focus public attention on this issue. As we noted in Chapter 3, the media regime of the mid-twentieth century created a unique public forum for what Colin Leys (2001, 150) called the "most important 'formative conversations.'" It was this ability to focus, for brief periods of time, intense and widespread attention on environmental issues that was one of the great achievements of this media regime. As we have argued throughout this book, however, the full power and significance of the ability to construct such media events is clear only if we expand our notion of political communication beyond traditional sources like news broadcasts. Indeed, when it comes to coverage of environmental media events, traditional sources of political information were only a small part, and were no more sophisticated or useful in their treatment, than less traditional outlets.

As an example of the ability of the passing media regime to foster a national conversation, we use the twentieth and thirtieth anniversaries of

TABLE 6.3. *Coverage of Earth Day, by Number of Stories*

	Washington Post	Network News	USA Today
1990	55	24	112
2000	19	4	10

Note: Results are based on a search for "Earth Day" in LexisNexis and the Vanderbilt Television News Archive for the four weeks surrounding Earth Day.

Earth Day in 1990 and 2000.[11] In both cases, it was a significant and predictable anniversary of an important event rather than any specific dramatic occurrence that pushed the environment onto the agenda. As we will see, between 1990 and 2000, we witnessed the significant erosion of the broadcast news media regime and a concomitant dramatic change in the way the two anniversaries were marked in the media.

In 1990, the twentieth anniversary of the first Earth Day brought a flurry of coverage across a broad spectrum of media. Newspapers and magazines featured stories on the preceding twenty years of environmental activism. Television shows were also aimed at celebrating the anniversary, from coverage on the network news broadcasts to special editions of television news magazines, docudramas, and other shows much more difficult to categorize. Two points are worth noting at the outset. First, much of the television programming marking the anniversary of Earth Day lay far outside the work of news divisions and other traditional sources of political information. Second, the wide-ranging array of programs, across genres and networks, created a sense of this being an important event that would have been hard for any viewers to miss, even if they avoided the nightly news broadcasts.

In short, the twentieth anniversary of Earth Day received a great deal of attention and provides an example of the agenda-setting power of the broadcast news regime, especially if we cast our net beyond traditional sources of political information. As Table 6.3 indicates, print media signaled the importance of the anniversary, with both the prestige press (here represented by the *Washington Post*) and more popular newspapers (here represented by *USA Today*) running a large number of stories on Earth Day in the two weeks leading up to and the two weeks following the anniversary. Also signaling the importance of the issue were the nightly

[11] The following discussion draws heavily on our own work in Delli Carpini and Williams (1994a).

network news broadcasts, which devoted twenty-four stories to the issue in the same four-week period, an unusually large amount of coverage of environmental issues.

To provide a sense of the range of formats used to celebrate Earth Day in 1990, in previously published work we analyzed three representative shows: an episode of the CBS news magazine *48 Hours* titled "Not on My Planet," hosted by then *CBS Evening News* anchor Dan Rather; a made-for-television docudrama on TBS titled *Incident at Dark River*, about toxic-waste pollution in a small town written by and starring Mike Farrell and costarring Helen Hunt; and "The Time-Warner Earth Day Special," a difficult-to-categorize, celebrity-driven show that aired on ABC.[12] Although the *48 Hours* episode devoted to environmental concerns was only the sixty-seventh most popular show out of ninety for the week (with a rating of 8.1 and a 14 share), this still meant it was watched by more than 8 million Americans.[13] "The Time Warner Earth Day Special," reflecting its airing in prime time on Sunday, the most popular television-viewing night of the week, was the sixteenth most watched show (with a rating of 14.6 and share of 24). No ratings are available for *Incident at Dark River*, which aired on TBS, but it was shown multiple times during the month of the Earth Day anniversary.

Reflecting the limitations of a single-axis media regime, although television, the dominant medium of 1990, dealt with environmental issues in a wide variety of genres, it did not deal with this issue in a wide variety of ways. In our own analysis of television coverage of the twentieth anniversary of Earth Day, we found almost no diversity in the shows that aired, regardless of genre (Delli Carpini and Williams 1994a).

First, they all employed a catastrophic perspective on environmental problems and the risks posed by pollution, assuming that pollution of all types was worse than ever, that each form of pollution posed a grave and immediate threat to humans and to nature, and that we must do

---

[12] The celebrities, who all participated in a series of skits organized around the threat to Mother Earth posed mainly by the production of needless waste, included Bette Midler (as Mother Earth), Robin Williams, Michael Moore, Morgan Freeman, Candice Bergen, Michael Keaton, Carl Sagan, and so forth.

[13] A rating refers to the number of households with televisions tuned into a show (in 1990, each ratings point equaled around one million households). A share, in contrast, is the percentage of all televisions in use that are tuned into a show. Both "The Time Warner Earth Day Special" and *48 Hours* drew a larger audience than *CBS Evening News with Katie Couric* attracts on any given evening (around 5.4 million viewers the week of April 4, 2011).

something now. Less serious attention was paid on any of these shows to scientific uncertainty or the relative risks posed by various forms of pollution.

Second, none of the shows seriously addressed the trade-offs between regulation and economic activity. The notion that reducing pollution may require reduced economic growth was not addressed or was ridiculed as a ploy by unscrupulous businesspeople, or the shows suggested that reducing pollution would be good for the economy.

Third, all the shows were critical of the problem-solving capabilities of political and economic institutions. Government is seen as corrupt, incompetent, and completely inadequate to deal with the problems posed by environmental pollution. The business sector is represented by either evasive corporate spokespersons or shady and disreputable owners, neither of whom can be trusted either to obey the law or to act responsibly.

Fourth, all the shows adopted a nostalgic individualism that served to blunt, in terms of political action, their more critical messages. The shows were almost entirely set in small-town America,[14] which allowed them to use the image of the New England town meeting as a forum for discussing public issues.

Fifth, although institutions were portrayed as flawed and inadequate, the solution is never political organization aimed at institutional reform or change. Rather, individuals, acting on their own as individuals, are seen as the solution to the problem. The shows' characters do not appeal to government to change; rather, they see the inevitable flaws of "big government" and "big business" and work instead on their own to solve our social problems. Hence, the mantra of the Earth Day special: "reuse, reduce, recycle."[15]

Although there was a real lack of diversity in the perspectives adopted by television in celebrating Earth Day, in 1990, the passing media regime was still intact enough to set the agenda, holding out the possibility of a public debate about the issue and, perhaps, a critique of the limitations

[14] Both *Incident at Dark River* and the skits of the Earth Day special are set in small towns. Four of the seven episodes on *48 Hours* are set in small towns (a fifth, though dealing with garbage in Los Angeles, was shot almost entirely in sparsely populated hills outside the city).

[15] This approach still shapes much of the media's treatment of all environmental issues, including global warming, which was virtually ignored in 1990 coverage. Yet as Ross Gelbspan (2004, 127) notes, "Unfortunately, though many environmental problems can be addressed through lifestyle changes, climate change is not one of them."

of the perspectives employed. Ten years later, the broadcast news media regime had largely collapsed and, with it, the ability of journalists or television executives to program a wide range of coverage that would attract large audiences. As Table 6.3 indicates, the celebration of the thirtieth anniversary of Earth Day in 2000 saw a dramatic decrease over 1990 in the amount of coverage in both newspapers and television news broadcasts.

Even more illustrative of the changing media environment was the 1990 "The Time Warner Earth Day Special" that aired on Sunday night and attracted 24 million viewers; in 2000, the only prime-time show drawing attention to Earth Day, "Planet Earth 2000," on ABC, aired on Saturday, the least-watched night, and drew 3.9 million viewers, finishing ninety-second out of ninety-three network shows for the week. In contrast to 1990, it would have been quite easy for the average citizen to avoid any knowledge of the anniversary.

Policing the Boundaries between News and Entertainment in Environmental Coverage

In 2000, the most publicized television event of the celebration became a flash point in the struggle over political information in the new media environment and the attempt to maintain the line between news and entertainment. ABC News's "Planet Earth 2000" was hosted by Leonardo DiCaprio. The young actor and environmental activist introduced the show's segments dealing with a number of environmental issues. However, what caused controversy was not the low ratings resulting from airing the show on Saturday night, the substantive topics of each segment, or any bias in the show's perspective but the fact DiCaprio conducted an interview with President Bill Clinton at the White House. When word leaked out that it would be the actor and not a journalist conducting the interview, David Westin, the head of ABC News, was swamped with e-mails from irate ABC employees who saw this as a violation of the appropriate role of journalists and, apropos of the subject of this book, a gross violation of the line between news and entertainment.

Westin's response is revealing for the grounds on which he chose to defend the DiCaprio interview. In an e-mail reply to employee criticisms, he first denied that the decision had even been made to air the interview, implying that the values of ABC News would be used to make the final edit of the show: "We'll take a look at whatever they've done and decide whether we can use any of it; it's quite possible we'll use none." He then went on to address the criticism that he was mixing news and entertainment: "All roles of journalists must be played by journalists (duh!)" (Last 2000). When the controversy wasn't stopped by this reply, ABC News issued a series of further explanations, claiming that the DiCaprio interview was not its idea but rather occurred after the Clinton administration invited ABC to do a tour of the environmental improvements made to the White House and the network asked if DiCaprio could be Clinton's guest on the tour. The White House released a statement challenging Westin's version of events: "In February, some time ago [ABC News asked] the president to answer some questions for an ABC News special. And ABC News indicated that it would be Leonardo DiCaprio that would ask the questions" (Last 2000).

That Westin found it so necessary to deny the news division's role in the DiCaprio interview reflects anxiety about the blurring of news and entertainment and the related insecurity of journalists trying to defend their turf.[16] Yet assuming that the line between news and entertainment is legitimate and self-evident begs the more fundamental question, Why should we be upset that President Clinton was interviewed by a movie star as opposed to a broadcast journalist? As we have argued throughout this book, rather than making knee-jerk assertions about the legitimacy of a particular genre or set of gatekeepers, we need to examine the actual content of the interview itself. Fortunately, a feature of the new media environment – the easy accessibility of many kinds of information unavailable before – makes this possible, as Salon.com posted the entire transcript of the interview (the full thirty minutes and not the briefer few minutes that actually aired). Here are the actual questions asked by DiCaprio (the questions that were included in the actual broadcast are in italics):

> 1. *Mr. President, I want to thank you very much for your time. And as you know, I'm neither a politician, nor a journalist, but being given the opportunity to sit down with you here and talk about an issue like global warming was an opportunity as a concerned citizen that I couldn't pass up. So my first question is, global warming is obviously a controversial topic among scientists and politicians. What*

---

[16] Unmentioned in Westin's denials was the allegation, noted by a Salon.com article, that the reason DiCaprio was picked for the interview was as part of the publicity campaign for his movie *Gangs of New York*, released by Miramax. Both Miramax and ABC are owned by the Disney Corporation (Last 2000).

is your understanding of what the effects of climate change will have on our future if preventative steps aren't taken immediately?

2. While growing up, I always felt that environmental issues were constantly overlooked, and I watched people band together for various causes which seemed to come and go, and it was almost like they were going in and out of style. So how do we take a misunderstood issue like climate change and not only raise awareness, but make its prevention an ongoing commitment?

3. Well, my other question pertaining to that is, if there was a profit incentive there, would that make us pay more attention?

4. Now, in Kyoto, in the 1997 Global Conference on Climate Change, it asked industrialized countries to drastically reduce their greenhouse gas emissions. And when we tried to enforce such protocols in developing countries, they came right back to us and said that the U.S. is responsible for a quarter of the greenhouse gases that are going into the atmosphere. How can we not practice what we preach?

5. *Why do you think this issue is so constantly overlooked, and why do you think people don't take it seriously enough? And for you, is it as important as something like health care or education?*

6. Now, the major polluters are obviously the big industries, such as the oil companies, who are one of the most powerful lobbies in the world. How do we convince them to change the way they've been doing business for the last century?

7. How do we get power companies to replace their coal plants with cleaner technologies? And why don't we make it so expensive for power companies to keep their old coal plants, that they have to invest in cleaner fuels?

8. Now, you've enacted tax credits for people who want to buy electric and fuel-cell vehicles. What are we doing to encourage oil companies to research alternative fuel technologies like fuel cells?

9. Many people have said in the past that the American dream was to buy a car and live in the suburbs. But it has created massive problems that have made us more reliant on our cars. Since it is so difficult for us to convince people to use mass transportation, how can we promote hybrid vehicles and convince people to give up their SUVs? For instance, if it only costs $575 a car to make them cleaner, why can't you make it a law, like seatbelts?

10. Now, Louisiana is the second largest consumer of fossil fuels and New Orleans the city most at risk for sea level rise. Can't something be done like in Atlanta where the government withheld highway funds, making it the model city for environmental responsibility?

11. *Now, I'm sure you've heard so many reports from scientists and politicians and citizens. What do you think the best course for American citizens is within the next 20 years as far as helping the environment is concerned?*

12. *Do you think we can eventually become a role model?*

It is easy to argue that these are not the best possible questions to ask a sitting president about environmental concerns: they are not very detailed about current or past governmental efforts or the administration's actual record; they also lack aggressive follow-up, and so forth. Even if we concede these shortcomings, the critique of the DiCaprio interview assumes that if a broadcast journalist had conducted the interview, these limitations would have been overcome. It is this implicit assumption with which we take issue. Given the dismal record of news divisions covering environmental issues, there is no reason to believe that the questions would have been sharper or the outcome more illuminating had a journalist "played the role of journalist" in this instance. Indeed, this assumption about the quality of journalists as interviewers in particular or as gatekeepers in general needs to be questioned beyond the specific arena of environmental issues. Consider as a point of comparison the first eight questions asked of President Clinton by the well-respected Jim Lehrer of PBS's *NewsHour* on the eve of the 2000 State of the Union Address, three months before the DiCaprio interview:

1. Can we assume, sir, that tomorrow night in the State of the Union you're going to declare the state of the union to be in pretty good shape?

2. The things that are good about this country right now, how much of that do you believe you deserve credit for?

3. Do you believe that history is going to give you credit for all the things you've just enumerated?

4. Are you worried about what the historians are going to write about you?

5. Let me read what the New York Times said in its lead editorial on Monday. They're talking about you – your legacy and

your presidency as you go into this last year. It said: "Historians are beginning to categorize Mr. Clinton as a politician of splendid natural talent and some significant accomplishments, who nonetheless missed the greatness that once seemed within his grasp." What's your reaction to that what might have been kind of thing?

6. All right. Let's talk about the one more hard year. Is there one particular thing that you really want to do before you leave this office?

7. What's the problem there, Mr. President, between Syria and Israel, what's the problem?

8. What about health care, what is it that you would like your legacy to be on health care? (*NewsHour* 2000).

To us, these questions do not seem any more hard-hitting, illuminating, or detailed than the DiCaprio questions. Our point is not that Jim Lehrer is a poor journalist or that DiCaprio would be a great one; it is to highlight the importance of making judgments based on the actual content and context of mediated political communication rather than on its source or genre. In the Age of Broadcast News, characterized by a single axis through which political information passed, the practices of professional journalists and the media organizations within which they were institutionalized were far more determinative than the identity of the specific individual who played the role of journalist.

Comparing the DiCaprio interview to an interview by a respected broadcast journalist focuses our attention on the actual rules used by gatekeepers as they pass on information to the public. Given the general similarity between the style and substance of the questions asked by Lehrer and DiCaprio, as well as the limitations of press coverage of the environment that we have already chronicled, it is significant to note that DiCaprio's questions that focused most specifically on substantive issues of environmental policy (questions 3, 4, 8, 9, and 10) were not aired in the actual broadcast. Neither was question 6, which focused on the significance of corporate capitalism, its disproportionate influence on the policy process, and its potential hostility to aggressive environmental policy – issues that have generally been ignored on television treatments of environmental concern, as we saw earlier. Understanding how little of the interview made it onto the actual show also draws our attention to the extremely limited time and attention devoted to the Earth Day anniversary in the American media in general.

Comparing the questions asked with those aired and with questions asked in other situations leads us away from a priori assumptions about genre and toward consideration of the processes that determine the content of the mediated political communication we actually consume. That is, the actual questioner plays only a small role in the content of the text, as decisions about which questions will air are made by others (here, presumably, those who regularly work for ABC News). As well, it is not at all clear who actually composed the questions asked by DiCaprio (or Lehrer, for that matter): was it the star himself, his advisers, or the writers of "Planet Earth 2000"? So, arguments about who is best suited to play the role of journalists – a Hollywood star or a highly paid on-air talent employed by the network's news division – obscures more significant questions about understanding who is actually speaking to us in any given mediated political text and the rules used to shape that dialogue; both are prerequisites for critical evaluation of any politically relevant communication. This was a difficult-enough problem in the Age of Broadcast News, but it becomes even more challenging in the new and multiaxial media environment, where both the number of gates through which mediated political information flows and the variety of norms and practices that shape what passes (and does not pass) through them has increased exponentially.

Finally, it is worth noting that, as with the problems we have analyzed with respect to the distinction between news and entertainment, the boundaries between the roles of broadcast journalist and celebrity are, to say the least, unclear. Many well-known broadcast journalists reach their positions as gatekeepers through achieving celebrity in fields that have only the slightest relationship to professional journalism. Further, many prominent broadcasters have little to do with what they actually read on air or the questions they ask of interviewees. It is, as we argue in detail in our concluding chapter, more important to know who has actually written the words and done the research behind the words that are spoken by politicians, journalists, movie stars, and other media figures.[17] This is especially so, because the new media environment introduces sources of political information of unclear provenance – blogs, web sites, YouTube

---

[17] It is worth noting that in Britain, the on-air talent who read the news on the BBC are called news readers, which is, in many cases, a more accurate description than our own anchorperson, with all its connotations of authorship of the news broadcast.

videos, links to numerous unfamiliar and familiar news sources, and so forth.

Avoiding a priori judgments and focusing on the actual content of DiCaprio's interview, including the parts that were not aired, also allows us to explore some of the potential advantages of having nonjournalists in the role of interviewer. This is especially significant in a multiaxial environment, where there is greater potential for realizing these advantages than in the Age of Broadcast News. First, DiCaprio identifies himself as a citizen, standing in for the citizen-viewers at home (albeit a much sexier citizen than most of the rest of us), and so someone who is part of the political system and deeply affected by the decisions made by government. This is in sharp contrast to the posture of neutral observer, somehow outside the political system, which professional journalists assume. Though not necessarily desirable in every situation, these two roles – involved citizen or neutral outside observer – clearly open up very different possibilities for providing political information to the broader polity. Second, flowing from this identification as citizen, DiCaprio's questions (unfortunately the ones that did not make it onto the program) can focus more on earnest questions about policy rather than the inside-baseball questions typical of journalists, which are aimed at revealing the president's strategic considerations in the struggle for partisan advantage. As a result, DiCaprio's questions seem much more consistent with what Thomas Patterson (1994) calls the governance schema, sought by citizens seeking to understand more about the substantive choices facing the political system, as opposed to the game schema, employed by most journalists, which sees the actions of political elites entirely in terms of strategic considerations in the struggle for partisan and electoral advantage.

Given the vital importance of environmental issues, and the poor job that the American mainstream press has done covering them, it is important to explore possibilities for improving this state of affairs in the emerging media regime. Yet journalists' anxiety around the DiCaprio interview is not an isolated example of the ways in which the erosion of their authority as gatekeepers and the resulting attempts at boundary maintenance block such serious and creative explorations of the potential of the new media environment.

Consider, for example, an event that occurred three years before the controversy over the DiCaprio interview. In 1997, as part of Breast Cancer Awareness Month, HBO aired a documentary titled *Rachel's Daughters* (Light and Saraf 1997) in which a group of ordinary women with breast cancer set out as "detectives" to find the cause of their cancer. Although the show employs many of the conventions of television news magazines, it also was remarkable for several reasons, all of which point to alternatives to the flawed conventional journalistic coverage of scientific issues.

The first innovative aspect of *Rachel's Daughters* was its treatment of scientific research and professional experts. The women consulted a wide variety of sources: some more activist and so less scientifically respectable (e.g., individuals convinced that high-voltage power lines cause cancer, someone from an unexplained "pesticide education center") but also more mainstream scientific researchers from Duke, Harvard, Berkeley, and the National Cancer Institute, who are all given ample time to introduce themselves, their research, and the reasons they became interested in the challenges of breast cancer research. In short, the show provided a wide variety of perspectives rooted in different knowledge bases.

To frame these segments and highlight the complex connections among research, political issues, and personal motivations, Cornell University professor Sandra Steingraber, a well-known environmental writer, biologist, poet, and herself a cancer survivor, speaks movingly of Rachel Carson, to whom the "Rachel" of the documentary's title refers. Steingraber recalls that Carson was dying of breast cancer as she wrote *Silent Spring*: "I often think of her, while she was undergoing radiation treatment, trying to piece together the scientific evidence to provide a compelling narrative for the rest of us" (Light and Saraf 1997).

Rachel's Daughters provides a vision of what could be accomplished in the medium of television if many of the assumptions of television journalism were rethought. Like much other television, the HBO documentary used the stories of the stricken women to create a powerful emotional tug. Unlike more usual treatments, however, this emotional appeal served to draw viewers into a quite nuanced and sophisticated treatment of a complicated issue. Reflecting the possibilities open to ordinary citizens in the new media environment, the show let the victims of disease themselves search through a wide variety of sources of information – some more scientifically reliable than others. In doing this, the show anticipated the opportunities for citizen-journalists that would dramatically expand in the new media environment, provided a model for viewers to search out information themselves, and embodied an important model of science in a democratic society.

Consistent with this view, as well as with the concerns of the movement for environmental justice, the show connects issues of race, class, gender, and disease. It also raises important questions about where and how public research dollars are allocated. The show recognizes that decisions about funding for research are not solely scientific issues, but rather are, in every sense of the word, political issues that need to be openly discussed. Reflecting the views of many scholarly analysts of science and science policy, the show rejects the idea that science is simply a body of objective knowledge that should be placed firmly in the hands of elites who will then make wise decisions on behalf of an ill-informed and emotionally volatile public. Finally, and most significantly, the show manages to do all of this without the "help" of professional journalists.

The day before *Rachel's Daughters* first aired, it was reviewed, along with another breast cancer documentary, in the *New York Times* by the science reporter Gina Kolata. Her analysis of the show was, to say the least, quite different from ours. She opens an exceptionally hostile review by saying:

All those who ever wondered to what extent breast cancer has become politicized should watch two shows that were produced to commemorate National Breast Cancer Awareness Month....

The women on these television programs are far removed from the universe of scientists and others who make distinctions between hypotheses and evidence, who believe that speculation is not proof and that when evidence fails to support a hypothesis, the hypothesis should be abandoned. the women on these programs believe none of the above. Their universe is emotional and scary, filled with corporate bogeymen and toxic wastes and young women dying of a dreaded disease. Its appeal is insidious, and that is its danger....

Rachel's Daughter's focuses on very young women with breast cancer, ignoring the fact that 85 percent of women who get breast cancer are over the age of 50 and that breast cancer is more common in men in their 70s than it is in women in their 20s. But no matter: the young women are so photogenic, and the environment is such an easy target. They are convinced that they were poisoned by their toxic environment. And so they venture out to interview kindred souls, hearing what they always suspected. Are crops sprayed with pesticides? Well, then, of course, pesticides cause breast cancer. (Kolata 1997)

To be fair, Kolata is correct to cite the cancer incidence figures, and if the show simply conformed to the normal television approach to risk, it would, indeed, be another case of statistical innumeracy. However, what Kolata fails to recognize is that her own review adopts its own model of science that, when measured against the views of science held by many philosophers and sociologists, or the model that emerges from *Rachel's Daughters*, is simplistic and naive in the extreme (i.e., that scientists are simply those who "make distinctions between hypotheses and evidence, who believe that speculation is not proof and that when evidence fails to support a hypothesis, the hypothesis should be abandoned"). *Rachel's Daughters* does indeed politicize the issue of breast cancer and environmental risk, but it is hardly unscientific to insist that such subjects are always political. Nor is it unscientific to insist that it is vital to recognize them as such and then deal with them in sophisticated and nuanced ways. As Steingraber (1998, 211) argues in her own book *Living Downstream*:

There are individuals who claim, as a form of dismissal, that links between cancer and environmental contamination are unproven and unprovable. There are others who believe that placing people in harm's way is wrong – whether the exact mechanism by which this harm is inflicted can be precisely deciphered or not. At the very least, they argue, we are obliged to investigate, however imperfect our scientific tools: with the right to know comes the duty to inquire. At the very least these two views constitute a clash of political, social and economic values, they do not define the boundaries between science and non-science.

Yet rather than seeing this as a debate between alternative views of science in a democratic society, Kolata dismisses the view expressed in *Rachel's Daughters* precisely as an attack on science itself. So, she concludes her review with the following:

The danger with this program is that anyone who is not deeply familiar with science will get the impression that we are all rapidly being poisoned by chemicals and radiation and that breast cancer is striking down young women with abandon. It is a normal human tendency to look about for something to blame when a tragedy like breast cancer strikes. But in displaying only the distorted parallel universe of some breast cancer activists, these programs should come with a prominent label: "Warning. What you are about to see may be heart-wrenching, but has little or no basis in fact." (Kolata 1997)

How could an otherwise fine science writer like Kolata present such a one-sided review of a sophisticated documentary like *Rachel's Daughters*? We offer two general answers to this question, both of which connect back to the very basic structures and rules of the passing media regime that we have implicated in the coverage of global warming and the environment throughout this chapter.[18]

---

[18] Our explanation avoids, but is by no means incompatible with, the more ad hominem perspective of a critical article about Kolata that appeared in the *Nation* (Dowie 1998).

First, Kolata's perspective reflects the difference between an advertiser-driven media outlet, like the *New York Times* or CBS, as opposed to a subscription-based outlet, like HBO. In the case of the former, there are severe structural pressures to avoid criticism of corporations or consumer culture, as the existence of advertiser-supported media depends on the financial support of corporate advertising, which promotes consumer culture. This severely restricts the discourse about environmental issues. Kolata's hostility to any criticisms of corporations and commercial culture is consistent with the economic interests of her employer, the *New York Times*, which depends on advertising revenue for its continuing existence. In contrast, HBO is a subscription-driven cable station that does not have to avoid taking controversial positions to attract the broadest possible audience required by advertisers. This hardly makes HBO, owned by Time Warner, a bastion of anticapitalist sentiments. However, it does allow the expression of more controversial political positions than is possible on the broadcast networks. Exploring the connection between various models of financing media outlets and their different impact on discourse is especially important as we move into a media environment where questions of how to pay for content on the web, cable, or satellite become the object of attention. Evaluation of these alternative business models should include their potential impact on the flow of political information.

Second, Kolata's hostility reflects the challenge to the role of professional reporters, like herself, posed by *Rachel's Daughters* specifically and the new media environment more generally. As the chief science writer for the *New York Times*, she holds the most prestigious position in the model of mass media that assumes that it is the job of trained, professional journalists to act as gatekeepers for the passage of scientific information to the general public. Yet arguably a program that dispenses entirely with professional journalists, like *Rachel's Daughters*, can provide a sophisticated, informative, and useful perspective on a complex scientific question, like the causes of and uncertainties about breast cancer. In short, such shows pose a challenge to the elitist assumption that only trained professionals can act in the public interest. The almost hysterical hostility of Kolata to *Rachel's Daughters* reflects (or at least presages) a defensiveness to the much broader challenge to journalists posed by the explosion of sources of information provided in the new media environment.

Absent more thoughtful reflections than those exemplified by Kolata, we run the risk of getting neither the presumed benefits of the old media system nor the benefits made possible by the emerging one. More productive would be a serious discussion about several issues fore-grounded by our critique of press coverage of environmental issues. It is vital if we are to have a more informed and engaged public regarding pressing issues such as climate control, that we evaluate new sources and forms of political information with a clear eye, devoid of unexamined presuppositions about the appropriateness of any given conduit and without unjustified assumptions about the degree to which past regimes were capable of fulfilling this vital democratic role. Given the dramatic changes in the media environment, it seems clear that new and currently unanticipated ways for communicating important issues such as environmental degradation to the public will continue to emerge. This suggests the need for agreed-upon norms regarding the construction and assessment of politically relevant media texts. And while such norms will necessarily vary by source and genre, it is ultimately no less important to scrutinize the claims of documentarians, novelists, and moviemakers than it is to understand the adequacy of the work of professional journalists.

Potentials and Pitfalls of the New Media Environment

How might certain qualities of the new media environment serve to improve public deliberation on issues such as the environment? One possibility revolves around alterations in the dynamics of agenda setting.

In his seminal work on press coverage of the Vietnam War, Dan Hallin (1986) explodes one of the assumptions held by many about the role played by journalists in turning public opinion against the war. He finds that critical press coverage became prominent only in 1968, when it followed rather than led the emergence of skepticism among political elites about the Johnson administration's policies and the turn of public opinion against the war. Hallin explains this finding by pointing to the rules used by journalists, especially their dependence on elite sources needed to define the two sides to a story at the heart of their definition of nonpartisanship.[19] He also notes the need to avoid offending public opinion, a result of the commercial basis of the American media. As we have seen, both dynamics were at work in coverage of environmental issues, which resulted in very little coverage of the issue.

---

[19] This insight is more fully elaborated by Lance Bennett (1990) in his influential work on "indexing": the idea that professional journalism does not provide us with a picture of the truth or of what is important to know about political issues so much as it reveals, or indexes, existing power dynamics in Washington. We return to this idea in Chapter 7.

As with the Vietnam War, it is useful to remember that throughout the thirty-year history of the contemporary environmental movement, media coverage was sparked not by investigative reporters but by organizers of the first Earth Day, new political organizations, and connected grassroots campaigns and their impact on public and elite opinion. Introducing the 1990 episode of *48 Hours* we discussed earlier, Dan Rather unintentionally recognizes the origins of the environmental movement and the need of journalists to wait for public opinion to validate their coverage: "For most people Earth Day used to conjure up images of long-haired activists in tie-died shirts. . . . [No] longer. . . . Most Americans say the air they breath and water they drink is worse than ever. . . . Americans say clean-up help isn't coming from government or business, so they're taking up the fight on their own" (qtd. in Delli Carpini and Williams 1994a, 79–80). In this context, it is worth noting that the first popular media attention to environmental concerns, which did indeed lead public opinion, was the decidedly nontraditional and unlikely best seller *Silent Spring*, published in 1962.

Several features of the new media environment might increase the ability of environmental groups, especially at the grass roots, and other nontraditional sources of environmental information to get their message out to the wider public, thereby avoiding the structural limits of more traditional sources. First, and most obvious, the multiaxiality of the new media environment makes possible a wide variety of approaches, perspectives, and voices in the gathering and circulating of information about the environment. This does not, of course, mean that any particular new conduit will improve on or provide an adequate alternative to the information provided during the Age of Broadcast News. It only means that a wider variety of ways of providing information are possible, and as we argue in Chapter 8, it is vital to develop adequate criteria for judging their relative and collective merits (some of which should reflect what was best about the norms and practices of professional journalism).

Second, there has been a dramatic increase in the ease with which information can be gathered by ordinary citizens. Although mainstream American media coverage may be sparse and flawed, the internet, for example, allows users to access and share information from a broad range of sources from around the world, including actual scientific reports, press coverage in other countries, and innumerable blogs and websites that focus on environmental issues. Many environmentally oriented portals, such as the Environmental News Service and

Grist.com, collect the latest information about environmental issues from a wide range of governmental, university, foundation, and press sources from around the world in easily accessible formats. The Environmental Protection Agency's toxic-release inventory collates all reports of hazardous-waste releases and allows citizens to search for such events in their own neighborhoods. In turn, these sites are often mentioned and linked to on more popular blog and news aggregators like the Huffington Post or Talking Points Memo.

Third, the significantly reduced cost of producing mediated messages that can then be widely distributed has made it much easier for environmental groups and even ordinary citizens to create powerful media messages. The highest-profile use of new media has thus far been by "the usual suspects" – already-well-known figures like Laurie David (StopGlobalWarming.org) and Al Gore (WeCanSolveIt.org). The latter has raised enough money to wage a multimedia campaign with both a sophisticated webpage and television ads featuring prominent figures who, one would assume, disagree with one another over everything but the need to address the climate crisis: Pat Robertson and Al Sharpton appear in one, Nancy Pelosi and Newt Gingrich in another. Yet the connection between visiting a webpage and clicking on a link to sign up for the Stop Global Warming Virtual March and other forms of political engagement is an open question (which, as with our earlier discussion of online gaming, deserves serious study). As with our analysis of television coverage of the twentieth anniversary of Earth Day, however, this appeal to very general agreement may mask sharp disputes over specific policy solutions. Most significant is the question of how effective politically such forms of new organizing will be in influencing the actions of policy makers.

By allowing grassroots groups in one place to publicize their work and communicate with similar groups in other parts of the country and the world, new media can strengthen the grassroots environmental groups that have been the site of many of the most dramatic successes but remain far below the radar of the mainstream national press, and so invisible to the wider public. To the extent that new media can effectively publicize grassroots efforts that have been quite successful at getting many universities, localities, and states to commit to lower greenhouse-gas emissions and to reduce their carbon footprint, they can raise public awareness and build political support for more aggressive action by the federal government. So, for instance, WeCanSolveIt.org provides links to local environmental groups searchable by zip code. StopGlobalWarming.org provides a list of cities that have agreed to the Kyoto protocol and suggestions for how to influence local officials to do so if they haven't already. In the end, the role of media is crucial, as it is only by raising broader public support that local actions can have a significant impact – ultimately, global climate change can be addressed only at the levels of national and international action.

A fourth relevant feature of the new media environment is its corrosive effect on the lines between producers and consumers, elites and the masses, and the blurring of the line between various formally distinct roles in the political and social systems. Even more than in the past, popular cultural figures have been able to parlay their fame into becoming influential spokespersons for social causes. As we noted earlier, Live Earth in 2007 led to a spike in mainstream press coverage of global warming. Laurie David, the ex-wife of the comedian Larry David and an influential Hollywood producer in her own right, has been the public face of the online StopGlobalWarming.com website, which, among other things, has attracted more than nine hundred thousand people to sign online petitions. The ability of such high-profile figures along with less well-known grassroots groups to use new media opens up paths around the dismal and limited coverage of environmental issues by mainstream media outlets. These new conduits clearly played a significant role in the mainstream media's acceptance, albeit late, of the consensus on the human causes of global warming.

Al Gore's postpresidential candidate career is a particularly revealing instance of the potentials created by the eroding lines between different social, cultural, and political roles. His movie *An Inconvenient Truth* was a surprising sensation, focusing attention on global warming and winning him both an Academy Award and Nobel Peace Prize. Media coverage highlighted how a formerly stiff and humorless policy wonk had become the darling of Hollywood and acquired the charisma of a rock star. Implicit and/or explicit in much of this coverage was the belief that this publicity would be used to launch a new Gore campaign for president. Such an assumption makes perfect sense if one accepts traditional beliefs that the route to real power and influence over public policy is by capturing elective office and a formal role in the political system. Yet Gore's trajectory may indicate something more profound at work: the blurring of roles creates new opportunities for the exercise of political power that lies outside formal roles in the political system. We need to remember that Al Gore was a U.S. senator and then vice president for eight years, during which time little was done to address global warming (Breslau 2006). Given the structural limitations on the ability of even the most prominent politicians to effect change, it may well be that Gore's emergence as a public celebrity able to exploit the many new conduits through which political information can flow provides him with more influence over climate policy than would a role as president.[20]

Yet these four characteristics of the new media environment represent only potentials, and it is far from clear that they will be institutionalized in a new media regime. Just as changes in the media environment open up possibilities for enriching public dialogue on environmental issues, they also contain the potential for undermining serious consideration of these issues. First, while the explosion of conduits through which political information flows opens up many more sources of information than ever before, it also means the collapse of a gatekeeping system that allowed, at least in theory, the vetting of information by professional journalists for its reliability and accuracy. So, although it is possible to gather information from a wide variety of sources, the origin and reliability of that information is often difficult to judge. For example, a Google search for "global warming" results in a very mixed bag of sources; when we did so, the second listing was a link to GlobalWarming.org, the website of the Cooler Heads Coalition. Although the website is professionally done and seems to provide an interesting range of information, it takes some digging to learn that it is the site of a global-warming skeptic's organization and created by Consumer Alert's National Consumer Coalition, a group with ties to the energy industry (Source Watch 2009). As we argue in Chapter 8, one of the fundamental impediments to the new media environment playing a role in vitalizing democratic debate is the difficulty of understanding who is actually creating the information we obtain so easily, a prerequisite for judging the reliability of and critically evaluating that information.

Second, making the evaluation of political information even more difficult is the ideological and informational segregation made possible in the new media environment. In the arena of environmental policy, as with most other issues, it is possible for even the most interested and motivated

---

[20] In this context, it is also important to note the degree to which Gore's public persona as a humorless policy wonk prone to excessive claims on his own behalf was actually the product of the narratives imposed on him by journalists during the 2000 election campaign – when this image was contrasted with the easygoing, more down-to-earth George W. Bush. For a reevaluation of this press coverage, including the regret expressed by the journalists themselves, see Peretz 2007.

citizen to spend all of his or her time with information and people with whom they are in ideological agreement. So, for example, as much of the mainstream press settled into a consensus position that global warming was real and that human causes were significant, those who doubted such conclusions could find their skeptical opinions regularly reinforced. For example, the Drudge Report in the unusually snowy winter of 2009–2010 (at least for those living in the mid-Atlantic states) prominently ran the headline about the numerous storms as sly evidence that warming was not as severe as many were claiming. Similarly, a regular viewer of Fox News would have found a story on August 19, 2005, citing the usual group of global-warming deniers, which took to task *USA Today* for its cover story pronouncing the anthropogenic causes of global warming as being a settled matter of consensus. In the winter of 2009–2010, a Fox viewer would have seen an image of Al Gore's book *An Inconvenient Truth* half buried in a snowdrift.

Finally, although the eroding boundaries between various social, political, and cultural roles has the potential to open up new axes of effective political influence, these changes raise many questions. How sustainable and effective over the long haul are organizations or causes that depend on the support of celebrities? What are the long-term impacts of virtual political organizing? Although web-based organizers have produced impressive numbers of online actions – clicking to join campaigns or sending e-mails to elected representatives – the effectiveness of such activities compared with more traditional forms of activism are very much open to debate. Does participation in virtual political activity lead to further action, or does it sap, with little time, effort, or commitment, the potential for arguably more meaningful political participation of those initially motivated to do more? Further, the ability to engage in political activity from the privacy of one's own home via computer may actually undermine ideas about collective action that underlie the most effective responses to environmental challenges:

Web sites and flyers too numerous to mention instruct anxious members of the public to run their dishwashers only when full, to wash their clothes in cool or warm rather than hot water, to insulate their hot water heaters and keep their tires properly inflated – even as the world's glaciers are disappearing, whole islands are going under from rising sea levels, and world food supplies are dropping at alarming rates. Of course, poor people are largely excluded from sharing this sense of righteousness, illusory as it might be. (Gelbspan 2004, 138–139)

Given these conflicting potentials, there is nothing inevitable about the impact of the changing media environment on environmental politics. At the most general level, on the one hand, the explosion in the number of conduits for political information and the incredible diversity in the form and substance of information about environmental issues creates heretofore-unimagined possibilities for educating citizens and fostering new forms of political organization and participation. On the other hand, this same diversity results in a fragmentation of the audience for information about the environment, which may serve to isolate citizens and prevent the engagement of different opinions that is at the heart of any coherent public discussion of the issue. What is certain is that any new media regime, shaping and naturalizing as it will the new media environment, will have significant impact on the ways in which environmental issues are addressed in the next several decades.

Paths toward Improving Coverage: Intertextuality, Social Practices, and Media Literacy

Although it is difficult to predict the ultimate characteristics of public environmental discourse over the coming few decades, there are nevertheless several key characteristics of the new media environment, currently in great flux, which will have an important influence on that discourse. The concept of intertextuality and the ways it comes to be institutionalized in a new media regime captures nicely what is likely to drive changes in environmental discourse. Communication scholars have long argued that any specific media text depends for its meaning on its relationship to other texts.[21] Fully understanding the meaning of, for example, a scene in *The Simpsons* that portrays the daughter Maggie trying to stab her father Homer repeatedly while eerie staccato string music plays in the background depends on knowing that this is a reference to another media text, the film *Psycho*. Intertextuality has always been an important part of the construction of meaning, but never more so than in today's media environment. The patterns and practices of referencing (and hyperlinking) across various media texts will help determine whether the new media environment reinforces the echo-chamber effect of reinforcing pre-existing opinions and dismissing challenging views or whether it will facilitate the use of new media for accessing diverse information, building new forms of community and allowing political debate across various communities.

---

[21] For a good summary of the significance of intertextuality, see Grossberg et al. 2006.

The Daily Show routinely shows clips from the news programs that it then satirizes. On February 2, 2010, for example, the show aired a number of clips from cable news networks, especially Fox, which had seized on recent snowstorms hammering the East Coast as a kind of challenge to the consensus over global warming.[22] Then the show had one of its "correspondents" file a report claiming that global warming had been disproved because average temperatures had been falling steadily since August.[23] This was challenged by another correspondent, appearing to be reporting from Australia, claiming that, because temperatures there were in the nineties every day in February, this proved that the globe was warming at an accelerating pace. Lest one miss the satirical point, a third correspondent reported that, because it had gotten dark outside, the sun had been destroyed and the world had been plunged into everlasting darkness. Although intertextual references have always been a component of political satire, the use of the actual clips and the potential (via internet video downloads) to explore more fully the stories in question is new and potentially important: allowing, for example, viewers to evaluate for themselves how fair the original cable news story and *The Daily Show* satire actually were.

Intertextuality takes on new shapes on the internet. Wikipedia and other sites like it go beyond simply citing sources (an old form of intertextuality) to providing hyperlinks that allow a reader to go almost instantly to the source in question. Such ability to easily follow the network of sources is especially important in an area like climate change, where, as we have seen, so many scientific findings seem to be referred to in other media texts (from editorials to news stories, movies, and novels), often out of context.

Several creative uses of intertextuality, if widely adopted, could dismantle the ideological silos within which much political discourse increasingly takes place, and in the area of climate change, might lead to the scientific consensus over global warming having a much greater impact on American public opinion and policy. Cass Sunstein (2001) has suggested that websites should be required to provide links to sites that express views with which it disagrees. His "must-carry requirement," a kind of Fairness Doctrine for the internet, would require, for example, a

---

[22] *The Daily Show* used the Fox image of Al Gore's book in a snowdrift, which we mentioned earlier.
[23] The humor of these reports depends on another sort of intertextuality, familiarity with the pomposity and exotic location settings of many network and cable reports.

site devoted to global-warming skeptics to provide links to scientific sites and environmental groups that accept its reality (and vice versa).[24] At the very least, such practices would make it much harder for those who consume an ideologically restricted media diet to assume that their views are shared by the rest of the public.[25]

Although regulatory action might be one solution, other possibilities exist at the level of developing new forms of more voluntary social practices. Jon Stewart, for instance, recently went beyond using actual Fox clips as a jumping-off point for satire to actually appearing on *The O'Reilly Factor* for a civil debate that was aired over two nights. Stewart's appearance and how to interpret it was discussed on both shows, and the entire interview was available for downloading on both shows' websites. Because there is little overlap between the audiences of the two shows (if demographics is any indicator), such engagements might help overcome some of the more pernicious effects of ideological audience fragmentation.

Much is often made about the potential of new media, especially the internet, to allow citizens themselves to fact-check and gain further information about the issues that concern them and to critically evaluate media coverage. A public aware of the nature of science and skilled at using new media to check on reliable scientific sources would be an important bulwark against the ability of climate-change skeptics to game media coverage. How critical media literacy is taught in schools and effectively practiced by the public will be part of determining the impact of a new media regime on this vital issue.

Yet even at its best, media literacy education can be only part of the solution. Most citizens have limited time and knowledge when it comes to the task of checking the accuracy and reliability of the sources used in debates over climate change or other issues with a heavy technical and/or scientific component. Consequently, the public may change its expectations about how it will receive and evaluate information, but the actual shaping of more reliable and useful mediated information will still fall to those who have the time (i.e., a paying job) and expertise to do

---

[24] In effect from 1949 to 1987, the Federal Communications Commission's Fairness Doctrine required broadcasters to deal with controversial public issues in an honest and balanced manner.

[25] The possibility of using actual regulatory requirements for such linking practices might be tested in the Obama administration, where Sunstein works in the White House Office of Information and Regulatory Affairs.

TABLE 6.4. *Number of Network News Stories on Economic Inequality*

	1970s	1980s	1990s	2000s
Inequality in the United States	3	1	3	5
Inequality elsewhere in the world	0	3	2	0

Note: Totals exclude mentions of religious, gender, and other forms of noneconomic inequality but include mentions of educational inequality, tax inequality, and so forth.
Source: Vanderbilt Television News Archive.

so. Such a task might be performed by a type of professional journalism rethought and redefined for the new media environment. We return to this issue in more detail in Chapter 8.

Conclusion

As we have argued throughout this book, there is nothing about the new media environment that will inevitably lead to either improvement or further erosion in the quality of democratic politics. Rather, the actual impact of new media depends on the specific features of an emerging media regime that will shape the ways citizens develop more or less stable patterns of media use. How the American political system responds to the challenge of global climate change will depend in large part on the contours of this new media regime. Moreover, we selected global warming as one example of media treatment of a long-enduring, slowly changing, and terribly significant issue. We expect that an examination of other such issues would reveal similar patterns of coverage with respect to both the Age of Broadcast News and the possibilities and limitations of a changing media environment. That is, we would predict exceptionally limited coverage of questionable quality in the passing broadcast news regime.

Take as an example the issue of growing economic inequality in the United States, a trend that is occurring slowly over time (and so shares many of the features of environmental change) and has profound implications for democratic politics.[26] Table 6.4 lists the total number of network news stories dealing with inequality between 1970 and 2007. To compile this table, we searched the Vanderbilt Television News Archive for

---

[26] On the growth of inequality and its impact on politics, see Bartells 2008; Hacker and Pierson 2010.

any story using the word *inequality*. We found thirty-four stories, but we didn't include those that dealt with noneconomic forms of inequality (e.g., gender or religious inequality, unless the story also dealt with economic issues like wages). Over the entire three decades, there were only seventeen stories, of which only twelve dealt with economic inequality in the United States. Although this finding is hardly definitive, it suggests that, as with climate change, if one believes that economic inequality is an important issue worthy of ongoing and sophisticated coverage, then using the Age of Broadcast News as a standard is misguided.

We must, in short, be careful to not romanticize the broadcast regime as we seek to maximize the ways in which the new media environment might provide higher-quality coverage that engages the wider public and encourages thoughtful deliberation and action. Developing standards appropriate to this new environment requires recognizing what Markus Prior (2007) describes as the fundamental differences between the broadcast regime, which provided political information in limited but unavoidable ways, and the new media environment, which provides abundant information that is easily avoidable. We take up this task more directly in Chapter 8, but a few observations that flow from this chapter's analysis are appropriate here.

The central role of media in shaping environmental policy is best explained by recalling two terms we introduced in Chapter 4: *hyperreality* and *multiaxiality*. There is no doubt that global climate change and the scientific consensus around the causes of this change constitute objective facts that operate quite independent of any mediated understanding of the environment. At the same time, political understanding of this crisis, attempts by all interested actors to influence public opinion, and the political consequences that flow from public opinion are almost entirely dependent on the mediated treatments of the environment. Indeed, the scientific facts of global warming are politically effective only to the extent that they come to be part of the hyperreality that constitutes mediated communications about the environment.

A good example of the significance of the hyperreality of environmental politics is provided by the study of Boykoff and Boykoff (2004), which we discussed earlier. They found that public opinion about climate change followed the path of the prestige press's coverage, which at first covered the issue as a matter of emerging scientific consensus but then adopted a frame that discussed the issue as one over which there was much legitimate scientific disagreement. American public opinion followed this arc, with declining percentages of people believing that climate change was occurring and supporting government action. In short, it was the hyper-reality of media treatment of climate change, operating as a social fact quite independent of scientific research, which helped to shape the lack of political action on global climate change.

The significance of the concept of hyperreality focuses our inquiry less on the facts of global climate change per se than on the ways in which such facts do or do not enter into media discourse. This, in turn, highlights the importance of multiaxiality – understanding the multiple axes of power that shape media discourse. As the older media regime breaks down, so, too, does its characteristic axis of influence: the contest between professional journalists and political elites to control the limited number of gates through which political information flows. The explosion of gates characteristic of the new media environment has disrupted this single axis and created the potential for new axes of influence. It is these new axes that have been employed by a wide number of environmental groups, celebrities, global-warming skeptics, and others to get their own perspective on the environment to the public. This multiaxiality does not, however, mean that the emerging system allows all groups or individuals equal opportunities for shaping media discourse: structures of political power are not abolished by new media. Indeed, policy decisions made by the government in shaping a new media regime are precisely about which interests will be allowed to make effective use of the opportunities opened up by the new media environment.[27]

This chapter's investigation of media coverage of environmental issues as well as the concepts of hyperreality and multiaxiality suggests several conclusions relevant to the decisions that will shape a new media regime. First, although the role of professional journalists needs to be rethought, this does not by any means suggest that they will or should be unim-portant in a new media regime. However, debate over the specifics of this role needs to be based on a realistic appraisal of the job done by journalists in the recent past that is free of unreflective attempts to pro-tect unwarranted professional privilege. Such debate might open the way for journalists to play a prominent role in fairly evaluating the claims made by the numerous groups that now have access to public debate over

---

[27] For example, as we write, Federal Communications Commission rules on cross-media ownership rules are being contested by both media organizations and activist groups. How many different types of media – newspapers, television, and radio stations – can be owned by a single corporation will have a decisive impact on the diversity of voices allowed to influence the information passing through the new gates created by new media.

environmental issues. In the new media environment, citizens have a pressing need for help in evaluating the truth claims made by novelists like Michael Crichton, a filmmaker like Roland Emmerich, or a celebrity like Laurie David. Such evaluation is useful only to the extent that it both recognizes the legitimacy of a wide range of sources of information, rather than making a priori judgments about the legitimacy of certain sources or genres, and actually checks the claims made, rather than assuming that providing two sides to a story fulfills the obligation of journalists.

Second, a central challenge of the new media regime will be to ensure that the fragmentation and segmenting of audience for political information is countered by mechanisms that guarantee the engagement of disparate political views. Scientific consensus over the anthropogenic causes of global warming has limited political impact if wide swaths of the public get all their information from sources that deny its existence. As well, given fragmentation of the public's attention, the occasions when the public does focus on a specific issue, as during media events, become especially significant. Here again, is a role that professional journalists might be uniquely suited to play in a new media regime.[28]

Third, as new actors, operating outside the negotiation between journalists and political elites, help to set the agenda in the numerous arenas of public policy, including environmental concern, there needs to be much fuller consideration of the rules they use and the expectations of the public with respect to the claims made. What are the responsibilities of filmmakers, for example, to accurately represent the science of climate change when they address these issues? How much can be fudged for the sake of dramatic impact without invalidating the broader truth claims of a filmmaker or novelist? What are the responsibilities of scientific researchers, including social scientists, to present their findings through the media to a wider public in a form that is both accessible and accurate? These are questions that, obviously, cannot be answered definitively or authoritatively by the state but that nevertheless underlie the influence such disparate sources of political information have on public discourse. As well, they are not unique to the new media environment. Rather, they have become more obvious and pressing as a changing media environment explodes the consensus over the appropriate sources of political information that obscured them in the past.

---

[28] Given the increasing rarity of such moments when the public is focused on environmental issues, it is particularly disturbing that an event like the thirtieth anniversary of Earth Day received even less media attention in 2000 than it had in 1990.

Fourth, while addressing the responsibilities of the widening number of actors who provide political information is vital, there is simply no getting around the degree to which the new media environment has altered the situation of ordinary citizens who now are left to negotiate an incredibly rich but fragmented media environment. Will citizens make use of this environment to improve their understanding of and participation in political life? Will the incredible increase in the availability of information be at all matched by an increase in its creative and critical use? For us, the answers to such questions will be crucial not only to future policies such as those regarding the environment, but also to the future health of our democracy.

7

9/11 and Its Aftermath

*Constructing a Political Spectacle
in the New Media Environment*

I had expected to find the annihilating economy of the event – the way in which it had concentrated the complicated arrangements and misarrangements of the last century into a single irreducible image – being explored, made legible. On the contrary, I found that what had happened was being processed, obscured, systematically leached of history and so of meaning, finally rendered less readable than it had seemed on the morning it happened. As if overnight, the irreconcilable event had been made manageable, reduced to the sentimental, to protective talismans, totems, garlands of garlic, repeated pieties that would come to seem in some ways as destructive as the event itself.

> – Joan Didion, "Fixed Opinions, or the Hinge of History." *New York Review of Books*, 2002

Propaganda is going to get really thick & deep and we should reserve judgment.

> – A poster on the chat room of the neo-Nazi website Stormfront

One good thing could come from this horror: it could spell the end of the age of irony.

> – Roger Rosenblatt, "The Age of Irony Comes to an End." *Time* 2001

ABU, PALM PILOT SALESMAN, DETAINED WITHOUT CHARGES BY THE FBI: "I'm not just being inconvenienced here! I could be sent to a military tribunal, tried in secret and *shot*! All perfectly legal now! Do you know where *else* they have trials like that, my friend? *Iraq*! The country I fled from to come to America!"

FBI AGENT: "Too bad irony's dead."

ABU: "Yes, that would have helped."

> – Gary Trudeau, *Doonesbury*, January 4, 2003

The terrorist attacks of September 11, 2001, profoundly disrupted the norms, processes, and content of both old and new media. All regular programming (including advertising) on broadcast and cable television was immediately suspended in favor of around-the-clock coverage of the attacks. Electronic and print news media ceased coverage of almost all issues or events that were not at least indirectly connected to the attacks. Websites and internet chat rooms normally devoted to a wide range of disparate topics either focused exclusively on the attacks or experienced dramatically reduced traffic. Cultural and sporting events were canceled. In short, the diversity of form and content characteristic of the new media environment gave way to a much more singular focus. At the same time, media coverage in the immediate aftermath of 9/11 was heralded as the reascendance of traditional journalism, as people of all ages returned to the news for the latest information about unfolding events.

As we write this, the tenth anniversary of the terrorist attacks is approaching, and it is possible to gain some perspective. For example, given the continued decline in the audience for the network news, the large numbers of newspaper bankruptcy filings, the continuing hemorrhaging of jobs for professional journalism, and the general recognition that there is a crisis in American journalism, it seems clear that 9/11 did not usher in a rebirth of supposedly serious outlets of political information. Coverage of the terrorist attacks of 2001 helped prepare the way for the Bush administration to make its dubious case for the invasion of Iraq in 2003, and it continues to help justify an American military presence, albeit much reduced in that country in 2011 (though the number of troops in Afghanistan, the first war emerging from the 9/11 attacks, has increased). At the same time, although there are many claims that 9/11 represented a dramatic rupture in how Americans understood the world, there is to date no consensus on what this new understanding actually is; nothing comparable to the Cold War frame we discussed in Chapter 3 has emerged. As a result, understanding of 9/11 remains essentially contested at the same time that its impact continues to haunt American politics in 2011.

The September 11 attacks occurred at a crucial time in the development of what we have been calling the new media environment. The essential technological changes were in place (e.g., the normalization of the internet, cable and satellite television, cell phones, and so forth) and the passing media regime – what we've been calling the Age of Broadcast News – had clearly lost its authority. But absent a new regime, no clearly established rules, norms, or strategic rituals for the "appropriate" role of various media in such a period of intense crisis had emerged. We can now see the ways in which various media struggled to respond to 9/11 and the longer-term impact of these responses on the subsequent invasions of Iraq and Afghanistan and the resulting involvement of the United States in two extended military conflicts.

One genre that struggled intensely over its appropriate role was the late-night talk show. The decision to cancel broadcasts following the 9/11 attacks clearly (and mistakenly, we would argue) signaled the belief that such shows were politically irrelevant and had nothing to contribute to public discourse on the issue. Equally telling were the decisions as to when and how to return to the air. As one media reporter put it, "The feds have been more forthcoming about their leads on terrorists than execs at NBC's and CBS's late-night talk shows have been about their efforts to return their shows to the air" (De Morales 2001a, C7). When the shows did return, anywhere from six to seven days after the attacks, they all adopted unusual formats to signal their relationship to the continuing discourse on 9/11. Jay Leno and David Letterman dispensed with their opening monologues, with the latter explaining that he did not trust his comic judgment at a time like this. The struggle to find the right tone was especially obvious in the genre-defying combination of guests on these shows. Dan Rather appeared on Letterman and twice broke down in tears discussing the attacks. His companion on the show was Regis Philbin, the New York–based television celebrity. Jay Leno hosted Senator John McCain and the geriatric rockers Crosby, Stills, and Nash, who sang "Find the Cost of Freedom" and "My Country 'Tis of Thee." Craig Kilborn hosted Lawrence O'Donnell, a political analyst on MSNBC and writer on *The West Wing*; Dr. Drew Pinsky, a TV health adviser; and *Everybody Loves Raymond* cast member Patricia Heaton, who was in New York City on September 11.

At one level, the struggles of these programs to strike the right tone seem unremarkable for television – a mixture of seemingly genuine emotion, maudlin sentimentality, and almost pure kitsch. What is significant, however, is that the usual fare of skeptical, cynical, and occasionally satirical political commentary was gone. This does not mean, however, that the shows' political relevance was also gone. Rather, in a different but equally important way as the traditional news media, the decision to take late-night talk shows off the air and to return in the way they did played an important, if unreflective, role in setting, priming, and framing the post-9/11 national agenda.

A telling exception to the response of most late-night talk shows was that of *Politically Incorrect*, hosted by Bill Maher. Like other shows, *Politically Incorrect* was initially taken off the air. When it returned, Maher left one chair empty in honor of the conservative columnist and frequent guest Barbara Olson, who had died on Flight 93 when it crashed in Pennsylvania. Unlike the other late-night hosts, Maher did not dispense with his opening monologue, although he told no jokes: "It's going to be a little more serious. I think that's okay. It's okay with you?... We've lived through shock, anger, grief, fear.... But you know what, we need a release too." But he also added, "I do not relinquish, nor should any of you, the right to criticize, even as we support our government. This is still a democracy and they're still politicians" (Gumbell 2001, 10).[1] His commitment to this principle was demonstrated later in the show. The conservative author and former Reagan administration appointee Dinesh D'Souza challenged President Bush's labeling of the terrorists as cowards: "These are warriors and we have to realize that the principles of our way of life are in conflict with people in the world." Maher agreed, adding, "We have been the cowards, lobbing cruise missiles from 2,000 miles away. That's cowardly. Staying in the airplane when it hits the building, say what you want about it, it's not cowardly" (Bohlen 2001).

The reaction was immediate and angry. The right-wing talk-show host Dan Patrick called on his listeners to call their local television stations and the show's sponsors to voice their displeasure.[2] Although this ground swell of calls failed to materialize (the station received a few hundred calls, less than it receives when it preempts a soap opera), Sears and Federal Express rapidly pulled their ads from the show (McDaniel 2001). Although ABC continued to run *Politically Incorrect* without sponsors, several affiliates owned by two broadcasting groups dropped the show. Maher apologized for his comments, trying to explain that he thought his job was to continue being provocative, that he was deeply affected by the loss of life in the attacks but felt uncomfortable expressing such private grief in public, and that he regretted the pain his comments might have caused. Over the following few days, the controversy seemed to be dying down, ratings for the show increased, and several affiliates that

[1] Interestingly, Gumbell, a British reporter was the only writer throughout the controversy to cite Maher's opening statement.

[2] Patrick, who owns the radio station from which his show originates, is also a Texas state senator who boasts on his webpage of "pass[ing] a bill placing 'In God We Trust' permanently in the Senate Chamber and was the Senate author to place 'Under God' in our state pledge."

had dropped the show started to broadcast it again (including WJLA in Washington, D.C.).

The controversy was reignited on September 27, when at a press briefing, the White House press secretary Ari Fleischer was asked about the president's response to Maher's remarks:

> Fleischer said he had not seen a transcript of the broadcast, but that did not stop him from commenting that 'it's a terrible thing to say; and it's unfortunate' and that 'the reminder is to all Americans that they need to watch what they say, watch what they do, and that this is not a time for remarks like that.' He added, "It never is." (De Morales 2001b, C7)

Again, WJLA pulled the show, this time for good, and the number of affiliates dropping *Politically Incorrect* rose to seventeen.

Then, ABC announced that it would stand by the show, and many newspapers ran editorials and op-ed pieces decrying the chilling effect of Fleischer's comments on free speech (although few defended what Maher had said). The columnist and frequent *Politically Incorrect* guest Arianna Huffington started an online petition to keep the show on the air. Interestingly, D'Souza disappeared from the controversy entirely – he was neither attacked nor defended and never issued a public apology for his comments.[3] Although the show was saved for the moment, it is clear that the controversy doomed Bill Maher and his show at ABC. In March, when the network tried to attract David Letterman to replace Ted Koppel and *Nightline*, it also saw this as a way to replace *Politically Incorrect*. In May 2002, the network announced the cancellation of Maher's show, which finally went off the air on June 28.

The comments and fate of Bill Maher and *Politically Incorrect* may seem a trivial event to open a discussion regarding media coverage of September 11 and its aftermath. To the contrary, we would suggest that the case of *Politically Incorrect* provides an ideal entry point for such an examination. First, it again demonstrates the difficulty and limited value of drawing stark distinctions between news and entertainment, and it highlights the role of the latter in public discourse about important issues. At a time when such discourse was closing down, it is revealing that alternative perspectives came not from the news but from a late-night entertainment show hosted by a stand-up comedian. In the years since 2001, the political significance of shows like *Politically Incorrect*, including *The Daily Show*, *The Colbert Report*, and *Real Time with Bill Maher*

---

[3] Based on a LexisNexis search.

on HBO (a restructured version of *Politically Incorrect*) has increased, especially as counterweights to the discourse of professional journalism. "Satirical fake news programs, such as Jon Stewart's *The Daily Show*, would be considered fiction by traditional journalism but, much like court jesters of medieval times, they regularly connect the dots and express insights more incisive than the network news" (Wedel 2009, 42).

Second, the controversy over Maher's comments highlights the absence of clearly understood and accepted rules regarding the appropriate role of non-news genres in public discourse and the consequences of this absence. Ironically, on the one hand, Maher had considerably more freedom to express his controversial views than did professional journalists, whose traditional roles as independent observers and balanced purveyors of facts are suspended in times of national crises. At the same time Maher delivered his comments, Dan Rather was saying (significantly, in his teary appearance on David Letterman) that "George Bush is the president, he makes the decisions and, you know, as just one American, [if] he wants [Americans] to line up, just tell me where" (Engel 2002, 3).

On the other hand, Maher had little protection against retaliation for his comments because he was defined as an entertainment figure and so not deemed part of the community of broadcast journalists. As a result, although there was spirited debate in newspapers and on the internet over his right to say what he did, the controversy was ignored by television journalists. There was only one story on any of the nightly network news shows (including CNN) that even mentioned the controversy: a two-minute, forty-second broadcast on ABC News on September 28 devoted to the confusion over how popular culture should address the terrorist attacks, which included Maher's comments as an example.[4] Further, newspaper editorials on the controversy tended to focus on the potentially chilling effects of Fleischer's comments rather than defending what Maher had said, his right to say it, or the forum in which he had said it. Most telling was a back-and-forth between the editors at the *Washington Post* and Albritton Communications, the owner of ABC's Washington affiliate, WJLA. After a September 26 *Post* editorial criticizing the decision to take *Politically Incorrect* off the air for a second time, a letter from Frederick J. Ryan Jr., president and chief operating officer

---

[4] This was the only story turned up in a search of the Vanderbilt Television News Archive for the end of 2001, using the terms "Bill Maher" and/or "*Politically Incorrect*." The archives include all three nightly network news broadcasts plus CNN's *Nightly News*, hosted by Aaron Brown.

of Albritton, was published under the heading "Proud to Pull 'Politically Incorrect'":

It is important to note that "Politically Incorrect" is produced by the Disney ABC Entertainment Division. It is not a product of ABC News. Further, Mr. Maher is a satirist, not a journalist. In his attempt at humor he is unguided by rules of journalism or the standards of ABC News, The Post or other major news organization follows. The First Amendment entitles Mr. Maher to speak his views no matter how outrageous or insensitive they may be. The First Amendment also gives WJLA the right to broadcast what it deems appropriate.[5] (Washington Post 2001)

This aspect of the story is more evidence of the insidious consequences of asserting information hierarchies based on unexamined, and in this case unsustainable, dichotomies like news versus entertainment. The result is an inability to understand in any sophisticated way the role that a wide variety of media play in shaping our understanding of a crisis like 9/11. As we noted in Chapter 4, the impact of popular culture is not limited to the general public but extends to elites, too. When it came to making decisions about enhanced interrogation techniques (i.e., torture), high-ranking Bush administration decision makers referenced Jack Bauer's actions in the show 24. However, unless we treat shows like 24 as politically relevant texts, worthy of serious study, we will never develop an understanding of political communication adequate to the needs of both citizens and scholars.

Third, the Maher controversy illustrates the degree to which the new media environment is characterized by multiaxiality, even during dramatic media events such as 9/11. For example, the campaign against Maher was orchestrated by a right-wing talk-radio host. Maher's defenders, including many prominent cultural figures, responded through an online petition. Though ignored by television journalists, the issue was the subject of lively discussions and coverage on a variety of websites. More generally, it is important to note that Maher's show started on Comedy Central, a cable network. In a multiaxial environment, basic cable stations provide the opportunity for such genre-defying shows as

---

[5] One wonders where Ryan would place someone like Bill O'Reilly of Fox News, who first became known as the host of *Entertainment Tonight*, or, for that matter, those journalists willing to "line up" where the president tells them. Would *Politically Incorrect* still be on WJLA if it had been produced by ABC News? If it were, would Maher have been free to say what he did? Obviously, we think it is futile to try and make such abstract distinctions. Instead, Maher's comments and the reaction they generated are better analyzed in terms of their political relevance and their role in furthering or frustrating democratic politics.

Politically Incorrect and *The Daily Show* to develop, find a voice, and attract an audience.[6] It is the inability of mainstream broadcasters to accommodate such shows, without destroying the very originality that made them attractive in the first place, which is central here:

Mr. Maher has always been an uneasy fit at the network, its acquisition of him a classic case of a mainstream media company seeking a youthful edge by raiding the rising and more permissive world of cable, where Mr. Maher honed his sarcastic wit.... [He] considers himself a libertarian. And that puts him at odds at times with conservatives, at times with liberals, and at times with executives of Disney, who are said, for example, to be no fan of his criticism of the war against drugs. Disputes with censors and advertising executives are common. (Rutenberg 2001a, C1)

Fourth, the episode illustrates the degree to which the processes of agenda setting and framing have been fundamentally altered in the new media environment, even during periods of crises. No longer are these functions controlled by a single axis defined by traditional gatekeepers such as professional journalists and political elites. Maher's comments, at odds with the messages found in most mainstream media, were unusual only because they were aired on a broadcast network. In this new multiaxial environment, critiques and counterarguments to mainstream U.S. journalists and political elites abounded in new media such as the internet, outlets that did not exist as recently as the 1991 Gulf War. Moreover, and quite ironically, the continuing controversy over Maher's remarks, stoked by this new media environment, increased the show's ratings and (for this and other reasons) made it more difficult for ABC to abandon the show: "In the mirror-like world of public relations, the uproar may have actually extended his time by making it unlikely the network will yank him for mediocre ratings. While that is an option that has been considered from time to time, it might now be seen as buckling under" (Rutenberg 2001a, C1).

---

[6] It's worth pointing out here that it was in the aftermath of 9/11 that *The Daily Show* emerged as a cultural and political force, largely by providing a satirical and critical perspective on the way professional journalists covered the events of the day. As we have seen in Chapter 1, this did not represent a dumbing down, as the audience of the show is more informed than those who rely primarily on either a daily newspaper or the nightly network news (see, for example, Program on International Policy Attitudes. 2006). Jon Stewart has turned down offers to move his show to one of the networks, fearing that doing so would increase censorship. Moreover, as we argue here, *The Daily Show* and *The Colbert Report* did their best to subvert the widely accepted narrative of the Bush administration, often passed on uncritically by the press to the public, with respect to the justification for the war and the resulting "Mess O'Potamia."

Fifth and finally, however, the existence of multiple gates through which public information passes does not automatically mean that all points of view are equally able to speak or be heard in public discourse. In a multiaxial environment, control of the public agenda remains a political struggle, even if more complex than in the past, with winners and losers still determined by the distribution of political and economic power. It is, therefore, no surprise that in the post-9/11 environment, the anti-Maher campaign, orchestrated by right-wing fringe media, abetted by the White House, and ignored by mainstream broadcast journalists, was ultimately successful. It is also no surprise that conservative commentator Dinesh D'Souza, who started the controversy, was left unscathed.

Media Events in the New Information Environment

Media "events," such as 9/11, serve a number of purposes. At a minimum, they provide the public with ongoing and up-to-date, if often partial and unreliable, information about the issue at hand. They also serve as powerful examples of the media's agenda-setting power by focusing public attention on a single issue in normally unprecedented ways. As noted by Daniel Dayan and Elihu Katz (1992), media events can also serve a more basic human function, acting as public rituals of grief, mourning, and reconciliation. Examples of past media events that have played this role are the Kennedy assassination, the death of Princess Diana, and the loss of the Challenger and Columbia space shuttles. Such mediated public experiences tap into shared foundational beliefs that can unify seemingly disparate segments of society. Although various media may cover these events in somewhat different ways, underlying assumptions about the public agenda are shared across both outlets and audiences.

Clearly, much of the coverage of 9/11 – and public reaction to it – was consistent with Dayan and Katz's notion of media events as public rituals. But the terrorist attacks also set off a political crisis that raised profound and contested questions about the role of the United States in the world and the most appropriate response to the attacks. As such, it also had many elements of a different definition of media event offered by the media scholar John Fiske (1996). Rather than rituals of reconciliation, Fiske argues that media events can provide opportunities for marginalized publics to enter mainstream discourse, thus challenging the hegemonic or uniform interpretations that normally dominate considerations of political and social issues.

At the same time, the abundance of diverse sources of information of unclear provenance and the ease with which analysts with dubious credentials can circulate their interpretation of events can create not just alternative publics but also alternative hyperrealities on which competing political discourses can then be based. A clear and troubling example of this congruence of multiaxiality and hyperreality is the spread of so-called 9/11 truthers, people whose challenge of mainstream accounts is expressed in a wide and bizarre range of conspiracy theories about what happened during the attacks and who was responsible.

In large part because of the complexity of the new media environment, we believe that both of these seemingly disparate functions of media events were at play in the coverage of the 9/11 terrorist attacks. Although the mainstream media initially adopted a largely hegemonic ritual of mourning, grief, and reconciliation, quite different discourses were available through alternative channels of information, and these eventually found their way back into parts of the mainstream. The result illustrates the consequences, for both better and worse, of the passing of the Age of Broadcast News and that regime's ability to construct a "single forum for [our] most important 'formative conversations'... a forum that... was more or less universally attended" (Leys 2001, 150). Consequently, control of the traditional news outlets, most often the outcome of the interaction between political elites and professional journalists, no longer necessarily structures public discourse. At the same time, the new and unstable multiaxial environment in no way ensures a more sophisticated and democratic public discourse.

Much of the complexity found in public opinion, both after the attacks and especially in the subsequent buildup to war in Iraq, was a consequence of this very different environment within which media events now play out. Understanding the political and social impact of the media during times of crisis requires that we extend our analyses to include the myriad new and evolving sources of politically relevant discourse.

Is Watching and Reading More News Good for You? Change and Continuity in Coverage of 9/11

Even in the new media environment in which we live, many things remain unchanged. As in the past, when dramatic events take place, Americans gather around the electronic hearth in huge numbers, turning to the news media for both information and solace. This was certainly the case after 9/11. For example, ACNielsen reported that, between 8 P.M. and 11 P.M. on September 11, 2001, an estimated 79.5 million viewers tuned in to the major broadcast and cable news outlets (ABC, CBS, NBC, CNN, CNN Headline News, Fox News, CNBC, MSNBC, and TBS or TNT – which were carrying CNN), as compared to 26 million viewers for a typical evening of network and cable news viewing.[7] Although ratings for nightly network news broadcasts soon returned to more normal levels, there was still a 3 percent overall increase for 2001, the first time in decades that audiences had grown.[8] The big winners were the cable news networks: "In the aftermath of the September 11 attacks, the Pew Research Center found 9 of 10 Americans were getting their news primarily from television – but 45 percent turned to cable, 30 percent to the broadcast networks" (Kurtz 2002, A1). Ratings for CNN were 50 percent higher in September 2002 than they had been in August 2001 (Engel 2002). Increased news viewing was especially dramatic among the young, who had been seen as abandoning "serious" news. In the wake of 9/11, 45 percent of eighteen-to thirty-four-year-olds tuned in to CNN, 30 percent to MSNBC, and 20 percent to Fox News, as compared to just 16 percent, 20 percent, and 12 percent, respectively, in August (Walker 2001). The increased audience for news was not limited to television. Newspaper circulation increased, as did the circulation of *Time* and *Newsweek* (up by almost 80 percent in the weeks after the attacks). The *Atlantic Monthly* also saw dramatically increased sales for its three-part series on the attacks.

Broadcast journalists were quick to interpret increased audiences as evidence that, when it really mattered, Americans turned to them. Walter Isaacson, the Chairman and CEO of CNN, said of the attacks, "It's helped all of us regain our focus. It's injected a note of real seriousness. And the things we think of doing to chase ratings now pale in comparison to the importance of doing this story seriously and reliably" (Rutenberg 2001b, C10). And Mel Karmazin, the president and CEO of Viacom, the parent company of CBS, remarked, "Over the past ten weeks, we've been reminded why we do what we do" (qtd. in Auletta 2001, 66).

---

[7] Although these are impressive figures, given the normal size of the television news audience, it is worth noting that the 2002 Super Bowl drew 86 million viewers.

[8] Yet despite the increase, the actual economics of the network news broadcasts have actually worsened, as modest increases in ratings were at the expense of dramatically increased costs of covering the terrorist attacks and the war in Afghanistan and not matched by any increase in advertising revenues in a depressed economy (Rutenberg and Schiesel 2002).

The return of the public to "serious" journalism proved transitory, however, and by September 2002, circulation and viewership for print and television journalism had returned to their pre-9/11 levels (Engel 2002). Though longer lasting than the increases for the broadcast news, even the boosted ratings for most cable news were not permanent: CNN, Headline News, MSNBC and CNBC all saw dramatic double-digit drops in ratings between late 2001 and late 2002 (Offman 2003).

And what was the public's reward for this significant, if temporary, return to the news? The findings of communications researchers suggest that it is during media events, when the greatest attention is focused on the news, that the contradictions in the social responsibility theory of the press are most glaring. In times of national crisis, journalists are more likely to act as the voice of the state than as independent professionals searching out competing perspectives on the day's events. Daniel Hallin (1986) illustrates this process in his study of media coverage of the Vietnam War. Professional journalism depends on "credible sources," defined primarily as political elites, in determining newsworthiness, maintaining objectivity, and providing balance. However, in times of national crises, and especially international crises, the public statements of political elites from different ideological or partisan camps often converge, partly out of a sense of patriotism and partly out of hesitancy to criticize the administration in power. As a result, the information provided to citizens becomes constrained, thus reflecting a limited range of political viewpoints.[9] This closing off of debate is reinforced by corporate media's sensitivity to ratings and public opinion. In times of national crisis, when there are strong rally-around-the-flag sentiments among the public, journalistic coverage is likely to be very cautious about offending a patriotically aroused audience by criticizing the actions of government officials.

Another limiting factor of coverage during high-profile media events, resulting from the norms of professional journalism but exacerbated in the new media environment, is the imperative to "get the story first." One of the effects of around-the-clock coverage of any event – whether the Clinton-Lewinsky scandal discussed in Chapter 5 or the terrorist attacks of September 11 – is to dramatically shorten the news cycle while increasing the pressure for journalists to have something new to report.

---

[9] Hallin (1986) finds that, before 1968, elite opinion about the war was united and so the "the sphere of legitimate controversy" was quite narrow. It was only after 1968 and the Tet offensive that elites were divided enough about the war to go on the record with their criticisms that journalists began to file stories critical of the Johnson administration's policies.

As a result, much of what is reported is not subject to the same scrutiny and fact-checking as would be the case during more placid periods. Elihu Katz (1993) noted this in his analysis of coverage of the 1991 Gulf War, when for the first time the twenty-four-hour cable networks began to drive media coverage. The result, he persuasively argued, was the abdication of the editing role for journalists. Combined with the convergence of elite opinion and a hesitancy to appear out of step with public opinion, journalists are even more susceptible to government manipulation.

In times when public consensus, reconciliation, and/or support for the government is either useful or harmless (e.g., the types of media events examined by Dayan and Katz 1992) this process might be viewed in a positive light. When, however, such consensus is artificially manufactured in ways that affect contestable policy outcomes, it becomes difficult to distinguish between socially responsible and totalitarian press systems. As Lance Bennett, Steven Livingston, and Regina Lawrence (2007) note, the irony is that when government is working as we expect it to in a democratic society – policy makers are debating a wide range of perspectives – the press works well. However, when government fails to consider a range of perspectives and options but coalesces around a single viewpoint – in short, when there is the most need for an aggressive and independent fourth estate – the press fails.

Murray Edelman (1995) goes so far as to argue that the implicit function of mainstream journalism during "political spectacles" is not to inform a democratic citizenry and enable them to form educated opinions about events but to mobilize the public in support of already-determined government policies. This argument is supported by the coverage of both the 9/11 attacks and the virtually uncritical treatment of Bush administration claims about justifications for the invasion of Iraq in 2003. Given this state of affairs, Edelman draws the conclusion that the only real option for citizens is to not pay attention.[10] Even if one accepted this depressing solution, however, it ignores the fact that it is precisely during such media spectacles or events that the social and political pressure for citizens to pay attention to "serious" coverage is the greatest.

It is not hard to find evidence that the mainstream media acted as described earlier in the aftermath of September 11, 2001. Dan Rather

---

[10] The new media environment, with its fragmentation of outlets, may make it much easier for citizens to ignore the efforts of government to mobilize opinion. On November 11, 2001, for example, when President Bush gave a speech celebrating the heroes of 9/11, only one of the four networks (ABC) interrupted regular programming to carry it (Rich 2006, 37).

was not the only journalist ready to "line up" for the administration. A study by the Pew Center for Excellence in Journalism (2002) concluded that post-9/11 coverage in newspapers and television heavily favored U.S. positions, with about half of the stories examined containing only viewpoints consistent with Bush administration policies. Television news was especially susceptible to this bias, rarely including any criticism of the administration (Jurkowitz 2002). Many network correspondents (including Tim Russert of NBC and most Fox News correspondents) and local broadcasters donned American-flag pins. Those who refused to adopt this practice were swiftly threatened with retaliation. In Missouri, Republican state legislators threatened to withhold funding from the University of Missouri's School of Journalism after the news director of the campus TV station banned wearing flag pins and putting ribbons on cameras. The news director's argument is worth quoting, appealing as it did to the values and procedures of professional journalism: "Our news broadcasts are not the place for personal statements of support for any cause – no matter how deserving the cause may seem to be. Our job is to deliver the news as free from outside influences as possible" (Brazaitis 2001, H3).

The loss of critical distance within mainstream journalism went beyond donning lapel pins or broadcasting American-flag logos in the corner of television screens. On Fox News, the anchor Brit Hume dismissed civilian deaths in Afghanistan as essentially unworthy of news coverage. The head of CNN, Walter Isaacson (quoted earlier lauding the values of serious, reliable reporting), required reporters to mention civilian casualties in Afghanistan only if they also recalled Americans killed in the September 11 attacks (this applied only to domestic, not international, CNN broadcasts; Hertsgaard 2002, 14). The seemingly blatant violations of the norms of professional journalism were not limited to television. For example, in October 2001, a Florida newspaper sent this message to its staff: "DO NOT USE photos dealing with civilian casualties from the war on Afghanistan on page A1.... DO NOT USE wire stories that lead with civilian casualties.... They should be mentioned further down in the story. If the story needs rewriting to play down the civilian casualties, Do It" (qtd. in Johnson 2008, 30). Newspaper columnists in Texas and Oregon were fired for publishing criticisms of the president's handling of the attacks (Carter and Barringer 2001).

It is easy enough to criticize the shortcomings of crisis journalism, and many have carried out detailed and convincing analyses of coverage of 9/11. Indeed, journalists themselves are among the most vigorous, if after-the-fact, critics of such coverage.[11] Our point is not to simply repeat these critiques but to make a more basic point about the role of journalism in the new media environment. Measured superficially against the norms and assumptions of the Age of Broadcast News, the media's response was entirely appropriate. "Entertainment" media was rightfully suspended. "News" coverage was expanded. And the public increased its attention to that expanded news. But what was suspended in the wake of the terrorist attacks was not just regularly scheduled programs and commercials but "normal" journalism as well. Thus, although there were increased audiences for traditional news outlets, the information provided by these outlets was far from ordinary – in terms of both the content and the rules used to produce it – and arguably far from useful.

Assessing Mainstream News Coverage of the 9/11 Media Spectacle: What Went Wrong and Why It Always Goes Wrong

During and after the September 11 attacks, familiar figures – Dan Rather, Tom Brokaw, Peter Jennings, and so forth – spoke to us from the familiar setting of the network newsroom. They employed the formats and rules of news discourse used during their usual nightly news broadcasts. These seemingly superficial trappings of the news serve to signal viewers that they are receiving information that is authoritative, trustworthy, objective, and balanced. Alterations in these strategic rituals that occur during times of crisis – for example, around-the-clock coverage of a single event, the showing of emotion, the wearing of flag lapel pins – signal the added importance of the event being covered. But they do not reduce (and perhaps enhance) the expectation of viewers that the information received from these familiar figures will conform to the rules of professional journalism. Indeed, it is for precisely this reason – and the reassurance provided by it – that viewers turn to television news in times of crises.

This "understanding" between news producers and consumers is problematic even during noncrisis periods for the reasons discussed earlier in this book. Nonetheless, to the extent that audiences are aware of these rules and that journalists follow them, there is at least the possibility

---

[11] They returned to their routine after-the-fact (and only after-the-fact) self-criticism in the remarkable apologies by the *New York Times* and *Washington Post* for their uncritical acceptance of false and dubious claims used by the Bush administration to justify the invasion of Iraq in 2003.

that citizens can critically assess the information they receive. However, during media events, even this level of transparency is threatened. Although we see the same faces and settings, the rules determining what is spoken change dramatically and invisibly. At such times, it becomes increasingly difficult to determine who exactly is speaking to us through mainstream news outlets or what rules are determining the content and substance of that information. The result is media coverage that undermines the critical abilities of even the most discerning viewers. Yet as critics as diverse as Murray Edelman and Bill Maher have suggested, it is during periods of crisis that a critical perspective is most necessary. Indeed, given the loss of independence that characterizes the mainstream media during such periods, it might be more honest if government spokespersons were to simply take over news broadcasts. At least there would be less confusion regarding who is speaking to the public.

This sort of confusion about who is actually speaking is carefully orchestrated by the government to shape public opinion through what we now call public relations but that is more accurately called propaganda campaigns. Indeed, the basic techniques used by governments to mobilize support have changed little since they were first outlined by Harold Lasswell (1971) in his analysis of the propaganda campaigns waged during World War I: demonization of the enemy leader, defining the decision to go to war as defensive, appeals to international law, specific targeting of different rationales for war to different audiences, and so forth (Williams 2004). Examples of such propaganda used by the Bush administration abound. What has changed, perhaps, is the level of sophistication. So, for example, the Pentagon employed "a production designer who had worked for Disney, MGM, Good Morning America, and the illusionist David Blaine...to give General Tommy Franks a confidence-inspiring $200,000 set for briefings at Central Command headquarters in Qatar" (Rich 2006, 74). More recently, it was revealed in the *New York Times* that many of the military experts used by the networks were part of a Pentagon military analyst program designed to parrot Defense Department talking points (Barstow 2008). The issue is less the conduct of government (after all, as Lasswell argued, mobilizing public opinion in support of war is to be expected and may be unavoidable) than it is the unacknowledged suspension of the professional practices of journalists to uncritically pass the propaganda along.

This confusion is driven not only by challenges to journalists' standard operating procedures (e.g., fact-checking, editing) created during times of crises but also by the more direct influence of ideology. Consider, for example, that whereas the cable networks were the big winners in the ratings gains that followed 9/11, CNN (the leading cable news network) was

overtaken by the News Corp-owned Fox News channel, which is altogether more feature-y, and by most reckonings, less straight. Its flagship evening show, the O'Reilly Factor, features Bill O'Reilly, a right-wing attack dog of more than normal ferocity who has gained an extraordinary degree of attention from the media pages in the elite press. (Engel 2002, 3)

Significantly, it was the Fox News network that, while using the tagline, "Real Journalism: News that is Balanced and Fair," most enthusiastically donned flag lapel pins and abandoned even the most minimally critical perspective of professional journalists. Our point is not that providing information from an ideological perspective is a problem – indeed, we would argue that it is impossible to do otherwise. As with the treatment of government propaganda, it is presenting consciously biased information under the guise of the traditional norms of journalism that is at issue here.

The seldom-acknowledged profit motive of news organizations and the short- and long-term impact of this motive on the quality of information provided also raise troubling issues. As we have seen, corporate executives such as Mel Karmazin of CBS were quick to take credit for the job done by their news divisions during the 9/11 crisis. As such, they represent themselves to the public as guardians of the media's public interest obligations. However, it is the very same executives who, with little public fanfare, also demand increased economic accountability of their news divisions. For example, the increased expenses of covering the terrorist attacks, coupled with dramatically decreased advertising revenues due to the withdrawal of commercials and a slumping economy, led executives such as Karmazin to cut back expenses in the months after September 2011 so as to meet corporate profit targets (Auletta 2001; Rutenberg and Schiesel 2002). These cutbacks make it unlikely that there will be the resources to provide high-quality, long-term coverage of issues such as terrorism, even when journalists have returned to their professional practices. In 2008, when there were still more than 150,000 American troops stationed in Iraq, CBS News no longer had a full-time correspondent in the country (Stelter 2008).

The influence of economic considerations (driven by a concern with ratings and advertising revenue) and ideology can intersect. Again, our emphasis here is on the lack of attention to these underlying forces. For example, the ratings success of the Fox News network's embrace of on-air patriotism was not lost on the executives at NBC. In March 2003, they gave Michael Savage, a controversial right-wing radio host, his own weekly show on MSNBC.[12] The network attempted to mask the underlying reason for this decision by using the language of professional journalism to defend the move, calling it an effort to "expand the marketplace of ideas." It is clear, however, that the driving force was an economic one (Fairness and Accuracy in Reporting 2003). In the same month that Savage was hired, MSNBC canceled *Donahue*, a liberal talk show. In this case, MSNBC justified the decision in economic terms, claiming that poor ratings were the reason for canceling the show. However, at the time it was taken off the air, *Donahue* was the highest-rated talk show on the cable network. The true reason behind the decision was revealed (significantly, not by the mainstream news media but by the website All Your TV[13]) with the publication of a confidential MSNBC internal memo, which called the show's host, Phil Donahue,

a tired, left-wing liberal out of touch with the current marketplace... He seems to delight in presenting guests who are anti-war, anti-Bush and skeptical of the administration's motives... [and his show might become] a home for the liberal antiwar agenda at the same time that our competitors are waving the flag at every opportunity." (Fairness and Accuracy in Reporting 2003)

In short, when Mel Karmazin, Walter Isaacson, Dan Rather, or Bill O'Reilly speak to us, they do so from multiple perspectives – from highly rewarded guardians of the corporate bottom line to guardians of the public interest – with multiple, often conflicting motives. Given the private-ownership model of journalism that dominates the American media, these contradictions have always been present and are unremarkable. However, the absence of transparency about this state of affairs, indeed the often conscious effort to disguise economic and ideological motives in the guise of serving the public interest, limits the ability of citizens to assess the information they receive. This is especially important and

---

[12] According to critics, on his radio show, Savage had called child victims of inner-city gunfire "ghetto slime," had referred to nonwhite countries as "turd world nations," had called homosexuality "perversion," and had asserted that Latinos "breed like rabbits." His MSNBC show was canceled in July 2003 after he made an ugly attack on a gay caller ("Why don't you just get AIDS and die?").

[13] The fact that this information was made public by a website is consistent with our broader argument that the new media environment alters the dynamics of media events, in that information that would have in past media regimes remained hidden was leaked to an internet site and then publicized more widely through e-mail by the liberal media watchdog group Fairness and Accuracy in Reporting.

obvious in periods of political crises, when the stakes for citizens, and thus the importance of their being aware of the limits of the information they have, are especially high, but it is also true during more routine periods.

Recall that a hallmark of Fiske's definition of media events is that they are characterized by multiaxiality: unlike treatment of routine events, multiple perspectives, many not usually heard, engage one another in public discourse. Yet this is precisely what did not happen in coverage of 9/11. The closing off of mediated public discourse resulted in the creation of a single narrative, put in place by political elites within the Bush administration, dutifully reported by mainstream journalists, and seamlessly leading from the terrorist attacks to the invasion of Afghanistan to the war in Iraq. This argument implicitly served as the basis for much of the criticisms leveled at 9/11 coverage, which were made (almost entirely retrospectively) in newspapers, magazines, and – to a lesser extent – television.

As we have seen, the norms of professional journalism, which generally limit the range of voices considered authoritative during periods of relative calm, are especially constraining during periods of political crises, when rallying around the flag; consensus among political elites; and nationalistic, ideological, and economic motivations of the news media are particularly intense. This was certainly true in post-9/11 coverage by the mainstream press. The coverage took for granted that American response must be military; that replying with nonviolence or diplomacy was not a serious option; that "we" would find who did this, track them down, and destroy them. Nearly two years after September 11, 2001, this dominant narrative was still firmly in place on most electronic and in most print news outlets as the administration made the case for war in Iraq. Yet as Steve Rendall of the media watchdog organization Fairness and Accuracy in Reporting put it: "The pundit offering is one-sided. Where are the experts on international law? Where are the experts who might take Martin Luther King Jr. and Mohandas Gandhi seriously? The peace experts? You might think that's a joke, but there are people who study these things as seriously as war" (qtd. In Brazaitis 2001, H3).

The closing off of alternative viewpoints is a familiar characteristic of many media events. However, given the changing media environment and the dramatic increase in gates through which political information can flow, there are rich possibilities for alternative voices. For this reason, the privileging of traditional news outlets, evidenced by the decision to take most other genres off the air during the week immediately following 9/11, was particularly problematic. So, too, were subsequent efforts to silence, marginalize, or demonize alternative voices, as exemplified by the orchestrated attacks on Bill Maher, the canceling of *Donahue*, and the firing of columnists voicing opposition to the dominant consensus. Tellingly, one of the few sources of alternative perspectives found on the news were Hollywood activists such as Martin Sheen, Janeane Garofalo, and Sean Penn, who were able to translate their celebrity into authoritative status. Even here, however, such celebrity activists were regularly challenged and discounted, not only because of their views but also because they lacked the presumed credentials necessary to speak out on public issues.

The attempt to forge a consensus view was not limited to discourse but also emerged from the very technology of the media itself. Here, we focus on the ability of television to broadcast the most powerful of "live" images. As we have seen, with the introduction of most new technologies, there is a tendency to see such innovations as ways to break through the distorting prism of existing media and get to an unmediated reality. This tantalizing promise is nowhere more evident than with the live coverage of the attacks of 9/11. Watching the towers of the World Trade Center collapse on themselves in real time as the usually glib television journalists went silent was an experience none of us will ever forget. The immediacy of the event and the power of those images create a temptation to believe that we are, indeed, seeing the truth with our own eyes. Yet the ability to broadcast images in real time, powerful as these particular scenes are, is not the same thing as presenting an unmediated and unedited picture of events. Inevitable, if obscured, editorial decisions have important ideological implications for the version of political truth favored by the images selected. From almost the first moments of the crisis, broadcasters faced a wide range of decisions about what to show, what not to show, what to show only once, and what to continuously repeat. For example, there was almost immediate controversy over whether to show images of people jumping to their death from the burning twin towers. In the end, the networks decided against showing those gruesome images. Yet what criteria were used in making these editorial decisions and what was their goal, given that these images were widely seen in outlets from the tabloid *New York Daily News* to the internet? Susan Sontag (2003, 68) points out that, given the degree to which scenes of graphic violence have become commonplace in our culture, from the nightly news to films to videos circulating on the internet, the decision to not show certain scenes of actual violence is actually quite problematic, with implications at the foundational level of politics: "Often [network journalists'] decisions are cast as judgments about "good taste" – always a repressive standard when invoked by institutions."

The contrast between the illusion of seeing reality and the politically freighted editorial decisions made by news divisions was even starker in coverage of the invasion of Iraq. So, as embedded reporters traveled with American and British troops and provided us with dramatic footage of what the conflict looked like from their perspective, the networks chose not to air footage of the civilian victims of the war. Later, CNN explained this decision as simply a "news judgment where we would of course be mindful of the sensibilities of our viewers" (qtd. in Rich 2006, 77). Yet it seems obvious that airing footage from the soldiers' perspective, emphasizing the precision weapons technology they employed, without showing what the bullets and bombs actually do when they reach their destination, creates a particular hyperreality that is an essential part of mobilizing and maintaining support for any war. The connection between the technology of waging war and the technology used to portray it through photography and film was made as early as the 1930s by Ernst Junger, a German author and veteran of World War I. He noted that it is not accidental that we use the same term to describe the "shooting" of a person with a gun and a camera, concluding, "It is the same intelligence, whose weapons of annihilation can locate the enemy to the exact second and meter that labors to preserve the great historical event in fine detail" (qtd. in Sontag 2003, 66–67).

We would add that the very idea that these decisions are simply based on "good taste," "news judgments," or the "sensibilities of viewers" depends on accepting the sharp distinction between news and entertainment that we have been troubling over throughout this book. Frank Rich (2006, 77) called the decision to limit images of graphic violence as "culturally counterintuitive," arguing:

Only a few years earlier, movies such as *Saving Private Ryan* and *Black Hawk Down* had been widely applauded for the innovative realism of their battle scenes. Wouldn't it have made sense for media depictions of an actual war at least occasionally to adhere to the same standard? Apparently not. The prewar joke – that the war would be the ultimate reality show – came true. Its life-and-death perils were airbrushed whenever possible in the same soothing style as the artificial perils on *Survivor*.

Now, as in the past, the ability of new technologies to get us to an unvarnished reality remains a myth – the closer media seem to get us to such a reality, the farther away that reality recedes and the more vital becomes understanding the significance of the hyperreal constructions on which public and elite perceptions depend. The danger of the myth lies in its promise of a way to avoid the hard, critical work of analyzing the connection between mediated political information and the inevitably contested vision of political truth to which it is connected. In the case of "live" coverage of 9/11 and the military response to the attacks, the myth is doubly difficult to avoid. First, because the images came to us in a seemingly but not truly unedited form. Second, because they are being presented by journalists who we assume, incorrectly, are acting according the usual tenets of their profession. In short, the images of 9/11 came to us with an aura of verisimilitude that was exceedingly difficult to resist and that had important consequences for the ability or inability of the public to understand the causes and context of the attacks or to critically analyze the decisions of the government about responses to the attacks. Put another way, do these live images help us to get to the political truth of the events? Do they further or retard our efforts to understand why nineteen men undertook a suicidal mission to kill so many innocent Americans?

The failures of professional journalists and the network and cable news divisions represented an important missed opportunity. Coverage of the attacks meant dramatically increased audiences, including young people, for traditional sources of political information. As such, it was a rare opportunity for enhancing the ability of a focused citizenry to participate in a public conversation about the causes, context, and appropriate responses to the attacks. Given the endless hours of coverage, much of it simply repeating what had already been reported, there was ample time to provide such perspective. Yet as we have seen, this opportunity to encourage democratic debate was missed, as journalists "lined up" for the administration. As Edelman suggests, the more we watch of mainstream media during such political spectacles, the less able we are to enter into a critical debate. It is not that the coverage did not affect public discourse. Rather, it did so in a way that made viewers less able to question government policies and thus more available for mobilization by the state, a mobilization that extended from 9/11 through the invasion of Afghanistan and the war in Iraq.

The waxing and waning of the audience make the behavior of journalists in the wake of 9/11 particularly troubling. As is usually the case, much like a drunk waking up with a hangover after a bender, many journalists look back at their performance during media events and find ample reason for self-criticism. So, for example, Dan Rather regretted his comments on David Letterman's show:

By May [of 2002], he was complaining on BBC2's Newsnight that patriotism had "run amok" in the US and insisting: "It's unpatriotic not to stand up, look them in the eye, and ask the questions they don't want to hear – they being those who have the ultimate responsibility... of sending our sons and daughters, our husbands and wives, our blood, to face death." (Engel 2002, 3)

In September 2007, speaking at the National Press Club, *CBS Evening News* anchor Katie Couric was even more critical:

Everyone in this room would agree that people in this country were misled in terms of the rationale of this war... The whole culture of wearing flags on our lapel and saying 'we' when referring to the United States and, even the 'shock and awe' of the initial stages, it was just too jubilant and just a little uncomfortable. And I remember feeling, when I was anchoring the 'Today' show, this inevitable march towards war and kind of feeling like, 'Will anybody put the brakes on this?' And is this really being properly challenged by the right people? And I think, at the time, anyone who questioned the administration was considered unpatriotic and it was a very difficult position to be in. (qtd. in Washington Examiner 2007)

Yet such self-criticism (either voiced on the BBC – and not *CBS Evening News with Katie Couric* – or six years later to a roomful of journalists) matters little when expressed so long after the fact and at a time when the large audiences gathered for media events have disappeared. This belated, ritualistic form of self-criticism is labeled "pressure without reform" by media scholar Robert Entman. He explains that this criticism, by audiences, elites, and journalists themselves, is unlikely to lead to actual change in media coverage because it fails to address the continuing economic and political pressure on professional journalists (Entman 1989). In any event, these institutional pressures mean that the opportunities for improving coverage remain largely unrealized. If more evidence of this cycle is needed, consider that, in 2003, a year after Rather's critique, the *New York Times*, the *Washington Post*, and virtually every network and cable news division accepted the administration's false claims for an invasion of Iraq.

The systematic failure of professional journalism makes the example of Bill Maher so tragic. The host of *Politically Incorrect* was ideally situated to provide a model of how we might discuss, in an engaging and accessible manner, the issues raised by the terrorist attacks. In our view, throughout its five-year run on ABC, the show demonstrated how a variety of conflicting political views could be debated with humor, wit, and civility that usually did not trivialize the issues being discussed. This was an especially notable achievement, as the show routinely attracted a relatively large audience (between 2.5 million and 3 million viewers) in an otherwise fragmented media system. Maher's opening comments on his return to the air after the attacks, quoted at the beginning of this chapter, indicated that he understood the responsibility he had to continue to model democratic practice. Indeed, his perspective was quite similar to that adopted a year later by Dan Rather – recall that Maher said, "I do not relinquish, nor should any of you, the right to criticize, even as we support our government. This is still a democracy and they're still politicians."[14] Yet his inability to continue in this vein in the wake of the furious reaction to his remarks and ultimate cancellation of his show was a great loss, especially when the rest of the mainstream media was so monolithic in its coverage of this media event.

Hyperreality and Multiaxiality in Mainstream News Coverage of 9/11

Hyperreality refers to a loss of certainty in one's ability to distinguish clearly and hierarchically between reality and its mediated representation. Almost by definition, media events such as 9/11 are hyperreal affairs, as they involve emotional, personalized, community-wide reactions to happenings that are, for most people, "experienced" solely through the mass media. In such circumstances, the norms of objectivity, fairness, and balance that underlie professional journalism are especially important if there is to be some meaningful relationship between reality and its representation. This is all the more the case when the political stakes are high, as they clearly were in the period following the September 11 attacks. But as we have seen, the representation of reality constructed through the mainstream news media was both hegemonic and ideologically skewed. At the same time, many aspects of the new media environment, such as twenty-four-hour news, live satellite broadcasts, portable video cameras, and the like, added to both the reach and the seductiveness – the hyperreality – of this mediated construction.

Our point here is not that hyperreality resulted from decisions made by the mainstream news media – such blurring of reality and its representation is an increasingly unavoidable aspect of the mass mediated environment in which we all live. Rather, we suggest that this inevitable state of affairs raises new concerns for the political implications of media

---

[14] It is worth emphasizing that Maher made his statement on the same night that Rather was offering to "line up" on *Late Show with David Letterman*.

coverage. In the case of 9/11 and its aftermath, for example, the expectation, ingrained over the latter half of the twentieth century, that the mainstream news media were functioning as "mirrors" on reality made it likely that citizens would mistakenly and uncritically equate media representations with the events being represented. This made public opinion particularly susceptible to mobilization by the state (Nacos, Bloch-Elkon, and Shapiro, 2011). Unlike with coverage of the Clinton scandals discussed in Chapter 5, where the multiaxiality of the new media environment allowed arguably fringe elements of the political right to set the agenda for mainstream news outlets, in the case of 9/11, it was more traditional political elites (the Bush administration) who were able to control the news agenda. In short, while the multiaxiality of the new media environment may provide greater opportunities for diverse and previously marginalized interests to shape media discourse, such an outcome is far from guaranteed. Elite control of the public agenda depends on influencing or even shutting down many more information conduits than it once did, but this is not impossible. As the case of 9/11 illustrates, its framing as an act of war (e.g., as opposed to a criminal act) and a national security crisis helped political elites limit the alternative discourses available to Americans, especially in the immediate aftermath of the event.

Without using the term *hyperreality*, the Bush administration recognized that it was no longer possible to distinguish between media representations and any objective reality that they purport to portray. In terms Jean Baudrillard might have used, shortly before the 2004 election, the journalist Ron Suskind in a *New York Times Magazine* story quoted a presidential adviser as saying that journalists were part of the "reality-based community.... [A] judicious study of discernible reality is not the way the world really works anymore.... We're an Empire now and when we act, we create our own reality" (qtd. in Rich 2006, 3). The effectiveness of the administration's approach is indicated by the enduring impact on public opinion of the hyperreality it created. A survey taken in 2004 by the Program on International Policy Attitudes at the University of Maryland (PIPA) showed that 35 percent of respondents still believed Iraq had weapons of mass destruction when the United States invaded, and another 19 percent felt that it "had a major program for developing them" at the time. Nearly two-thirds of respondents said that they believed that most experts said Iraq did have weapons of mass destruction (30 percent) or that experts were evenly divided on the issue (35 percent). Half believed that Iraq was either closely linked with al-Qaeda before the war (35 percent) or was directly involved in the 9/11 attacks (15 percent).

Eighty-two percent said either that "experts mostly agree Iraq was providing substantial support to al-Qaeda" (47 percent) or that "experts are evenly divided on the question" (35 percent). Only 15 percent said it was their impression that "experts mostly agree [that] Iraq was not providing substantial support to al-Qaeda."

In March 2006, PIPA repeated these questions in a new survey and found that many Americans still believed in these falsehoods but that such beliefs were starkly divided along party lines:

> Though their numbers are declining, a majority of Republicans continue to believe that before the war, Iraq had weapons of mass destruction or a major program for developing them and do not think that most experts believe Iraq did not have [weapons of mass destruction]. A growing majority of Democrats believe the opposite on both points.

> A majority of Republicans, though declining, maintains the belief that Iraq was providing substantial support to al-Qaeda and that clear evidence of this support has been found, in contrast to large majorities of Democrats who hold opposing beliefs. A slight majority of Republicans believe that most experts agree that Iraq was providing support to al-Qaeda. Only 1 in 4 Democrats holds this view, but only a minority (and a declining one) perceives that most experts agree that Iraq was not providing support. (Program on International Policy Attitudes 2006)

In terms consistent with the notion of hyperreality, the PIPA report concluded, "Indeed it seems fair to say that in regard to the Iraq war, Republicans and Democrats are living in separate realities" (World Public Opinion.org 2006).

Thus far, one might conclude that, at least in times of crises, politics in the new media environment looks very much like it did during the Age of Broadcast News, with traditional elites setting the public agenda and the news media serving as information gatekeepers in this process. If, however, we expand our notion of politically relevant media beyond traditional news sources, a much more complex, less easily characterized picture emerges.

Saying What We Want When We're Supposed to Watch What We Say: The New Media Environment and Resistance to the Political Spectacle

Despite the limitations of professional journalism's coverage of the 9/11 terrorist attacks, the larger media environment provided the public with a much more diverse range of information than has typically been the case during media events. To be sure, some aspects of what we have characterized as part of this new environment, such as the more central role of comedy and satire, were shut down in the immediate aftermath of the terrorist attacks. The Bill Maher example is particularly revealing in this regard, as his show lay at the boundaries between traditional and new approaches to providing politically relevant information. The "censoring" of his critical views and the absence of any norms to prevent this from happening demonstrate both the democratic limits and the continued power of the late-twentieth-century media regime. This closing off of discourse was not uniform. Reflecting the new conduits opened up by the multiaxiality of a changing media environment, as one moved further from traditional genres, such as news, or traditional media, such as broadcast television, the diversity of alternative discourses increased.

Two central, if tentative, observations emerge out of our examination of the broader media environment following the 9/11 terrorist attacks, observations that hint at the democratic potential of this environment. First, the relationship between traditional and nontraditional sources of politically relevant information is dynamic and interactive. For example, it appears that as mainstream news sources became more hegemonic and hierarchical in their coverage, alternative venues such as highly politicized websites and online chat rooms became more open, providing rich and vibrant forums for political discussion. In a phrase, these new media outlets provided a place for Americans to say what they want at precisely the moment when they were being warned by political elites (through the mainstream media) to watch what they say. Second, parts of the nontraditional media provided a space for citizens to critically and collectively interrogate mainstream media coverage and elite discourse. This space presents a potential alternative to Murray Edelman's (1995) dismal conclusion that the only way for citizens to avoid making themselves available for uncritical mobilization by the state during periods of political crises is to ignore media representations, and thus abdicate their civic roles in a democracy.

To be sure, these observations, tentative and based on one reading of a single media event as they are, come with many caveats. The current media environment is still very much in flux. Neither citizens nor political elites currently take full advantage of the new media's democratic potential.[15] Nor are they likely to do so unless new norms and strategic

---

[15] Yet the numbers of citizens who regularly read blogs, send news stories or hyperlinks to friends via e-mail, and actually post in online discussions are all rising, especially among the young (Pew Research Center Internet and American Life Project 2009, 2010).

rituals for the role of media in democracy – that is, a new media regime – are consciously developed. Nonetheless, they do suggest that this environment offers new avenues for potentially strengthening democratic discourse and reintroducing citizens into that discourse in new and empowering ways.

Patterns of News Media Use in the Aftermath of 9/11

As noted earlier, citizens appeared to return to traditional news media in the aftermath of the September 11 terrorist attacks. However, a closer look at the overall patterns of media consumption during this crisis suggests that journalists are "whistling past the graveyard" if they conclude that Americans once again relied on them as they had in a past era. The very insistence that in times of crisis people come back to the traditional news media is evidence of the contestation around the boundaries of news and non-news that is currently occurring.

According to a 2001 ABC News poll, almost half of all Americans sought out news through the internet, and more than a third of these internet users reported increasing their reliance on online sources after September 11, 2001. And although many of the most popular websites immediately following 9/11 were affiliated with mainstream print or broadcast media (e.g., CNN's AllPolitics), the form and content of the information provided on such sites differed, often dramatically, from that available in the more traditional news outlets. Taking advantage of this multiaxial environment, when seeking out information online, people did not limit their search to traditional news sources. For example, the website of Matt Drudge, the notorious political gossip, was the twentieth most popular destination on the internet for the week following the terrorist attacks, the first time it had ever rated that highly. This made it more popular than the websites for the *New York Times*, the *Washington Post*, and *USA Today*.

Even the pattern of increased viewership of television news can be misleading. Recall that while the total number of minutes per day spent by Americans watching "news programming" has remained largely unchanged over the past few decades, the meaning of this category has changed in recent years to include a wide range of talk shows, celebrity-focused television magazines, and so forth. This pattern is evident in the post-9/11 audience for cable news networks. Despite temporary increases following 9/11, within a year audiences for most cable news stations had returned to their pre-9/11 levels. The only exception was Fox News, now the most popular cable news station, which saw its ratings increase by

44 percent during 2002 (Offman 2003). Yet the consistently conservative Fox, which is led by the former Reagan adviser Roger Ailes and features former *Entertainment Tonight* host Bill O'Reilly, is hardly the poster child of traditional journalism. It is also worth noting that, even with its expanded audience, Fox drew an average of 667,000 viewers in 2002 – or .2% of the American population – compared to an average for the network nightly news of 31 million viewers, or of 2 to 3 million viewers for the canceled *Politically Incorrect* (Engel 2002).[16]

The new information environment has changed the meaning of "following the news" in yet another way, dramatically increasing the availability of nonmainstream and non-U.S. sources. For instance, three weeks after 9/11, when we entered "Afghanistan" (one of the five most popular search terms used by people in the week following 9/11) into the search engine of Yahoo!, the result was a long list of links to news articles, many of which came from abroad. One of the articles came from a Pakistani English-language newspaper and provided a detailed analysis of the Northern Alliance (a group of Afghani anti-Taliban dissidents – primarily local warlords – with whom the U.S. military worked closely). This easily accessed story provided much more factual and historical information on this crucial alliance than appeared anywhere in the American press. In addition, despite being printed in a military dictatorship, the article was far more critical of U.S. and Pakistani policy than anything in the linked articles published in the American press. Also available was a September 14 *Independent* (London) commentary connecting the terrorist attacks to U.S. foreign policy and calling for a reconsideration of the U.S.-led sanctions against Iraq and unreflexive support for Israel. In short, although the mainstream news media in the U.S. generally closed ranks behind the administration, the broader news environment made possible by new technology such as the internet provided a much more pluralistic range of information and viewpoints.

The availability of diverse perspectives was not limited to print journalism, as the role of the Arab satellite station Al Jazeera indicates. It was through Al Jazeera that Osama bin Laden and others associated with the al-Qaeda network chose to speak, sending the station videotapes and offering interviews with its correspondents. The use of one particular interview with bin Laden highlights both the way in which the new media environment affects traditional journalism and the ongoing efforts of

---

[16] Even in 2009, when Fox News dominated the cable news ratings, it drew an average of 2.25 million viewers for its prime-time lineup (Shea 2009).

traditional journalism to deal with these changes. American news media outlets were torn between their desire to air the tape (both because it was newsworthy and because it was likely to attract audiences) and their tendency to rally around the flag during times of crisis. Indeed, the Bush administration tried to halt the airing of the tape on American networks under the pretext that it might contain hidden instructions to terrorist cells. In addition, Secretary of State Colin Powell called for the government of Qatar to reign in the Arab news station. In the end, American news outlets opted to repeatedly air the bin Laden interview, justifying their decision by saying that it was already widely available through other sources. However, they did so while making frequent and awkward disclaimers warning that Al Jazeera was an unreliable and biased source of information and that viewers should watch the tape with caution. As one newspaper columnist noted, "On MSNBC, Brian Williams was almost apologetic about showing the bin Laden tape so often, saying with a tone of resignation that we do have a free press and, anyway, the tape would have gotten out somehow. (In the pre-cable, pre-internet era, it probably would not have)" (James 2001, B8). In short, it was the availability of new communication technologies that both made coordinating the attack possible and allowed the perpetrators to publicize their reasons. As George Packer (2006) noted: "If bin Laden didn't have access to global media, satellite communications, and the Internet, he'd just be a cranky guy in a cave."

The increasing complexities of the new media environment are further highlighted when one considers that, before September 11, 2001, CNN had been negotiating with Al Jazeera to work together and share resources. However, the negotiations were put on hold in the wake of September 11, when Al Jazeera reacted angrily to CNN's use of the bin Laden footage. Al Jazeera had actually never aired the Osama bin Laden interview, even though it was conducted by its correspondent, because it felt the correspondent had been intimidated and had acted unprofessionally. Then CNN aired the tape without permission. In short, although "Al-Jazeera [was] much maligned [in the U.S. after 9/11] even by those with no knowledge of Arabic and thus no direct understanding of exactly what's being broadcast, the Arab news network was arguably abiding more closely by the norms of professional journalism than was CNN" (Sullivan 2001). Al Jazeera became even more accessible when it began an English-language station and an English-language website. However, this accessibility has not gone unchallenged. For example, during the invasion of Iraq, Al Jazeera correspondents had their press credentials withdrawn by the New York Stock Exchange. Illustrating the struggle for control of the new, multiaxial information environment, when the station launched its English website in April 2003, it was immediately criticized for bias by the *Wall Street Journal* and then crashed by a hacker attack. Even as recently as 2010, its English-language television station, available on many cable and satellite systems throughout the world (even Israel), was available in the United States only on a very few cable systems (Buckeye Cable, Toledo, Ohio; Burlington Cable, Burlington, Vermont; Global-Cast World TV; Washington Cable, Washington, D.C.) and the satellite Dish Network.

In the end, of course, most Americans' exposure to news about 9/11 and its aftermath was through the mainstream news outlets, and so was limited to the perspectives that dominated these traditional outlets. Nonetheless, the examples here suggest the potential for the new media environment to provide citizens with a much wider and diverse array of information and viewpoints than was previously possible during major media events. With this diversity comes greater responsibility for citizens, however, who will increasingly be called on to critically analyze and assess the sources and content of the information they receive. If this responsibility can be met (which will depend as much on the actions of government and the media as on the actions of citizens themselves), the possibility exists that citizens, by critically analyzing and comparing the perspectives of quite different sources of information, can gain new insights into both who is speaking to them and the rules used by various sources to produce politically relevant information. In short, the new media environment holds out the potential for dramatic democratic possibilities as compared to the Age of Broadcast News. Whether these gains are realized will, of course, depend on the outcome of political struggle over the structure of the media regime emerging and the emphasis placed on educating citizens within this new regime.

Some commentators immediately recognized the implications of a changing media environment for the public. Significantly, one of the most insightful observations was not from a political reporter but from a media critic. On October 10, 2001, Caryn James (2001, B8) wrote in the *New York Times*: "Instead of a monolithic American point of view, the audience today is receiving a global perspective, seeing news from the BBC and from Al Jazeera, the Arab television station that first carried the bin Laden and Al-Qaeda tapes. The diversity of sources exists whether the American networks want to admit it or not." She goes on to note the discomfort of electronic journalists with this multiplicity of perspectives:

[A]lmost all American anchors have seemed flummoxed by what to do with so much information from so many perspectives.... Today there is not one propaganda voice but many, including that of the United States....

[T]he anchors have done little to put comments from American pundits and officials into perspective. The networks are overloaded with military analysis, mostly retired officers who do less analyzing than cheerleading (James 2001, B8).

James ends by addressing the issue of how individual citizens will respond to these changes and the unwillingness of mainstream journalism to see that the tools of critical analysis can be drawn from a wide range of sources, and not just what is labeled "the news": "The audience is now in the position of juggling multiple viewpoints, like the reader of a novel with several unreliable narrators.... As technology races ahead, our images outpacing our understanding, television desperately needs cultural analysis" (James 2001, B8).

Evidence abounds that citizens need help in critically analyzing the new media environment. One way in which the new media has been used by citizens to reject the dominant media narrative is the belief in fantastic conspiracy theories. Despite the seeming irrefutable evidence of constant and repeated videos and eyewitness accounts, the power of both multiaxiality and hyperreality is illustrated by the 9/11 Truth movement. Common among this group is the belief that planes did not actually hit the twin towers but that the buildings were brought down by explosives planted within them. This alternative hyperreality is based on the closest possible analysis of videos and official accounts for the tiniest discrepancies (inevitable in any complex narrative that is itself a hyperreal construction), which when considered in toto seem to support the idea of official lies, conspiracies, and cover-ups. The Truth movement's movie *Loose Change*, which purports to debunk the official story that the twin towers were destroyed as a result of a terrorist attack, was distributed on the internet and was viewed more than a million times (Hayes 2006). The power of such alternative hyperrealities is evidenced by findings like a 2006 Scripps Howard–Ohio University Poll that found that "one-third of Americans think the government either carried out the 9/11 attacks or intentionally allowed them to happen in order to provide a pretext for war in the Middle East" (Hargrove 2006).

Beyond the News: Politics as Culture and Culture as Politics

As James (2001) indicates, the new media environment requires a rethinking of the role of journalists, especially during high-profile events when they are most likely to dominate the media soapbox. The multiplicity of available viewpoints renders the norms of professional journalism, especially the injunction to simply present two sides of a story or to rely on a limited set of authoritative sources, as outmoded. Instead, there is a need to contextualize multiple perspectives and increasing demands on individual citizens to seek out and sort through conflicting sources of information. It is this task that a reoriented professional journalism might help citizens with. Moreover, we find James's suggestion that this task may be helped more by the skills one learns from reading a novel or analyzing other cultural texts than from traditional journalistic approaches to political information as an interesting echo of the Realist movement we discussed in Chapter 1. Recall that the Realists, in the shadow of the new media environment created by photography, movies, and advertising, sought to uncover political truth through a variety of genres – poetry and novels, as well as journalism.

The degree to which the new media environment has challenged the ability of mainstream journalists to control the political agenda is further understood if we look beyond the availability of information from nonmainstream and/or non-American journalists to consider an even broader range of politically relevant genres.[17] As we noted in the previous chapter, the connections among various media texts – intertextuality – is an important concept for appreciating the ways in which citizens make meaning. And the internet, through hyperlinks, e-mail, social networking sites, and so on, makes it easier than ever to quickly compare and contrast various media. For example, in the immediate aftermath of 9/11, there were numerous and widely circulated e-mail jokes ("Television psychic Miss Cleo predicted that Osama bin Laden would die on a national holiday, since 'Any day you die gwan be an American holiday'"), interactive games ("Nuke-Bin Laden"), and animated cartoons posted on the Web (a cartoon bin Laden being sexually assaulted by the Gimp from the movie, *Pulp Fiction*) (Wiltz 2001, C1).

---

[17] Of course, popular culture has always played a role in political discourse – we are not arguing that this is new, and we leave open the question of whether it is more common now than in the recent past. We argue instead that the significance of such alternative discourses has been obscured and discounted by the news-entertainment distinction characteristic of the latter half of the twentieth century and is becoming more visible as a result of the challenge to this distinction brought on by the new media environment.

Cultural figures such as television and movie actors and musicians also added to the diversity of voices and viewpoints (the multiaxiality) found in the post-9/11 media environment. On occasion, such figures (e.g., Janeane Garofalo, Mike Farrell) were able to use their celebrity status to directly enter mainstream news coverage, appearing as guests on political talk shows. In other circumstances, the blending of politics and culture took place (initially at least) outside the news genre, as when a member of the musical group the Dixie Chicks announced at a concert that the group was "ashamed the President of the United States is from [their own state of] Texas." Even the sports pages were not immune from post-9/11 politics, as when the president of the Baseball Hall of Fame (former Reagan appointee Dale Petroskey) revoked actors' Susan Sarandon and Tim Robbins invitations to a planned fifteenth-anniversary showing of their film *Bull Durham* because of their vocal opposition to the war in Iraq. In a telling postscript to this incident, Sarandon and Robbins were then invited to appear on HBO's *On the Record with Bob Costas* to talk about both the movie and their political views. "It just seemed so logical," said Costas in explaining his decision. "Our show is a hybrid of sports, entertainment and a little bit of news. It's a perfect fit for us" (*New York Times* 2003). This logic appeared lost on mainstream journalists who, though often cover the views and actions of celebrity activists, generally treat them with the same combination of fascination, condescension, and outright ridicule as they did the Al Jazeera network. When one is willing to look for it, political discourse about pressing issues of the day can be found in surprising places, such as in the post-9/11 music of Bruce Springsteen ("The Rising") and Steve Earle ("Jerusalem"). Both works consciously addressed issues raised by the terrorist attacks, albeit in distinct, subtle, and personal ways. Both also provided perspectives that were at odds with the prevailing mood of much mainstream media coverage (or, for that matter, with the works of other musicians, such as the jingoist "Courtesy of the Red, White and Blue" by the country singer Toby Keith).

By abandoning a priori distinctions between news and entertainment for a more inclusive definition of politically relevant media, one begins to see that even during a media event such as that created by the terrorist attacks of 9/11, when mainstream journalism becomes more hegemonic in its coverage, the larger media environment can still resemble the river of discourses suggested by Fiske (1996). Recall from the previous chapter that, for Fiske, public discourse is never a single conversation but rather a set of conversations, much like a river containing various

currents and undercurrents. During major media events, these undercurrents can "erupt into turbulence" producing "eddies and counter-
currents" and even reversing the main flow of the river (Fiske 1996,
7). Carrying Fiske's metaphor further, in the new media environment, we
need to think not only about the mainstream and its various undercurrents
but also about the entire river system that produces them. Clearly, the
most powerful current in mainstream discourse about 9/11 was created
by professional journalists and the elites who dominated that discourse.
This fast-moving current often overwhelmed smaller undercurrents and
countercurrents. It also swamped (as public attention turned to journalists
covering the attacks) and dammed (through the removal of other regularly scheduled programming on television or other topics in print) many
tributaries that fed into and emerged out of the mainstream. Nonetheless,
these tributaries did not disappear, continuing to provide alternative if
less well-traveled routes for navigating in and out of mainstream discussion in the post-9/11 world, and even occasionally finding their way into
the discussion with enough strength to at least muddy the waters, if not
change the direction in which the mainstream flowed.

Cultural Politics and the Foundations of Politically Relevant Discourse

Although nontraditional media (and nontraditional sources) may have
had a limited direct impact on the mainstream flow of public discourse
once the events of 9/11 occurred, it is important to keep in mind that discourse during times of crisis builds on preexisting opinions and beliefs.
Put in terms of Fiske's river-of-discourses metaphor, understanding the
media's impact on public thinking after 9/11 requires considering what
has happened upstream, before the various tributaries and currents con-
verged at the site of the terrorist attacks. It is here that politically relevant
but nontraditional media can be especially important in shaping or priming the dynamics of public opinion, especially at the foundational level
of politics (i.e., the values and assumptions that underlie politics at the
institutional and policy levels). Indeed, at this premedia-event, foundational level, these nontraditional sources may be more important than
professional journalism, given the significantly larger audiences for the
former than for the latter.

In the case of 9/11, much of the popular media had served to prime
citizens to accept the interpretation of events that dominated mainstream
journalism. Such influence operated at explicit and obvious levels, as when
David Broder and Morton Kondracke both compared President Bush's

"Mission Accomplished" appearance on an aircraft carrier in 2003 to the fictional fighter-pilot president in the film *Independence Day*, or when the NBC news anchor Brian Williams reported how emotionally affecting he found the movie *United 93* (Rich 2006, 89; Kurtz 2007, 135). Popular movies also entered into a kind of debate about American policies as a series of after-the-fact movies critical of the Iraq War were released in 2007 (e.g., *In the Valley of Elah*, *Redacted*). Such movies were, correctly in our view, seen as political statements of their makers and discussed in this way by critics and some cable television talking heads but rarely by professional journalists in their gatekeeping role. Taking advantage of the conjunction of multiaxiality and hyperreality, the Bush administration entered into this debate when it sought out the Hollywood blockbuster producer and director Jerry Bruckheimer to make a more favorable film about the Iraq War (Rich 2006, 33).

Given the strength of the mainstream of discourse following an event like 9/11 or the invasions of Iraq and Afghanistan, however, movies or television shows made after the fact are probably unlikely to have a significant political impact. It is worth noting in this context that none of the movies dealing with 9/11, Iraq, Afghanistan, or the revelations about the torture of detainees were either popular or critical successes. In some cases, this has to do with films not being very good (i.e., Robert Redford's *Lions for Lambs*). But even thoughtful, albeit mildly, antiwar films like *In the Valley of Elah* or straightforward depictions of the American soldiers' experience, like the cable television series *Over There* and *Generation Kill*, also failed to find an audience. Nine years after 9/11 and seven years into the wars in Iraq and Afghanistan, *The Hurt Locker*, a film about an American bomb squad in Iraq became the first such critical and box-office success.

But movies made before important events can have significant political implications that are missed unless we adopt an expansive notion of political communication. The popularity of the movie *Saving Private Ryan* (1998, directed by Steven Spielberg), the highest-grossing film of the year, reversed more than a decade of largely critical films about the American military by portraying altruistic and honorable American soldiers fighting the Good War and helped prepare the public for the use of military force in both Afghanistan and Iraq (Williams 2010).

At an even subtler level, consider the treatment of Arabs and Muslims in Hollywood movies before 9/11. In the wake of the Cold War, the Arab terrorist had become the bogeyman for many Hollywood thrillers. It was possible to stereotype and demonize such figures in ways that were no longer acceptable for other "outsiders" long dehumanized by Hollywood, such as African Americans or gays and lesbians. Dining on a constant fare of such portrayals, especially when one has little other information or personal experiences to draw on, made it more likely that citizens would be primed for mobilization by the state once it became clear that a segment of the Arab Muslim community was behind the 9/11 attacks.[18]

Consider the 1994 movie *True Lies*, directed by James Cameron of *Avatar*, *Titanic*, and *Terminator* fame. The movie might be considered just another Hollywood blockbuster, far below the radar of most scholars and journalists who write about politics. It cost $110 million to make, grossed $146 million in its American release, and made another $80 million in rentals.[19] *True Lies* stars Arnold Schwarzenegger as Harry Trasker, America's top secret agent, and Jamie Lee Curtis as his unsuspecting wife, who believes that her husband is a boring computer salesman. She finds out Harry's true calling when they both become involved in chasing Salim Abu Aziz (played by Art Malik), a completely diabolical "Arab terrorist" who has gotten his hands on four nuclear weapons, one of which he eventually sets off in the Florida Keys. Although it's hard to imagine anyone taking the plot of this comedy seriously, the same cannot be as easily said regarding the depiction of Aziz and his Arab followers, who are portrayed as scarcely human, stupid to the point of idiocy, and evil beyond redemption. They wave "Arab" flags, dedicate their actions to Allah, and create and/or reinforce stereotypes and prejudices. Presenting such images, especially of a group that is rarely seen in either the popular or the news media except in connection to terrorism, cannot help but prime audiences to draw on these images when Arabs or Muslims become the focus of real-world events such as 9/11. Yet although *True Lies* received decidedly mixed reviews, none of the movie's critics addressed this stereotyping in any serious way. Indeed, we could find only one review that mentioned the issue at all, noting that Malik's role "doesn't do wonders for the Arab community" (Howe 1994, W38). We would add that the movie doesn't do wonders for American democracy either.

Popular media need not automatically serve to reinforce stereotypes and/or the policy preferences of elites, however, and are equally capable of

---

[18] This kind of priming effect was dramatically visible after the Oklahoma City bombing, when Arabs and Muslims were immediately suspected, even though they had nothing to do with the attacks.

[19] All figures about film cost and business, here and below, are from the Internet Movie Database (http://www.imdb.com). Rental business is included when available.

priming citizens to react in subtler and more nuanced ways. For example, *The Siege* (1998) uses the conventions of the Hollywood terrorist thriller to question some of the very issues glossed over not only by movies like *True Lies* but also by much of journalistic coverage of terrorism. The film was far from a box-office success, costing an estimated $70 million to make but only earning $42 million at the box office in its American run. Directed by Edward Zwick (*Glory, Legends of the Fall, Courage Under under Fire*), the movie stars Denzel Washington as Anthony Hubbard, an FBI counterintelligence agent whose partner Frank Haddad (played by Tony Shalhoub) happens to be an Arab American. After the American military abducts a Muslim religious leader in the Middle East, terrorists retaliate by targeting New York City for a series of bombings. Unable to stop the bombings, the government decides to declare martial law and send in the U.S. Army, commanded by General Devereaux (Bruce Willis), who launches searches through Arab neighborhoods and indiscriminately rounds up young Arabs and puts them in detention camps. The plot turns on the trade-offs between civil liberties and the fear of terrorism, as well as the relationship between stereotypes about Arab Americans and the very real threat of terrorism. So, for example, Haddad's own son is rounded up and placed in a camp, leading the FBI agent to resign and struggle to free his innocent son. At the same time, the CIA agent Elise Kraft (played by Annette Bening) begins to work with Hubbard to track down the terrorists. Raising another set of thorny issues about the war on terrorism, it turns out that one of the members of the terrorist cell is a CIA operative, and the cell is run by Kraft.

We are not claiming that *The Siege* is a great film. It does, however, show that it is possible to deal in a nuanced way with issues too often caricatured and/or ignored in both the popular media and the mainstream news media. Clearly, its treatment of the trade-offs between security and civil liberties suggests the need to consider alternative perspectives on the issues raised in combating terrorist attacks and, as such, prepares audiences for pluralistic perspectives on events like the 9/11 attacks. The movie primes viewers to think about the complex issues raised when the government responds to terrorism by targeting specific groups and suspending civil liberties. It also endorses acts of conscience and not simply the following of orders: Haddad gives up his job in a principled rejection of the racist policies of the government he works for, and Hubbard is forced to choose between the conflicting obligations of his job and his friend. In the end, his commitment to his friend triumphs, highlighting the moral choices many of us face in day-to-day life.

Interestingly, unlike with *True Lies*, *The Siege* was sharply criticized by the Arab American community and others for being racist in its portrayal of the terrorists. The *New York Times* movie critic Janet Maslin (1998) wrote, "Caught up in the crossfire is New York's Arab-American community, which has raised understandable objections to images seen in *The Siege*. Though the screenplay ... is strenuously even-handed and even incorporates a nice-guy, Beirut-born sidekick for Hub (played ably by Tony Shalhoub), the film's stark images of scheming Arab villains often speak louder than its diplomatic words." What matters here is not whether one sees the movie as fair or not in its portrayal of Arabs and Arab Americans so much as that it attempted to address an important, timely, and controversial set of issues, and it generated at least a limited public discussion about those issues – the very essence of the media's role in a democratic society. This could not have happened if the film had been seen as simply Hollywood entertainment and not as a political text as well, the latter view making it entirely appropriate for the filmmakers to be called to account for their work's impact on public dialogue. This is much preferable to the approach taken in *The Sum of All Fears* (2002, directed by Phil Alden Robinson), which, significantly, was produced following the events of 9/11. The film did quite well, costing $68 million to make and grossing more than $118 million in its American theater run. In the movie, the Palestinian terrorists of the novel were replaced by a shadowy group of German neo-Nazis. Although no one (or at least no one whom Hollywood will listen to) objected to the villainous portrayal of neo-Nazis, avoiding the uncomfortable issues raised by the attacks of 9/11 does nothing to improve the practice of democratic politics and reinforces the artificial and counterproductive divide between news and entertainment.

Although we make no claims that in and of themselves the specific movies we have briefly discussed had a major impact on public reaction to the events of 9/11 or on the public's views on the Iraqi conflict, we do believe that the larger media environment (including both news and non-news genres) can collectively shape the values and beliefs that citizens draw on. Consider, for example, that in an eerie echo of *The Siege*, immediately following 9/11 the Immigration and Naturalization Service (INS) instituted a policy requiring all male, non-U.S. citizens older than sixteen who emigrated from eighteen Middle Eastern and predominantly Muslim countries to register in person. When the men showed up, swamping INS processing capacities, many were detained in overcrowded detention centers at undisclosed locations for indeterminate periods of time.

Although the INS's actions were briefly covered on the news, public reaction was largely muted and accepting of the decision as a necessary evil. The exception to this was a December 2002 protest by two thousand Iranian Americans outside the INS building in Los Angeles (CNN 2002).

It is not too much of a stretch to suggest that citizens' reactions (or lack thereof) to this and similar policies were influenced by the ways in which popular culture addressed issues of terrorism, Arabs, and Arab Americans. Popular culture provides a potentially powerful venue for providing the foundational values on which citizens draw when actually participating in democratic politics by addressing fictional or fictionalized public issues in ways that allow citizens to think about, discuss, and consider their responsibility before facing them in the real world. In this way, citizens are better able to engage in actual democratic practice when such issues actually emerge. But this potential is seldom realized, in part because of norms that see popular culture as mere entertainment. In movies such as *True Lies* (which we think is typical of most mainstream popular culture and news genres), Arabs and Muslims are clearly portrayed as "others" to whom we have no connection or obligation. Even if we are concerned with the question of civil liberties, we would be less likely to see the detention of such "others" as a threat to us, as they lie outside the boundaries of our moral community, and the protection of our laws and values extends only as far as those boundaries. In contrast, a central point of *The Siege* was that Hubbard realizes his obligation is to his friend, whose son has been unjustly detained. Here, Arabs and Muslims were defined not as "others" but as friends and coworkers to whom, despite differences, we have a dense web of moral obligation. Were this perspective more commonly found in popular culture (and more openly discussed and debated as a result of these popular culture portrayals), policies such as those instituted by the INS following 9/11 would be seen as aimed at members of our own community, and so would impose on us moral obligations when these fellow community members are threatened. Perhaps, if this were the case, it would not have been only Iranian Americans demonstrating against the INS in Los Angeles.

This argument is applicable to the film and television treatments of the Iraq War that we mentioned earlier. In all these texts, whatever their artistic merits or political leaning, there are virtually no attempts to humanize Iraqi civilians or soldiers. In *Generation Kill*, for example, the only Iraqi portrayed is a rather cowardly and cartoonish translator for the American marines. The notable exception to this is the sympathetic treatment of Iraqi children, who are most often seen as playing or calling for and being given candy or treats by the Americans. These scenes, which recall World War II films portraying cheering Italian, French, and even German and Japanese civilians welcoming the victorious Americans and being rewarded with chewing gum and chocolate bars, serve not to bring the Iraqis into our moral community but to reinforce the idea that Americans deserve to be greeted as liberators.

The Intersection of News and Popular Culture in the Mainstream Media

As many of the examples we have discussed indicate, and as our central argument in this book suggests, the boundaries between news and entertainment are artificial and increasingly dysfunctional, supported more by norms and rituals than by their content or political relevance. One telling example of this eroding boundary erupted over the dropping of singer Toby Keith from ABC's 2002 "In Search of America: A July 4th Musical Celebration." Keith claimed he was dropped, at the insistence of the show's host Peter Jennings, because of the lyrics to his song, "Courtesy of the Red, White and Blue," which included the refrain:

> Oh, justice will be served, and the battle will rage.
> This big dog will fight when you rattle his cage.
> You'll be sorry that you messed with the U. S. of A.
> Cause we'll put a boot in your ass, that's the American way.[20]

The alleged interference of Jennings with Keith's "free speech" became the gleeful focus of other electronic journalists. As a *Washington Post* article reported, "CNN had a field day with the story yesterday, making it the centerpiece of its afternoon 'Talkback Live,' and the final story on 'Wolf Blitzer Reports,' including a long interview with Keith" (de Morales 2002, C7). Jennings's response was to deny that he had anything to do with the cancellation (although at a minimum he clearly acquiesced to it). Seeking to avoid controversy, the show's producers claimed that Keith had only been considered for the program but that no firm offer had ever been made and that it had nothing to do with the singer's politics.

Certainly ABC's decision (whether made by network executives or Jennings himself) was understandable and arguably served to avoid fanning the flames of intolerance that were still burning in the aftermath of 9/11.

---

[20] Though too incendiary for a network special, the song was regularly played at sporting events.

Within the confines of the mainstream media system and its logic, producers were exercising their social responsibility in deciding that Keith's song reinforced a mindless nationalism, especially given the tendency of most television coverage to adopt a patriotic and pro-administration perspective. Yet a better outcome would have been one that challenged Keith's perspective through engagement rather than exclusion:[21] perhaps allowing Keith to appear along with artists who disagreed with his perspective, such as Bruce Springsteen, Steve Earle, Meshell Ndegeocello, or – perhaps most appropriately – fellow country singers the Dixie Chicks.[22]

Equally problematic is the role of Peter Jennings, illustrating as it does the futility of trying to distinguish between news and entertainment. What are we to make of a professional journalist hosting a prime-time entertainment show with no obvious or formal connections to the goals and purposes of the ABC News division?[23] About his (alleged) role in determining who would appear on the show? And perhaps most important, in what role was he appearing before the public? As a journalist? A network anchor? A high-level network employee? A celebrity? A citizen? On reflection, he clearly appeared in all these roles. But the lack of transparency in this, especially as demonstrated by the confusion created by the controversy over Keith and the obfuscation by Jennings and ABC, highlights the need for a new set of more clearly articulated and widely understood norms in the new media environment.

Citizens in the New Media Environment: Internet Chat Rooms and Public Discussion of 9/11

One of the most important characteristics of the multiaxial new media environment (especially the internet) is its ability to provide citizens not only access to a wide range of information sources but also opportunities to enter into exchanges with fellow citizens about issues of the day. As part of a separate project to map the connection between political

---

[21] We explain our preference for engagement more fully in Chapter 8.

[22] Keith's right-wing brand of patriotism was not limited to his song – in concerts, he regularly flashes concocted screen images of the Dixie Chicks' Natalie Maines, who had made the anti-Bush statement quoted earlier, standing next to Saddam Hussein (*DeLuca* 2003).

[23] Jennings was not the only network anchor to play this genre-crossing role – Tom Brokaw served as host of the September 11, 2002, prime-time anniversary special "A Concert for America," broadcast on *NBC*.

ideologies and their expression in cyberspace, we had been monitoring websites and their chat room discussions on eleven different sites (chosen for their ideological diversity) for quite some time before September 11, 2001.[24] Representing the far right were the neo-Nazi sites Stormfront and Crosstar. On the more moderate right were Conservative Politics and the Conservative Political Action Conference's Free Republic Forum. On the more moderate left were MC Forums, hosted by Media Channel, and Salon.com. Further left were AlterNet, the Anarchist Anti-Defamation League, and the Guerrilla News Network. Finally, reflecting less easily classified perspectives, were the Forum of the Black Entertainment Television Network and the chat rooms of the *Jerusalem Post*. Tracking discussion in these chat rooms provided us with a fortuitous opportunity to see how users of these sites reacted to the terrorist attacks on September 11, 2001, and the days immediately following. What is clear is that, despite Ari Fleischer's injunction, the chat rooms provided a place for Americans to say what they wanted when the government was warning them to watch what they were saying.

In the ordinary course of events, when public attention was not focused on a specific media event like the 9/11 attacks, we found that most of the sites left much to be desired as forums for enlightened political discussion. The chat room discourse tended to be hegemonic in the perspectives voiced, with quick and severe discipline through vicious attacks (i.e., flaming) used to enforce political conformity to a site's perspectives. There was little effort, especially on the more politically extreme sites, to establish the origin of information used in arguments or the background and qualifications of posters. It says much about the level of tolerance for dissent, or its lack thereof, that we were forced to use only moderated sites (where there was someone responsible for screening messages before they were actually posted to the chat rooms), as unmoderated sites were so disjointed and subject to lack of tolerance and abuse that they proved unsuitable for analysis. Indeed, the requirement that there be a moderator to edit what did and did not get posted to a site is a good example of how, even in the new media environment, there is a need for gatekeepers.[25] It also illustrates the arguments of advocates of deliberative democracy as the preferred form of political decision making that public discussion always

---

[24] For a fuller discussion of this project, see Williams 2003.

[25] It is also another example of how, despite the beliefs of some cyber-utopians, sustaining serious debate and avoiding anarchy on the internet is never self-sustaining but inevitably requires the exercise of authority.

requires an able facilitator. Significantly, however, these gatekeepers are not journalists or political elites, but in the case of the internet, chat room moderators, search engines, and so forth.

Despite these limitations in the quality of chat room discussions, we found a striking transformation in the tenor of conversation on these sites in the immediate wake of 9/11, with the level of sophistication and tolerance increasing dramatically. This change points to significant possibilities for opening up political discourse during media events. These new possibilities, unavailable in prior media environments, depend on the dynamic relationship between new and more traditional sources of political information. Alternative new media, like chat rooms, have a subtle and changing relationship to the patterns, practices, and diversity of mainstream journalism.

Professional journalists are beginning to take advantage of the internet and, more generally, the possibilities created by much of new media for gathering information, often from citizens who would ordinarily have little voice in news broadcasts or large circulation print outlets. Many journalists keep blogs (including the network anchors Katie Couric and Brian Williams) and/or provide their e-mail address allowing readers and viewers to react to what has been broadcast or printed. Brian Williams regularly exchanged e-mails with soldiers in Iraq ("his own private intelligence channel on the war") and so got around the military's ban on talking to journalists (Kurtz 2007, 187). However, it may be that this new openness has less to do with new media than with the collapse of the Age of Broadcast News. During the Civil War, for example, the *Sunday Mercury* solicited and then printed written commentaries from ordinary soldiers.

The debates within journalism over how to use new media usually presuppose the authoritative role of professional journalists as gatekeepers. Even here there is much less attention to how to treat the comments and new types and sources of information that journalists actually receive. Many complain that there is little guidance on what to do with these reactions and point to the impossibility of keeping track of the thousands of e-mails and comments prominent journalists receive. Although there is beginning to be high-quality work on the Internet from social scientists, it seems clear that this new medium's impact on democratic discourse and participation for ordinary citizens has not been thoroughly thought through. If we are to fully understand the pitfalls and possibilities of the new media environment, it is especially important to understand what happens on the Internet during media events, when it is difficult to escape the hegemonic perspective reflected in so much of the mass media.[26]

More specifically, when we analyzed all discussion threads relevant to the 9/11 attacks on the eleven sites in our study, we found at least five ways in which they allowed a space for the development of a broad and critical perspective, unavailable in mainstream journalism's coverage of the terrorist attacks: interactivity, the availability and use of diverse sources of information, critical and collective examination of mainstream media texts, insularity of conversation, and civility.

Interactivity

Posters to the chat room discussions took advantage of the interactivity of the internet, through both synchronous and asynchronous discussions among individuals separated by vast distances but united by common political, cultural, or social concerns. This meant that, from the first moments of the attacks, while television broadcast images of the World Trade Center collapsing, many citizens turned simultaneously to chat rooms in an attempt to collectively make sense of what they were seeing. The possibilities opened up by interactivity resulted in fascinating, diverse, and quite sophisticated critical conversation among participants as they struggled, almost in real time, to interpret events being reported in the mainstream media. For example, on Salon.com, one participant identified Osama bin Laden as the primary suspect almost immediately (9:31 A.M. Eastern Time on September 11), long before the mainstream media broadcast this speculation.

Participants didn't abandon their political ideologies. For example, on the extreme right-wing sites Stormfront and Crosstar, racist and anti-Semitic attitudes were still in evidence. On the former site, there was immediate speculation that the attacks were engineered by the Israeli Mossad because Arabs were not sophisticated enough to pull off such attacks on their own. One participant noted, "It's all running on a ZOG script" (ZOG stands for "Zionist Occupation Government," the "true" rulers of the United States). But participants clearly wrestled with where such values left them with respect to the terrorist attacks. Another Stormfront poster cautioned about leaping to conclusions about who was to blame: "Propaganda is going to get really thick & deep and we should

---

[26] We use the term *mass media* to signal that, during media events, the fragmentation of the media, which we discussed in Chapter 2, declines significantly as television and the major news divisions of media corporations assemble the mass audiences of the Age of Broadcast News.

reserve judgment."[27] The result was a pattern of much more diverse, reflective opinions than was the usual case on these sites, or, as we have seen, was the case in most mainstream coverage of the attacks.

The Availability and Use of Diverse Sources of Information

Chat rooms and their host sites took advantage of the ease with which diverse sources of information could be accessed in the new media environment, especially over the internet. The chat room participants themselves provided many cross-postings of articles from a wide range of sources. These diverse sources were almost always examined from the perspective of the chat room's ideological position and used to buttress arguments made by participants. Some sources were obviously dubious but used nevertheless. So, for example, there was much reference on Stormfront to a story, originally published in the Arab-language press, that Jews had been warned to not show up at their World Trade Center offices on the day of the attacks. This was used as evidence to buttress the arguments, noted earlier, that the Mossad was behind the attacks. Yet as we will see, this site also saw the posting of an article from 1911 by Emma Goldman.

On the moderate left-wing Media Channel chat room, in response to television's repeated showing of a video of cheering Palestinians, there were links to a *Guardian* (London) story on how the United States fails to understand anti-American sentiment abroad, as well as links to articles in Singapore newspapers warning against blaming all Muslims for the attack. Another participant posted the text of a 1983 presidential proclamation praising Afghan freedom fighters, many of whom went on to establish the Taliban-run state.

Critical and Collective Interrogation of Mainstream Media

Interactivity and the ease with which diverse sources of information can be accessed led to a third characteristic of these conversations: the critical and collective examination of mainstream media coverage and, more broadly, government responses to the attacks. Across the ideological spectrum, conversations routinely interrogated the connection between U.S. foreign policy and the terrorist attacks. This sort of critical examination of the images provided by the mainstream coverage was not limited to moderate sites. On Stormfront, in response to repeated showing of the cheering Palestinians video just mentioned, one poster asked, "What is the difference between Arabs dancing in the streets and us celebrating

---

[27] All chat room quotes are from Williams (2003).

the bombing of Yugoslavia?" On September 13, a thread titled "Patriotic Idiots" started and one poster asked, "What about U.S. bombing of
Serbia or pharmaceutical factory in Afghanistan [*sic*]."

At the other end of the ideological spectrum, on the Anarchist Anti-
Defamation League site, one participant asked: "Have you seen the Palestinians and the Egyptians celebrating these attacks? The sad thing is most
Muslims are actually glad this happened." Another poster immediately
replied:

That is absolute crap. You saw the unreflecting, instant reaction of about 20
Palestinians over and over, who have had their lives torn apart by American
hardware. Their reaction was of course totally wrong. You are allowing the
media to draw you in to their war drum beating. Obscenity was seen on a much
larger scale in 1991 when thousands of Americans cheered in pubs the deaths
of 200,000 Iraqis. You know now what the destruction of 2 buildings is like.
Imagine whole cities destroyed, if that is possible without experiencing it. WE
DON'T WANT MORE WAR. Stay Sane. Keep Cool. God bless.

Indeed, on chat rooms across the ideological spectrum, there was vigorous debate about the connection between U.S. support for Israel and
the 9/11 attacks. This sort of analysis was common in the foreign press.
For instance, on September 14, the *Independent* (London) ran a commentary calling for a reconsideration of U.S.-led anti-Iraq sanctions and
unreflexive support for Israel. Yet as we have seen, in the mainstream
U.S. press, any examination of the connection between U.S. foreign policy and the attack was virtually absent, and if voiced, it was labeled as
treasonous – as Susan Sontag found out after publishing a critical piece in
the *New Yorker*. In chat rooms, and often in the most politically extreme
ones, such arguments were seriously debated, however. For example, on
Stormfront, one participant posted a quote from Osama bin Laden claiming that attacks were in retaliation for U.S. support of Israel. And on the
far-left Guerrilla News Network, a participant wrote:

What really lies at the heart of this issue is the painting of all Arabs as terrorists or
nameless/faceless religious heretics who don't really DESERVE their own country,
their own freedoms, their own rights. Given this attitude of the American people,
who, on average, don't give a F**K about Arab rights, the political machine is
free to outright (i.e. outrageous) support of Israel regardless of the atrocities they
commit. Granted the problems in the M/E are not easily resolved, but the Israelis
and Bush are moving towards policies of intolerance, which is only inflaming
the Palestinian refugees who have no hope other than that provided by (a) the
solidarity of the international community towards their plight or, failing that
(b) the armed resistance against their oppressors. Its NOT an attack on freedom (duh), its a wake up call to the Americans. The export of terrorism WILL
boomerang back. Remember that there are some 6M Palestinians in camps who

have never known any of the freedoms that America espouses. The suicide bombers come from these camps, second and third generation welfare recipients with no hope for a normal life.

The Insularity of Conversations

A fourth feature follows from the way chat rooms create the opportunity for relatively insular conversation among only like-minded individuals who may be separated by time and space. While the mainstream media reiterated themes of national unity, the chat rooms allowed different groups of Americans to debate what the impact of the attacks meant to and for them specifically. This allowed the critical interrogation of the role of the state (and the use of the media to mobilize support for administration policies).

At a time when many online chat rooms were seeing a dramatic increase in traffic, many by new participants, there were often debates over how (or whether) to maintain group boundaries and ideological purity. On Stormfront, for example, there was both concern over the need to guard against "blind haters" and concern about "liberals" coming into the chat room to foment discord. On Crosstar, a chat room that had much less traffic than Stormfront, there was an initial flurry of discussion about keeping "dissident voices" (i.e., liberals) off the board. One poster objected to allowing a particularly argumentative participant (Crimson) to contribute posting to this moderated discussion:

There are plenty of chat rooms where "Crimson" (appropriately named) can spout his ideology, but this is not one of them. Neither is Crosstar receptive to those trying to "disguise" themselves as "one of us," to try to smear or distort us. Crosstar is for Nationalists, those seeking information about Nationalism and Nationalists dissecting points and sharing information among themselves.

This boundary maintenance was defended by another poster who argued, ominously:

Crosstar Forum is moderated to be free of "noise" by would-be detractors, as well. Nationalists have fought hard for their internet "place in the sun" and they are not about to waste time arguing with their foes on their own turf. And it will be the same when we say of all of America: "This land is our land."[28]

Though disturbing when defended in this manner, in many ways, insular conversations, not easily accessible to the wider public, play a positive role

---

[28] Even during more ordinary times, sites like Stormfront and other extremist sites wrestle with the balance between being available to a wider audience, which they know to be hostile, and providing a relatively insulated forum for true believers. An interesting solution adopted by Stormfront is the maintenance of a specific section in their chat room for postings made by those who disagree with the ideology of the group.

by allowing marginalized groups to clarify their distinct values in relationship to those of the society at large within the safety of a sympathetic, homogeneous forum. This is especially important during media events, when the perspective of mainstream coverage is particularly hegemonic. So, for example, on a chat room hosted by the Black Entertainment Television, there was a thoughtful discussion of how African Americans were responding to 9/11. The conversation centered on whether it was possible to reconcile black beliefs about racist police and fire departments with the heroic images of these institutions in the wake of the terrorist attacks. A particularly interesting thread was prompted by the appearance on the television show *Saturday Night Live* of surviving firefighters – all of whom were white. Posters wrestled with how the undeniable heroism of these individuals contrasted with their participation in the fire department's discrimination against blacks. Such debate is avoided in mainstream coverage on network television. In 2005, for example, during another media event prompted by Hurricane Katrina, during a live telethon for the victims of the storm, the rap star Kanye West said, "George Bush doesn't care about black people." These sentiments were prominent on the BET chat room and, according to polling, to say nothing of voting, widespread among the black population more generally. Nevertheless, reflecting the attempt to portray the nation as entirely united, NBC immediately cut off West's microphone and deleted his remarks from the tape, which was delayed for its West Coast broadcast (Gold and Collins 2005).

Interesting debates also took place on left- and right-wing sites about the degree to which the current crisis did or did not justify forgetting past criticisms of liberals or conservatives, as the case may be. On the anarchist AlterNet, there was much admiration of the actions of Mayor Rudy Giuliani and defense of President Bush's failure to return quickly to the White House. What makes these perspectives distinct from their expression in the mainstream media is the degree to which they were offered in an environment where they are always challenged, interrogated, and debated. This is precisely what makes these chat rooms so interesting and important. During media events, they are not immune to or insulated from the values of more mainstream coverage (as they are to a greater extent during more routine times). Rather, they provide a collective forum for the interrogation of those values. So, although admiration for Giuliani and Bush might echo the perspective of broadcast coverage, the response to this support was quite different from what was found in mainstream coverage. For example, an attack on the defenders of these two usually vilified politicians on AlterNet started by saying, "So tell me, all you wimps." And on Salon.com a participant wrote: "I absolutely cannot stand George W. Bush, but this is just one of those times to rally behind the President, as well as Cheney, Powell, and Rumsfeld. Sometimes extraordinary events spur ordinary men to greatness. I hope this is one of those times." On this same board, after attacks on defenders of Bush, a participant wrote (placing the remarks of another poster in italics):

I would like to say a few things.... A lot of you have said some incredibly stupid things, and it reveals a stupidity that runs pretty deep. *"This would have never happened if Clinton were in office!"* Bullshit. Who was in office the last time the WTC was bombed? *"Where's Bush now? We need leadership! His response is ineffective!"* What the hell do you expect him to do? He's the President, he's in a secure location, and he's formulating a response. That's what Presidents do. *"In his first address, he acted like it was over, and it wasn't!"* How was he supposed to know? If he would have waited, you would have screamed and whined because he didn't come out and say something to you. *"Bush should resign for this. His job is to protect the people, and he didn't do that!"* Good grief... that doesn't even warrant a response. Let's drop the partisan crap, for one brief moment, and look at what we're saying. Thousands of innocent people have died, and some of you would like to think that GWB did this? ON PURPOSE?!! Or that he's HAPPY ABOUT IT? Good God, people, listen to yourselves. Whether or not you like his politics, he is human, like the rest of us. This is a tragedy for America, and the world. This administration may not be perfect, and you may disagree with them on policy, but I guarantee they are grieving just as much as you are. With the thousands of people dead, do you think they don't have friends and family affected by this?

Think before you post, please.

Perhaps the most interesting debate we found occurred on Stormfront. Some posters immediately called for closing the nation's borders and excluding all immigrants (here, they reflected the sentiments voiced by many political leaders on television). However, many disagreed, expressing concern about the closing down of civil liberties and the implications for domestic right-wing groups who might be blamed for the attacks. On the "Patriotic Idiots" thread, noted earlier, debates developed over how white racists should respond to the attacks. One poster asked: "Why be sad over attack on NYC/WTC which are hubs of anti-white, anti-human activity?" But another responded: "My grandfather enlisted the day after Pearl Harbor.... All politics/ideology aside, our COUNTRY WAS ATTACKED YESTERDAY."

One Stormfront poster launched a diatribe against ZOG arguing that Jews don't fight for their country; they only manipulate others to do so. She went on to argue that it was the manipulation of patriotism and nationalism by the media, in the service of the state (both, in her view, controlled by Jews), thus resulting in a tendency to drop any specific grievances that groups might have against the government, which was the greatest danger during times of crisis (compare this argument, minus the Jewish conspiracy, of course, with Edelman's (1995) arguments, discussed earlier). Ironically, she posted an article from 1911 by the Jewish writer Emma Goldman criticizing the uses of patriotism for just these purposes. However, this argument was attacked by a participant who pointed out that Jews have actually served and died in the armed forces well out of proportion to their small number in the population.

On September 14, a Stormfront participant quoted John Locke's warning about the dangers of giving up power to the legislature in support of a thoughtful critique of the power of government to act unaccountably in times of crisis. Finally, there was a poster who argued that American Aryans have far more in common with Jews than with Arabs and called for "a non-racist white nationalism."

Civility

The final characteristic of the chat room discussions we followed was their general tenor of tolerance to those with whom one might disagree. In the immediate wake of 9/11, even the most extreme sites adopted, or tried to adopt, a tolerance to divergent views, which was decidedly uncharacteristic of their rhetorical styles in ordinary times. Such civility is essential for political debate, and here it greatly expanded the range of views expressed, even on the most ideologically extreme sites. For example, on the moderate Conservative Political Action Conference, one poster, adopting the usual tone of the board, blamed Clinton and liberals:

They've put down our President over the past 8 months plus – That contributed to showing our Country as being WEAK enough to prompt outsiders to Attack Us? Bad enough that so many backed and defended Clinton cutting our defense so much during his years. So NOW can we at least rally and all come together?

However, the response was quite atypical for this board:

It's really impolitic to use this occasion as a means to launch into partisan political arguments. One could just as easily criticize the Bush decision to spend money on his missile defense system. I've been arguing to people on this forum for months now that the real threat now to our national security is HERE, in THIS country, from people like those who did what happened on Tuesday. This event bears out what I was arguing. Clinton's policies probably deserve some criticism, but so do Bush's. What's important is that we can now move in a definite direction. I think we all can come together now and agree. The battle has been joined by everyone.

Similarly, on the moderate left-wing Salon.com, after a poster argued that President Bush was cowardly for not returning immediately to the White House after the attacks, another participant responded:

> I hate Bush as much as anyone here but these comments about him protecting his ass as though he were cowering under a school desk somewhere instead of broadcasting from the oval office where he belongs are every bit as asinine as the idiots who are inciting violence against the "towel heads in 7–11." Grow up, people. This is likely an act of war, not a photo op for the shrub.

To which another poster added: "He's not the President we want, but he has to do the job. Let's let him do that."

At a more extreme position on the ideological spectrum, the anarchist AlterNet hosted an interesting debate over the meaning of displaying the American flag and whether participants were going to attend antiwar rallies. Many argued that, although they usually supported such demonstrations, they could not attend given the magnitude of the attack on the United States. The divergent viewpoints and the (relative) civility with which these positions were treated were strikingly different from the more normal ideological uniformity, enforced by vicious flaming.

We are not claiming, however, that this tone of tolerance was universal, either within or across sites. So, on the Anarchist Anti-Defamation League site, when a participant from the United Kingdom said: "It's about time someone showed those yanks a lesson, if I knew who was behind it I would shake them firmly by the hand." The responses were first: "What are you talking about, Limey?" And then: "Turn on the TV! REMEMBER THE TOWERS! KILL SAND NIGGERS!" And on Stormfront, to the argument mentioned earlier that Jews had actually served in the armed forces out of proportion to their numbers, came this response (by the same person who posted the article by Emma Goldman): "You little Jew commie socialist lover." To which the target of this attack replies simply: "This conversation is over."

In addition, even when a spirit of tolerance did emerge, it was quite short-lived on most sites. It was the all-encompassing characteristics of 9/11 as a media event that kept these sites engaged with mainstream media and so more open than usual to the moderating influences we have discussed. By a month after the attacks, even the limited pluralism, tolerance, and civility of discourse in these chat rooms had closed down and, just as the mainstream media returned to normal, so, too, did the political websites.

It is even more difficult to assess any lasting effects, if any, on the broader public of the increasing reliance on the internet and other non-mainstream sites for their information about 9/11. We know, as we mentioned earlier, that the belief of large segments of the public in falsehoods (e.g., the existence of Iraqi weapons of mass destruction) has been remarkably stable, despite the attempts of the press to apologize for critically accepting them. Both the declining authority of that press and the ability of new media, like chat rooms and blogs, to reinforce and recirculate discredited arguments and evidence no doubt play a role. As well, there is no denying (as we discussed in Chapter 5), the spaces opened up by new media for grassroots political discussion, and mobilization plays a significant role in the belief of many in the most outlandish conspiracy theories.[29] What we can say is that the impact on democratic politics of these new media will be shaped by the ways in which a new media regime can develop public policies, public norms, and social practices that shape the future of new media (e.g., "must carry" requirements for linking to sources and opposing points of view, the development of a media-literate polity that can critically evaluate the myriad sources of information, a broadened sense of responsibility among those who produce politically relevant media).

Conclusion

It seems to us that this analysis of media coverage in the wake of the 9/11 attack has important implications for how we think about the possibilities for improving the quality of political information available to citizens. First, it is important to acknowledge that, despite the changes we have discussed throughout this book, the mainstream news media dominated much of public discourse and did so in ways consistent with their behavior during earlier political crises and the media events created by them. That said, we find evidence of (and the potential for) a more diverse information environment than an examination of only the mainstream news would suggest. Even during this intense media event, when professional journalists seemed to regain the prominence they had during the Age of Broadcast News, elements of the new media environment provided alternative sources of information, points of view, and spaces for deliberation.

---

[29] In the 2006 Scripps Howard–Ohio University survey, which we discussed earlier, 36 percent of respondents suspected that the U.S. government promoted the attacks or intentionally sat on its hands. Sixteen percent believed that explosives brought down the towers. Twelve percent believed that a cruise missile hit the Pentagon (Hargrove 2006).

This diversity emerges from the multiaxiality of the new media environment and the consequent ability of a wide variety of groups to develop alternative interpretations of events dominating more mainstream media.

For example, shows like *The Daily Show* and *The Colbert Report*, along with significant segments of the blogosphere (in both the run-up to the invasion of Iraq and the subsequent decade of fighting in Afghanistan and Iraq), kept a critical light on the conflicts. Major news organizations scaled back the resources devoted to covering those conflicts (as a result of both the shorter-term budget pressures resulting from the coverage of 9/11 and the longer-term economic crisis of commercial journalism), and as a consequence, the fact that the country was engaged in two wars involving hundreds of thousands of troops and a military establishment strained to the breaking point threatened to become invisible to large segments of the public. During this period, *The Daily Show*'s ongoing segments "Mess O'Potamia" became especially significant politically relevant texts in their attempt to keep a media flashlight on the conflicts.[30] At the same time, the trips to Iraq of *Daily Show* contributor (and ex-marine) Rob Riggle and Stephen Colbert (who had his head shaved by the commander of American troops) reinforced the essential point that criticism of the administration's policies (and the media's coverage of those policies) was entirely consistent with supporting the troops.

To be sure, neither these multiple media outlets nor most citizens took full advantage of the democratic opportunities of the new media environment. Much of the broader media environment often served to directly and indirectly reinforce the hegemonic views that dominated the mainstream news media. At best, the examples we presented in this chapter offer tantalizing glimpses into what a truly open and diverse media regime might look like were it to more fully take advantage of the possibilities of the new media environment. Evidence that such possibilities are still unrealized is the ease with which political elites, using the media, were able to transform public horror over the terrorist attacks of September 11 into an invasion of Iraq, despite the lack of credible evidence that Iraq had weapons of mass destruction or was linked to al-Qaeda.[31] Indeed, this

---

[30] A similar role was played by *Countdown* host Keith Olbermann's daily reminder of the number of days American troops had been in Iraq, a technique borrowed from *Nightline's* coverage of the Iranian Hostage crises three decades earlier.

[31] Polls conducted before and during the Iraqi conflict consistently showed that large percentages of Americans wrongly believed that Saddam Hussein was behind the 9/11 attacks, that some or all of the hijackers were Iraqi, that Iraq used chemical or biological weapons during the war, and that weapons of mass destruction were found in Iraq once

successful use of the media to orchestrate a well-choreographed march to war demonstrates not only how public reactions to events such as 9/11 are shaped by the river of mediated discourses (in popular culture as well as the news) that existed before the terrorist attacks but also how the mediated representations of those events in turn shape subsequent discourse that occurs down river. Yet it is important to also note that even though this mobilization by the state was ultimately successful, public opinion was remarkably slow to rally around the invasion of Iraq, especially without U.N. endorsement, the possible result of the more diverse media environment found outside the mainstream news.

Even when successful at critiquing and resisting state mobilization, the new media environment raises many troubling issues about its impact on democratic politics. Though providing space for critiques of mainstream discourse, the unifying rituals of 9/11 as a media event kept even the most extreme groups engaged with the wider public. Once the media event ended, so, too, did this engagement. In some cases, the multiaxial environment then allowed the development and circulation of not just alternative interpretations but also alternative hyperrealties on which those interpretations depended. Of course, political groups outside the mainstream have always constructed their own counterreality on which to base their political analysis.[32] As the 9/11 Truth movement illustrates, what is different now is the ease with which it is possible to construct and then circulate such alternatives and the rejection of even the most widely accepted and basic facts of the matter (e.g., that planes piloted by terrorists crashed into the twin towers and the Pentagon on 9/11).

At a minimum, our examination of the media's representation of 9/11 makes clear that the democratic promise and pitfalls presented by the hyperreal and multiaxial new media environment are important to more fully understand. Explorations of the role of the media in times of political crises – whether by scholars or practitioners – must include films, dramas, comedies, and late-night talk shows as well as news broadcasts; foreign as well as domestic sources; chat rooms as well as newsrooms;

the war ended (Davies 2003). As we noted earlier, these misconceptions were enduring. For an excellent and definitive study of the way in which the Bush administration successfully manipulated mainstream news coverage in years following 9/11 and its impact on public opinion and public policy, see Nacos, Bloch-Elkon, and Shapiro (2011).

[32] In this sentence, we use the term *reality* rather than *hyperreality*. We reserve the latter term for application to the more recent media environment in which the construction of a politically significant reality (including those constructed by political elites themselves) can occur almost entirely within the media.

and so on – failing to do so risks badly misreading the impact of the media on public opinion, public action, and public policy. But understanding is not enough. The democratic potential of the new media is also worth struggling to preserve and enhance. This will be no easy task. The ever-present pressures to commercialize and control new media rather than to see it as a primary resource for democratic politics may well prevent their potential from ever being truly realized. The questions we face are how or if this potential will be nurtured and expanded in a new media regime, and as important, whether we can build a citizenry capable of effectively taking advantage of this potential in the way it formulates, discusses, and acts in the political world.

8

Shaping a New Media Regime

It is hard to picture the contemporary world, even in the face of a technology that makes each of us potentially equal senders and receivers of information, without a specialized institution of journalism.

— Michael Schudson, *The Power of News*, 1995

Political beliefs and actions spring from assumptions, biases, and news reports. In this critical sense politics is a drama taking place in an assumed and reported world that evokes threats and hopes, a world people do not directly observe or touch. . . . The models, scenarios, narratives, and images into which audiences for political news translate that news are social capital, not individual inventions. They come from works of art in all genres: novels, paintings, stories, films, dramas, television sitcoms, striking rumors, even memorable jokes. For each type of news report there is likely to be a small set of striking images that are influential with large numbers of people, both spectators of the political scene and policymakers themselves.

— Murray Edelman, *From Art to Politics*, 1996

Truth is so great a thing that we ought not to despise any medium that will conduct it to us.

— Michel de Montaigne, *Essays*, 1575

Between December 2004 and April 2005, all three anchor positions for the nightly network news became open when Tom Brokaw retired, Peter Jennings was diagnosed with lung cancer, and Dan Rather was forced out as a result of allegations (tellingly driven by conservative bloggers, talk-show hosts and other elements of the new media environment) about the use of forged documents in CBS's coverage of George W. Bush's Air National Guard service. The sudden changes at all three networks came amid greater uncertainty about the shape and even the survival of broadcast news. As we discussed in Chapter 3, audiences for the network news have precipitously declined and aged over the past two decades. Between March 2007 and March 2008 alone, CBS nightly news lost 21 percent of its eighteen- to thirty-four-year-old viewers, ABC lost 13.5 percent, and NBC lost 10.1 percent, with the average age for viewers of all three newscasts increasing to sixty-one (Fitzgerald 2008).

These declines cannot be blamed on citizen apathy about politics, as evidenced by the fact that they continued unabated during a presidential primary season that saw significant increases in voter interest and turnout. Rather, they are a result of the dramatic changes in the media environment we have been chronicling in this book. Cable news networks were the beneficiary of some of this exodus, with ratings increasing substantially, especially among younger viewers, during the 2008 presidential campaign. But this increase appears to have been temporary and limited. For example, the average age of viewers of *The O'Reilly Factor* remains older than sixty-five, and perhaps as old as seventy-one (Carter 2006). More important, cable "news" is so fundamentally different from traditional broadcast news in form and content that it would be a mistake to see audience shifts from the latter to the former as the equivalent of switching from CBS to ABC during the Age of Broadcast News. Internet use also helps explain the decline in broadcast news viewing – a 2008 Zogby poll reported that 55 percent of eighteen- to twenty-nine-year-olds said the internet was their primary news source about that campaign (Fitzgerald 2008). Yet although much of internet news traffic finds its way to websites operated by more traditional news sources (Hindman 2009), these sites are significantly different in form, content, and use from their broadcast parents, and even more than the latter are struggling to find a viable economic model to allow them to survive.

The situation is even worse when it comes to print journalism. Between 2005 and 2009, newspaper ad revenues dropped 44 percent, from $49.43 billion to $27.6 billion (Sass 2010). In a commercial media system, declining ad revenues is bad news for employees, and in just two months of 2008 (May and June) major newspaper chains cut more than 3,500 jobs (Sass 2008). And in October 2009, the venerable *New York Times*, once considered immune from the industry's larger woes, announced that it would be cutting 8 percent of its newsroom staff (Perez-Pena 2009). Such changes are not lost on journalists who tend, unsurprisingly, to be quite pessimistic about the future of their profession. A 2008 survey conducted by the Pew Research Center Project for Excellence in Journalism concluded:

> Certainly there is a clear but complex sense of pessimism pervading journalism. It cuts across print and broadcast and across local and national journalists. At the national level, more than six in ten journalists and senior executives now think journalism is headed in the wrong direction; less than a third are optimistic. TV and radio journalists at national news networks, many of whom entered 2007 with hopes of growth as online video became more widely used, are among the most pessimistic of all. All of these numbers are up from 2004. (Mitchell and Rosenstiel 2008)

Among corporate media executives, however, the dominant concern was not the future of journalism but the future of the news industry. At ABC, for instance, a debate raged over whether the new anchor would be sixty-three-year-old Charlie Gibson, the eventual choice (who was almost exactly the average age of his audience) or whether the network would create "a bold new program" by introducing two younger coanchors, Elizabeth Vargas and Bob Woodruff (forty-five and forty-six years old, respectively; Kurtz 2007, 207). In the end, in part because of Woodruff's being seriously injured while covering the war in Iraq, the only "significant" change made was to alter the name of the broadcast from *World News Tonight with Charles Gibson* to *World News with Charles Gibson*. In December 2009, Gibson, in turn, was replaced on his retirement by the sixty-four-year-old Diane Sawyer, the longtime host of *Good Morning America*, and the news broadcast was renamed *World News with Diane Sawyer*. Meanwhile, at CBS, the seat vacated by Dan Rather and once occupied by the iconic Walter Cronkite was given to Katie Couric, whose central qualification was being the longtime host of NBC's *Today Show*. Although the choice did generate concerns that her hiring signaled a shift to a more soft news, feature-oriented approach, most of the debate swirled around such vital issues as what she would wear, the characteristics and expense of a redesigned set, using pop music to set up stories, whether she would be standing or sitting when the show opened, and whether she would do a voiceover of the stories to follow or let an announcer perform that task (Kurtz 2007, 250–252).[1] The

---

[1] Couric's claim that much of this specific criticism resulted from sexism has some merit. More to the point, however, the presumption that the other broadcast networks were engaging in "serious" journalism is not a defensible claim. For example, during the time that CBS was under fire for going soft, ABC's Charles Gibson did a feature on what would happen if you tried to dig a hole to China, another on the fiftieth anniversary of

rearranging-deck-chairs-on-the-Titanic quality of these and similar debates seemed lost on its corporate participants. Indeed, Steve Capus, the president of NBC News, accused CBS of trying to change too much (Kurtz 2007, 273).

Even when the dramatically changing media environment was addressed by the broadcast news industry, it was done in ways that again missed its broader implications and potential. For example, CBS News introduced a new feature on what was "hot" on the internet. NBC's Brian Williams became the first network anchor to create his own blog. Not to be outdone, Couric established her own blog with video chats about the stories on the broadcast. In this escalating blog war, Williams soon introduced video chat to his blog.

One of the few public moments in which the new media's potential for reshaping the structure and assumptions of broadcast journalism specifically, and professional journalism more broadly, was provided by ABC's anchor. Following the injuries Woodruff suffered in Iraq, Gibson questioned whether the war was enough of a justification for asking journalists to risk their lives: "Maybe they could give video cameras to ordinary Iraqis to get footage of what life was like, but would that put them at risk?" (Kurtz 2007, 211). Though driven by an understandable concern for the physical safety of both colleagues and ordinary citizens, this question raises a host of other, arguably more central, ones: What role can and/or should citizens play in providing facts on the ground? What values and skills might be useful in guiding citizens as they gathered such information? What legal and physical protections can be offered to citizens as they gather such information? What would these changes mean for the role of professional journalists? But such questions were and are rarely asked as journalists and news executives ponder the fate of their profession. Nor are even more fundamental questions regarding the relationship among media, professional journalism, citizens, and democracy in the new information age.[2] At most, mainstream media have either attempted to incorporate aspects of this new environment at the margins by occasionally inviting citizens to provide content (as with CNN's highly orchestrated 2008 YouTube presidential primary debates or its online iReports) or have been reactive to this new landscape (as when

---

The Cat in the Hat (with him reciting the item in rhyme), and a story about a teenager who completed coursework for an undergraduate degree at the University of Virginia in a single year (Kurtz 2007, 317).

[2] For attempts to rethink journalism with these questions in mind, see the Knight Foundation's News Challenge (http://www.newschallenge.org).

the expulsion of journalists from Iran after the 2009 elections forced the news media to depend on the video, text messages, and tweets provided by local citizens).

This resistance to change might be more justifiable – though still ultimately wrongheaded – if there were evidence that the goal was to truly preserve the best of twentieth-century journalism. But the facts regularly belie this conclusion, at least as far as network executives are concerned. For example, in April 2008, it was reported that CBS News was in negotiations with Time Warner to "outsource some of its news gathering operations to CNN" (Arango 2008). The reduction in costs of using news feeds from the cable network would allow *CBS* to retain such high-priced on-air celebrity talent as Katie Couric. Of course, pooling is neither new nor limited to broadcast journalism: currently, only four American newspapers maintain any foreign bureaus, with the rest relying on the wire services or reprint articles from these four papers (Kristof 2008). What is disturbing is that decisions such as this one are the norm, driven primarily by profit considerations and made without serious and imaginative thinking by journalists themselves, let alone the broader public.

Past Media Regimes, the Current Media Environment, and Democratically Useful Media

The new media environment creates myriad alterations in the way political information is and can be communicated to the public, and as significantly, it creates new conduits for large segments of the citizenry to communicate with both elites and one another. In creating these new axes of communication, it has dissolved the assumptions, distinctions, and hierarchies of the Age of Broadcast News. These changes have been regularly noted by many scholars and journalists. As exemplified by the reaction of news anchors and executives illustrated earlier, however, they have been viewed from the perspective of the very media regime that is being challenged. As a result, the crisis of this particular regime is seen as a crisis of democracy itself. Viewed from a broader historical vantage, however, it is the Age of Broadcast News that is exceptional in its attempts to limit politically relevant media to a single genre ("news") and a single authority ("professional journalists"). More significant, as we have seen, there is little evidence that the Age of Broadcast News did a measurably better job than previous regimes at informing the public, encouraging enlightened democratic dialogue, or – in short – serving the broader interests of a democratic society.

In this book, we have attempted to put the current crises of U.S. journalism in just such an historical context. Six conclusions can be drawn from this interpretive review. First, the framers of the Constitution and Bill of Rights recognized that an informed, vigilant, and active citizenry is central to democracy. Second, the framers also recognized that an independent press, coupled with protections for the rights of free speech and assembly, are necessary to ensuring such a citizenry. Third, the specific meanings of *active citizens*, an *independent press*, *free speech*, and *free assembly* have been contested and redefined over our history. Fourth, these contestations have ebbed and flowed, with periods in which institutionalized norms (media regimes) have "naturalized" extant practices punctuated by moments in which disjunctures between theory and practice become too obvious to ignore. Fifth, these disjunctures have been driven by sometimes gradual, sometimes sudden economic, political, cultural, and technological changes. And sixth, to date at least, new media regimes inevitably emerge, the result of political struggle with clear winners and losers, eventually becoming naturalized until the next disjuncture occurs.

As we also have argued throughout this book, we are at such a critical disjuncture in the United States today, one in which the media regime in place for the latter half of the twentieth century has been dismantled and the contours of a new regime have yet to be formed. In the past, such moments have provided significant and rare occasions for reconsidering the relationship between media and democracy, often in very public and even organized ways. For example, the Rockefeller Seminars of the 1930s and the Hutchins Commission of the 1940s brought together a broad range of public figures to consider the implications of a changing media environment for American democracy. Although we make no claim that these past efforts produced results that advanced democratic practice (in many cases, quite the opposite could be argued), we do believe that the current moment affords us yet another chance to "get it right."

But what does "getting it right" entail? At a minimum, it requires serious consideration of what was most beneficial and most problematic about past regimes, what is potentially most beneficial and most problematic about the new information environment in which we live, and in each case how best to nurture the former and avoid the latter. Firm answers to these questions not only go beyond the scope of this book but also violate one of its central themes: that such answers ought to emerge from deliberations that include all of the actors – citizens as well – who are affected by them. We do, however, have suggestions for shaping the issues with which such a deliberation might deal, as well as some starting principles for assessing the democratic potential of the media and how well it meets this potential. These principles are based on a consideration of the qualities of past media regimes, the qualities of the information environment in which we currently live, and a more expansive notion of what we mean by both politically relevant and democratically useful media.

Lessons from Past Media Regimes

Past media regimes had several distinct but overlapping qualities that are relevant to any discussion of the current and future role of the media in U.S. democracy. Relevant because they were the product of similar discussions from earlier eras, because they are drawn from actual experience rather than purely theoretical speculations, and because they can provide useful counterpoints to more reified assumptions that are based solely on recent practices.[3] Although many such qualities might be emphasized, several strike us as particularly noteworthy. Cutting across the three regimes that dominated from the late eighteenth to the early twentieth century (the partisan press, the penny press, and the age of Realism) are the relative absence of distinctions between fact and opinion, politics and culture, news and entertainment, personal and political, journalist and citizen, and so forth, which were much more common in recent periods. Also characteristic of these earlier regimes was the notion, articulated and instituted in various ways, that mediated representations of the public world were midpoints on the continuum from the occurrence of events and emergence of issues to their interpretation and use, a continuum along which citizens themselves played an active, deliberative role at all points. Additional noteworthy qualities that were more specific to particular regimes from this earlier period include the partisan press's (unsurprising given its name) explicitly partisan affiliation and slant, as well as its elite-controlled content; the penny press's mass-oriented, nationalized content (made possible both by direct and by indirect subsidies provided by the government and by new technology such as the telegraph), its competition-driven model in which single communities featured numerous papers, its independent partisan slant, and its regular use of citizen journalists (a.k.a. correspondents); and the age

---

[3] This is not to say that our characterizations of these past qualities are not subject to debate or refinement, or that historical context may make some past experiences moot. But we believe that drawing on the past tethers more contemporary discussions in a useful, practical way, pointing to the possible without limiting such possibilities.

of Realism's multigenre approach for uncovering the "truth" of things, its acceptance of science and data as a journalistic tool without abandoning a more narrative reporting style, and its explicit efforts to uncover social inequities and push for social change. Each of these qualities both presumed and reinforced notions of media and democracy that differed in significant ways from what followed.

The media regime emerging within the Progressive Era of the latter nineteenth and early twentieth centuries marked a more dramatic and arguably limiting notion of both politically relevant media and politically engaged citizens. Its fundamental qualities – professionalized journalism, fact-based objective reporting, the separation of politics from popular culture, elite-dominated politics, citizens as observers – became further institutionalized and reified in the Age of Broadcast News. Layered onto these qualities in the latter regime were increasingly centralized (in terms of ownership, outlets, and content) media, increasingly routinized formats, and a growing emphasis on the watchdog function of the press.

Throughout this book, we have emphasized the Age of Broadcast News's limitations as a way to counter the frequent tendency of many analysts to uncritically accept its underlying assumptions, to romanticize its actual characteristics, and then to use them as the standards to which any new regime should aspire. At the same time, however, it is important to not lose sight of this passing regime's considerable achievements and lofty goals. As we have noted at several points, this regime developed a nightly ritual of citizenship – watching the evening news – which engaged most Americans and created a common political agenda, an achievement that seems increasingly remarkable in light of an increasingly fragmented media that seems to reinforce polarization and make civil engagement across political difference difficult.

Certainly – as the quote from Michael Schudson with which we opened this chapter suggests – a profession devoted to holding elites accountable by providing citizens with timely, useful, and otherwise inaccessible information, gathered and disseminated in a disinterested manner, has an important place in any new media regime. The problem, from our perspective, with the passing regime was both its regular failure to meet these goals and the hegemonic role it played as the purveyor of politically relevant information. Whether or not one agrees with this critique, however, there is no going back. The rapidly changing media environment makes it incumbent on us to rethink how the best goals and practices of prior regimes, including the Age of Broadcast News, might be incorporated into a new media regime.

Emergent Qualities of the New Information Environment
The qualities of past media regimes provide a useful starting point for thinking about the contours of a future regime. But as should be clear, one must also consider the emerging qualities of the information environment in which we currently live, qualities that, though not determinant, will be crucial in developing norms and practices that might encourage its most democratically useful tendencies and discourage its least democratic ones. As is now commonly accepted, this new environment, driven largely by technological changes, has unprecedented potential to dramatically increase the volume and range of information (broadly defined) available to and about citizens; to increase the speed with which information can be gathered, retrieved, and transmitted; to decentralize the sources of information; to alter the media consumption habits of individuals and groups and thus increase the control they have over the information they receive; to increase the ability to target specific messages to specific audiences; to increase the number and range of information producers and alter the relationship between producers and consumers; to increase both vertical and horizontal communication among citizens and between citizens and elites (one to one, one to many, many to one, and many to many); and to increase the interactivity of communication (for a prescient and still relevant overview of the qualities of new media, see Abramson, Arterton, and Orren 1988).

In turn, these technological innovations have intersected with and been shaped by changes in the cultural, economic, and political environments of the late twentieth and early twenty-first centuries. The result has been the emergence of a media environment whose central qualities are, we have argued, multiaxiality and hyperreality. These qualities are anathema to many of the core tenets of the Age of Broadcast News but not necessarily to a democratically useful media regime. To the contrary, we believe they open up the possibility of a new regime that incorporates the best of the Age of Broadcast News while also making possible the reemergence of useful qualities found in earlier regimes.

Defining Democratically Useful Media
The third requisite for assessing the promises and pitfalls of the new information environment, and the efficacy of any new regime that emerges from it, is establishing a common understanding of democratically useful media. As a starting point, we return to our definition of politically relevant media: media texts that shape opportunities for understanding, deliberating, and acting on (1) the conditions of one's everyday life, (2)

the life of fellow community members, and (3) the norms and structures of power that shape these relationships. Recall that this definition is sufficiently broad to include communication that is not automatically tied to particular genres (e.g., the nightly news), sources (e.g., professional journalists), or media (e.g., newspapers) while still allowing one to distinguish between more or less relevant texts. It also includes admittedly consciously normative assumptions regarding what democratic citizenship (i.e., understanding, deliberation, and action) and politics (i.e., self-interest, collective interests, and institutional power) entail.

Finally, it treats mediated texts as politically relevant not only when they encourage democratic citizenship but also when they discourage it (i.e., a text can shape opportunities by constraining understanding, deliberation, and action, as well as by enhancing them). In turn, however, our definition of politically relevant media can be easily transformed into a yardstick for measuring the democratic utility of media texts (and the regimes producing them) by focusing on their potential for enhancing democratic citizenship. In short, a broadcast news story, newspaper article, blog entry, or fictional television drama that reduces public understanding, deliberation, and/or participation – and the media regimes that produce them – are politically relevant but not democratically useful.

Building Blocks for Constructing and Assessing a New Media Regime

What are needed are criteria for a new media regime that preserve the best of the past while taking advantage of the opportunities created by a dramatically changed media environment. Such criteria are vital given the challenges to democratic life that have emerged in this new environment. For example, we have seen how multiaxiality can foster the development of insular communities that base their discourse not only on competing political values but also on idiosyncratic and incompatible views of reality – what we have called hyperrealities. This is a considerable change from the Age of Broadcast News, which managed to create, for better or worse, a hegemonic hyperreality, one that marginalized and/or limited the expression of alternative political perspectives deemed unworthy of "serious" attention. Absent such a hegemonic authority, a central challenge for a new and democratic media regime is to create an environment that brings diverse communities into civil engagement with one another. In turn, this requires developing widely shared norms regarding what such discourse should look like (with respect to both basic facts of the matter and more normative values) while acknowledging the inherent contestability of these facts and values. And it requires creating inclusive, accessible spaces for these ongoing conversations and debates to take place. In short, any new media regime, if it is to be democratic, must be deliberative.

A promising characteristic of the new media environment in this regard is its interactivity and several features that flow from it. By allowing almost anyone to create his or her own media – through websites, blogs, Facebook pages, or YouTube videos – the new environment significantly blurs the line between producers and consumers of political information. At a minimum, this allows a wide range of citizens to develop an appreciation for the challenges of gathering and disseminating information. As significantly, individual citizens increasingly move between the roles of consumer and producer of media, a process that can help prepare them for active civic and political engagement (whether mediated or not). Even privileged gatekeepers (e.g., political elites, professional journalists) who in the recent past could legitimately see themselves as exclusively the producers of media to be consumed by a largely passive public are increasingly forced to play the role of consumer as well. Journalists, for example, routinely list their e-mail addresses and increasingly mention reader comments in what they write. Other producers of media, from cable news commentators to television and movie producers, increasingly attend to fan sites, blogs, e-mails, and so on. Public officials, too, have increased their efforts to use new media to both talk to and listen to their various constituencies. To date, however, much of this "exchange" has been more akin to surveillance than dialogue, and the democratic possibilities of today's more interactive environment will remain unfulfilled unless they are clearly defined and forcefully argued in the debates and policies that ultimately will shape a new media regime.

Drawing on lessons from past media regimes, the emergent characteristics of the current information environment, and our definitions of politically relevant and democratically useful media, we suggest four criteria that we believe should underpin these debates. We believe that these criteria – transparency, pluralism, verisimilitude, and practice – salvage the spirit and intent of past efforts to create a democratic media environment while taking into consideration both the limitations of these earlier efforts and the promise and pitfalls evident in the new media environment.

We understand that these four criteria are debatable in their own right (as any democratic dialogue must consider such key values as essentially contestable) and so may not be the best or only ones to consider. As such, they are offered as informed suggestions, aimed to open rather than to settle debate. But we also believe that explicit criteria and debate over them are desperately needed now, as the very relationship among media, citizens, and politics is in flux. Without such a public debate, and a set of expectations to tether and shape that debate, the democratic potential of this new environment will likely be lost to a series of incremental decisions largely driven by market forces and entrenched political interests.

Transparency

To be democratically useful, communication requires some degree of familiarity and trust among the participants. This can be especially difficult in mass-mediated communication, where the physical and interpersonal connections between sender and receiver are often distant. It is more difficult still in the multiaxial and hyperreal media environment of the twenty-first century. Although the trustworthiness of information and its source is something that is determined over time and case by case, media regimes can vary in the extent to which they make such assessments possible. We believe a minimal requirement for this crucial condition is "transparency," by which we mean the ability of participants in politically relevant, mediated communication to know who is speaking to them. As such, it might be seen as the mass-mediated, systemic prerequisite for rhetoric's emphasis on ethos (from the Greek, "to be accustomed to") or the demonstration of a speaker's moral and ethical character.

The importance (if not the specific concept or term) of transparency can be seen in various and sometimes problematic ways in all the media regimes discussed in this book: the use of pseudonyms or surrogates during the late eighteenth and early twentieth centuries; the explicit, stated alignment of publications with a particular party or ideology that defined the partisan press; public, debated challenges to the authenticity of various correspondences; and so forth. It can also be seen in more formal ways in professional journalism's norms regarding the disclosure or protection of one's sources, the use of multiple sources, the inclusion of bylines, acknowledging when a story involves the economic interests of the media organization, and so on.

But our notion of transparency in the new information environment is more encompassing than this in three ways. First, because politically relevant media can include more than traditional news, norms of transparency must be extended to other genres, media figures, and media organizations as well. It becomes as important to know the motivations and professional ethics of Jon Stewart as to know those of Brian Williams, to know the economic interests of a movie studio as to know those of a newspaper chain, to know the "sources" of a songwriter as to know the sources of a reporter, to know the political views or affiliations of a blogger as to know those of a columnist. Second, transparency should be not only a norm for those who act as mediators in the public sphere but also a central part of their responsibility as mediators. By this, we mean that one of the central responsibilities of democratically useful media should be to make it possible for us to assess the authenticity and sincerity of the people, organizations, and institutions they mediate. And just as the range of media from whom transparency is expected has expanded, so, too, has the range of their mediated subjects, be they the president of the United States, a summer intern from Beverly Hills, a little-known governor of Alaska, an unemployed plumber from Ohio, or a 527 political action committee claiming to represent the 3,500 swift-boat veterans of the Vietnam War.

Third and finally, our definition of transparency assumes that, in the absence of reliable standards for judging accuracy, objectivity, and the other core (albeit questionable) assumptions that defined journalism in the Age of Broadcast News, it is crucial for audiences to be familiar with the rules (i.e., the norms, processes, institutions, and rituals) used in constructing the information they receive. As such, transparency includes not only traditional journalistic norms but also broader notions of disclosure, authenticity, sincerity, and ultimately familiarity. This inclusion of audiences in the process of constructing mediated interpretations of political reality must be done in a way that is clear and obvious; that is ongoing and foregrounded; and most important, that provides formal and informal opportunities for deliberation and contestation.[4] In a comment that applies as well to professional journalism, political blogging, or television satire as to reality programming, Jeff Gaspin, the executive vice president of alternative series at NBC, said in response to criticisms that "reality television" had been edited for dramatic purposes:

We all have to sort of establish our own rules. One of the things that you do to cover yourself is to put a disclaimer on there. You need to be fair to the audience, and you need to tell them whatever you have done. And it shouldn't necessarily be in fine print that you can't read. (qtd. in Schlosser and McConnell 2001, 12)

---

[4] Of course, as with most elements of the new media environment, distinguishing among senders, subjects, and receivers of politically relevant information is often difficult. Our point is that all users of the media must know one another at some level, and the responsibility for creating an environment where in which such judgments are possible is a shared one.

To play a democratic role in a new media regime, transparency cannot, as Gaspin noted, be "in the fine print that you can't read."

How might transparency in the way we conceptualize it contribute to the quality of democratic discourse? Consider, for example, issue advocacy ads and other all-too-common forms of mass mediated communications that are sponsored by large corporations or (as we saw in Chapter 5) by well-funded ideologues hiding under the guise of shell organizations with populist, grassroots-sounding names (Jamieson 2000). Under a media regime that valued transparency, such practices would, at minimum, be understood by citizens and ideally would be violations of commonly accepted norms and possibly formal regulations.[5] And if it did occur, it would be made transparent by those mediating the public world for us, be it Anderson Cooper, Stephen Colbert, or Lisa Simpson. Or, less obviously, viewers of a presidential address should understand that such addresses are often crafted by others and should have some sense of how this process works, who these others are, and what the president's own contribution to the text was.[6] This practice should be extended to include routine consideration of the ways in which the public statements of all political officials (and other public figures) are crafted. Similarly, the inner workings of Congress regarding the crafting of legislation should be more transparent. In all these examples, the responsibility for ensuring this level of transparency lies with the media, the political actor, and the public alike.

Transparency also applies to the inner workings of the media itself. Audiences need to know who is really speaking to them when they watch a

---

[5] As if it needed further criticism, the Supreme Court decision (*Citizens United v. Federal Election Commission*) removing all restrictions from corporate political contributions has been made even worse by strategies being developed by lobbying firms to hide a specific firm's contributions (lest they be unpopular with customers or shareholders) by pooling them in shell organizations, which can offer anonymity. In an age when political contributions go primarily to purchase advertisements, the violation of norms of transparency is both obvious and alarming.

[6] Indeed, what we are calling transparency was used for political advantage in the 2008 presidential campaign, when candidate Barack Obama let it be known that he was writing his speech on race himself (Pin 2008). Obama (or more accurately, the Obama campaign team) recognized that the public's skeptical, even cynical understanding of modern politics assumes that politicians simply speak the words prepared by their handlers. It therefore became necessary to alert the public that this time, if only this time, he was actually speaking in his own words. In 2000, Al Gore used the same technique when his campaign let it be known that he himself had written his acceptance speech at the Democratic National Convention, and Ross Perot followed a similar strategy in 1992. Although the public announcement that a candidate has actually written his or her own speech is largely a campaign tactic designed to appeal to the public's skepticism about the nature of political discourse, it highlights the need for greater transparency regarding the procedures through which public figures communicate to citizens.

segment of Fox's *The Sean Hannity Show* (are they hearing talking points from Republican Party operatives?), read a political blog (what are the political and economic affiliations of the author?), watch Jay Leno make a joke about the president (what are the political views of Leno and/or his writers?), or view an HBO miniseries about the lives of inner-city African Americans (do the writers have any real-world experience with the subject matter?). In the end, transparency is important not only so that viewers can assess the trustworthiness of what they are viewing, reading, or hearing but also because it encourages those who step onto the media soapbox to take responsibility for what they are saying.

Although truly embedding the value of transparency in a media regime is ultimately a cultural shift dependent on voluntary and professional norms and practices, government regulations can and, we argue, must play an important role in fostering such an environment. Cass Sunstein (2001), for example, has suggested the need for right-to-know legislation that would require media corporations to regularly and visibly (i.e., not in the fine print you can't read) report to relevant communities on their public service and public interest activities. He argues that this simply extends to the media existing requirements in the environmental arena that require corporations to make public information about their use and disposal of hazardous substances. This emergence of community right to know has been central to empowering citizens and local environmental groups who are now able to hold corporations more accountable for the environmental impacts of their behavior (Williams and Matheny 1995). In support of his argument, Sunstein reflects a value at the heart of transparency when he cites Justice Brandeis's famous comment that "sunlight is the best disinfectant." This approach is evocative of Federal Communications Commission (FCC) regulations requiring radio and television stations to periodically defend their public interest contributions in exchange for the right to broadcast. But following the logic of this argument in a way that reflects the characteristics of the new media environment and an expansion of what we mean by public service in this changed system, we would extend the right to know to include, for example, ownership of media corporations and clear statements about who produced any particular media text. To serve its intended purposes, there would have to be experimentation with the most effective way of presenting right-to-know information. For example, if we move such information from the fine print, how should it be presented so that citizens will actually attend to it? Would a prominent voiceover or written statement at the beginning of a particular show, website, or newspaper revealing ownership, who actually worked on it, and so forth, suffice (as measured, perhaps, by studies of increased levels of awareness on the part of the audience)?

The extension of public service requirements to nontraditional forms of political communication such as blogs, films, or non-news television programming in response to a changing media environment is not a new phenomenon. For example, the FCC struggled in the 1980s over whether to extend the fairness doctrine to non-news daytime talk shows like *The Donahue Show*:[7]

That doctrine requires a broadcaster or, in some instances, a cable system, to provide equal opportunities to competing candidates to appear on the air. In the most common situation, if one candidate buys commercial time on a broadcast station, the station must treat other candidates in the same race equally, and allow them to buy equal amounts of time on the station at equivalent rates to those paid by the first candidate. If a candidate is given free time, all his or her opponents are entitled to the same amount of free time, if they request it within seven days of the first candidate's appearance. (Oxenford 2007)

However, recognizing that certain forms of broadcasting (mainly broadcast journalism) required more autonomy, news programs were deemed exempt. This exemption allows journalists to exercise their discretion about what to cover without having to provide equal coverage to all candidates. The FCC extended this "bona fide news" exemption to daytime talk shows on the grounds that they were also providing a type of news coverage to their audience. Our point is not that this was the right decision; one might argue that allowing an exemption for talk shows was a mistake. Indeed, one might further argue that removing the news exemption for broadcast journalism would actually improve the quality of campaign coverage by forcing equal coverage of all candidates. Rather, the point is that the FCC has a history of wrestling with the challenges new forms of communication raise regarding the distinction between news and entertainment and has decided that some shows that seem to fall in the latter category actually play an important role in providing political information to the public.[8] In the face of a dramatically

---

[7] We are grateful to the media lawyer Richard Marks for bringing these deliberations to our attention.

[8] Supporting our argument that considerations of the public interest should be extended beyond traditional sources of political information was the struggle of the National Organization of Women (NOW) during the 1970s to have included in a station's licensing renewal an evaluation of the portrayal of women across all of its programming, not just the news. The carefully thought-out understanding of television's full range of programming that animated NOW's intervention into licensing is also an illustration of how the assumptions of the Age of Broadcast News blinkered journalists and many scholars to the political relevance of programming labeled "entertainment" (Perlman 2007).

changed media environment, there needs to be broader and more explicit consideration of just such issues.

What does all this suggest for professional journalism? Just as the goal of transparency implies new roles and responsibilities for nontraditional media, cultural figures, government, and citizens, it creates new roles and responsibilities for journalists. In the Age of Broadcast News, the value of transparency was at least partially served when journalists were scrupulous about revealing their sources, balancing their stories, and so forth. These rituals signaled to viewers that the information they were receiving was assembled according to a set of known, agreed-on rules. The new media environment, with its changing incentives (e.g., market populism), formats (e.g., twenty-four-hour "live" cable stations or news websites), and technologies (e.g., computer graphics, the ability to edit screen images), requires that journalists reassess both their role and the strategic rituals necessary to fill that role.

Even at the height of the Age of Broadcast News, the practices of journalists were often less than ideal and far from transparent. As we noted in Chapter 7, this was most evident during media events, when the combination of an expanded news hole and the pace of incoming information made following traditional norms and procedures more difficult and thus momentarily more visible by their absence. However, in the new faster-paced and competitive media environment, the demands of getting the latest, "breaking" news on the air means that journalists are routinely far less able to perform the writing and editing functions that have been at the heart of their profession (Katz 1993). As a result, the traditional rules of journalism face a triple challenge when it comes to transparency. First, their institutionalization over time has made them and their inherent limitations increasingly "naturalized" and so invisible. Second, the changed media environment has made these rules even less applicable than in the past. And third, these practices are increasingly violated by the news media themselves, as the very same people (journalists and experts), appearing on the very same programs, and using the very same discourse are employing quite different rules to construct the information they provide. How to construct a new set of transparent norms and procedures that can operate in this new, complex, and constantly shifting information environment is a major issue to be addressed by professional journalists and others dependent on them if they are to remain relevant to democratic discourse.

In addition to reconceptualizing their own norms and rules, journalists must also rethink their role, especially in light of continuing cutbacks in funding for basic reporting, the increasing reliance on press releases as the basis for news stories, and the growth in importance of unfamiliar citizen-journalists.

One possible and promising function – one for which we believe professional journalists are well positioned – is to play a leading role in making transparent the processes used to construct politically relevant media texts created outside the realm of professional journalism.[9] Journalists could provide insight into the ways various websites operate; how politicians write speeches; the source and uses of corporate political contributions; how particular images from ordinary citizens were selected, edited, and circulated; how Hollywood movie productions deal with issues of political relevance; and so forth. In short, making the norms and rules by which public information is communicated more transparent is not only an issue facing journalists within their own profession; it may be one of the core contributions that defines professional journalism in the next media regime, shifting from a gatekeeping role to one that focuses more on explication, education, and facilitation of public discourse.

Pluralism

Transparency, though important to any democratic communications environment, is in and of itself not enough – for example, knowing that almost all the information one receives about nuclear energy is from a media organization heavily invested in that industry does not make the information environment democratic. The second key quality for a new media regime is pluralism, or the openness of the media environment to diverse points of view and the equal accessibility of these different views. As such, it is related to qualities seen in past regimes, such as the numerous, competing papers found during the eras of the partisan and penny press, the multigenre environment of the Realist Era, and the rules regarding balance and equal time during the Age of Broadcast News. But as with transparency, we see pluralism as a broader concept when applied to the new media environment, drawing on both past experiences and approaches but combining them in ways that take advantage of emerging opportunities for expanded deliberation.

Pluralism, as we use the term, relates to issues of both structure and content. Structurally, a pluralistic media regime is one that, much like

---

[9] We are not suggesting that this is the only role to be played by professional journalism (or a new conceptualization of its values and practices). As we argued earlier, any media regime will need the investigative reporting and disinterested gathering of information necessary to a well-functioning democratic society.

the Age of Realism, consciously acknowledges the potential political relevance and facilitates the democratic utility of a wide range of media and genres. Newspapers, magazines, photographs, radio, movies, television, websites, blogs, social networking sites, instant messaging, tweets, and so on, though different in their strengths and weaknesses, are no more or less privileged. Nor are news; columns; talk shows; documentaries; docudramas; dramas; comedies; personal narratives; reality programs; and the multitude of other, shifting forms that representation of the public world can take. Second, structural pluralism acknowledges, values, and facilitates diversity in the economic models underlying the media, including a mix of private and public; of local, regional, national, and global; and of centralized and decentralized ownership and control. Third, it supports diversity in the producers of politically relevant media texts, from professional journalists to public figures from other sectors of society, citizen-journalists, and "average" citizens. And fourth, it strives for equal access (as consumers and, where appropriate and possible, as potential producers) to the variety of mediums, genres, and sources of politically relevant information available more broadly.

Pluralism also foregrounds the importance of diverse and accessible content, the sought-after outcome of the structural criterion highlighted earlier. The diversity of political opinion expressed (implicitly or explicitly) in the movies, prime-time television, talk radio, and the blogosphere is as important as that found on the nightly news or in daily newspapers. This aspect of pluralism is not intended as a way to assess single media texts, unless of course that text is part of a genre claiming this quality as part of what defines it (as, for example, with most professional news broadcasts or daily newspapers). What we are advocating is a more ecological consideration of the range of perspectives and their interconnections that characterize the politically relevant media as a field of discourse. For example, finding that politicians are consistently portrayed in a cynical, mono-motive fashion within and across the full range of media, genres, and texts available to citizens would be viewed as a problem because it would fail to capture the more nuanced "reality" in which public officials struggle between a self-interested concern with political advantage and a genuine commitment to principle. The absence of pluralism in the treatment of politicians – confirmed in several studies of both news and entertainment media – is made even more troubling by findings that suggest a connection between viewing such treatments of politicians with the public's cynical attitudes about politics (Lichter, Lichter, and Amundson 2000; Cappella and

Hall Jamieson 1997; Patterson 2002; Morgan, Shanahan, and Signorielli 2009).[10]

Although individual media texts need not be pluralistic, they can be the catalyst for expanding the range of public discourse. For example, in 1991, the director Oliver Stone's *JFK* precipitated an extended debate over the "truth" about the 1963 Kennedy assassination. Stone's movie presented a story of a conspiracy to assassinate President Kennedy and government cover-ups, implicated Lyndon Johnson, and portrayed the controversial New Orleans attorney Jim Garrison in a heroic light. The movie was far from pluralistic in its treatment of the assassination and was roundly criticized for what was seen by many as an overwrought and unbalanced (in multiple senses of the term) treatment. Nevertheless, the movie precipitated an extended discussion in the media that raised many issues about the coverage of the assassination in the mainstream press; led to the publication of many new books on the assassination (most notably the persuasive anticonspiracy book *Case Closed*, by Gerald Posner [1993]); and perhaps most significantly, led to Congressional action to open the Warren Commission files to public scrutiny. In short, the movie led to an exceptionally pluralistic media discussion. Further, because the movie as a text was arguably very transparent – it was clearly the perspective of Oliver Stone – viewers were able to understand who was speaking to them and how to interpret the movie's perspective. More recent examples of opinionated media texts sparking pluralistic debate include Michael Moore's *Fahrenheit 9/11* (regarding the Iraq War) and *Sicko* (regarding health care), Al Gore's *An Inconvenient Truth* and 20th Century Fox's *The Day after Tomorrow* (both about global warming), and ABC's *The Path to 9/11* (regarding the 2001 terrorist attacks).

Pluralism as applied to content also suggests a shrinking of what Hallin (1986, 116–118) calls the "spheres of consensus and deviance" and an expanding of the "sphere of legitimate controversy." One cannot simply assume, a priori, that certain viewpoints (e.g., that the United States is experiencing an "economic boom" or a "recession") are universally agreed on or uncontrovertibly facts. Determinations of what constitutes all but the most basic facts, what constitutes opinion, and for whom this is the case are almost always inherently contestable. Indeed, drawing

---

[10] A notable and tellingly popular exception to this tendency was the television drama *The West Wing*. More recently, the critically acclaimed HBO series *The Wire* portrayed urban political leaders in nuanced and diverse ways.

the boundary between issues of fact that are assumed to be insulated from concerns of balance or pluralistic analysis and issues of opinion that are assumed to require such balance is one of the most profoundly ideological gatekeeping roles that the media traditionally played in the latter half of the twentieth century. Pluralistic treatment of, for example, the economy would mean constantly problematizing simplistic notions such as economic expansions and recessions opening up questions of how evenly distributed are the fruits of economic growth and the pain of decline. Alternative viewpoints must be readily and regularly available, such as those of environmentalists who might question the desirability of economic growth in the first place, or of Appalachian, inner-city, and developing-country residents who might question the very existence of an expansion for themselves and their communities.

A third criterion of pluralism as applied to content assumes that any issue is likely to have multiple dimensions of contestation rather than the single-axis assumption (e.g., liberal versus conservative, Democrat versus Republican) that underlies current notions of fairness and equal access but that could be found in earlier media regimes as well. For example, the two-party, single-axis model of the mid-nineteenth century resulted in a failure to deal with the issue of slavery within the mainstream press.[11] Only in the abolitionist press, which implicitly rejected the single-axis assumption of balance for a multidimensional model in which views that went beyond those of the two dominant parties were emphasized, produced a more pluralistic perspective.

Although pluralism is important to a democratic media under any circumstances, the potential for realizing it in the current environment is promising. This is so because new technology and the blurring of genres increase the possibility for a new media regime characterized by a much richer, diverse conversation. New media such as the internet and mobile phones make it possible for previously ignored or marginalized groups to become part of public discourse in ways that would have been impossible in an earlier era. Similarly, shows like the canceled *Politically Incorrect*, *The Daily Show*, or *The Colbert Report*, and websites and blogs of various political stripes, make it possible to discuss public issues such as gun control, drugs, school violence, religion and politics, gender roles, international affairs, and so forth, in ways that are much less bound (in form and substance) by the norms of professional journalism.

---

[11] It is interesting that a key text in forcing this issue of slavery onto the public agenda was the novel *Uncle Tom's Cabin*.

Indeed, and as we have shown throughout this book, such mediated spaces provide opportunities to critique more mainstream sources and viewpoints.

However, as we have also shown throughout this book, the pluralistic potential of the new media environment will not be automatically realized, as it also has characteristics that can narrow the diversity of public debate. The increasing ability to target specific audiences coupled with the ability of individuals to pick and choose the information they attend to make it quite possible that public discourse will become more fragmented and disjointed, thus creating a combination of information rich and information poor citizens (Prior 2007) and distinct "publics" that are in isolation of each other (Sunstein 2001). The multiaxial nature of the new environment can easily tip from pluralism to instability, with different interests capturing the public agenda at different points in time. Its hyperreal quality can transform legitimate needs for multiple interpretations of the facts to an anarchic relativism or, in the words of Stephen Colbert, "truthiness." And the relaxation of media regulations and the dominance of market capitalism can concentrate corporate control over multiple media conduits in ways that make pluralism more illusion than reality.

Ensuring a meaningful pluralism requires a conscious, public, and ongoing effort to include it as one of the guiding principles of the new media regime, a principle that applies to a wide range of media producers. An open discussion and debate about the responsibility of those who make movies, music, television shows, and so on, is vital to developing a media regime that maximizes the pluralism of political discourse. Many cultural figures explicitly recognize this responsibility. For example, the screen icon Robert Redford, well known for his liberal views, articulated his vision of the political role of moviemakers as he expressed his own opposition to a U.S. invasion of Iraq:

Independent films "might carry a lot of weight in terms of how a government behaves, what information they are allowing out and what their attitude is about freedom of expression," he said. "One of the virtues of independent films is not only that they needn't be burdened by commercial dogma, but that they shouldn't be hindered in expressing different points of view. Freedom of expression is our most precious virtue," he said. "We have to be on our guard not to be careless with it." (BBC News World Edition 2003)

This view is far from universal, however. Many conservative critics of the so-called liberal bias of Hollywood respond to such statements by dismissing the idea that "mere entertainers" have a role to play in "serious" political debate. This reassertion of the boundary between news and entertainment is often policed in right-wing media (e.g., the online Drudge Report, *The O'Reilly Factor*, Rush Limbaugh's radio show) by ridiculing the factual mistakes, political naïveté, or alleged disingenuousness of celebrity activists such as Barbara Streisand, Madonna, Martin Sheen, and Norman Lear. The irony of these attacks being made by celebrity figures such as Drudge and Limbaugh aside, such policing efforts – like those of many traditional journalists – are misguided both because they rely on unworkable distinctions between politically relevant and nonrelevant media and because they are contrary to the value of pluralism. A conservative response that is more in tune with the realities of the new media environment and the value of pluralism has been suggested by the former Republican senator, presidential candidate, and television and movie actor Fred Thompson. Criticizing the public antiwar stance of politically liberal actor Martin Sheen (who played the liberal President Bartlett on *The West Wing*), Thompson (who, at the time, played a district attorney on *Law and Order*) challenged Sheen to a debate (Kaplan 2003). Rather than closing off the arenas within which politics is legitimately considered, such a debate would have served to expand public discourse in an entertaining (in the very best sense of the term) and forthright fashion.[12]

New conduits for political information created by the internet, public-access television, portable recording equipment, and so on, suggest the need to reconsider the role of "average" citizens in contributing to a pluralistic media environment. Clearly, many more citizens can now produce and disseminate political information. The potential for these conduits to influence politics through new axes of political power is illustrated by the blogger Joshua Marshall's significant role in keeping Trent Lott from becoming the Senate majority leader in 2003. Since then, the role and diversity of bloggers as part of the agenda-setting process has dramatically increased.

Blogs and other new media, such as Independent Media Centers, offer the possibility for expanding the number of citizens who can act as "personal" (as opposed to professional) journalists, by providing their own vision – to a potentially unlimited audience – of what the significant political issues of the day are and how to tell the story of such

---

[12] We are less certain what to make of Thompson's later suggestion that he be allowed to run against President Bartlett on *The West Wing*! Perhaps, frustration at being refused was a reason for his decision to run for the actual presidency in 2008.

issues.[13] For example, during the 2003 war in Iraq, the blog of a young Iraqi in Baghdad during the U.S. bombing campaign became one of the most popular on the internet.[14] As is the case with so many other boundaries, new media also blur the line between professional and personal journalism. During the Iraq War, many reporters and photographers for the major networks maintained personal blogs of material that did not make it into their on-air reports. For example, the CNN reporter Kevin Sites maintained a blog to which he posted his observations and photographs about life in Iraq, providing a "very human side to life" to the country and the war (Dembart 2003, 2).

Here again, the new media environment offers an opportunity to rethink the role of professional journalists. As with all such opportunities, however, whether this potential is realized will depend in large part on how they are integrated into a new media regime. This struggle over new rules is already evident. One response to the openness of the new environment is an attempt to reassert the line between professional journalism and other sources of information. For example, CNN ordered Kevin Sites to stop posting material to his blog, saying, "Covering a war for CNN . . . is a full-time job, so we asked Kevin to concentrate on that for the time being" (Dembart 2003, 2). Not surprisingly, we think this response is both wrong and ultimately indefensible. If the values of professional journalism are to survive and prosper, its defenders must be able to offer clear and reasoned explanations of their contribution to advancing the democratic features of a new media regime. The significance of information gathering and investigative reporting to any democratic media regime makes the profession's standards and values enduring. Indeed, if trained to share these values, nonprofessional citizen-journalists may expand the amount of information available to the public at the same time that they demonstrate the importance of journalism itself. Rather than seeking to restore their lost monopoly on gatekeeping, journalists

---

[13] Independent Media Centers are a large number of locally based but interlinked web-based resources. They grew out of the antiglobalization demonstrations in Seattle in 2000 and are run by local activists, across the globe. Although each center has its own local "flavor," in general, the centers provide information about a variety of progressive political causes; host chat rooms; provide opportunities for local citizens to report on issues of interest by offering training, equipment, and a web-based outlet for this citizen journalism; and sometimes offer venues for a variety of local and national artists to perform.

[14] Bloggers from Iraq (including the series of short videos produced by Iraqi college students called "Hometown Baghdad" and widely circulated on YouTube) provided an example of how new media can create new moral communities, which challenge state appeals to nationalism, even during times of war.

could carve out a new role as critical guides to the multitude of sources and perspectives available to citizens. In addition, they could use these new conduits to provide a broader array of perspectives themselves. Realizing this potential, the BBC, in contrast to CNN, actually encouraged its reporters to maintain blogs of their own personal experiences, hosting them on the network's internet site. As well, rather than attempting to draw lines between news and non-news, journalists could directly enter, and even facilitate, public debates occurring in and generated by movies, music, television, the internet, talk radio, and so forth.

Finally, the current moment calls for discussion regarding the role of government in facilitating pluralism. Despite the dreams of utopian libertarians, the market will not automatically deliver the diversity promised by the new media environment. Instead, decisions by government regulators to allow or retard the increasing concentration of media ownership, or to weaken or reassert the public interest obligations of the media, will play a central role. The connection between economic concentration, made possible by government decisions, and the narrowing of political debate was illustrated by the actions of the media conglomerate Clear Channel during the 2003 invasion of Iraq. Clear Channel, which at the time owned more than 1,200 radio stations across the country, emerged as the dominant force in the industry after the 1996 Telecommunications Act loosened restrictions on media ownership. It has been the focus of much criticism for its tight control over what plays on all its stations and the pressure it has exerted on recording artists to tour with its concert management division. As revealed by Paul Krugman (2003) in the *New York Times*, Clear Channel used its control over its affiliates to organize pro-war demonstrations across the country. Whether the motivations of the San Antonio–based corporation were a result of honest political beliefs or, as Krugman suggests, an attempt to curry favor with the Bush administration and so head off attempts to tighten regulations on ownership, the ability of a single corporation to surreptitiously control the political opinions expressed on more than 1,200 local radio stations violates the principles of both transparency and pluralism and illustrates the political implications of government action for the quality of the mediated political information provided to citizens.[15]

---

[15] Another example of the potential costs of highly centralized media is MSNBC's decision to cancel the political talk show *Donahue* during the war against Iraq, which we discussed in Chapter 7. At the same time, the current strategy of the station to become the Fox News of the left, though perhaps increasing pluralism, may be quite problematic when it comes to the next values we suggest, verisimilitude and practice.

Verisimilitude

Both transparency and pluralism take as a given that truth and objectivity are problematic concepts that have lost their authority. But in the absence of these modernist concepts, one can slip too deeply into the relativist perspective we hope to avoid. Indeed, as we noted in Chapters 3 and 4, it was a reaction to the fragmenting qualities of subjectivity that led in part to the rise of the doctrine of journalistic objectivity. We attempt to salvage the intent of these modernist concepts while recognizing the potency of the postmodern critique by including verisimilitude as our third quality of a democratic media regime. We use the word *verisimilitude* not to mean "the appearance or illusion of truth" (although this definition should always be kept in mind) but to mean "the likelihood or probability of truth." As such, it is a term that acknowledges the uncertainty of things (and thus is less authoritative than connoted by *truth* or *objectivity*) while at the same time acknowledging the importance of seeking common understanding through efforts to approach an essentially contested truth. In this way, it contains elements of the concept of logos (or rational, informed discourse) found in Aristotelian rhetoric, although it allows for the importance of pathos – or emotion – as well, especially but not exclusively for genres outside of traditional news (Chambers 2009). More specifically, when we talk about verisimilitude in the media, we mean that sources of political communications must take responsibility for the truth claims they explicitly and implicitly make. Part of such responsibility is recognizing that the assumptions about the nature of political truth, because inevitably contested, must be made explicit. We capture part of this responsibility with the criterion of transparency, as only if we know who is speaking can we know who is responsible. Additionally, making clear who is speaking increases the likelihood of those parties taking responsibility and being accountable for the texts they author. However, the media (especially in its new forms and hyper-real implications) have tremendous ability to mimic and hence influence reality. With this power comes the responsibility to represent reality in a way that has the likelihood or probability of being true. Pluralism further helps in this endeavor by ensuring that any single declaration of truth can be debated, challenged, or refined. But verisimilitude goes beyond these two qualities.

In the quote with which we began Chapter 1, Walter Lippmann (1922, 10) rejected any a priori distinction between fact and fiction and used the word *fidelity* much as we use *verisimilitude*: "The range of fiction extends all the way from complete hallucinations to the scientist's perfectly self-conscious use of a schematic model, or his decision that for his particular problem accuracy beyond a certain number of decimal places is not important. A work of fiction may have almost any degree of Fidelity, and so long as the degree of Fidelity can be taken into account, fiction is not misleading." At the most basic level, verisimilitude implies that the creator of any politically relevant communication is responsible for getting its verifiable facts right – it is not enough to qualify dubious claims or escape responsibility with a brief disclaimer.

For instance, when HBO aired a fictionalized account of CNN's coverage of the 1991 Persian Gulf War, it included scenes that made it seem as if Iraqi soldiers had taken babies out of incubators in Kuwaiti hospitals, a claim long since demonstrated as the false product of propaganda (Fairness and Accuracy in Reporting 2003). Despite numerous protests, the network aired the program, acknowledging the controversy by including a brief (and we would argue insufficient) note during the end credits: "While the allegations of Iraqi soldiers taking babies from incubators were widely circulated during the run-up to the Gulf War (the time frame of the drama of our film), these allegations were never substantiated." Similar controversies surrounded truth claims made in CBS's docudrama *The Reagans*, ABC's docudrama *The Path to 9/11*, and Michael Moore's documentaries *Fahrenheit 9/11* and *Sicko*.

This rather straightforward aspect of verisimilitude applies to visual truth claims as well. For example, if CBS News claims to be broadcasting a live camera shot from Times Square in New York, it should not (as it did) alter the images presented so as to "erase" a billboard advertising a competitor's news program and insert an ad for its own show. Similarly, ABC News should not (as it did) show film footage it claims to be an FBI surveillance tape when in fact it was a re-creation of such a tape. Nor should any of the cable and broadcast news networks have rebroadcast the iconic footage of the toppling of Saddam Hussein's statue in Baghdad (as they continue to do) once it became clear that this event was staged.

As with transparency, verisimilitude also requires educating audiences – in this case, about the processes underlying truth claims. For example, the wide use by journalists and political elites of polling is based on a powerful truth claim that it is a scientific way to measure the preferences of the American public. However, such claims are legitimate only if the assumptions on which the polls are based can be examined (e.g., random sampling, response rates, sample sizes, question wording). Yet despite the efforts of professional organizations such as the American Association for Public Opinion Research, polling methods are often treated as proprietary (as with exit polls or preelection polls of likely voters), results are often reported without appropriate information about how the poll was conducted, and many polls lack even the rudimentary requisites of scientific survey research (as with call-in, text, and many internet polls), which make it impossible to evaluate their truth claims. Similar critiques could be extended to the methods – and the need for education about them – underlying the truth claims made in movies, television shows, and blogs.

At a more fundamental level, however, verisimilitude requires that the authors of any media text be aware of and take responsibility for its deeper truth claims, even if these claims are not strictly verifiable in any formal sense. The representation of public officials or business executives as always greedy and corrupt, of inner-city youths as only victims or criminals, of young adults as politically apathetic, of Muslims as terrorists, and so forth – these are truth claims that cut to the foundations of political life, truth claims that cannot be justified by simply getting the quote right, demonstrating that the video is accurate, or (in the case of non-news) stating that "any resemblance to real people or events is purely coincidental." At this foundational level, verisimilitude hinges more on the overall combination of feeling (pathos) and understanding (logos) that a reader, viewer, listener, or user is left with than on factual accuracy in the narrow sense of the term. Viewed in this way, a novel or movie such as *Primary Colors* arguably does more to portray the inner workings of a campaign or of Bill Clinton the person – that is, more closely approaches the "truth" – than most of what has been broadcast on the news. An episode of a television show like *The West Wing* can be more informative about Washington politics than a typical news broadcast. A daily blog from an Iraqi teenager or a U.S. soldier can tell us more about the Iraq War than a Pentagon debriefing.

As with transparency and pluralism, we make no claims that verisimilitude can be assessed mechanically, easily, or consensually. Nor do we argue that the same criteria for judging the truth claims of a news story would apply to a docudrama, fictional movie, satirical television show, or personal blog. Rather, verisimilitude is meant to serve as a way for media producers to remain cognizant of their public interest obligations and for media users to think about the democratic utility of both particular texts and the media environment more broadly. As such, it serves to open and shape public discussion about the relationship between a particular politically relevant media text, the politic truth it purports to represent, and the media regime that produced it.

Take, for example, the historical fiction of Russell Banks's (1998) *Cloudsplitter* and Jane Smiley's (1998) *The All-True Travels and Adventures of Lidie Newton*. Both novels deal with the abolitionist movement in pre–Civil War America. The former is a fictionalized account of the life of John Brown as told by his only surviving son, whereas the latter tells the story of a fictionalized woman who confronts the issue of slavery in "Bloody Kansas." Both are clearly novels and, as such, cannot be judged as if they were the nonfiction works of historians. Nevertheless, because they deal with the history of race in America, they seem to us clearly politically relevant texts, and so readers must be able to count on a certain degree of verisimilitude in such texts. At the most basic level, we must assume that the authors have done their homework so that the dates are correct and the atmosphere of the period is faithfully rendered as best as it can be from the work of historians and other sources. Only if this norm has been met, we would argue, can we enjoy the sort of deeper truth that novels can reveal but that historians are often blocked from achieving: a subjective sense of what it might have been like to actually live during a particular time, of what people of the time felt or believed, or of what we might have done in the same situation. It is this sense of truth that lay at the heart of the Realist movement's use of poetry and novels, as well as reporting, to get at the lived experience of ordinary people. Indeed, both Banks and Smiley explicitly address this issue in forewords and afterwords, by citing their sources and describing the sort of research they did while also reminding the reader that their works are novels and not, strictly speaking, history.

Through the routinization of such practices (and subsequent discourse sparked by and about such novels), the reader can better evaluate the verisimilitude of a text along with the vision of truth held by the author. In *The Age of American Unreason*, Susan Jacoby (2008) makes a related point when she argues that a significant virtue of the middlebrow historical novels of the 1950s (e.g., James Michener's *Hawaii* or Irving Stone's *The Agony and the Ecstasy*), so mistakenly criticized by writers like Dwight Macdonald and Lionel Trilling, was that the authors based their works on a prodigious amount of historical research. Consequently, when Americans read these best sellers, they were also learning a considerable amount about their subjects. In stark contrast, many current historical best sellers (Jacoby singles out Dan Brown's *Angels and Demons* and *The Da Vinci Code*) are often sloppily done, with many historical inaccuracies that, if anything, misinform their readers. In our terms, whatever their literary shortcomings, Stone and Michener paid careful attention to the value of verisimilitude, whereas Brown did not.

Consequently, the former served a democratically useful public purpose, whereas the latter did not.

The importance of verisimilitude extends far beyond historical novels to other mediums and genres. In Britain, for example, the use of re-creations and docudramas has a longer history than in the United States. What the British call dramadocs have been produced by network news divisions and have been long seen as a way for journalists to take us where news cameras could not go – a truth claim quite similar to the one made for historical novels. This structural choice has resulted in an approach to the production of dramadocs that is virtually the same as for traditional documentaries (indeed, the two types of programs are frequently produced by the same people; Paget 1998). As a result, dramadocs undergo a more rigorous ritual of research and fact-checking than is the case for the average story on a nightly news broadcast. In turn, the collusion between producers and audiences that determines the meaning of any television genre is very different in Britain from in the United States, with viewers in the former approaching the broadcast knowing that it has been subject to a rigorous review that included concerns of verisimilitude.[16]

Some recent American television shows represent models of what we mean by verisimilitude. Especially noteworthy is HBO's *The Wire*, created by the former crime reporter David Simon and the former Baltimore homicide police officer Ed Burns. Before working on *The Wire*, Simon wrote an account of his year spent with Baltimore homicide police, and the two coauthored an ethnography of a drug corner in the city (Simon and Burns 1991, 1997). These nonfictional accounts inform virtually every aspect of the fictional program, thus providing an unrivaled picture (by either fictional or nonfictional television) of the workings of an American city from the inner-city residents to the police, the political system, the public schools, and the media.

It is important to see that seriously addressing the truth claims of a media text is not the same thing as the traditional journalistic process of fact-checking. Indeed, too great a focus on fact-checking can lessen rather than increase verisimilitude. For example, the equating of truth with accuracy in American news culture often leads journalists to be little more than stenographers to power. And as British television has moved more toward an American model, the role of legal departments in vetting dramadocs has increased proportionately. The result is the

---

[16] Such differences may be part of the reason that, as we discuss here, British viewers express much higher level of trust in political information received from television news than do their American counterparts.

oversight of dramadocs by lawyers, nicknamed "fact fascists" by producers (Paget 1998, 15). The lawyers are resented because they limit scripts
to claims that would be defensible as factual in a court of law and, as a
result, producers claim, undermine the advantages of the genre as a way
to get at deeper truths. Consider the issue of verisimilitude as it applies to
Hurricane, a powerful movie about the life of Rubin "Hurricane" Carter,
a black boxer falsely convicted of murder and imprisoned for nineteen
years before being freed after a prolonged and complex legal struggle. In
addressing the racism of the criminal justice system, the movie is clearly
a politically relevant text. Further, because the central narrative of the
film is the life and struggles of an actual person, we would expect that
its producers have gotten the basic facts of the story right, just as we
would expect Smiley, Banks, the producers of television dramadocs, and
the producers of television news to have done. As a fictionalized account,
of course, there is room for negotiation with the facts. So, for example, the movie created a fictional detective who is meant to embody the
racism that leads to Carter's initial conviction and continued imprisonment. Allowing for devices to simplify a story line should not free writers
and producers from their public obligations to verisimilitude, however.
Hurricane received a great deal of criticism revolving around the fictional
racist detective because, by blaming Carter's plight on the actions of an
individual villain who is ultimately (very ultimately) foiled, it diverted
attention from the more general racism of the criminal justice system.
The decision to create the fictional character and have him serve as the
symbolic cause of the injustice at the heart of the film arguably undermined the ability of the movie to get to the truth of Carter's experience
in particular or the truth of race relations in America more generally.

Three final points about verisimilitude and its application as a standard for assessing politically relevant media need to be made. First, the
verisimilitude of a particular media text is and should be open to debate.
This includes our brief assessments of the truth claims contained in
Hurricane or the novels of Banks and Smiley, which were meant as examples of how one might employ verisimilitude as a way to stimulate debate
rather than as a definitive statement on their relationship to the truth
or reality. Second, we intend our arguments to apply only to the extent
that one also argues that a particular media text is politically relevant.
For example, criticisms quite similar to those we made about *Hurricane*
were leveled at *A Beautiful Mind*, the movie biography of the troubled
Nobel Prize–winning physicist John Nash. Critics argued that the movie
had gotten many of the facts wrong, especially crucial details of Nash's
breakdown, his relationship with his wife, and so forth. Whatever the

merits of these criticisms, their political significance is arguably less than those aimed at *Hurricane*, as the latter deals with issues of race and the criminal justice system, whereas the former was less clearly relevant to the foundations, issues, and processes of politics. Of course, even this conclusion is open to debate – once again demonstrating the inherent contestability of politics and the need for a communications system that accepts this as its fundamental guiding principle.

Finally, like transparency but unlike pluralism, verisimilitude is a criterion that can be applied to both individual media texts and the larger media environment and the media regime that shapes that environment. For instance, what made the dubious truth claims of *Hurricane* so significant is the degree to which they echo the claims made in the whole field of media discourse about race: the movie repeats the focus on individual rather than institutional explanations for racism adopted in many other genres, including the news. The media scholars Robert Entman and Andrew Rojecki (2001, 156), in their study of the portrayal of race relations on television, found the show *NYPD Blue* typical: "The racism, however, is located in lapsed and weak Whites rather than in the institutions themselves." This is quite similar to the conclusions that Benjamin DeMott (1998) reached in his survey of American popular culture's treatment of racism: that it is a problem solvable by the actions of well-meaning individuals rather than the reform of institutions. *The Wire* stands in stark contrast, with its systematic focus on institutions – the criminal justice system, the political system, urban public schools, and the press.

In the end, assessing the verisimilitude of individual texts and the structures that produce them is an ongoing process requiring a pluralistic and transparent environment. Professional journalism can play a central role in this process, serving as facilitators of the process and as one of the central mediated spaces in which it occurs.

Practice

Our final suggested criterion for assessing the democratic utility of politically relevant media is practice. We use this term in two, related ways. The first is preparing citizens for political and civic engagement through the media's ability to model and be a place to rehearse such behavior. The second is the media's ability to facilitate actual participation and increasingly to be the place where such political engagement occurs. Consistent with our definitions of politically relevant and democratically useful media, we include political talk and deliberation as an important component of civic and political engagement (Jacobs, et al., 2009).

Unlike transparency, pluralism, and verisimilitude, treating practice as an explicit goal of politically relevant media has few roots in the Age of Broadcast News, although to some degree it can be found in earlier regimes such as the partisan press, the penny press, the Realist Era and – thanks in no small part to John Dewey – the Progressive Era. Practice as a criterion can also be seen in recent challenges to the view that professional journalists should be removed and disinterested observers, such as James Lemert's (1981) notion of mobilizing information, and the civic or public journalism movement (Rosen 1999; Sirianni and Friedland 2001).

Despite its somewhat tenuous connection to the past, in many ways, practice is the criterion most directly connected to the health of democratic politics. It is also the criterion against which the Age of Broadcast News most clearly falls short. The latter half of the twentieth century is marked in the United States by numerous indicators of the civic and political disengagement of citizens, including relatively steady declines in voter turnout and other forms of political participation, in political interest, in news media use, and in political and social trust (Zukin et al. 2006; Patterson 2002; Putnam 2000).[17] And despite the broader availability of higher education, the ubiquitous availability of broadcast news, and the slow but real integration of women and minorities into public life, aggregate levels of political knowledge have remained low and inequitably distributed (Delli Carpini and Keeter 1996).

At the same time, however, other forms of participation seem to be increasing. At the local level, citizen groups have become much more organized and powerful, spoiling many development plans and spawning their own acronym – NIMBY (not in my backyard). At the global level, there have been unprecedented worldwide protests against the World Trade Organization, the U.S. invasion of Iraq, the publication of anti-Muslim cartoons in Denmark, the 2009 elections in Iran, and, most recently, authoritarian rulers throughout the Middle East. The London *Guardian* newspaper columnist Madeline Bunting (2003, 21) notes this new pattern of citizen action:

What has changed is the pattern of participation; political parties and turnouts may be declining, but intense episodic political engagement is on the increase. In recent years we have seen both the lowest turnouts and the biggest demonstrations in British political history – there's a conundrum to keep hundreds of political scientists busy.

---

[17] Although our focus is on U.S. media and politics, we suspect that our arguments could be extended, with some important caveats, to at least other Western democracies and possibly more globally.

It is no coincidence that these local, national, and global trends in political and civic participation have largely paralleled the rise and fall of the Age of Broadcast News. The norms of professional journalism and its monopoly on gatekeeping reinforced an elitist view of the political world that, as Walter Lippmann (1922) argued, was needed to limit the potentially disruptive effect of unruly mass participation. At the same time, the horse-race frame of professional journalists; the media's emphasis on public officials' and candidates' self-serving interests and personal shortcomings; the privileging of crime, disaster, and crisis news; and the generally decontextualized nature of political reporting has added to public cynicism and thus to generally declining civic and political engagement – a trend occasionally punctuated by moments of frustration or protectionist-motivated forays into the public world (Patterson 1993; Cappella and Hall Jamieson 1997; Schudson 1998). From our perspective, it is these characteristics that render so much of what is commonly labeled "political communication" to be politically relevant but in a way that is debilitating to the practice of democratic politics.

We believe that the evolving media environment offers intriguing possibilities for encouraging and enriching the practice of politics among citizens through the provision of new and varied sources of information, new possibilities for creating political community, new means for discussing politics, new forms of political and civic organizing, and even new ways of participating. Information and communication technologies such as the internet, computers, and mobile communication devices provide the most obvious example of these possibilities and how one might use "practice" as a criterion for assessing and encouraging the democratic utility of this medium. The internet already includes numerous sites explicitly devoted to public affairs: mainstream (e.g., NYTimes.com, CNN.com) and alternative news websites that allow citizens to monitor public issues and events (e.g., Indymedia.org); opinionated sites (e.g., HuffingtonPost.com or FoxNews.com) that place these issues and events in more explicitly ideological perspective; nonprofit sites that assist citizens in their political decision making (e.g., VoteSmart.org); government sites that provide citizens with basic information, online access to many services, and the ability to contact public officials (e.g., USA.gov); party, campaign, and issue advocacy sites that can inform, motivate, and mobilize supporters (e.g., MyBarackObama.com; MoveOn.org; RockTheVote.com; and ICBL.org, the site of the International Campaign to Ban Landmines); sites designed to facilitate local volunteerism (e.g., CityYear.org, VolunteerMatch.org); blogs and social networking sites that encourage face-to-face and online conversation and deliberation about issues of the day (e.g., SpeakOut.com, AmericaSpeaks.org); and even political games (e.g., NationStates.net, USGovSim.net, SimCivic.org). Online resources such as these could be assessed, individually and collectively, for how well they model democratic engagement in their form and content, as well as for the opportunities they provide citizens to rehearse and participate in civic and political life. For example, consistent with the norms of professional journalism, traditional news sites generally provide little in the way of explicitly encouraging or facilitating practice relative to more avowedly political or advocacy-oriented sites.

Of course, even the latter sites can and often do fall short on this score. Many limit their calls to action to financial contributions, scripted e-mail messages to elected officials, registering an opinion, or at most voting. On the one hand, practice of this kind might still be seen as a valuable way for individuals to learn a little about an issue of public import, begin to feel connected to larger communities, and take a small step toward engagement through limited and relatively costless action. On the other hand, it might simply serve as a substitute for more direct, costly, but ultimately more effective forms of civic and political engagement, modeling a thin form of plebiscitary democracy rather than a more deliberative or deeply participatory one (Abramson, Arterton, and Orren 1988). Our point is not to claim that one interpretation is more valid than the other but to suggest that the implications for civic and political practice must be part of any discussion regarding the design of a new media regime.

As we have argued throughout this book, one of the central characteristics of the new media environment is the blurring of genres. With this in mind, it is important that practice as a criterion be applied to media that are not overtly organized around politics. The architecture of the internet, especially the hyperlink, is especially relevant in this regard, as it has the potential for users to easily and instantaneously see and make the link to politics from what at first blush seem like apolitical searches and sites. Someone going online to find out more about a health-related issue for a friend can literally and figuratively make the connection to government policies. Followers of a popular rock group might find themselves chatting online about the lead singer's recent comments about poverty, war, or the environment. Online shoppers looking to purchase a hot new athletic shoe might find themselves learning about issues of consumer protection, international trade, and child labor. Fans of a popular television show might find themselves contributing to a thread on a recent episode involving racism or sexism. Such connections are partly serendipitous, but the likelihood of their occurring and how far into the world of politics they lead ultimately depend on things such as the content and design of a website, the algorithm of a search engine, the network of links connecting various sites, or government regulations regarding net neutrality.

As with other aspects of the new media environment, the implications of this blurring of entertainment, culture, consumption, and politics is not always clear or simple. Consider, for example, the popular computer game, The Sims, which allows players to create and then manage virtual families as they work, sleep, eat, shop, and perform all manner of mundane tasks. The game has spawned a large number of downloadable add-ons created by other players, which allow gamers to customize their own Sim families and communities. One popular download was an Iraq War add-on, which included antiwar posters, T-shirts, and so forth, that could be hung on walls and worn by characters in the game. What is the connection between this expression of political sentiment, in the context of a computer game or within a chat room or on a website, and engagement in political deliberation and action in the physical world? Does it constitute modeling? Rehearsing? The expression of public opinion? Or is it simply a diversion from or substitute for more meaningful participation? Again, our point is not to answer these questions but to suggest that, although the internet offers possibilities for reinvigorating political and civic life, there is no guarantee that this evolving medium will continue to develop this potential. As we have shown throughout this book, to date the new media environment has produced mixed results at best and contains elements that can just as easily lead citizens away from public involvement as toward it (Prior 2007). Indeed, compared to the creativity and resources that have gone into making the internet a good and safe place to shop and play, efforts to make it a good and safe place to both prepare for and actually engage in political action seem malnourished.

Practice as a measure of the media's democratic utility is not limited to the internet. Consider talk-radio shows such as Rush Limbaugh's or partisan cable television shows like those of Bill O'Reilly or Keith Olbermann. How might we assess their contributions to democratic practice?[18] Talk

---

[18] We are not here considering the degree to which these shows meet the standards of transparency, verisimilitude, or (collectively) pluralism, standards against which they would arguably fall quite short.

television and radio often involve engaged dialogue among the host, his or her guest, and (especially for talk radio) the listeners, the latter of whom are encouraged to call in, discuss, and sometimes even disagree about the issues of the day. To their credit, these shows also regularly encourage and facilitate political action such as getting in touch with political representatives, voting, and discussing politics with others not listening to or watching the show. Of course, whether one would consider the form and content of the exchanges that take place as appropriate models of democratic deliberation is an open question (here, the interview segments conducted by Jon Stewart on *The Daily Show* stand out as much better models of informative, civil, yet entertaining discourse; Baym 2010). But criticisms of talk radio and television often conflate what we consider legitimate concerns about the quality of the discourse with outmoded notions of both politics and the media.

For example, in November 2002, the Democratic Senate leader Tom Daschle accused Limbaugh and other right-wing talk show hosts of adding "a shrill tone" to political debate for the sake of their ratings and thus of turning "politics into entertainment." He went on to say:

What happens when (radio talk show host) Rush Limbaugh attacks those of us in public life is that people aren't satisfied just to listen. They want to act because they get emotionally invested. And so, you know, the threats to those of us in public life go up dramatically, on our families and on us, in a way that's very disconcerting. (Reuters 2002)

In addition to the dubious attempt to draw a causal connection between Limbaugh's comments and threats of violence, we think that Daschle's critique misses the point for two reasons.[19] First, it treats "politics" and "entertainment" as mutually exclusive categories. Much of Limbaugh's appeal is that his show is entertaining, something not to be criticized but applauded. In the same way that right-wing commentators (including Limbaugh) dismiss politically active liberal celebrities, Daschle's comments seek to reassert the authority of traditional elites (of which he is a part) characteristic of the Age of Broadcast News. Second, his criticism echoes the elitist tone of that past regime when he treats as a

[19] Especially because the comments made by Limbaugh were often taken out of context, as when he refers to Daschle as El Diablo. To the liberal Fairness and Accuracy in Reporting, this is evidence of Limbaugh's efforts to demonize the democratic senator. However, to anyone who listens to the show, this label is part of the often humorous, if quite pointed and conservative, perspective of the show and its host. That listeners actually believe this means Daschle is the devil and thus worthy of being eliminated is quite hard to believe.

threat the notion that people become emotionally invested in politics and so want to do more than listen. The essence of good practice is that citizens should be encouraged to do more than just listen. Although there may be much to criticize about the connections between right-wing media and the rise of the Tea Party movement, there is also much to learn about the potential (and problems) of the new media environment for mobilizing citizen participation that can challenge entrenched elites. The problem is not that right-wing talk shows encourage practice but the absence of both alternatives from competing political perspectives and consideration of the implications for democratic practice of different approaches to media mobilization. Again, however, this absence of pluralism (in both political perspectives and modes of mobilization) cannot be remedied by the market, especially given the increasingly centralized ownership of media by corporate conglomerates such as Clear Channel. Rather, it will require a conscious effort to hold the media to its public interest obligations. In short, Senator Daschle's criticisms would be more effectively aimed at FCC decisions, as was actually the case in 2008, rather than at the rhetoric of Rush Limbaugh.

Practice as a means of assessing the democratic utility of the media can be extended to entertainment television and film as well, although by their nature these media are largely limited to modeling civic and political citizenship. For the most part, prime-time television dramas, comedies and reality shows, and in-theater films are silent on the civic and political lives of the many characters we come to know, and when they do address the world of formal politics, it is most often presented in cynical and simplistic ways. As such, their contributions to democratic practice are arguably negative and insidious. But exceptions exist. Consider, for example, the character of Lisa Simpson on Fox's long-running animated show *The Simpsons*. Although the show is often a wickedly funny political satire, it is saved from falling into the easy cynicism so characteristic of much political comedy (and amply represented by the characters of Bart and Homer) by Lisa, who is, in many ways, the ideal citizen.[20] She is informed, public minded, and regularly participates in the political life of her school and community. Dramatic series such as *The West Wing* (now available in syndication or on DVD) also arguably encouraged practice by modeling political engagement in more positive, efficacious ways than is usually found on prime-time television. The USA Network, building on

---

[20] For a wonderful attempt to use all of the Simpson family to illustrate different models of citizenship, see Schudson (2009).

its catch phrase, "Characters Welcome," has used its promotional spots to celebrate the racial, ethnic, and religious diversity of its stars and (with mixed results in terms of democratic practice) to encourage viewers to continue and expand this conversation on its website. CBS has promoted the CBS Cares page of its website where viewers can learn about, discuss, and volunteer to work on issues such as HIV/AIDS, breast cancer, child abduction, and tolerance. And Hollywood films such as *Milk* model active citizenship in a positive and inspiring light.

Finally, media's responsibility to encourage and facilitate democratic practice extends to the civic and political roles of those engaged in the process of cultural production. For example, given the centrality of movies, television, and music in influencing the ways in which white Americans perceive African Americans, Robert Entman and Andrew Rojecki (2001) argue that media critics have a responsibility to highlight the ways in which race is portrayed in the works they review. If they were conscious of the racial subtexts of movies and the difficult issues raised by various treatments (in our terms, if they practice good citizenship and understand the broad meaning of political relevance), critics "could even be leading forces in reshaping White audiences' sensibilities, tastes, and ultimately market demand" (Entman and Rojecki 2001, 188–189). Yet as currently practiced, little attention is given to such issues: in surveying movie reviews, Entman and Rojecki found virtually no attention was paid to troubling portrayals of race.[21] Indeed, we think that in the new media environment, critics have a democratic obligation to fully explore the political implications with respect to practice (as well as pluralism, transparency, and verisimilitude) of the politically relevant texts they review. Claims that critics can or should restrict themselves to aesthetic values are themselves embedded in the untenable distinctions between political and other forms of media that we have criticized throughout this book. In a democratic new media regime, criticism would be seen clearly as the civic activity it is.[22]

---

[21] So, for example, in the reviews they examined of the movies *Independence Day*, *A Time to Kill*, and *Jerry Maguire*, there was not a single mention of racial stereotyping.

[22] We take the phrase "criticism as civics" from Hector Amaya (2003). In a fascinating comparison of reviews of Cuban films of the 1960s written by American and Cuban film critics, he shows how the claims of the former to a nonpolitical aesthetic criticism actually reinforced the political agenda of the U.S. government. In contrast, Cuban critics, recognizing the political nature of their work because of strict government censorship, were able to develop strategies that allowed for a contextualization of the political element of criticism.

Entman and Rojecki provide another example of how cultural figures can further the practice of democratic politics in their discussion of the popular television show *ER*. Significantly, given the fragmentation of the television audience along racial lines, this was, at the time of their research, the only show in the top twenty for both whites and African Americans. Not coincidentally, this was also the only show they examined that portrayed an affair between a black man and a white woman. But, in an example of an actor recognizing the broader political implications of his work, the African American actor Eriq La Salle (who played Dr. Benton) used his considerable leverage with the show's producers to end the affair because he thought it perpetuated stereotypes about black men and white women. Further, he objected to the way his character was portrayed as loving toward a white colleague but prickly toward two black female characters. La Salle said, "We have to take care of the message that we're sending as African-Americans, or any other group of minorities . . . that we have the exact same type of exchanges with our mates that we get to see our white counterparts have" (Entman and Rojecki 2001, 157). La Salle's contribution to practice was in raising the issue of racial stereotyping to the level of public debate, where it could become an explicit consideration in the production and critical analysis of politically relevant communication.

As Entman and Rojecki's argument suggests, creating and maintaining a media regime that maximizes its democratic utility requires that the goal of democratic practice – as well as of transparency, pluralism, and verisimilitude – be the responsibility of all people who have access to or control of the numerous public soapboxes available today: professional journalists; anchors and hosts; writers, directors, and producers; photographers and videographers; actors and artists; bloggers and web masters; researchers and teachers; corporate and nonprofit executives; candidates and public officials; consumers, producers, and users; and so on. As such, it requires a cultural shift of admittedly dramatic proportion, one that is supported by mutually reinforcing norms, rituals, practices, and expectations, as well as by laws and regulations, and that collectively serve to remind us that whatever our specific profession or avocation, we are also all citizens of local, national, and global communities. Such a culture would have, for example, seen ABC's corporate decision to cancel *Politically Incorrect* (discussed in Chapter 6) as an abdication of the network's public interest obligations given the program's modeling of entertaining yet informative, civil, and serious debate on important issues of the day. More broadly, it would change the terms and scope of debate regarding how best to encourage and maintain the democratic utility of the new media environment.

Creating a National Dialogue

That American professional journalism is in crises is painfully clear. But crises are also opportunities, in this case, the opportunity to radically rethink the relationship between media and democracy in the twenty-first century. This opportunity will be squandered, however, if a new media regime were to be shaped by incremental decisions driven almost exclusively by market considerations and made solely by the economic, political, and professional elites most closely bound to the passing regime. The new media environment has made evident the limitations of the Age of Broadcast News as well as the degree to which its institutionalization both obscured and retarded the democratic potential of a much wider range of politically relevant communications.

Because fully realizing this potential represents a challenge to existing gatekeepers, any meaningful debate about the shape of a new media regime will require the inclusion of a broad range of voices, must be public and structured, and must consider both the limitations of the past and the democratic (as opposed to purely economic) opportunities and challenges opened up by the new media environment. Markus Prior (2007) illustrates the need for involving a wide range of actors in debate over the shape of a new media regime in his insightful analysis of what he calls "post-broadcast democracy." He notes that, from the perspective of satisfying the specific demands of viewers, the Age of Broadcast News was quite inefficient. Television constituted a kind of oligopoly rather than a free market: given the small number of broadcast outlets and the efforts of networks to assemble the largest possible audience, individual viewers were routinely required to watch much that they were not specifically searching for when they turned on the television. Being exposed to a regular newscast was a sort of positive externality of this market failure: whether they specifically sought it out or not, viewers tended to watch the nightly news, as there were no other options. In sharp contrast, the post-broadcast system, what we have been calling the new media environment, is much more efficient when it comes to satisfying the demands of citizens. Given the geometric increase in the outlets for all sorts of mediated texts, someone can much more finely tune their media diet to their own individual demands. Consequently, the increase in market or media efficiency eliminates the market failure of the old regime and, with it, the positive externality of being exposed to a daily news broadcast. We take this analysis one step further and suggest that this post-broadcast world, in which citizens can avoid traditional news sources, increases both the public interest obligations of the non-news media and the importance of including them in discussions of what these responsibilities are and how they should be facilitated. When it comes to debate over the democratic utility of political communications and the institutions that shape them, journalists and scholars have a role to play, but so, too, do movie producers, television writers, musicians, and – most important – ordinary citizens themselves. It is simply not acceptable, for example, for filmmakers who create movies with clear political relevance to escape responsibility for the content or impact of their work by claiming to be artists and so immune from having to engage in debate over the implications for democratic politics of their creations.

We believe that such an encompassing debate is urgent because, if the past is a guide, the current instability and uncertainty created by the political, cultural, economic, and technological changes documented in this book will give way to a new, structured media regime, the shape of which will have enormous implications for U.S. democracy. But even if, as some might legitimately argue, inherent anarchic qualities of the new media environment make it ungovernable, such a discussion remains crucial if we are to salvage any meaningful relationship between media and democracy. Indeed, regardless of whether a new media regime forms, reflection, deliberation, and critique should be viewed as an ongoing necessity: the democratic utility of the media will most likely be maximized and maintained if their public interest obligations (assessed by qualities such as transparency, pluralism, verisimilitude, and practice) and the rules governing these obligations remain a constant and foregrounded topic of debate.

What might such a debate entail? Certainly it would raise difficult and fundamental questions about the role of professional journalism and its current and future contributions to democracy. At the most basic level, we must ask what professional journalists contribute that cannot be obtained through other means. Is there a necessary relationship between journalism as a profession and the media (e.g., private newspapers, television networks) that employ them? Do we, for example, actually benefit from the resources devoted to reporting by the networks when, as Howard Kurtz (2007, 247) puts it, the nightly news broadcasts are simply "repackagers" of the news, "perfectly content to wait until [a] story [is] so widely reported that it . . . congeal[s] into conventional wisdom"? What should we make of the Pew Research Center Project for Excellence in Journalism's 2008 conclusion:

In the end, if the problems of network news can be mostly attributed to the decline in the overall audience of broadcast network television generally rather than something having to do with the newscasts in particular, then the survival of the networks' news divisions in some ways may well depend on their liberating themselves from the broadcast television platform on which they were founded – and even perhaps from the networks themselves. (Qtd. in Arango 2008)

Are their viable alternative models for sustaining professional journalism's core functions: for example, the nonprofit investigative journalism organization ProPublica, started by former *Wall Street Journal* managing editor Paul Steiger, or the various proposals suggested by Leonard Downie Jr. and Michael Schudson (2009) or by Robert McChesney and John Nichols (2009)? Raising these and related questions (e.g., how journalists are trained and paid; how their stories are constructed, disseminated, and used) is not to suggest that professional journalists are no longer needed. To the contrary, we believe that a well-functioning twenty-first-century democracy cannot survive without them. To fully address the possibilities opened by the new media environment, however, we need to more fully articulate the specific contributions of this profession qua a profession to democracy.

Following from this, any debate regarding the shape of a new media regime must address the role to be played by citizen-journalists and their relationship to professional journalism and other forms of politically relevant communication.[23] What might a serious consideration of Charlie Gibson's musing (discussed earlier in this chapter) about giving Iraqi citizens the equipment to provide on-the-ground reporting look like? How might the potential hinted at in the Iranian Twitter revolution be more effectively and systematically harnessed? The *New York Times* writer Nicholas Kristof (2008) expresses well the ambivalent position of professional journalists when it comes to considering the opportunities now available to citizen journalists:

[R]eaders who want global news can find it now on the Web, more easily than ever. And there have been some interesting efforts at citizen journalism or blogging

---

[23] The term *citizen-journalist* has become a commonly used and contested phrase. We use it here to capture the degree to which "ordinary" citizens can fulfill many of the functions of journalists (the common use of the term), but we remind readers that all journalists (professional or otherwise) are citizens.

from hot spots around the world. One new venture is Demotix, which offers aspiring journalists a chance to upload their articles and photos for others to see – and some possibility that news outlets will publish them. I don't know whether to be horrified, since it represents a further erosion of the newspaper business model, or to applaud another avenue to get international news coverage. The latter, I guess.

Debate regarding the shape of a future media regime should also include consideration of the role of cultural elites such as entertainment television and film executives, writers, directors, producers, and actors. What are the rights and responsibilities of these citizens when they address issues of public import? How might these obligations be met without risking the artistic freedom necessary for their crafts? How might such forms of politically relevant media be brought more effectively in public discourse about pressing issues of the day? How can professional journalists, citizen journalists, and cultural producers complement and supplement one another so that the whole is greater than the sum of its parts? Controversies over television docudramas such as *The Reagans* and *The Path to 9/11*, or films such as *The Day after Tomorrow*, *Fahrenheit 9/11*, and *Sicko* point to the political relevance of entertainment media, the need for agreed-on norms for assessing them, and the inevitability of ongoing deliberations regarding their democratic utility.

Finally, consideration of the contours of a new media regime should consider the role of "average" citizens and how to encourage and facilitate their negotiation of the complex information environment in which they now live. In the Age of Broadcast News, with its very limited options for acquiring political information, it may well have made sense to assume that the best use of a citizen's time would be to watch a single source of reliable information (i.e., one of the thirty-minute nightly network news shows). However, even acknowledging that the time and energy citizens are willing and able to devote to public affairs is limited, the notion that a responsible citizen should privilege the nightly news is no longer tenable or normatively justifiable. One might argue that citizens today might be better informed if they adopted a "grazing" strategy in which they sampled from a number of different sources of information. For example, a citizen who moved between the network news broadcasts, a political blog, and *The Daily Show* arguably would have been both earlier and better informed about the inconsistencies in Vice President Cheney's justifications for the invasion of Iraq than a citizen who just watched a network news broadcast or even one who regularly read a daily newspaper.[24] This is so because absent news constraints, such as only reporting what happened in the previous twenty-four hours or limiting statements of public officials to sound bites, *The Daily Show* could run back-to-back videotapes of Cheney's public statements from different points in time, demonstrating that he had significantly shifted his arguments. The irony here is that, although such a technique would be out of bounds for the nightly news broadcasts or most newspapers, "using actual footage of public figures to demonstrate their actual positions over time is not advocacy journalism, but the rawest form of objectivity" (Kurtz 2007, 107). Strategies such as grazing might also have the added advantage of increasing the amount of time citizens spend acquiring politically relevant information, as many of the sources (e.g., *The Daily Show*) would include media and genres that also satisfy other desires such as entertainment.

In the end, the shape of a new media regime will be strongly influenced by political decisions, and so such decisions should be central to the public debate we are advocating. For example, in March 2009, the U.S. House of Representatives passed legislation that would shield journalists from federal prosecution for refusing to reveal their sources to government officials. The bill that was approved extends these protections to anyone "who regularly gathers, prepares, collects, photographs, records, writes, edits, reports, or publishes news or information that concerns local, national, or international events or other matters of public interest for dissemination to the public *for a substantial portion of the person's livelihood or for substantial financial gain* and includes a supervisor, employer, parent, subsidiary, or affiliate of such covered person" (Ardia 2007). The italicized passage makes clear that protection extends only to those who make their living working in conventional media organizations, excluding the myriad other providers of political information found in the new media environment. Similar legislation was passed by the Senate Judiciary Committee in December 2009, but significantly, its version of the bill excludes the italicized limitation (an amendment offered by Senators Dianne Feinstein and Richard Durbin that would have similarly restricted

---

[24] And recall from Chapter 1 that survey results indicate that those who say they rely primarily on *The Daily Show* for their political information tend to be better informed than those who say they rely primarily on either the network news broadcasts or a newspaper. At the same time, those who failed to explore sources other than *The Daily Show* would have been unable to understand the context or significance of the story on Cheney.

the definition of a journalist and that was supported by professional news organizations was narrowly defeated).

Although the final outcome of this legislation still remains uncertain, it points to the complexity of the very notion of a journalist in the new information environment, the reticence of many political and media elites to accept these changes, and the need for debates such as this one to be more public and more integrated into a broader discussion of the future of the media and its role in democracy (Hendler 2010).[25] Numerous other policy debates recently or currently in play, the outcomes of which will significantly affect the shape of a new media regime, include the protection of network neutrality, regulations on the concentration of media ownership, rights to privacy in a number of new platforms, the ending of subsidized postal rates for smaller magazines, and the extension of copyright laws in digital media (e.g., the Digital Millennium Copyright Act).

Policy decisions such as these have enormous implications that will last long after a new regime has emerged. Again, the past offers important lessons in this regard. Decisions made in the early nineteenth century about the political role of the mail helped shape dramatic changes in the expansion of American democracy, especially subsidization of postal rates for newspapers and magazines. Though currently under challenge, this principle has helped allow smaller, politically significant magazines like the *Nation*, the *National Review*, and the *New Republic* to survive and, like their intellectual forebear, the abolitionist *Liberator*, to maintain an influence on political debate far beyond their small circulations. Similarly, the principle that, regardless of its content, all mail must be treated the same and not be opened by officials without a warrant helped influence decisions about the privacy of telephone conversations and provides the precedent for current battles over issues like net neutrality and privacy rights on the internet. Had decisions about the developing postal system been different, so, too, would be the shape of subsequent media regimes. Likewise, the outcome of debates over issues such as net neutrality will have a significant impact on the ease with which nonmainstream political voices can find an audience for their views (heavily affecting pluralism) and so shape the discursive environment in a new media regime.

In the same way, decisions reached in the 1930s that established a privately owned, advertising-driven media system with only minimal public service obligations continues to limit and shape current possibilities for

---

[25] Consider, for example, the implications of such legislation and who is protected by it for websites such as WikiLeaks and their contributors?

American media policy. For example, the presence of a strong and vibrant public service broadcasting system in the United Kingdom creates a very different context for responding to the fragmenting implications of new media. Significantly, public trust in the BBC and its continued status as the most relied-on source of political information set the standards for newer commercial stations and might provide a forum for a less fragmented and polarized public discourse than would be possible in the United States.[26] In *The Death and Life of American Journalism*, McChesney and Nichols (2009) argue that the twentieth-century adoption of this commercial model and its current acceptance as natural and inevitable leads to a failure to consider both the role of public subsidy for political media throughout American history and the success of public service models throughout the democratic world today.

The new media environment itself makes it possible to imagine new forms of public deliberation, less limited to elites and involving the broader public. As the growing media reform movement and its at least limited success in altering FCC decision making in the areas of media concentration and net neutrality illustrate, new conduits of political communication – from e-mail to YouTube to blogs – have created new and significant axes of political power in the making of media policy (McChesney 2007). Such dynamics may widen the range of policies that may be seriously considered in a new media regime.

Concluding Thoughts

The challenge we collectively face is not how to re-create the authoritative hierarchy of the past – for better or worse, that battle has already been lost. Instead, it is to create a new media regime that, through explicitly defined values like transparency, pluralism, verisimilitude, and practice, provides the opportunities for a wide variety of voices, interests, and perspectives to vie for the public's attention and action. We believe that such an environment is preferable – more democratic – to assuming a priori that any particular group or interest should have the power to set the agenda.

---

[26] Recent surveys of the British public reveal that 70 percent of BBC viewers said they trust it in general, and 79 percent reported trusting its news broadcasts (Glover 2009). About three-fifths said that they trust commercial news broadcasts. In contrast, a 2009 survey conducted by the Pew Research Center for the People and the Press found that 60 percent of those interviewed thought U.S. media was biased, 63 percent said news stories were often inaccurate, and 74 percent said the news media favored particular sides in covering political and social issues (2009b).

Ultimately, this new information environment requires not only new definitions of political relevance and democratic utility but also an expanded definition of democratic citizenship. The distinctions between political, cultural, and economic elites, between information producers and consumers, even between elites and "the masses" are becoming more fluid in this new context. As such, the notions of press responsibility that underlie traditional models of media and politics must be expanded to other individuals and institutions that influence politically relevant media texts. Similarly, notions of civic responsibility that are applied to the general public must be expanded to also apply to traditional political, cultural, and economic elites – to any individual or organization that is given access to the soapbox in our expanded public square.[27]

The type of mediated environment we envision – and that we believe is feasible as an aspiration – is one that draws on but is not constrained by all the past regimes that have defined the relationship between media and democracy in the United States. But in concluding this book, we would like to draw the reader's attention to two of these periods in particular. Elements of Realism strikes us as being particularly relevant, promising, and challenging as we imagine what a democratic media regime of the twenty-first century might look like. Promising because of its use of multiple mediums and genres, its blending of culture and politics, its balance of reason and emotion, its concern for social progress and justice, and its methodologies for seeking "truth" while remaining cognizant of its contested nature and encouraging of competing, dialectical interpretations of it. Relevant because many of the technological, political, and cultural qualities of the new media environment are amenable to these Realist goals and approaches. But challenging because the hyperreal quality of the new environment would seem, at first blush, to be anathema to realism. Yet on closer inspection, it becomes clearer that the Realist Era, with its use of a wide range of mediated constructions of the social and political world, was in its own way hyperreal. The point is that hyperreality can obscure our understanding of the social and political world, but it need not do so. The key, we believe, is not to deny the hyperreality of today's mediated environment but to develop norms and practices that help ensure that this hyperreality is used to better understand the truth of things.

---

[27] As we noted earlier, it is for this reason that we embrace the term *citizen-journalist* because it signals both that ordinary citizens can sometimes perform the duties of journalists and that journalists are also citizens. A similar case could be made for terms like citizen-artist, citizen-actor, or citizen-politician.

The second regime of particular note – one that tellingly followed immediately on and in some ways overlapped with the Age of Realism – is the Progressive Era. In the end, the issues raised by the current media environment are not unlike those underlying the debate between John Dewey and Walter Lippmann of nearly a century ago. At its core remains the issue of the limitations of the public – the public and its problems as Dewey called it. In most ways, Lippmann's (1922) arguments about the need for elite democracy, given the limited capacity of the public, triumphed and were underwritten by the structures of the Age of Broadcast News. The changes of the past twenty years that we have chronicled in this book have thoroughly undermined this system and increased geometrically the conduits through which politically relevant communication flows, thus making it increasingly difficult for the professional elites called on by Lippmann to shape the information to which the public attends. In turn, this requires citizens – both "elite" and "average" – to ethically and critically consider the democratic utility of the politically relevant information they produce and consume.

It is not too dramatic a leap to suggest that the fate of democratic politics in the twenty-first century now depends, as Dewey argued in the 1920s, on the ability of political systems to produce sophisticated and critical citizens, and to provide them with the motivations. resources, and opportunities to act on this newly developed identity. Unlike Lippmann, we do not believe that the "problem" of the public is an intractable one on which more participatory democracy must inevitably founder. Rather, like Dewey, we see this problem as one that is the responsibility of all of us, the media included, to overcome.

References

Abramson, Jeffery, F. Christopher Arterton, and Gary Orren. 1988. *The Electronic Commonwealth: The Impact of New Media on Democratic Politics.* New York: Basic Books.

ACNielsen. 2009. "A2/M2 Three Screen Report: Television, Internet and Mobile Usage in the U.S." December 18. http://kr.en.nielsen.com/site/documents/3_Screen_Report_US_2Q09.pdf.

Adorno, Theodor W., and Max Horkheimer. [1947]2002. "The Culture Industry: Enlightenment as Mass Deception." In *Dialectic of Enlightenment*, trans. Edmund Jephcott, 94–136. Stanford, CA: Stanford University Press.

Aldrich, Gary. 1996. *Unlimited Access: An FBI Agent inside the Clinton White House.* Washington, D.C.: Regnery Publishing.

Amaya, Hector. 2003. "Viewing political selves in film: A comparative reception study of Cuban films in Cuba and the United States." Ph.D. Dissertation. University of Texas at Austin.

Anderson, Benedict. 1983. *Imagined Communities: Reflections on the Origin and Spread of Nationalism.* London: Verso.

Ang, Ien. 1991. *Desperately Seeking the Audience.* London: Routledge.

Arango, Tim. 2008. "CBS Said to Consider Use of CNN in Reporting." *New York Times*, April 8. http://www.nytimes.com/2008/04/08/business/media/08cbs.html.

Ardia, David. 2007. "U.S. House Overwhelmingly Passes Federal Shield Bill, Changes Definition of Who is Covered," October 17. http://www.citmedialaw.org/blog/2007/us-house-overwhelmingly-passes-federal-shield-bill-changes-definition-who-covered.

Auletta, Ken. 2001. "Battle Stations." *New Yorker*, December 10, 66–67.

Bagdikian, Ben. 1997. *The Media Monopoly.* 5th ed. Boston: Beacon Press.

Baker, G. Edwin. 2007. *Media Concentration and Democracy: Why Ownership Matters.* New York: Cambridge University Press.

Balkin, Jack M. 2009. "The Presidency and the Rise of the New Partisan Press." *Balkinization*, October 23. http://balkin.blogspot.com/2009/10/presidency-and-rise-of-new-partisan.html.

327

Banks, Russell. 1998. *Cloudsplitter*. New York: Harper Collins.

Bark, Ed. 2004. "'American Candidate' Program Is Television's Ultimate Also-Ran." *Dallas Morning News*, August 8. http://community.seattletimes .nwsource.com/archive/?date=20040808&slug=candidate08.

Barney, Darin. 2000. *Prometheus Wired: The Hope for Democracy in the Age of Network Technology*. Chicago: University of Chicago Press.

Barnhurst, Kevin, and John Nerone. 2001. *The Form of News: A History*. New York: Guilford Press.

Barstow, David. 2008. "Behind TV Analysts, Pentagon's Hidden Hand." *New York Times*. April 20.

Bartells, Larry. 2008. *Unequal Democracy: The Political Economy of the New Gilded Age*. New York: Russell Sage Foundation and Princeton University Press.

Baym, Geoffry. 2010. *From Cronkite to Colbert: The Evolution of Broadcast News*. Boulder, CO: Paradigm Publishers.

BBC News World Edition. 2003. "Redford Speaks Out Against War." January 21. http://news.bbc.co.uk/2/hi/entertainment/2679235.stm.

Bennett, W. Lance. 2008. "Changing Citizenship in the Digital Age." In *Civic Life Online*, edited by Lance Bennett, 1–24. Cambridge: Massachusetts Institute of Technology Press.

————. 1990. "Toward a Theory of Press-State Relations in the United States" *Journal of Communication* 40, No. 2, 103–127.

————. 1988. *News: The Politics of Illusion*. New York: Longman.

Bennett, W. Lance, Regina Lawrence, and Steven Livingston. 2007. *When the Press Fails: Political Power and the News Media from Iraq to Katrina*. Chicago: University of Chicago Press.

Bennett, W. Lance, Terris Givens, and Christian Breunig. 2008. "Communication and Political Mobilization: Digital Media Use and Protest Organization among Anti-Iraq War Demonstrators in the U.S." *Political Communication* 25, 269–289.

Bennett, William J. 1997. *The Death of Outrage: Bill Clinton and the Assault on American Ideals*. New York: Free Press.

Benson, Rodney, and Daniel Hallin. 2007. "How States, Markets and Globalization Shape the News: The French and U.S. National Press, 1965–1997." *European Journal of Communication* 22, no. 1, 27–48.

Berkowitz, Dan. 1990. "Refining the Gatekeeping Metaphor for Local Television News." *Journal of Broadcasting and Electronic Media* 34, 55–68.

Bimber, Bruce. 2003. *Information and American Democracy: Technology in the Evolution of Political Power*. New York: Cambridge University Press.

Bleske, Glen L. 1991. "Ms. Gates Takes Over: An Updated Version of a 1949 Case Study." *Newspaper Research Journal* 12, 88–97.

Bloom, Alan. 1988. *The Closing of the American Mind*. New York: Simon and Schuster.

Bogart, Leo. 1989. *Press and Public*. Hillsdale, NJ: Lawrence Erlbaum Associates.

Bogost, Ian. 2007. *Persuasive Games: The Expressive Power of Videogames*. Cambridge: Massachusetts Institute of Technology Press.

Bohlen, Celestine. 2001. "THINK TANK; In New War on Terrorism, Words Are Weapons Too." *New York Times*, September 29. http://query.nytimes.com/gst/fullpage.html?res=9B04EFDA163DF93AA1575AC0A9679C8B63

Booth, Michael. 2004. "The Science of Disaster Films 'Day after Tomorrow' Stokes the Debate over Global Warming." *Denver Post*, May 23.

Bord, Richard J., Ann Fisher, and Robert E. O'Conner. 1995. "Is Accurate Understanding of Global Warming Necessary to Promote Willingness to Sacrifice?" *RISK: Health, Safety and Environment* 4, no. 3, 339–354.

Boulton, Clint. 2006. "Yahoo's Earnings Message to Google: We're Bigger Than You." *eWeek Google Watch*. April 18. http://googlewatch.eweek.com/content/archive/yahoos_earnings_message_to_google_were_bigger_than_you.html.

Boykoff, Maxwell T. and Jules M. Boykoff. 2004. "Balance as Bias: Global Warming and the U.S. Prestige Press." *Global Environmental Change* 14, no. 1, 125–136.

Braudy, Leo. 1997. *The Frenzy of Renown: Fame and Its History*. New York: Vintage Books.

Brazaitis, Tim. 2001. "Lamenting the Loss of Free Speech." *Cleveland Plain Dealer*, September 30, H3.

Breen, Steven. 2009. "Political Animal." *Washington Monthly*, February 17.

Breslau, Karen. 2006. "The Resurrection of Al Gore." *Wired* 14, no. 5, May. http://www.wired.com/wired/archive/14.05/gore.html.

Brock, David. 2003. *Blinded by the Right: The Conscience of an Ex-Conservative*. New York: Three Rivers Press.

Bunting, Madeline. 2003. "We Are the People." *(London) Guardian*, February 17, 21.

Burke, Kenneth. 1966. *Language as Symbolic Action*. Berkeley: University of California Press.

Burkeman, Oliver. "Bloggers Catch What Washington Post Missed." *(London) Guardian*, December 21.

Burr, Ty. 2004. "Storm Warning: Not Only Action-Film Fans Are Awaiting 'The Day after Tomorrow.' Will Watching Global Warming Wreak Climactic Havoc on Film Make It Seem More Real, or Less?" *Boston Globe*, May 23.

Campbell, Kim. 2002. "'Newsblaster' Software Scans, Summarizes News." *Christian Science Monitor*, February 28. http://www.csmonitor.com/2002/0228/p12s02-stct.html.

Cappella, Joseph, and Kathleen Hall Jamieson. 1997. *The Spiral of Cynicism: The Press and the Public Good*. New York: Oxford University Press.

Carey, James W. 1997. "The Roots of Modern Media Analysis: Lewis Mumford and Marshall McLuhan." In *James Carey: A Critical Reader*, edited by Eve Stryker Munson and Catherine A. Warren, 34–59. Minneapolis: University of Minnesota Press.

———. 1989. *Culture as Communication*. Boston: Unwin Hyman.

Carter, Bill. 2006. "MSNBC Star Carves Anti-Fox Niche." *New York Times*, July 11.

Carter, Bill, and Felicity Barringer. 2001. "A Nation Challenged: Speech and Expression; in Patriotic Times, Dissent Is Muted." *New York Times*, September 28.

Chambers, Simone. 2009. "Rhetoric and the Public Sphere: Has Deliberative Democracy Abandoned Mass Democracy?" *Political Theory* 37, no. 3, 323–350.

Chandler, Alfred D. 1977. *The Visible Hand.* Cambridge, MA: Harvard University Press.

Chapman, Glenn. 2007. "Internet Users Transformed into News Reporters" Agence France-Presse, February 11. http://groups.yahoo.com/group/nhnenews/message/12589.

Christians, Clifford G. 2000. "An Intellectual History of Media Ethics." In *Media Ethics: Opening Social Dialogue*, edited by Bart Pattyn, 15–46. Leuven, Belgium: Peeters.

CNN. 2002. "Iranian-Americans Protest Immigration Policy." CNN.com, December 18. http://articles.cnn.com/2002-12-18/us/ins.protest_1_immigration-policy-immigration-officials-ins-detains?_s=PM:US.

Cohen, Patricia Cline. 1982. *A Calculating People: The Spread of Numeracy in Early America.* Chicago: University of Chicago Press.

Conason, Joe, and Gene Lyons. 2000. *The Hunting of the President: The Ten Year Campaign to Destroy Bill and Hillary Clinton.* New York: St. Martin's Press.

Crampton, Thomas. 2007. "More in Europe Worry about Climate Than in US, Poll Shows." *New York Times*, January 4. http://www.nytimes.com/2007/01/04/health/04iht-poll.4102536.html.

Davidson, Keay. 2004. "Film's Tale of Icy Disaster Leaves Experts Cold." *San Francisco Chronicle*, June 1.

Davies, Frank. 2003. "War poll uncovers fact gap. Many mistakenly believe U.S. found WMDs in Iraq." *Philadelphia Inquirer.* June 14, A1.

Dayan, Daniel, and Elihu Katz. 1992. *Media Events: The Live Broadcasting of History.* Cambridge, MA: Harvard University Press.

Dell, Kristina. 2008. "How Second Life Affects Real Life." *Time*, May 12. http://www.time.com/time/health/article/0,8599,1739601,00.html.

Delli Carpini, Michael X., and Scott Keeter. 1996. *What Americans Know About Politics and Why It Matters.* New Haven, CT: Yale University Press.

Delli Carpini, Michael X., and Bruce A. Williams. 2001. "Let Us Infotain You: The Politics of Popular Media." In *Mediated Politics: The Future of Political Communication*, edited by W. Lance Bennett and Robert Entman, 160–181. New York: Cambridge University Press.

———. 1994a. "Fictional and Non-Fictional Television Celebrates Earth Day: Or, Politics Is Comedy Plus Pretense." *Cultural Studies* 8, no. 1, 74–98.

———. 1994b. "Methods, Metaphors, and Media Research: The Uses of Television in Political Conversations." *Communication Research* 21, no. 6, 782–812.

DeLuca, Dan. 2003. "Divided country, Bashing and boycotting the Dixie Chicks may do them some harm, but it hurts country music even more." *Philadelphia Inquirer* – June 14.

Dembart, Lee. 2003. "Web Logs Offer Up-Close and Uncensored Views on the War." *International Herald Tribune*, March 24.

De Morales, Lisa. 2002. "Sunday's Best: Schieffer Topples Russert." *Washington Post*, June 14.

———. 2001a. "Letterman's Back Tonight, but Don't Expect a Biting Mono-logue." *Washington Post*, September 17.

———. 2001b. "WJLA Pulls 'PI' a Second Time." *Washington Post*, September 28.

DeMott, Benjamin. 1998. *The Trouble with Friendship: Why Americans Can't Think Straight about Race*. New Haven, CT: Yale University Press.

Dewey, John. 1946. *The Public and Its Problems: An Essay in Political Inquiry*. Chicago: Gateway Books. (Originally published 1927)

Didion, Joan. 2002. "Fixed Opinions, or the Hinge of History." *New York Review of Books*, January 16, 54–59.

Diner, Steven J. 1998. *A Very Different Age: Americans of the Progressive Era*. New York: Hill and Wang.

Dowie, Mark. 1998. "What's Wrong with the New York Times's Science Report-ing." *Nation*, July 6.

Downie, Leonard, and Michael Schudson. 2009. "The Reconstruction of Amer-ican Journalism." *Columbia Journalism Review*, October 19. http://www.cjr.org/reconstruction/the_reconstruction_of_american.php.

Easton, David. 1965. *A Systems Analyses of Political Life*. New York: John Wiley and Sons.

Edelman, Murray. 1995. *Constructing the Political Spectacle*. Chicago: University of Chicago Press.

Edgerton, David. 2007. *The Shock of the Old*. New York: Oxford University Press.

Emery, Michael, and Edwin Emery. 1988. *The Press and America: An Interpretive History of the Mass Media*. New York: Allyn and Bacon.

Engel, Matthew. 2002. "Has Anything Changed?" *(London) Guardian*, Septem-ber 2, G2.

Entman, Robert. 2004. *Projections of Power: Framing News, Public Opinion, and U.S. Foreign Policy*. Chicago: University of Chicago Press.

———. 1989. *Democracy without Citizens: Media and the Decay of American Politics*. New York: Oxford University Press.

Entman, Robert, and Andrew Rojecki. 2001. *The Black Image in the White Mind: Media and Race in America*. Chicago: University of Chicago Press.

Evans, Harold. 2001. *War Stories: Reporting in the Time of Conflict*. Arlington, VA: Freedom Forum Newseum.

Fairness and Accuracy in Reporting. 2003. "MSNBC's Double Standard on Free Speech: 'Turd World' Is OK – 'Anti-War, Anti-Bush' Is Not." March 3.

———. 2003. "HBO Adds Disclaimer to Gulf War Movie." January 3.

Farrall, Kenneth. 2009. "Suspect until Proven Guilty: A Problematization of State Dossier Systems via Two Case Studies: The United States and China." Ph.D. diss., Annenberg School for Communication, University of Pennsylvania.

Fish, Stanley. 1994. *There's No Such Thing as Free Speech: And It's a Good Thing, Too*. New York: Oxford University Press.

Fishkin, James S. 2009. *When the People Speak: Deliberative Democracy and Public Consultation*. New York: Oxford University Press.

Fiske, John. 1996. *Media Matters: Race and Gender in U.S. Politics*. Minneapolis: University of Minnesota Press.

Fitzgerald, Toni. 2008. "Network News Sees Big Slide in 18–34s." *Media Life*, March 13. http://www.medialifemagazine.com/artman2/publish/ Dayparts_update_51/Network_news_sees_big_slide_in_18-34s.asp.

Foremski, Tom. 2006. "How the Secret Identity of LonelyGirl15 Was Found." *Silicon Valley Watcher*. September 12. http://www.siliconvalleywatcher.com/ mt/archives/2006/09/how_the_secret.php.

Fox New. 2004. "Jon Stewart Delivers News for the MTV Generation." FoxNews.com, March 2. http://www.foxnews.com/story/0,2933, 113003,00.html.

Frank, Thomas. 2000. *One Market under God: Extreme Capitalism, Market Populism, and the End of Market Democracy*. New York: Doubleday.

Franken, Al. 1999. *Rush Limbaugh Is a Big Fat Idiot and Other Observations*. New York: Dell.

Fukuyama, Francis. 1993. *The End of History and the Last Man*. New York: Avon Books.

GamePolitics.com. 2008. "Top 20 Video Game Moments from Presidential Campaign." November 5.

Gary, Brett. 1996. "Communication Research, the Rockefeller Foundation, and Mobilization for the War of Words." *Journal of Communication* 46, no. 3, 124–148.

Gelbspan, Ross. 2004. *Boiling Point: How Politicians, Big Oil and Coal, Journalists, and Activists Have Fueled the Climate Crisis – And What We Can Do to Avert Disaster*. New York: Basic Books.

———. 1997. *The Heat Is On: The Climate Crisis, the Cover-Up, the Prescription*. Cambridge: Perseus Books.

Gerbner, George, Larry Gross, Michael Morgan, and Nancy Signorielli. 1986. "Living with Television: The Dynamics of the Cultivation Process." In *Perspectives on Media Effects*, edited by J. Bryant and D. Zillmann, 17–40. Hillsdale, NJ: Lawrence Erlbaum Associates.

Gerson, Michael. 2007. "Where the Avatars Roam." *Washington Post*, July 6.

Gitelman, Lisa. 2006. *Always Already New: Media, History, and the Data of Culture*. Cambridge: Massachusetts Institute of Technology Press.

Gitlin, Todd. 2001. *Media Unlimited: How the Torrent of Images and Sounds Overwhelms Our Lives*. New York: Metropolitan Books.

———. 1996. *The Twilight of Common Dreams: Why America Is Wracked by Culture Wars*. New York: Metropolitan/Holt.

Glover, Julian. 2009. "Public rejects Murdoch view of BBC, says ICM poll: Trust in corporation grows despite attacks by Murdoch and politicians." *Guardian.co.uk*. September 4. http://www.guardian.co.uk/media/2009/sep/04/ bbc-icm-poll-james-murdoch.

Gold, Matea and Scott Collins. 2005. "NBC Deleted Kanye's Comments on Bush from Telethon Re-Broadcast." *Los Angeles Times*, September 5.

Goldfarb, Charles B. 2003. "Market Structure of the Video Programming Industry and Emerging Public Policy Issues." Congressional Research Service Report to Congress. http://congressionalresearch.com/RL32027/document.

php?study=Market+Structure+of+the+Video+Programming+Industry+and+ Emerging+Public+Policy+Issues.

Grindstaff, Laura. 2002. *The Money Shot: Trash, Class, and the Making of TV Talk Shows*. Chicago: University of Chicago Press.

Grossberg, Lawrence, Ellen Wartella, Charles Whitney, and J. MacGregor Wise. 2006. *MediaMaking: Mass Media in a Popular Culture*, 2nd ed. Thousand Oaks, CA: Sage Publications.

Gumbell, Andrew. 2001. "War on Terrorism: Dissenting Voices – Free Speech Has Become Second Casualty of War." *(London) Independent*, September 28.

Habermas, Jürgen. 1991. *The Structural Transformation of the Public Sphere*. Cambridge: Massachusetts Institute of Technology Press.

Hacker, Jacob S. and Paul Pierson. 2010. Winner-Take-All Politics: How Washington Made the Rich Richer – and Turned Its Back on the Middle Class. New York: Simon & Schuster.

Hallin, Dan. 1986. *The Uncensored War: The Media and the Vietnam War*. New York: Oxford University Press.

Hansell, Saul. 2007. "AOL Will Watch How You Behave." NewYorkTimes. com. July 24. http://bits.blogs.nytimes.com/2007/07/24/aol-will-watch-how-you-behave/.

Hanson, Russell L. 1985. *The Democratic Imagination in America*. Princeton, NJ: Princeton University Press.

Hardt, Michael, and Antonio Negri. 2000. *Empire*. Cambridge, MA: Harvard University Press.

Hargrove, Thomas. 2006. "Third of Americans Suspect 9–11 Government Conspiracy." Scripps Howard News Service, August 1. http://www.scrippsnews. com/911poll.

Harp, D. M., J. Loke, and I. Bachmann. 2009. "Pit Bulls, Politics, and Gender Performance: A Feminist Analysis of Sarah Palin on Major News Websites." Paper presented at the annual meeting of the International Communication Association, Chicago. May 21–25.

Harvey, Fiona. 2005. "The Heat Is On." *Financial Times*, July 2, 19.

Hayes, Christopher. 2006. "9/11: The Roots of Paranoia." *Nation*, December 8. http://www.thenation.com/article/911-roots-paranoia.

Hechtkopf, Kevin. 2008. "Palin Speech Scores Big Ratings." CBSNews.com. September 4. http://www.cbsnews.com/8301-502163_162-4417245-502163. html.

Hendler, Clint. 2010. "Will the Shield Bill Become Law?" *Columbia Journalism Review*, August 9. http://www.cjr.org/campaign_desk/will_the_shield_bill_ become_la.php.

Hertsgaard, Mark. 2002. *The Eagle's Shadow: Why America Fascinates and Infuriates the World*. London: Bloomsbury Books.

Hindman, Matthew. 2009. *The Myth of Digital Democracy*. Princeton, NJ: Princeton University Press.

———. 2008. "What is the Online Public Sphere Good for?" In *The Hyperlinked Society*, edited by Joseph Turow, 268–288. Ann Arbor: University of Michigan Press.

Hobsbawm, Eric. 1994. *Age of Extremes: The Short Twentieth Century, 1914–1991*. London: Abacus.

Hofstadter, Richard. 1955. *The Age of Reform*. New York: Vintage Books.

Howe, Desson. 1998. "Primary Colors: Elect to See It." *Washington Post*, March 20.

———. 1994. "True Lies." *Washington Post*, July 15.

Isikoff, Michael. 1997. *Uncovering Clinton: A Reporter's Story*. New York: Crown Books.

Israel, Jerry. 1972. *Building the Organizational Society*. New York: Free Press.

Itzkoff, David. 2010. "'Family Guy,' Palin and the Limits of Laughter." *New York Times*, February 19.

Iyengar, Shanto. 2001. *Is Anyone Responsible? How Television Frames Political Issues*. Chicago: University of Chicago Press.

Iyengar, Shanto, and Donald Kinder. 1987. *News That Matters Television and American Opinion*. Chicago: University of Chicago Press.

Jacobs, Lawrence, Fay Lomax Cook, and Michael X. Delli Carpini. *Talking Together. Public Deliberation and Political Participation in America*. Chicago: University of Chicago Press. 2009.

Jacoby, Susan. 2008. *The Age of American Unreason*. New York: Pantheon Books.

James, Caryn. 2001. "A Public Flooded with Images from Friend and Foe Alike." *New York Times*, October 10.

Jamieson, Kathleen Hall. 2000. "Issue Advocacy in a Changing Discourse Environment." In *Mediated Politics: Communication in the Future of Democracy*, edited by W. Lance Bennett and Robert M. Entman, 323–341. New York: Cambridge University Press.

Jenkins, Henry. 2006. *Convergence Culture: Where Old and New Media Collide*. New York: New York University Press.

Johnson, Chalmers. 2008. *Nemesis: The Last Days of the American Republic*. New York: Henry Holt.

Jones, Alex. 2009. *Losing the News: The Future of News that Feeds Democracy*. New York: Oxford University Press.

Jurkowitz, M. 2002. "Fighting Terror; The Home Front The Media; Pro-US Tendency Is Seen in Survey." *Boston Globe*, January 28.

Kakutani, Michiko. 2001. "The Age of Irony Isn't over After All." *New York Times*, October 9.

Kaplan, Don. 2003. "Activist TV Duo Square Off in Ideological War." *New York Post*, February 28.

Kaplan, Robert D. 2001. *The Coming Anarchy: Shattering the Dreams of the Post Cold War*. New York: Vintage.

Katz, Elihu. 1996. "And Deliver Us From Segmentation." *Annals of the American Academy of Political and Social Sciences*. 546, July, 22–33.

———. 1993. "The End of Journalism? Notes on Watching the Gulf War." *Journal of Communication* 42, no. 3, 5–13.

Katz, Jon. 1997. *Media Rants: Postpolitics in the Digital Nation*. San Francisco: Hardwired.

Keeter, Scott. 1999. "The Perplexing Case of Public Opinion about the Clinton Scandal." Paper presented at the annual conference of the American Association for Public Opinion Research, May 13–16, St. Pete Beach, FL.

Keller, Evelyn Fox. 1994. "The Paradox of Scientific Subjectivity." In *Rethinking Objectivity*, edited by Allan Megill, 313–332. Durham, NC: Duke University Press.

Keller, Jared. 2010. "Evaluating Iran's Twitter Revolution." *Atlantic*, June 18. http://www.theatlantic.com/technology/archive/2010/06/evaluating-irans-twitter-revolution/58337/.

Kelly, Jack. 2004. "An Educational Good Read: The Creator of 'Jurassic Park' Debunks the Coming Environmental Crisis." *Pittsburgh Post-Gazette*, December 26, J7.

Kirn, Walter. 2001. *Up in the Air*. New York: Random House.

Klapper, Joseph. 1960. *The Effects of the Mass Media*. Glencoe, IL: Free Press.

Klein, Joe. 2008. "Sarah Palin's Myth of America." *Time*, September 10. http://www.time.com/time/politics/article/0,8599,1840388,00.html.

Klein, Maury. 1997. *Days of Defiance: Sumter, Secession, and the Coming of the Civil War*. New York: Vintage Books.

Klinenberg, Eric. 2007. *Fighting for Air: The Battle to Control America's Media*. New York: Henry Holt.

Kolata, Gina. 1997. *"television review*; Seeking Something to Blame When Breast Cancer Strikes." *New York Times*, October 1. http://www.nytimes.com/1997/10/01/arts/television-review-seeking-something-to-blame-when-breast-cancer-strikes.html

Kolbert, Elizabeth. 2006. *Field Notes from a Catastrophe: Man, Nature, and Climate Change*. New York: Bloomsbury.

———. 2001. "Pimps and Dragons." *New Yorker*, May 28. http://www.newyorker.com/archive/2001/05/28/010528fa_FACT.

Konner, Joan. 1996. "A Journalist Is..." *Columbia Journalism Review*, November–December, p. 4.

Kovach, Bill, and Tom Rosenstiel. 1999. *Warp Speed: America in the Age of Mixed Media*. New York: Century Foundation Press.

Kraidy, Marwan. 2009. *Reality Television and Arab Politics: Contention in Public Life*. New York: Cambridge University Press.

Krakauer, John. 2009. *Where Men Win Glory: The Odyssey of Pat Tillman*. New York: Doubleday, 2009.

Kristof, Nicholas. 2008. "Citizen Foreign Correspondence." *New York Times*, July 24. http://kristof.blogs.nytimes.com/2008/07/24/citizen-foreign-correspondence/.

———. 2007. "The Big Melt." *New York Times*, August 16.

Krugman, Paul. 2003. "Channels of Influence." *New York Times*, March 25.

Kuczynski, Alex. 2000. "On CBS News Some of What You See Isn't There." *New York Times*, January 12.

Kurtz, Howard. 2007. *Reality Show: Inside the Last Great Television News War*. New York: Free Press.

———. 2002. "Troubled Times for Network Evening News." *Washington Post*, March 10, A1.

————. 1998. *Spin Cycle: How the White House and the Media Manipulate the News*. New York: Touchstone Books.

Lasswell, Harold D. 1971. *Propaganda Technique in World War I*. Cambridge: Massachusetts Institute of Technology Press.

Last, Jonathan V. 2000. "Leonardo DiCaprio, Cub Reporter." Salon.com, April 5. http://www1.salon.com/politics2000/feature/2000/04/05/dicaprio/index.html.

Lemert, James. 1981. *Does Mass Communication Change Public Opinion After All?* Chicago: Nelson Hall.

Levine, Lawrence. 1997. *The Opening of the American Mind*. New York: Beacon.

————. 1988. *High Brow, Low Brow: The Emergence of Cultural Hierarchy in America*. Cambridge, MA: Harvard University Press.

Lewin, Kurt. 1947. "Frontiers in Group Dynamics." *Human Relations* 1 no. 2, 5–41.

Lewis, Eugene. 1988. *American Politics in a Bureaucratic Age*. New York: University Press of America.

Lewis, Michael. 2000. "Boom Box." *New York Times Magazine*, August 13. http://www.nytimes.com/2000/08/13/magazine/boom-box.html.

Leys, Colin. 2001. *Market-Driven Politics: Neoliberal Democracy and the Public Interest*. London: Verso.

Lichter, S. Robert, Linda S. Lichter, and Daniel Amundson. 2000. "Government Goes Down the Tube: Images of Government in TV Entertainment, 1955–1998." *Press/Politics* 5, no. 2, 96–103.

Liebes, Tamar, and Bruce A. Williams. 2000. "Public Affairs Talk Shows in Israel and the United States: The Interaction of the New Media Environment and Political Culture." Paper presented at the annual meeting of the International Communication Association. Acapulco, Mexico, May 2000.

Light, Allie and Irving Saraf. 1997. *Rachel's Daughters: Searching for the Causes of Breast Cancer*.

Lilla, Mark. 2003. "The New Age of Tyranny." *New York Review of Books*, October 24, 28.

Lippmann, Walter. 1922. *Public Opinion*. New York: Harcourt, Brace.

Livingstone, Sonia and Peter Lunt. 1994. *Talk on Television: Audience Participation and Public Debate*. New York: Routledge.

Lodge, David. 2002, "Sense and Sensibility." *Guardian Review*, November 2, 4–6.

Lott, John R., Jr. 2008. "Bad Impression: Did the Media Take Swipes at Sarah Palin?" FoxNews.com. September 2. http://www.foxnews.com/story/0,2933,414943,00.html.

Lustig, Jeffrey R. 1982. *Corporate Liberalism*. Berkeley: University of California Press.

Lyons, Patrick. 2007. "YouTube and the Censors: An Update." NewYorkTimes.com. August 31. http://thelede.blogs.nytimes.com/2007/08/31/youtube-and-the-censors-an-update/.

Madden, Mike. 2008. "How Democrats Are Fighting Back against Sarah Palin." Salon.com. September 10. http://www.salon.com/news/feature/2008/09/10/fight_back.

Margolick, David. 1990. "Ignorance of 'L.A. Law' Is No Excuse for Lawyers." *New York Times*, May 6.

Maslin, Janet. 1998. "'The Siege': New York as Battleground of Terrorists and Troops." *New York Times*, November 6. http://partners.nytimes.com/library/film/110698siege-film-review.html.

Mayer, Jane. 2008. *The Dark Side: The Inside Story of How the War on Terror Turned into a War on American Ideals*. New York: Random House.

McChesney, Robert. 2007. *The Real Communication Revolution: Critical Junctures and the Future of Media*. New York: New Press.

———. 1999. *Rich Media, Poor Democracy: Communication Politics in Dubious Times*. Urbana: University of Illinois Press.

McChesney, Robert, and John Nichols. 2009. *The Death and Life of American Journalism*. Philadelphia: Nation Books.

McCombs, M. E., and D. L. Shaw. 1972. "The Agenda-Setting Function of Mass Media." *Public Opinion Quarterly* 36, 176–187.

McCullough, David. 2001. *John Adams*. New York: Simon and Schuster.

McDaniel, Mike. 2001. "Politically Incorrect Comes under Fire for Comments about Terrorists." *Houston Chronicle*, September 19.

McLuhan, Marshall. 1995. "Media as the New Nature." In *Essential McLuhan*, edited by Eric McLuhan and Frank Zingrove, 270–276. New York: Basic Books.

Media Dynamics, Inc. 2010. *TV Dimensions 2010*. New York: Media Dynamics, Inc.

———. 2004. *TV Dimensions 2004*. New York: Media Dynamics, Inc.

Meserve, Jean, and Mike M. Ahlers. 2010. "Google Reports China-Based Attack, Says Pullout Possible." CNN.com. January 13. http://articles.cnn.com/2010-01-12/tech/google.china_1_google-search-engine-david-drummond?_s=PM:TECH.

Miller, Toby. 1998. *Technologies of Truth: Cultural Citizenship and Popular Media*. Minneapolis: University of Minnesota Press.

Mindich, David T. Z. 1998. *Just the Facts: How "Objectivity" Came to Define American Journalism*. New York: New York University Press.

Mitchell, Amy, and Tom Rosenstiel. 2008. "Financial Woes Now Overshadow All Other Concerns for Journalists. The Web: Alarming, Appealing and a Challenge to Journalistic Values." Pew Project for Excellence in Journalism. March 17. http://people-press.org/2008/03/17/2008-journalist-survey-a-commentary-of-the-findings/.

Moeller, Susan D. 1999. *Compassion Fatigue: How the Media Sell Disease, Famine, War, and Death*. New York: Routledge.

———. 2007. *Storm World: Hurricanes, Politics, and the Battle over Global Warming*. Orlando, FL: Harcourt.

Mooney, Chris. 2005. "Checking Crichton's Footnotes." *Boston Globe*, February 6.

Moore, David W. 2003. "Half of Young People Expect to Strike It Rich." Gallup Poll. March 11. http://www.gallup.com/poll/7981/half-young-people-expect-strike-rich.aspx.

Morgan, Michael J., M. J. Shanahan, and Nancy Signorielli. 2009. "Growing Up with Television: Cultivation Processes." In *Media Effects: Advances in Theory and Research*, edited by Jennings Bryant and Mary Beth Oliver, 34–49. New York: Routledge.

Morrison, Scott. 2010. "2nd UPDATE: Google Says Its Web Search Service in China Operating Normally." *Wall Street Journal*, July 29.

Murray, Susan, and Laurie Ouellette. 2009. *Reality TV: Remaking Television Culture*. New York: New York University Press.

Mutz, Diana. 1998. *Impersonal Influence: How Perceptions of Mass Collectives Affect Political Attitudes*. New York: Cambridge University Press.

Mutz, Diana, Paul Sniderman, and Richard Brody, eds. 1996. *Political Persuasion and Attitude Change*. Ann Arbor: University of Michigan Press.

Nacos, Brigitte, Yaeli Bloch-Elkon, and Robert Shapiro, 2011. *Selling Fear. Counterterrorism, The Media and Public Opinion*. Chicago: Chicago University Press.

Nagourney, Adam. 2009. "If White House Is Her Goal, Palin's Route Is Risky." *New York Times*, July 5.

Nasaw, David. 2000. *The Chief: The Life of William Randolph Hearst*. New York: Houghton Mifflin.

Nash, Gary B. 1979. *The Urban Crucible: Social Change, Political Consciousness, and the Origins of the American Revolution*. Cambridge, MA: Harvard University Press.

New York Times. 2007. "Yahoo Executives Defend Company in China Case." NewYorkTimes.com, November 6. http://www.nytimes.com/aponline/technology/AP-Yahoo-China.html?ex=1352005200&en=cb4ffb53f0354017&ei=5090&partner=rssuserland&emc=rss

New York Times. 2003. "'Bull Durham' Stars on HBO." April 3. http://www.nytimes.com/2003/04/23/sports/bull-durham-stars-on-hbo.html.

NewsHour. 2000. "President Clinton." http://www.pbs.org/newshour/bb/white_house/jan-june00/clinton_1-26.html

Nizza, Mike. 2007. "A Long Way to the Bottom of a U.N. Index." *New York Times*. November 27.

Offman, Craig. 2003. "Bad Tidings for Cable News Pack." *Variety*, January 1.

Ohlemacher, Stephen. 2006. "Americans Breathe to Live, but Mostly They Live for TV." Associated Press. December 16.

O'Neill, Onora. 1996. *Toward Justice and Virtue*. New York: Cambridge University Press.

Online NewsHour. 2000. "A NewsHour with Jim Lehrer Transcript, President Clinton." January 26.

Oxenford, David. 2007. "Barack Obama and the Daily Show, Hillary Clinton and David Letterman, Fred Thompson and Law and Order – What about Equal Time?" *Broadcast Law Blog*, August 30.

Packer, George. 2006. "Knowing the Enemy." *The New Yorker*. December 18. http://www.newyorker.com/archive/2006/12/18/061218fa_fact2

Paget, Derek. 1998. *No Other Way to Tell It: Dramadoc/Docudrama on Television*. Manchester, U.K.: Manchester University Press.

Pasick, Adam. 2006. "Virtual Economies Attract Real-World Tax Attention." Reuters. October 16. http://msl1.mit.edu/furdlog/docs/2006-10-16_reuters_2ndlife_tax.pdf.

Patterson, Thomas. 2002. *The Vanishing Voter: Public Involvement in an Age of Uncertainty*. New York: Alfred A. Knopf.

———. 1994. *Out of Order*. New York: Vintage Books.

Pein, Corey. 2005. "Blog-Gate: Yes, CBS Screwed Up Badly in 'Memogate' – but So Did Those Who Covered the Affair." *Columbia Journalism Review*, no. 1 January–February.

Peretz, Evgenia. 2007. "Going after Gore." *Vanity Fair*. October. http://www.vanityfair.com/politics/features/2007/10/gore200710.

Perez-Pena, Richard. 2009. "Times Moves to Trim 100 in Newsroom." *New York Times*, October 20.

Perkins, Joseph. 2004. "Disaster Movie Destroys the Truth." *San Diego Union-Tribune*, May 7.

Perlman, Allison. 2007. "Feminists in the Wasteland." *Feminist Media Studies* 7, no. 4, 413–431.

Perlstein, Rick. 2008. *Nixonland: The Rise of a President and the Fracturing of America*. New York: Scribner.

Peterson, Theodore. 1956. "The Social Responsibility Theory." In *Four Theories of the Press*, edited by Fred Siebert, Theodore Peterson, and Wilbur Schramm, 73–104. Urbana: University of Illinois Press.

Pew Research Center for the People and the Press. 2009a. "Stewart-Cramer Registers Less than Rihanna-Chris Brown; Public Sees More of a Mix of Good and Bad Economic News." March 18. http://people-press.org/http://people-press.org/files/legacy-pdf/499.pdf.

———. 2009b. "Public Evaluations of the News Media: 1985–2009; Press Accuracy Ratings Hits Two Decade Low." September 12. http://people-press.org/files/legacy-pdf/543.pdf.

———. 2008a. "Internet's Broader Role in Campaign 2008: Social Networking and Online Videos Take Off," January 18. http://people-press.org/http://people-press.org/files/legacy-pdf/384.pdf.

———. 2008b. "Positive Ratings for Coverage of Financial Crisis: Many say Press has been too Tough on Palin." October 9. http://people-press.org/files/legacy-pdf/460.pdf.

———. 2004a. "Cable and Internet Loom Large in Fragmented Political News Universe." January 11. http://people-press.org/2004/01/11/cable-and-internet-loom-large-in-fragmented-political-news-universe/.

———. 2004b. "News Audiences Increasingly Politicized: Online News Audience Larger, More Diverse." Pew Research Center Biennial News Consumption Survey. June 8. http://www.pewtrusts.org/uploadedFiles/wwwpewtrustsorg/Public_Opinion/Public_opinion_and_polls/pew_research_news_060804.pdf.

———. 2000. "The Tough Job of Communicating with Voters." February 5. http://people-press.org/2000/02/05/the-tough-job-of-communicating-with-voters/.

Pew Research Center Global Attitudes Project. 2007. "Rising Environmental Concern in 47-Nation Survey." June 27. http://pewglobal.org/2007/06/27/global-unease-with-major-world-powers/.

Pew Research Center Internet and American Life Project. 2010. "Understanding the Participatory News Consumer." March 1. http://www.pewinternet.org/Reports/2010/Online-News.aspx.

――――. 2009. "Usage of Time Spreadsheet: 2000–2009." http://www. pewinternet.org/Static-Pages/Trend-Data/Usage-Over-Time.aspx.

Pew Research Center's Project for Excellence in Journalism. 2010a. "The State of the News Media." http://www.stateofthemedia.org/2010/index.php.

――――. 2010b. "How News Happens: A Study of the News Ecosystem of One American City." http://www.journalism.org/analysis_report/how_news_happens.

――――. 2010c. "Social Media Tackles Controversial Issues." PEJ New Media Index, February 1–5. http://www.journalism.org/index_report/social_media_tackles_controversial_issues.

――――. 2009. "State of the News Media 2009." http://stateofthemedia.org/2009/.

――――. 2008. "Key News Audiences Now Blend Online and Traditional Sources: Audience Segments in a Changing News Environment." August 17. http://people-press.org/2008/08/17/key-news-audiences-now-blend-online-and-traditional-sources/.

――――. 2002. "Return to Normalcy? How the Media Have Covered the War on Terrorism." January 28. http://www.journalism.org/node/281.

Pickard, Victor. 2010. "Reopening the Postwar Settlement for U.S. Media: The Origins and Implications of the Social Contract between Media, the State, and the Polity." *Communication, Culture and Critique* 3, no. 2, 170–189.

Pin, Daniel H. 2008. "In Your Own Words – Please." *New York Times*, August 15.

Polanyi, Karl. 1944. *The Great Transformation*. Boston: Beacon Press.

Poovey, Mary. 1998. *A History of the Modern Fact: Problems of Knowledge in the Sciences of Wealth and Society*. Chicago: University of Chicago Press.

Porter, Theodore M. 1994. "Objectivity as Standardization: The Rhetoric of Impersonality in Measurement, Statistics, and Cost-Benefit Analysis." In *Rethinking Objectivity*, edited by Allan Megill, 197–237. Durham, NC: Duke University Press.

Posner, Gerald L. 1993. *Case Closed: Lee Harvey Oswald and the Assassination of JFK*. New York: Random House.

Postman, Neil. 1985. *Amusing Ourselves to Death: Public Discourse in the Age of Show Business*. New York: Penguin.

Prior, Markus. 2007. *Post-Broadcast Democracy: How Media Choice Increases Inequality in Political Involvement and Polarizes Elections*. New York: Cambridge University Press.

Pruitt, Gary. 2000. "Roadmap 2005: National vs. Regional Journalism Strategies for a Successful Future." Pew Center for Civic Journalism. http://www.pewcenter.org/doingcj/pubs/roadmap.html.

Putnam, Robert D. 2000. *Bowling Alone: The Collapse and Revival of American Community*. New York: Simon and Schuster.

Reuters. 2007a. "Blocked China Web Users Rage against Great Firewall." June 22. http://www.reuters.com/article/2007/06/19/us-privacy-china-idUSPEK21813920070619.

――――. 2007b. "Google to Provide Internet Content in China." CNBC.com. June 20.

———. 2002. "Daschle: Shrill Political Talk Spurs Threat." Yahoo! News, November 20.

Reville William. 2005. "A Warming World Needs the Temperature Turned Down." *Irish Times*, April 28.

Rhodes, Richard. 2008. *Arsenals of Folly: The Making of the Nuclear Arms Race.* New York: Vintage Books.

Rich, Frank. 2006. *The Greatest Story Ever Sold: The Decline and Fall of Truth from 9/11 to Katrina.* New York: Penguin Books.

———. 2002. "Live by Showbiz, Die by Showbiz." *New York Times*, March 16.

Ringle, Ken. 1998. "Uncovering the Sex Lives of Politicians." *Washington Post*, February 5.

Rogers, Everett M. 1994. *A History of Communication Study: A Biographical Approach.* New York: Free Press.

Rosen, Jay. 1999. *What Are Journalists For?* New Haven, CT: Yale University Press.

Rosenblatt, Roger. 2001. "The Age of Irony Comes to an End." *Time*, September 16. http://www.time.com/time/covers/1101010924/esroger.html.

Rosenfeld, Richard N. 1997. *American Aurora: A Democratic-Republican Returns.* New York: St. Martin's Press.

Rutenberg, Jim. 2001a. "Bill Maher Still Secure in ABC Slot, at Least Now." *New York Times*, October 8.

———. 2001b. "A Nation Challenged: The Coverage; Networks Move to Revive Foreign News." *New York Times*, September 24.

Rutenberg, Jim, and Seth Schiesel. 2002. "Doubted as Business, Valued as Asset, Network News Will Be Hard to Displace." *New York Times*, March 18.

Safire, William. 2002. "You Are a Suspect." NewYorkTimes.com, November 14. http://www.nytimes.com/2002/11/14/opinion/you-are-a-suspect.html.

Salon.com. 1998. "Why We Ran the Henry Hyde Story." September 16. http://www.salon.com/news/1998/09/16newsc.html.

Samuelson, Robert J. 2007. "Greenhouse Simplicities." *Newsweek*, August 20. http://www.newsweek.com/2007/08/15/greenhouse-simplicities.html.

Sass, Erik. 2010. "Analysts: Slight Uptick in Radio, Newspapers Slide." *Media Daily News*, March 26. http://www.mediapost.com/publications/?fa=Articles.showArticle&art_aid=125071.

———. 2008. "Grim Reaper: Newspapers Cut 3,500+ Jobs in Two Months." *Media Daily News*, July 18. http://www.mediapost.com/publications/?fa=Articles.showArticle&art_aid=86831&passFuseAction=PublicationsSearch.showSearchReslts&art_searched=&page_number=0.

Savadove, Bill, and Tony Munrow. 2001. "AOL, Legend Set China Internet Joint Venture." Yahoo! News, June 11.

Schaefer, Louisa. 2007. "Germany: United States Could Pave the Way by Going Green." Deutsche Welle, July 26, http://www.dw-world.de/dw/article/0,2705033,00.html.

Schlosser, Joe, and Bill McConnell. 2001. "What Is Real, Really?" *Broadcasting and Cable*, August 27, 12.

Schudson, Michael. 2009. "A Family of Public Spheres." Talk at the mini-plenary "Keywords: The Public Sphere, Public Culture and Reasoned Public Choice" of the fifty-ninth annual International Communication Association conference, May 22, Chicago.

————. 1998. *The Good Citizen: A History of American Civic Life.* New York: Free Press.

————. 1978. *Discovering the News: A Social History of American Newspapers.* New York: Basic Books.

Schweitzer, N.J. and Michael J. Saks. 2007. "The CSI Effect: Popular Fiction About Forensic Science Affects the Public's Expectations About Real Forensic Science Jurimetrics 47 357–364.

Shattuc, Jane. 1997. *The Talking Cure: TV Talk Shows and Women.* New York: Routledge.

Shea, Danny. 2009. "Fox News Dominates 3Q 2009 Cable News Ratings." Huffington Post, September 30. http://www.huffingtonpost.com/2009/09/30/fox-news-dominates-3q-200_n_304260.html.

Sheppard, Noel. 2008. "Gore Used Fictional Video to Illustrate 'Inconvenient Truth.'" Newsbusters.org, April 22. http://newsbusters.org/blogs/noel-sheppard/2008/04/22/abc-s-20-20-gore-used-fictional-film-clip-inconvenient-truth

Shi, David. 1995. *Facing Facts: Realism in American Thought and Culture, 1850–1920.* New York: Oxford University Press.

Simmons, John. 2008. "The Networks' New Advertising Model." *Fortune,* May 5.

Simon, David, and Edward Burns. 1997. *The Corner: A Year in the Life of an Inner City Neighborhood.* New York: Bantam Books.

————. 1991. *Homicide: A Year on the Killing Streets.* Boston: Houghton Mifflin.

Simpson, Christopher. 1994. *The Science of Coercion.* New York: Oxford University Press.

Singer, Adam. 2009. "49 Amazing Social Media, Web 2.0 and Internet Stats." TheFutureBuzz.com. January 12. http://thefuturebuzz.com/2009/01/12/social-media-web-20-internet-numbers-stats/.

Sirianni, Carmen, and Lewis Friedland. 2001. *Civic Innovation in America: Community Empowerment, Public Policy, and the Movement for Civic Renewal.* Berkeley: University of California Press.

Smiley, Jane. 1998. *The All-True Travels and Adventures of Lidie Newton.* New York: Alfred A. Knopf.

Smith, R. Jeffrey. 2009. "Judge Questions Justice Department Effort to Keep Cheney Remarks Secret." *Washington Post,* June 19. http://www.washingtonpost.com/wp-dyn/content/article/2009/06/18/AR2009061803879.html?hpid=moreheadlines.

Sontag, Susan. 2003. *Regarding the Pain of Others.* New York: Picador.

Source Watch. 2009. "Cooler Heads Coalition." June 25. http://www.sourcewatch.org/index.php?title=Cooler_Heads_Coalition.

Spillius, Alex. 2008. "Sarah Palin: Tina Fey Could Be Her Strongest Opponent." *(London) Telegraph.* September 14. http://blogs.telegraph.co.uk/news/alexspillius/5231857/Sarah_Palin_Tina_Fey_could_be_her_strongest_opponent/.

Standage, Tom. 1998. *The Victorian Internet: The Remarkable Story of the Telegraph and the Nineteenth Centuries On-Line Pioneers*. New York: Berkley Books.

Standora, Leo, and Paul H. B. Shin. 2004. "'Day after Tomorrow' Scenario Could Play Out Here." *New York Daily News*, December 28.

Starr, Kenneth. 1998. *The Starr Report*. Washington, D.C.: Office of the Independent Counsel of the U.S. Congress.

Starr, Paul. 2005. *The Creation of the Media: Political Origins of Modern Communications*. New York: Basic Books.

Statistical Abstract of the United States. 2009. "Survey of Income and program Participation." U.S. Census Bureau. http://www.census.gov/sipp/

Steel, Ronald. 1980. *Walter Lippmann and the American Century*. New York: Vintage Books.

Steinberg, Jacques. 2005. "CNN Seeks New Ways to Battle Fox News." *New York Times*, March 23.

Steingraber, Sandra. 1998. *Living Downstream: A Scientist's Personal Investigation of Cancer and the Environment*. New York: Vintage Books.

Stelter, Brian. 2008. "Reporters Say Networks Put Wars on Back Burner." *New York Times*, June 23. http://www.nytimes.com/2008/06/23/business/media/23logan.html.

Sullivan, Sarah. 2001. "Courting Al-Jazeera, the Sequel: Estrangement and Signs of Reconciliation." *TBS Journal*, Fall–Winter. http://www.tbsjournal.com/Archives/Fall01/Jazeera_special.htm.

Sunstein, Cass. 2001. *Republic.com*. Princeton, NJ: Princeton University Press.

Suskind, Ron. 2004. *The Price of Loyalty: George W. Bush, the White House, and the Education of Paul O'Neill*. New York: Simon and Schuster.

Suzuki, David. 2006. "Public Doesn't Understand Global Warming." August 18. PLACE: David Suzuki Foundation. http://www.greenbiz.com/blog/2006/08/21/public-doesnt-understand-global-warming.

Sweney, Mark. 2006. "American Idol Outvotes the President." *(London) Guardian*, May 26. http://www.guardian.co.uk/media/2006/may/26/realitytv.usnews.

Tanenhaus, Sam. 2009. "North Star." *New Yorker*, December 7.

Tanner, Lindsey. 2007. "AMA Won't Call Video Gaming an Addiction." Associated Press, June 28. http://walkingthefenceline.wordpress.com/2007/10/18/ama-wont-call-video-gaming-an-addiction/.

Taub, Eric. 2002. "How It Works: Where Little but the News Is Real." *New York Times*, March 14.

Teachout, Zephyr and Tim Wu. 2006. "You Tube? It's So Yesterday." *Washington Post*. November 5. http://www.washingtonpost.com/wp-dyn/content/article/2006/11/03/AR2006110301472_pf.html.

Teixeira, Ruy. 2007. "What the Public Really Wants on Energy and the Environment." Center for American Progress. http://www.americanprogress.org/issues/2007/03/wtprw.html.

Tewksbury, David. 2003. "What Do Americans Really Want to Know? Tracking the Behavior of News Readers on the Internet." *Journal of Communication* 53, no. 4, 694–710.

Thaves, Tom. 2000. "Frank and Ernest." August 14.

Thomson, Elizabeth A. 2005. "Hurricanes Growing Fiercer with Global Warming." *MITnews*, July 31. http://web.mit.edu/newsoffice/2005/hurricanes.html.

Time. 2009. "Now That Walter Cronkite Has Passed On, Who Is America's Most Trusted Newscaster?" http://www.timepolls.com/hppolls/archive/poll_results_417.html.

Trippi, Joe. 2004. *The Revolution Will Not Be Televised: Democracy, the Internet, and the Overthrow of Everything*. New York: HarperCollins.

Tucher, Andie. 1997. "You News." *Columbia Journalism Review*, 35 May–June, 26–30.

Turow, Joseph. 2006. *Niche Envy: Marketing Discrimination in the Digital Age*. Cambridge: Massachusetts Institute of Technology Press.

———. 1997. *Breaking Up America: Advertisers and the New Media*. Chicago: University of Chicago Press.

Tygiel, Jules. 2000. *Past Time: Baseball as History*. New York: Oxford University Press.

Vaidhyanathan, Siva. 2011. *The Googlization of Everything*. San Francisco: University of California Press.

Variety. 2007. "'Anchorwoman': Over and out." August 23. http://weblogs.variety.com/on_the_air/anchorwoman/.

Walker, Jerry. 2001. "Younger Audiences." *Media News* 34, no. 44, 4.

Washington Examiner. 2007. "Couric weighs in on Iraq, Rather." September 26. http://washingtonexaminer.com/blogs/couric-weighs-iraq-rather.

Washington Times. 2007. "Poll: Bias 'Alive and Well' in Press." March 15. http://www.washingtontimes.com/news/2007/mar/15/20070315-114454-8075r/.

Weart, Spencer R. 2008. *The Discovery of Global Warming*. Cambridge, MA: Harvard University Press.

Weber, Max. 1948. *From Max Weber: Essays in Sociology*, trans. H. H. Gerth and C. Wright Mills. London: Routledge.

Webster, James G., and Patricia F. Phalen. 1997. *The Mass Audience: Rediscovering the Dominant Model*. Mahwah, NJ: Laurence Erlbaum Associates.

Wedel, Janine R. 2009. *Shadow Elite: How the World's New Power Brokers Undermine Democracy, Government, and the Free Market*. New York: Basic Books.

Wheen, Francis. 1999. *Karl Marx*. London: Fourth Estate.

White, David Manning. 1964. "The 'Gatekeeper': A Case Study In the Selection of News." In *People, Society and Mass Communications*, edited by Lewis A. Dexter and David M. White, 143–159. New York: Free Press.

Wiebe, Robert H. 1967. *The Search for Order, 1877–1920*. New York: Hill and Wang.

Wilentz, Sean. 2005. *The Rise of American Democracy: Jefferson to Lincoln*. New York: W.W. Norton.

Will, George F. 2009. "Dark Green Doomsayers." *Washington Post*, February 15.

———. 2004. "Global Warming? Hot Air." *Washington Post*, December 23.

Williams, Bruce. 2010. "From True Love to Collateral Damage: American Media's Changing Treatment of Civilians in Wartime." *Communication Review* 12, no. 3, 227–238.

————. 2004. "War Rhetoric's Toll on Democracy." *Chronicle of Higher Education*, April 4. http://chronicle.com/article/War-Rhetoric-s-Toll-on/31813.

————. 2003. "Internet Chatrooms, and Public Discourse after 9/11." In *Reporting Conflict: War and the Media*, edited by Daya Thussu, 176–189. London: Sage Publications.

Williams, Bruce A., and Albert R. Matheny. 1995. *Democracy, Dialogue, and Environmental Disputes: The Contested Languages of Social Regulation*. New Haven, CT: Yale University Press.

Williams, Raymond. 2003. *Television: Technological and Cultural Form*, 3rd ed. London: Routledge. (Originally published in 1974.)

Wilson, Christopher P. 1985. *The Labor of Words: Literary Professionalism in the Progressive Era*. Athens: University of Georgia Press.

Wiltz, Teresa. 2001. "Playing in the Shadows: Popular Culture in the Aftermath of Sept. 11 Is a Chorus without a Hook, a Movie without an Ending." *Washington Post*, November 19.

World Public Opinion.org. 2006. "Iraq: The Separate Realities of Republicans and Democrats." March 28. http://www.worldpublicopinion.org/pipa/articles/brunitedstatescanadara/186.php?nid=&id=&pnt=186

Yergin, Daniel, and Joseph Stanislaw. 1998. *The Commanding Heights: The Battle between Government and the Marketplace That Is Remaking the Modern World*. New York: Simon and Schuster.

Zaller, John. 1998. "Monica Lewinsky's Contribution to Political Science." *PS* 31, No. 2, 182–184.

Zuckerman, Michael. 1998. "Tocqueville, Turner, and Turds: Four Stories of Manners in Early America." *Journal of American History* 85, no. 1, 13–42.

Zukin, Cliff, Scott Keeter, Molly Andolina, Krista Jenkins, and Michael X. Delli Carpini. 2006. *A New Engagement? Political Participation, Civic Life and the Changing American Citizen*. New York: Oxford University Press.

Index